ADVANCES IN CONNECTIONIST AND NEURAL COMPUTATION THEORY
Volume 3

John A. Barnden, Series Editor

Analogy, Metaphor, and Reminding

edited by
John A. Barnden and Keith J. Holyoak

**ABLEX PUBLISHING CORPORATION
NORWOOD, NEW JERSEY**

Copyright © 1994 by Ablex Publishing Corporation

All rights reserved. No part of this publication may be reproduced, stored in a retrieval system, or transmitted, in any form or by any means, electronic, mechanical, photocopying, microfilming, recording or otherwise, without permission of the publisher.

Printed in the United States of America

ISBN: 1-56750-101-X   ISSN: 1060-2410

Ablex Publishing Corporation
355 Chestnut Street
Norwood, New Jersey 07648

Table of Contents

List of Contributors	iv
Description of Series	v
Contents of Previous Volumes	vi
Preface	ix
Introduction	1

1 REMIND: Retrieval From Episodic Memory by Inferencing and Disambiguation — 29
Trent E. Lange & Charles M. Wharton

2 The Role of Goals in Retrieving Analogical Cases — 95
Colleen M. Seifert

3 A Case Study of Case Indexing: Designing Index Feature Sets to Suit Task Demands and Support Parallelism — 126
Eric A. Domeshek

4 The Case for Nonconnectionist Associative Retrieval in Case-Based Reasoning Systems — 169
Piero P. Bonissone, Lisa F. Rau, & George Berg

5 What Is Metaphor? — 203
George Lakoff

TABLE OF CONTENTS

6 A Structured Connectionist Model of Figurative Adjective-Noun Combinations **259**
Susan H. Weber

7 Back-Propagation Representations for the Rule-Analogy Continuum **282**
Catherine L. Harris

8 On the Connectionist Implementation of Analogy and Working Memory Matching **327**
John A. Barnden

Author Index **375**

Subject Index **380**

List of Contributors

John A. Barnden, Computing Research Laboratory & Computer Science Department, New Mexico State University, Las Cruces, NM

George Berg, Computer Science Department, State University of New York, Albany, NY

Piero P. Bonissone, GE Corporate Research & Development, Schenectady, NY

Eric A. Domeshek, College of Computing, Georgia Institute of Technology, Atlanta, GA

Catherine L. Harris, Department of Psychology, Boston University, Boston, MA

George Lakoff, Department of Linguistics, University of California, Berkeley, CA

Trent E. Lange, Artificial Intelligence Laboratory & Department of Computer Science, University of California, Los Angeles, CA

Lisa F. Rau, GE Corporate Research & Development, Schenectady, NY

Colleen M. Seifert, University of Michigan, Ann Arbor, MI

Susan H. Weber, Elan Computer Group, Inc., Mountain View, CA

Charles M. Wharton, Department of Psychology, University of California, Los Angeles, CA

Description of the Series

The books in this series present research on the computational abilities of systems that are partially or wholly connectionist or neurally inspired. The series is distinctive in its main emphasis: the question of how connectionist or neural network models could be made to perform rapid, short-term types of computation that appear useful in higher level cognitive processes. Issues of perceptual pattern recognition and slow learning or adaptation are de-emphasized (though not rigidly excluded), as they have been receiving extensive coverage elsewhere. The phrase "Computation Theory" in the series title is not intended to indicate that the articles in the volumes are mathematically rigorous treatises in the foundations of computer science. The primary intent behind the word "Computation" emphasizes more of an orientation towards the computational aspects of neural networks than to the electronic, psychological, biological, or philosophical aspects. Nevertheless, such aspects are not unwelcome and are present in a number of contributions to the volumes in the series. The use of the word "Theory" in the series title emphasizes that contributions can engage in general discussion or point towards new types of systems, rather than necessarily presenting implemented systems.

Although Volumes 1, 2, and 3 of the series are collections of articles (mostly written for the books, rather than reprints of previously published papers), there is room for future volumes to be research monographs.

Contents of Previous Volumes

Volume 1

Introduction: Problems for High-level Connectionism, *John A. Barnden & Jordan B. Pollack*
Connectionism and Compositional Semantics, *David S. Touretzky*
Symbolic NeuroEngineering for Natural Language Processing: A Multilevel Research Approach, *Michael G. Dyer*
Schema Recognition for Text Understanding: An Analog Semantic Feature Approach, *Lawrence A. Bookman & Richard Alterman*
A Context-Free Connectionist Parser Which is Not Connectionist, But Then it is Not Really Context-Free Either, *Eugene Charniak & Eugene Santos, Jr.*
Symbolic/Subsymbolic Sentence Analysis: Exploiting the Best of Two Worlds, *Wendy G. Lehnert*
Developing Hybrid Symbolic/Connectionist Models, *James Hendler*
Encoding Complex Symbolic Data Structures with Some Unusual Connectionist Techniques, *John A. Barnden*
Finding a Maximally Plausible Model of an Inconsistent Theory, *Mark Derthick*
The Relevance of Connectionism to AI: A Representation and Reasoning Perspective, *Lokendra Shastri*
Steps Toward Knowledge-Intensive Connectionist Learning, *Joachim Diederich*
Learning Simple Arithmetic Procedures, *Garrison W. Cottrell & Fu-Sheng Tsung*
The Similarity Between Connectionist and Other Parallel Computation Models, *Jiawei Hong & Xiaonan Tan*
Complex Features in Planning and Understanding: Problems and Opportunities for Connectionism, *Lawrence Birnbaum*
Conclusion, *Jordan Pollack & John Barnden*
Author Index
Subject Index

Volume 2

Introduction, *Keith J. Holyoak & John A. Barnden*
The Copycat Project: A Model of Mental Fluidity and Analogy-Making, *Douglas R. Hofstader & Melanie Mitchell*
Component Processes in Analogical Transfer: Mapping, Pattern Completion, and Adaptation, *Keith J. Holyoak, Laura R. Novick, & Eric R. Melz*
Integrating Analogy With Rules and Explanations, *Greg Nelson, Paul Thagard, & Susan Hardy*
A Hybrid Model of Continuous Analogical Reasoning, *Thomas C. Eskridge*

A Hybrid Model of Continuous Analogical Reasoning, *Thomas C. Eskridge*
A Hybrid Model of Reasoning by Analogy, *Boicho N. Kokinov*
Similarity, Interactive Activation, and Mapping: An Overview, *Robert L. Goldstone & Douglas L. Medin*
Connectionist Implications for Processing Capacity Limitations in Analogies, *Graeme S. Halford, Wiliam H. Wilson, Jian Guo, Ross W. Gayler, Janet Wiles, & J.E.M. Stewart*
Analogical Mapping by Dynamic Binding: Preliminary Investigations, *John E. Hummel, Bruce Burns, & Keith J. Holyoak*
Spatial Inclusion and Set Membership: A Case Study of Analogy at Work, *Keith Stenning & Jon Oberlander*
Author Index
Subject Index

Preface

This book and Volume 2 of the same series are closely related in content. Although they can be read independently, a reader interested in one is strongly encouraged to consult the other as well. To encourage further reading into the series the chapters found in all volumes are listed at the front of the present book. In addition, both this volume and Volume 2 have the same introductory chapter, which discusses some issues that underlie both volumes and summarizes the contents of all the chapters of both volumes.

The main emphasis of *Advances in Connectionist and Neural Computation Theory* is on the question of how connectionist or "neurally inspired" models can be made to perform rapid types of computation that appear useful in high-level cognitive processes. The first volume, edited by John Barnden and Jordan Pollack and entitled *High-Level Connectionist Models*, appeared in 1991. The chapters in that volume addressed a wide range of fundamental theoretical problems for which any successful model of cognition must find solutions: the need for knowledge representations with the requisite expressive power to encode propositional information, the need for mechanisms that permit the rapid encoding and manipulation of structured representations in working memory, and the need for learning techniques that can be applied to representations of the necessary complexity. Many of the contributions focused on issues that are particularly salient in dealing with natural language processing and reasoning.

As Volume 1 neared completion, John Barnden, the series editor, decided that a natural follow-up would be a book dealing with the topic of analogy, broadly construed to include cross-domain structure mapping, metaphor generation and understanding, complex episodic memory retrieval, and case-based reasoning. Analogy involves essentially all the core issues considered in Volume 1, and is closely tied to both natural language processing and human reasoning. In January 1990, John Barnden asked Keith Holyoak, who had been working on models of analogical thinking based on connectionist parallel constraint satisfaction, if he would share in the editorial work for a second volume. Despite a certain amount of misgiving as to whether the time was yet ripe for a book-length treatment of a topic that had not yet received much detailed attention within the connectionist community, we agreed to jointly undertake the project.

We began by soliciting chapters from a number of researchers in the relevant topic areas, as well as by widely disseminating a call for papers. We encouraged a broad range of contributions from cognitive scientists drawn from the disciplines of artificial intelligence, cognitive psychology, and linguistics. In addition to "pure" connectionist models (if such can be defined), we solicited contributions based on other types of subsymbolic models, on hybrid models that integrated symbolic and connectionist components, on more traditional symbolic models that may exhibit some of the desirable properties of connectionist models, as well as critical discussions of the potential limits of connectionist approaches to modeling analogy.

We were extremely pleased to find that we received a large number of excellent contributions, from cognitive scientists in Europe and Australia as well as North America, spanning the entire range of topics that we had hoped the book would cover. Indeed, the number of contributions and their individual size ultimately led us to produce the present two volumes rather than the single one originally planned.

The contributors to the two volumes are mainly psychologists and computer scientists, but philosophy and linguistics are also represented. The application of connectionist-style ideas to high-level cognition in general, and to analogical thinking in particular, is still at a very early stage. Many of the projects described in the chapters have blossomed over the time the volumes were in preparation. Many different approaches are represented; where they will eventually lead remains to be seen. Our goal was to "let a hundred flowers bloom," and in that we believe we have succeeded. This pair of books may well have been a little premature in its conception; but the field grew as the contributions were compiled, and we think the project's completion is timely indeed.

The present volume is distinguished from Volume 2 by containing those chapters that explicitly focus on: (a) metaphor, (b) the involvement of analogy in natural language, or (c) the retrieval/reminding aspects of analogical and case-based reasoning. The chapters form a unity, partly because the chapters on topic (c) are in fact mostly concerned with cognitive tasks related to natural language input, and partly, of course, because metaphor is bound up with analogy and natural language. Indeed, although there are only two chapters that focus explicitly on metaphor, much of the content of both volumes is of potential application to metaphor simply by virtue of addressing analogy.

Volume 2 is entitled *Analogical Connections*, and contains chapters of two sorts. Some describe specific connectionist or partially connectionist systems aimed at performing a large part of the whole task of analogy-based reasoning, rather than concentrating on just one stage such as mapping. The remaining chapters of Volume 2, on the other hand, are more restricted in focus, and concentrate on the mapping phase of analogy. They address particular analogical mapping techniques and constraints, the role of mapping in similarity judgments, and the nature of connectionist support for analogical mapping.

It goes without saying that the quality of this volume and its companion is due above all else to the hard work of our authors. Early drafts of chapters were selectively circulated among the authors, many of whom contributed detailed reviews of other chapters. The final versions reflect serious revisions (sometimes multiple) based on the reviews each chapter received. Where chapters were seen as interrelated, authors added sections relating their work to that described in other chapters, an effort which we feel has contributed a great deal to the integrative nature of the pair of volumes as a whole.

We took the unusual step of preserving anonymity in the commentary that chapters received from other authors (other than from ourselves, the editors). Also, we obtained anonymous peer commentary from 15 other researchers. We thank all these reviewers—authors and nonauthors alike—for their hard reviewing work and the extremely useful comments that resulted.

The assembling of these books was aided by the use of facilities at the Computing Research Laboratory and Computer Science Department, New Mexico State University. We would like to thank Bea Guzman of that Laboratory and Peary Brug of the Cognitive Science Research Program, University of California, Los Angeles, for a great deal of secretarial help. Support for preparation of both volumes was provided by Grant SBR-9310614 from The National Science Foundation.

The volumes are directed mainly at researchers in connectionism, analogy, metaphor, and case-based reasoning, but would also be suitable for graduate courses in those areas, particularly analogy and connectionism. The books make contributions to connectionism and to analogy as such, rather than just to their interaction.

J.A.B., Las Cruces, New Mexico
K.J.H., Los Angeles, California
June, 1994

Introduction*

Keith J. Holyoak
John A. Barnden

1. ANALOGICAL CONNECTIONS AND CONCEPTUAL BRIDGES

This book and its companion volume (see Preface) bring together a set of papers exploring "analogical connections"—a deliberately prismatic term referring primarily to connectionist approaches to analogy, but alluding also to connections between different facets of analogy, and to links that analogy has with metaphor, case-based reasoning, human similarity judgment, and perception.

The aim, therefore, is to build conceptual bridges between areas that have often been investigated separately, but that invite theoretical integration. This theme is intentionally open-ended. Researchers in the area of analogy are only just beginning to build links to work on connectionist models of cognition and learning. Conversely, connectionists have barely considered the question of achieving analogical processing, except insofar as the familiar types of connectionist similarity-based generalization can already be regarded as limited forms of analogy. We need not apologize, therefore, for the fact that many of the investigations in the present volume are at a relatively early stage. Our hope is that they will stimulate further research in the same vein.

Many of the chapters illustrate some opportunities for connectionism to aid the analogy researcher, notably because of the connectionist facility with highly parallel soft constraint satisfaction and associative retrieval of memories. At the same time, however, the complexity of analogical processing as traditionally conceived presents a considerable challenge to connectionism. This is because analogy has mostly been studied within the symbolic paradigm, and traditionally rests on complex symbolic representations and manipulations that are not

---

* We thank Bobbie Spellman, Imre Balogh, and Tom Eskridge for helpful comments on an earlier draft of this chapter, and Balogh also for help with Figure 1. We are grateful to the chapter authors for allowing edited versions of their own text to serve as the core of the chapter summaries in Section 6.

easily implemented or emulated by connectionist systems. Paradoxically, however, analogical reasoning may itself be able to act as a bridge over this gap between the symbolic and connectionist paradigms, promising to combine the advantages of both. This point is argued in Barnden's chapter. Other views on how the gap could be bridged are presented elsewhere (Barnden & Pollack, 1991a; Dinsmore, 1992; Hinton, 1991a).

Little work has been done on applying connectionism directly to metaphor. Only two of the chapters (Lakoff & Weber, Volume 3) explicitly focus on metaphor, although some of the instances of linguistic analogy addressed in Harris's chapter (Volume 3) could well be classed as metaphor (see also Chandler, 1991). However, given that metaphor generally involves the use of an analogy between the vehicle (source) and the tenor (target), and that most of the chapters favor the application of connectionism to analogical processing, it follows that they do contribute implicitly to the issue of how metaphor could be handled in connectionist systems.

Sections 2 to 5 of this Introduction discuss themes underlying various chapters in the two books. These sections are all relevant to both volumes, although Sections 3 and 4 are more directly connected to Volume 2 than to Volume 3. Section 6 provides summaries of all chapters in both volumes.

2. CONNECTIONISM AND HYBRIDISM

The existence of the symbolic/connectionist gap just mentioned explains why many of the models presented in Volume 2 are hybrid ones, as opposed to being completely connectionist. For the purposes of this introduction, a *hybrid* system is one that has both some connectionist aspects and some symbolic aspects with no specified connectionist realization. Notice that this does not require there to be separate symbolic and connectionist *modules* in any simple sense. For instance, a system consisting of a network that performs both symbolic marker passing and connectionist activation-spread, over the same links and nodes, is hybrid under our definition. Also, the notion does not imply that the symbolic aspects cannot be given a connectionist realization, but only that they have not, in fact, been given one. A type of system that is *not* hybrid under our definition is one that can be described as symbolic at a high level of description but in which all structures and processes are also given a fully connectionist realization.

Two central but implicit assumptions in both volumes are that it is indeed important for psychologists, AI researchers, and others to provide accounts of analogy and metaphor, and that it is worthwhile to develop connectionist or partially connectionist accounts of cognition. It is not the task of these volumes to define connectionism, something that is difficult to do even informally. We assume that the reader is already reasonably familiar with the general nature of connectionism. Nevertheless, it may be helpful to quote here the description used in another introductory chapter (Barnden & Pollack, 1991b):

> Typically, a connectionist system is a *large weighted network* of processing units that communicate with each other by means of *simple numeric messages*. A unit transforms incoming messages by a *simple function* which may depend on the unit's *state*. Units operate in a *massively parallel* fashion. In response to an environment, the weights in such networks can often be *slowly adapted* by local modification rules.
>
> We preceded the above definition by the term "typically" because such systems do not form a precise class, but hold family resemblances to each other. Furthermore, our definition is completely framed in computational terms, and lacks the conceptual vocabulary of psychology and biology. (p. 1)

Often, other features are stipulated, such as that the network should have no central controller. We list and discuss some standard restrictions on the computational nature of connectionist systems in Section 5 below.

We should emphasize that we use the term "connectionism" to cover both the "localist" (or "structured") variety and the "distributed" variety. What this distinction comes down to is itself unclear (see van Gelder, 1991, for an untangling of issues). Roughly, a localist system uses individual units in the network to represent the entities that are of interest at a high level of description of the system, whereas a distributed system uses activation patterns across many units for that purpose (its individual nodes represent, if anything at all, entities that are of interest at a relatively low level of description of the system). Most of the connectionism in these two volumes is localist, but the distributed variety plays an important role in some chapters in each book.

3. THINKING AND PERCEPTION

The connections that arguably have had the greatest historical impact on developments in the study of analogy are those between analogy and perception. This is reflected directly or indirectly in Harris's chapter in Volume 3 and some of the chapters in Volume 2 (Hofstadter & Mitchell; Goldstone & Medin; Stenning & Oberlander; and see Indurkhya, 1991). In a broad sense, an analogy can potentially be drawn between thinking and perception: perhaps we can view thinking as a kind of seeing. The very fact that it is natural to use the word "view" as a metaphor in phrasing the possibility suggests how deeply entrenched is the connection between thought and perception in everyday language (cf. Lakoff & Johnson, 1980; Lakoff, Volume 3; Richards, 1989; Sweetser, 1990). Among the psychological progenitors of cognitive science, the analogy has actually been bidirectional. Over a century ago, Helmholtz, the father of the scientific study of vision, argued that perception is like thinking in that it, too, depends upon inferences, albeit inferences drawn below the level of conscious awareness (Helmholtz, 1962). For example, the visual system uses information derived from the disparity between the two retinal images to "infer" the appearance of a unified scene. But over the past century much more was learned about perception than about thought, so that perception is now the (partially) understood source analog, while thinking is the poorly understood target analog.

How is thinking like seeing? Early in this century, the Gestalt psychologists emphasized that both thinking and seeing depend on the construction of internal representations in which elements were integrated within an overarching relational structure. What we see is more than a set of isolated visual features, and what we think is more than a set of ideas; in both domains the person imposes an organization so that "the whole is different from the sum of its parts." Given this emphasis on the centrality of relational structure, it was natural to consider the possibility of reorganization, or restructuring, of elements. What does it mean to restructure a percept or concept? The Gestalt psychologists provided tantalizing glimmers of insight, as in this passage by Maier (1930):

> First one has one or no gestalt, then suddenly a new or different gestalt is formed out of the old elements. The sudden appearance of the new gestalt, that is, the solution, is the process of reasoning. How and why it comes is not explained. It is like perception: certain elements which one minute are only one unity suddenly become an altogether different unity. (p. 116)

Tantalizing, yes, but all too vague and devoid of any computational basis. Now, over 60 years later, we see the reemergence of the Gestalt emphasis on the primacy of relational structure, but now with far more powerful computational models to aid in theoretical developments. In particular, certain aspects of connectionism—most notably, its emphasis on the interpretation of inputs by parallel constraint satisfaction—may help to understand the analogical connections between thinking and perception. In the present volumes this fundamental analogy is most clearly expressed by Hofstadter and Mitchell, as they introduce their Copycat model of analogical mapping and the construction of representations:

> The present characterization will...read very much like a description of a computer model of *perception*. This is not a coincidence; one of the main ideas of the project is that even the most abstract and sophisticated mental acts deeply resemble perception....[T]he essence of understanding a situation is...the awakening from dormancy of a relatively small number of prior concepts—...precisely the relevant ones—and applying them judiciously so as to identify key entities, roles, and relationships in the situation. (Volume 2, p. 36)

4. CONSTRAINT SATISFACTION AND ANALOGICAL MAPPING

The analogy between thinking and perception can be further developed by focusing on particular forms of thinking for which the resemblance is most compelling. The present volumes, as the chapter on Hofstadter and Mitchell's Copycat model exemplifies, focuses on analogical reasoning itself. To use an analogy is to "see" one thing as another, to focus on a set of structured correspondences—a mapping—between source and target. Prior knowledge of the source and application of the correspondences will impose a new unity on the target situation, providing a new understanding of key roles and relations. Here we can pursue analogical connections that lead from Gestalt perception to analogical mapping, bridged by one of the core contributions of modern connectionism—the idea that coherent active representations can be dynamically constructed by parallel constraint satisfaction.

Figure 1 depicts a Necker cube—a subtly distorted two-dimensional representation of a cube, which allows two alternative interpretations of the assignment of vertices in the drawing to vertices of a canonical cube. Each node in the upper half of the figure stands for a hypothesis that the line drawing vertex it is connected to is a particular cube vertex (e.g., FLR: Front Lower Right). Note that each hypothesis label, such as FLR, appears on two different nodes, one for each of the two alternative interpretations. The hypothesis labels for one of the interpretations are in italics, while the nonitalic labels are for the other interpretation. Blobbed and arrowed lines indicate inhibitory and excitatory connections respectively. Not all connections are shown. Both Feldman and Ballard (1982) and Rumelhart, Smolensky, McClelland, and Hinton (1986) have used the Necker cube to illustrate the power of parallel constraint satisfaction as a mechanism for resolving ambiguity of relational structure. The crucial insight is that each of the two global interpretations can be defined in terms of a set of more elementary interpretations of the elements of the drawing. For example, under one interpretation the lower-left vertex of the drawing is the front-lower-left (FLL) vertex of the cube, whereas under the other interpretation the same point is interpreted as the back-lower-left (BLL) vertex.

Furthermore, the possible local interpretations are highly interdependent, tending to either support or compete with each other in accord with the structural relations embodied in the canonical cube. Thus, if the lower-left vertex of the drawing point is the FLL vertex of the cube, then the vertex directly above it in the drawing should be the front upper left (FUL) of the cube, as indicated by an excitatory connection between the two units representing the two hypotheses. In contrast, the alternative interpretations of a single vertex as FLL or BLL are mutually incompatible, as indicated by an inhibitory connection between these two units. Given a constraint network such as that illustrated in

Figure 1, a connectionist relaxation algorithm will tend to converge on one or the other of the two possible views, activating a subset of units that collectively represent a coherent interpretation, and deactivating the others. The network is thus bistable. Small changes in the initial state of the network, such as prior support for a particular interpretation of one corner of the cube, can generate cascading changes in the activation pattern over the interconnected units, driving the network toward the global interpretation consistent with the entering bias.

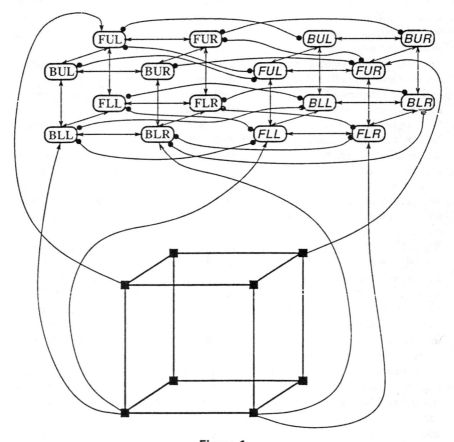

Figure 1.
A simple network representing some of the constraints involved in perceiving the Necker cube. (Adapted from "Schemata and Sequential Thought Processes in PDP Models," by D.E. Rumelhart et al., 1986, *Parallel Distributed Processing* (Vol. 2; ed. by J.L. McClelland, D.E. Rumelhart, & the PDP Research Group), Cambridge, MA: MIT press. Reprinted by permission.)

The above connectionist analysis of the dual interpretations of a Necker cube had a direct connection, via analogical transfer, to the development of one theory of analogical mapping—Holyoak and Thagard's (1989) Analogical Constraint Mapping Engine (ACME). This theory is developed further in Holyoak, Novick, and Melz's chapter in Volume 2. Note that the problem of interpreting a Necker cube can be construed as one of finding a set of mappings between points in the drawing and points in a canonical "cube schema." Therefore, each unit in Figure 1 can be interpreted as a localist representation of a mapping hypothesis. For example, the unit FLL in effect represents the hypothesis, "the lower-left vertex of the drawing maps to the front-lower-left vertex of the cube." The connections between units reflect structural constraints based on spatial relations, which drive the network toward a globally consistent set of mappings.

Holyoak and Thagard (1989) generalized this basic constraint-satisfaction approach to model how people might find coherent mappings between representations of structured situations, such as problems or stories. The major constraints assumed by ACME are isomorphism (a preference for mappings that are structurally consistent and one-to-one), semantic similarity (a preference for mapping between predicates that are similar in meaning), and pragmatic centrality (a preference for mappings of particular importance for achieving the goal to which the analogy is believed to be relevant). In another illustration of the analogical connections between analogy and perception, Holyoak and Thagard (1989) pointed out that an abstract analogy can be drawn between some of ACME's constraints and those postulated by Marr and Poggio (1976) in their constraint-satisfaction model of stereoscopic vision (an aspect of vision that Helmholtz [1962] considered a prime example of "unconscious inference"). Just as mapping involves finding systematic correspondences between elements of two analogs, stereopsis involves finding systematic correspondences between points in two retinal images.

As in Hofstadter and Mitchell's Copycat model, ACME's constraints are construed as soft pressures, rather than hard requirements. Once a constraint network of "mapping units" is dynamically created for a particular source and target analog, ACME employs essentially the same interactive-activation mechanism as illustrated for the Necker-cube example, relaxing into a stable state in which the most active mapping units collectively define the "optimal" overall mapping between the two situations.

Examples of mappings can be found that exhibit a type of ambiguity similar to that of the Necker cube—two sets of correspondences, each incompatible with the other, may constitute plausible rival "views" of the mapping between the elements of the analogs. One such example, adapted from Hinton's (1986) "family tree" problem, is discussed in the chapter by Holyoak, Novick, and Melz in Volume 2. A more naturalistic case of a bistable mapping involves the Persian Gulf War of 1991. When the Gulf War began, there were serious arguments in the United States and elsewhere concerning the degree to which

Iraq's military seizure of neighboring Kuwait was analogous to Nazi Germany's seizure of Czechoslovakia and other countries at the outset of World War II. President George Bush argued that Saddam Hussein, the leader of Iraq, was analogous to Adolf Hitler. This analogy was hotly debated in the media at the time because the mapping strongly implied that early military intervention was warranted. During the period international attention was focused on the analogy, Spellman and Holyoak (1992) asked American college students to provide correspondences between the major leaders and countries involved in the Gulf War and those involved in World War II, assuming (for the sake of the argument) that Saddam Hussein in fact corresponded to Hitler.

One interesting aspect of the mappings students provided is that part of the analogy proved to be bistable, with two alternative sets of correspondences. These correspondences are illustrated in Figure 2. The basic ambiguity is that if Bush is FDR then the U.S.-'91 (United States during the Persian Gulf War) is the U.S.-WW2 (United States during World War II) and Saudi Arabia is Great Britain; whereas if Bush is Churchill then the U.S.-'91 is Great Britain and Saudi Arabia is France. In the figure, dotted lines indicate mappings that result when Bush is mapped to FDR. Large dashed lines indicate mappings that result when Bush is mapped to Churchill. Solid lines represent mappings that are constant regardless of the mapping for Bush.

Semantic similarity supports the mapping of the U.S. to the U.S; in addition, some structural pressures provide support because (at least according to American history books) the U.S. played the leading role in the eventual victory of the Allied forces, just as the U.S. was doing in the war against Iraq. On the other hand, it was in fact Great Britain which provided the earliest response to the German aggression, a fact that provides structural support for the alternative mapping. As Figure 2 illustrates, the mapping of U.S.-'91 to U.S.-WW2 supports the corresponding mapping between the respective leaders, Bush and Franklin Delano Roosevelt; whereas the alternative mapping of U.S.-'91 to Great Britain supports a mapping of Bush to Winston Churchill. Each of the alternative mappings has an inhibitory connection to its rival.

As the ACME model predicted, Spellman and Holyoak (1992) found that the great majority of subjects who produced mappings of these parties selected one of the two "consistent" patterns (U.S.-'91 = U.S.-WW2 and Bush = FDR; or U.S.-'91 = Great Britain and Bush = Churchill), rather than a pattern that mixed leaders and countries. Furthermore, as also illustrated in Figure 2, the choice between these two alternatives was coupled with consistent patterns for other correspondences. Saudi Arabia, a major ally of the U.S. in the Gulf War, was often mapped to Great Britain, but only if the U.S.-'91 was not mapped to England. If Great Britain was "captured" by the U.S.-'91 as its preferred correspondent, the mapping for Saudi Arabia shifted to some other country involved in World War II, such as France. Thus, much as the Necker cube has two alternative views, the analogy between the Gulf War and World War II

Figure 2.
Bistable mapping. (From "If Saddam is Hitler then Who is George Bush? Analogical Mapping Between Systems of Social Roles," by B.A. Spellman & K.J. Holyoak, 1992, *Journal of Personality and Social Psychology, 62*. Reprinted by permission.)

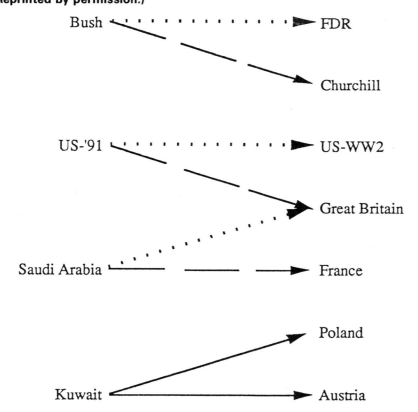

yielded two alternative sets of mappings—either those indicated by dotted or else by dashed lines in Figure 2—each set of which tended to "stand or fall together."

Such examples provide concrete illustrations of the "perception-like" nature of analogical thinking—in particular, the fact that people tend to find coherent mappings, rather than intermingling multiple incompatible interpretations. Furthermore, for both perception and analogy, constraint-satisfaction models provide good accounts of human intuitions about the relational structure of complex situations. In Volume 2, Goldstone and Medin's chapter presents a constraint-satisfaction model of the influence of shared relational structure on human judgments of the similarity of visual forms, thus illustrating a very direct link between mapping and perception. More generally, the fact that constraint-satisfaction models can help us to understand the human ability to see links between previously unrelated situations encourages further exploration of how connectionist concepts can be applied to analogical thinking. Where this exploration will lead remains to be determined. One important function of this volume is to examine some of the possible directions.

5. ANALOGY AND CONNECTIONISM: OPPORTUNITIES AND CHALLENGES

Analogical thinking manifests itself in many guises, which lie along a continuum from the metaphorical to the literal. The continuum ranges from comprehending metaphors, which involves understanding concepts from one domain of knowledge in terms of superficially dissimilar concepts from a different domain, to case-based reasoning, in which different but closely related examples, typically drawn from a single domain, are used to solve problems or build explanations. The contributions to these volumes span this full range. In addition, as many theorists have noted (e.g., Carbonell, 1983; Gentner, 1983; Gick & Holyoak, 1980; Hall, 1989), analogical thinking involves several constituent processes. Major steps in analogy usage include retrieving and selecting a potentially useful source analog, finding a mapping between the elements of the source and target, deriving inferences based on the mapping, evaluating and possibly adapting the inferences to satisfy constraints required by the target situation, and learning in the aftermath of analogical transfer. To varying extents, each of these steps is discussed within the present collection of papers.

The different types of analogical thinking, and the different steps in the overall reasoning process, offer both opportunities for and challenges to connectionism. Some of these are discussed in the following paragraphs.

We have already discussed the usefulness of connectionist constraint satisfaction in the mapping and mapping-based inference stages of analogy. Another way in which connectionism could help the mapping stage is through the use of "reduced" or "compressed" representations (see, e.g., Hinton, 1988, 1991b; Plate, 1991; Pollack, 1991; Sumida & Dyer, 1989). These representations have been developed as a way of compressing data structures that have diverse sizes, and possibly several levels of nesting, into flat activation vectors of uniform width. Crucially, the hope is that similarities between the structures before reduction are captured to some useful degree by similarities between the reduced versions. Such compression would then open up the possibility of using standard connectionist tools, which are essentially for fixed-width vector transformation, to get the effect of complex manipulations of symbolic data structures that are not of fixed size. Moreover, the idea is that the manipulations be done "holistically" (i.e., without needing to unpack the reduced representations into their individual parts). (The possibility of holistic processing has been partially ratified: see, e.g., Blank, Meeden, & Marshall, 1992; Chalmers, 1990; Pollack, 1991; Stolcke & Wu, 1992.) Reduced representations have therefore been used as a defense against Fodor and Pylyshyn's (1988) claim that connectionism cannot match the abilities of symbolic systems other than by the (allegedly) uninteresting device of directly implementing those abilities.[1]

The way that reduced representations might help in analogical mapping is as follows. The mapping process involves matching complex structures in the source analog to complex structures in the target. Perhaps, then, a reduced representation of a source structure might be similar to a reduced representation of a matching target structure, where the similarity is one that can be holistically and rapidly measured by a connectionist subnetwork. Connectionism *may* thus be able to provide an efficient matching method. It would be distinctly different from the matching in, for instance, ACME, because that relies on a dynamically constructed mapping network for each mapping task, whereas the reduced representation approach would work with a predetermined network. Holistic connectionist similarity detection using reduced representations has been demonstrated (Stolcke & Wu, 1992), although so far only in forms considerably simpler than what is needed for analogical processing. Holistic similarity detection is also exploited in Barnden's chapter in Volume 3.

Another opportunity for connectionism arises because the analogical mapping problem is a special case of the binding problem—the fruit of the mapping process is meant to be a set of temporary links between source items and target items. Therefore, connectionist approaches to the binding problem are candidates for being used in representing the results of analogical mapping. This usage occurs, for instance, in the chapter by Hummel, Burns, and Holyoak (Volume 2) where the synchrony approach to binding is used as part of a method for encoding mappings. A distinctly different connection between analogical mapping and connectionist binding arises in Stenning and Oberlander's chapter in Volume 2. This rests in part on their view that people's mental bindings are based on experience with particular content areas and that some bindings are therefore more easily maintained than others. This possibility could have important implications for the bindings set up by analogical mapping.

The parallel activation-spread aspect of connectionism could serve to provide analogy systems with an efficient means of associatively retrieving source analogs that are relevant to a given target. (This idea is exploited in the chapters in Volume 2 by Eskridge and Kokinov; and in Volume 3 by Barnden; Domeshek; Lange & Wharton; and Weber.[2]) The story is by no means simple, though, since

---

[1] We say *allegedly* uninteresting, because in fact it is quite difficult to use connectionism to implement practical forms of traditional symbolic processing directly, without creating a very cumbersome system. See Barnden (1984) and Barnden and Srinivas (1991).

[2] However, the chapter by Bonissone, Rau, and Berg in Volume 3 argues that, for the purpose of analog retrieval, symbolic marker passing combined with other symbolic processing is superior to parallel distributed processing techniques.

it is not obvious how a fully connectionist system would use *structures* within a target analog as retrieval keys, as opposed to using more basic items such as individual predicates and object names. Structured retrieval cues are a major problem in symbolic analog retrieval, not to mention the connectionist variety. Again, reduced representations may be a promising approach. A target substructure encoded as a reduced representation could perhaps be spread throughout the long-term memory of source analogs, themselves encoded as reduced representations, causing the retrieval of source analogs that contain substructures similar to the target substructure. (A version of the method is proposed in Barnden's chapter.) There is, however, some way to go before the method can be said to be of proven worth, since it is by no means clear that the right types of structural similarity can indeed be captured in reduced-representation similarity.

Lange and Wharton's chapter throws an interesting light on retrieval for analogy. The authors claim that the use of elaborative inferencing to enlarge a retrieval cue, so to speak, can obviate the need for a target/source matching process that explicitly checks for (partial) isomorphism during retrieval. Rather, structural differences between target structures that are composed of similar sets of components lead to differences in the resulting elaborative inferences, and hence cause differences in retrievals anyway, just by virtue of the connectionist spreading-activation process.

There is less reason to think that connectionism has anything special to offer the posttransfer stages of analogy, in which mapping-based inferences are possibly adapted, rejected, or extended, and in which learning may occur, leading to changes in the long-term memory of source analogs. Standard connectionist adaptation techniques could support some aspects of analogical learning, such as strengthening of links between source analogs in memory, but the techniques have less obvious application to "one-shot" learning events such as rapidly converting the target analog into a new source analog in long-term memory, or rapidly forming a generalization spanning the target and the source(s) that have been likened to it. This is especially so because of the complex structural nature of targets and sources.

As a final word on the opportunities for connectionism, we refer again to the point that standard sorts of similarity-based generalization in connectionism can be construed as a type of analogy making. This is the crux of Harris's chapter (Volume 3), which is about a type of linguistic analogy. However, current generalizing connectionist systems are weak in their abilities to encode and manipulate complex information structures such as those involved in analogy as understood in the symbolic paradigm. (And it has by no means been shown that holistic processing of reduced representations, though promising, could adequately overcome the weakness.) It is therefore hard to maintain that standard connectionist similarity-based generalization is of itself a *complete* solution to the problem of analogy.

The challenges that analogy presents to connectionism largely arise from the traditional view of analogy as being a matter of complex symbolic representations and manipulations. Such representations and manipulations (whether used for analogy or not) are often recognized as not being readily implementable or emulatable in connectionism. Unfortunately, few authors spend much time showing exactly and technically *why* the difficulties arise; rather, the perception of difficulty is part of the folk culture of the field.[3] One reason for this is the lack of a precise definition of what a connectionist system is, and claims that connectionism cannot do so-and-so can often be deflected by adding new techniques and thereby suitably redrawing its boundaries. Also, even without boundary massaging, discussion is difficult because the large variety of existing connectionist systems makes it awkward to state succinct generalizations, and forces one to proceed case by case.

The difficulties in implementing or emulating complex representations and manipulations in connectionism are ultimately to do with the following features of the information structures that seem to be required by high-level cognitive processing:

- They can be highly temporary—for instance, sentence-meaning representations and intermediate reasoning products need to be rapidly created and modified, and, possibly, rapidly destroyed.
- The structures can combine information items (e.g., word senses) that have never been combined before, or never been combined in quite the same way.
- The structures can be of widely varying complexity, as can be seen, for instance, by considering natural language sentences.
- In particular, the structures can be multiply nested; consider, for instance, the proposition that *John believes that Peter's anger with Mary caused him to write her a strongly worded letter.*
- Also, a given type of information can appear at different levels of nesting: as Hinton (1991b) stresses, a system might have to represent a room that has a wall that bears a picture that itself depicts a room.
- A given type of information may also have to be multiply instantiated in other ways, as when, for instance, there are three love relationships that need to be simultaneously represented.

Turning to manipulations, systems must exhibit strong properties of *structure-sensitive systematicity* of processing—each information structure X that one cares to mention has an extremely large class of variants that must be able to be

---

[3] Nevertheless, Barnden (1984), Barnden and Srinivas (1991), and Fodor and Pylyshyn (1988) provide some detailed analyses. (Barnden's views differ, however, from those of Fodor and Pylyshyn, and some critique of the latter appears in Barnden, 1992.) For another discussion see, e.g., Section 7 of Hofstadter and Mitchell, Volume 2; the chapters by Touretzky, Hinton, Smolensky, and Pollack in Hinton (1991a); and the chapters by Dyer and Birnbaum in Barnden and Pollack (1991a).

subjected to the same sort of processing as X is; and the class is far too large to imagine that each variant is processed by a separate piece of network. So, we must have networks capable of very flexible and general processing. The (in)famous variable-binding problem is one manifestation of this point. Systematicity is championed by Fodor and Pylyshyn (1988). Although connectionists tend to feel that those authors overstated the case and are wrong in supposing that systematicity and related desiderata force us to adopt classical symbolic structures, there is general recognition that some strong form of systematicity is important.

These features of structures and manipulations combine to distinguish the types of information that "high-level" connectionist systems (ones directed at common-sense reasoning and natural language understanding, for instance) must deal with from the types for which more typical connectionist systems and neural networks must cater. The divergence is wide enough to cause difficulty in the application of traditional connectionist techniques. It is fair to say that the techniques were originally developed largely with specific "low-level" tasks, such as restricted forms of visual pattern recognition, in mind. The difficulties arise because of the following restrictions traditionally adhered to in fully connectionist systems (although almost every restriction is violated by some systems):

- Connectionism traditionally does not allow the dynamic, rapid creation of nodes and links. (However, many hybrid symbolic/connectionist systems do, including those of Holyoak et al. and Eskridge, Volume 2.)
- The effect of such creation could in principle be obtained by allowing connections to have zero weight, and assuming that weights can be very rapidly changed by large amounts, but this ability is only countenanced in somewhat atypical connectionist research (e.g., in Pollack, 1987).

In any case, the encoding of temporary associations as rapidly created/facilitated links does not lend itself very well to the desired types of processing of those associations (Barnden, 1984; Barnden & Srinivas, 1991). This is because connection weights (traditionally) cannot be processed as data items in the way that activation values can.

- Connections are not labeled in the sense that links in a semantic network are.
- Connections in connectionism lack flexibility in another sense as well. A connection that is not symmetric (i.e., bidirectional, with equal weight in each direction) only allows activation to flow in one direction. In a symbolic system such as a semantic network, however, processing may be able to "flow" in either direction across a link, even though it is directed.

These two restrictions force information that could be put into link labels and directionality to be encoded somehow in extra links, activation values, weights, or other features of network topology, adding significantly to the cumbersomeness of the net and its processing (see Barnden & Srinivas, 1991, for evidence of this).

INTRODUCTION 15

- The resolution of connectionist activation values is generally not fine enough to allow them individually to encode complex symbolic structures. Most typically, activation values encode confidence levels of some sort, and small changes in activation values tend to lead only to small changes in processing.
- Pointers are usually not allowed. That is, connections are not generally allowed to transmit activation values, or groups or sequences of them, that are to be thought of as names or addresses of parts of the network.
- Stored programs are not allowed, in any conventional sense. That is, connections are not generally allowed to transmit activation values, or groups or sequences of them, that are to be thought of as names of internal computational actions to be performed.
- Connectionist systems are generally not supposed to have central controllers.

Apart from wondering why these features cause difficulty, one might well ask why they are imposed in the first place. The real, though often unspoken, reason seems to be a desire not to stray too far from the presumed nature of biological neural networks, even in connectionist research that does not explicitly purport to be biologically realistic.[5] Even granting that this desire is reasonable, however, we are left with some questions, such as whether there is any evidence that signals in mammalian brains do not, in fact, encode pointers or names of internal computational actions. Also, as Barnden and Srinivas (1991) argue, the very notion of a pointer becomes intrinsically slippery as soon as one leaves behind the architectural precepts of conventional computers.

The present volumes do not seek to answer these questions about the nature and motivations of connectionism. With the exception of Bonissone et al.'s contribution, the chapters make the implicit assumption that it is methodologically worthwhile to see whether connectionist techniques that mostly obey the above restrictions can be used to achieve analogical processing.

The reader interested in how the general difficulties faced by high-level connectionism can be overcome may wish to consult Volume 1 in the present series (Barnden & Pollack, 1991a; Dinsmore, 1992; Hinton, 1991a).

6. OVERVIEW OF THE CHAPTERS

This pair of volumes is logically organized into three parts. The first two parts comprise Volume 2, and the third part is Volume 3.

---

[4] However, it is difficult to make clear sense of this feature, given the metaphorical nature of the words "central" and "controller." Indeed, most connectionist models do, implicitly, have a central controller, which, for instance, tells units when to adjust their weights and when not to; but the controller is usually hidden from view in the simulation program or the modeler's mind, rather than being cased out in connectionist terms. (For further observations of this sort, see Aizawa, 1992.)

[5] However, Shastri (1991) provides some in-principle arguments for the validity of some of the restrictions.

Volume 2, Part I—Integrated Models of Analogical Thinking

This part contains five chapters focusing on connectionist or partially connectionist systems aimed at performing a large part of the whole task of analogy-based reasoning, rather than focusing on just one stage such as mapping.

Hofstadter and Mitchell (Chapter 1) describe Copycat, a nondeterministic model of analogy making aiming at psychological realism. Copycat is hybrid in the general sense used in this introduction (see Section 2).[6] The authors maintain that the hybrid middle ground in cognitive modeling occupied by Copycat is, at present, the most useful level at which to attempt to understand the fluidity of concepts and perception that is so clearly apparent in human analogy making. Copycat discovers analogies between abstract situations in a microworld designed to capture many basic issues in analogy making. A central tenet is that analogy making cannot be divorced from perception. Copycat's perceptual interpretations of and mappings between the situations it is given are constructed in parallel, each activity influencing the other; and all processing aims at building up structures representing perceptions, at various levels of abstraction. In mapping, inexact matches are allowed by "conceptual slippages," which are enabled when concepts are sufficiently close in the Slipnet (Copycat's concept repository). Each Slipnet node represents a concept's core, with the full concept being a probabilistically defined "halo" surrounding the core. As perceptions are made, the Slipnet flexes in response, adjusting interconcept distances and spreading activation among nodes. Reciprocally, the Slipnet's changing state serves, along with dynamic saliences of objects, as a source of biases guiding the parallel terraced scan, a probabilistic mode of search by which promising routes are explored rapidly and "dark horses" more slowly, avoiding a combinatorial explosion. As perception deepens, bottom-up yields to top-down processing, in which concepts discovered to be relevant are imposed on the situation; global order thus tends to emerge. Numerous simulation runs reveal Copycat's robust behavior despite its nondeterministic substrate. It almost always steers clear of bizarre pathways, usually arrives quickly at reasonable answers, and occasionally discovers creative analogies. On a philosophical level, Hofstadter and Mitchell argue that nondeterminism is necessary for flexible cognition, and claim that their architecture, being essentially a model of fluid concepts and mental pressures, has validity beyond analogy making.

Holyoak, Novick, and Melz argue in their chapter (Chapter 2) that the commonly distinguished processes of analogical mapping, inference, and evaluation/adaptation—collectively making up the process of analogical transfer but commonly distinguished from each other—are indeed psychologically distinct. For example, an analogist may succeed in deriving a reasonable

---

[6] Hofstadter and Mitchell state that their system is not hybrid, but they assign a narrower meaning to the term than we do in this introduction.

mapping between a solved source problem and an unsolved target problem yet be unable to perform the inference and/or evaluation processes required to use the mapping to generate a useful solution to the target problem. The chapter considers the extent to which the three subprocesses of analogical transfer are amenable to modeling using connectionist-style mechanisms. The theoretical starting point is the ACME system for analogical mapping (see Section 4). The authors agree that with some simple extensions ACME can also account for basic postmapping analogical inferences, but that without much more extensive augmentation the more open-ended process of evaluation and adaptation lie beyond the model's capabilities. More generally, the differential success of humans at various stages of analogical transfer may suggest the need to integrate connectionist mechanisms with rule-based reasoning (cf. the chapters by Nelson, Thagard, and Hardy and by Kokinov). The extended ACME system, like ACME itself, is hybrid in the sense that a mapping network is dynamically constructed by symbolic processing of the provided target and source analogs. However, the constructed network itself is entirely connectionist.

The chapter by Nelson, Thagard, and Hardy (Chapter 3) presents part of a theory that ties together three important factors in high-level cognition: analogy, rule-based reasoning, and explanation (including hypothesis generation and evaluation). The chapter concentrates on the integration of analogy-based reasoning and rule-based processing. The authors believe there are deep affinities between these two types of processing, and that both can be viewed as processes of parallel satisfaction of semantic, structural, and pragmatic constraints within a connectionist network. The chapter describes an implemented system called CARE (Connecting Analogies with Rules and Explanations). CARE illustrates a novel kind of rule-based processing complementary with the authors' previous connectionist work on analogy. CARE is based on a connectionist network, but overall is a hybrid symbolic/connectionist system because, as noted in Section 6.2 of the chapter, new nodes and links are added in the course of problem solving, and variable binding is done by means of a symbolic technique.

Eskridge's chapter (Chapter 4) proposes a theory of analogical reasoning termed Continuous Analogical Reasoning, and partially realized in an implemented, hybrid symbolic/connectionist analogy system (ASTRA). The theory is designed to encompass the major aspects of analogical reasoning rather than to isolate a single stage of the process. It is motivated by the belief that the main problem hindering much of the research on analogical reasoning is that only one portion of the analogical reasoning process is studied while interactions with other aspects of the process are ignored. Eskridge argues that while many researchers are quick to agree that indeed the stages should be integrated, few produce models which lend themselves well to integration. One justification for modeling only one portion of the analogy process is that it is easier to implement one portion at a time, with the idea that once components are developed for each stage of analogy the components can be tied together to create a complete system. However, Eskridge maintains that modeling a single stage of the analogical reasoning process will produce an inadequate model of that stage when viewed in isolation or when viewed as part of the complete analogical reasoning process. One reason for this is that isolating a stage of the process clouds the issue of what processes compose that stage. This is because the individually modeled stage will include mechanisms to perform processing that would normally be done by another stage. ASTRA is hybrid in that network links have type labels, symbolic marker passing is used, and new links are created as a result of symbolic processing.

Kokinov's chapter (Chapter 5) also presents a hybrid symbolic/connectionist model of human analogical reasoning (AMBR). In both chapters the symbolic and connectionist aspects are intimately intertwined rather than being confined to separate modules; and, in both, the symbolic aspects facilitate the encoding and manipulation of complex bodies of information, while the connectionist aspects facilitate associative retrieval. Again, Kokinov addresses retrieval, mapping, mapping-based inference, and other processes, rather than concentrating on one stage of analogical reasoning, and casts them as processes running in parallel rather than as sequential stages. Kokinov's driving concern is to account for the context-dependent variability and flexibility of human problem-solving behavior, a matter that is ignored by most models of analogy. In particular, his model is directed at accounting for the dependence of reasoning on recent memory accesses. Accordingly, the model's memory is not a static store, but instead a dynamic process running in parallel to all other reasoning components. Kokinov's system is hybrid much in the sense that Eskridge's system is: network links have type labels, symbolic processing (including marker passing) as well as connectionist activation spread occurs over the network, and new nodes and links are created by symbolic processing.

There is a great deal of high-level similarity between Kokinov's approach and that of Hofstadter and Mitchell's. All the different stages of analogy making should occur in parallel, not in serial (see also Eskridge). Semantic similarity should be dynamic and context dependent and should depend (at least in part) on the activation levels of certain key concepts. Dynamic activation levels of concept nodes should control the focus of attention and determine pragmatic factors such as the relevance of concepts and the salience of objects. The parallelism should be governed by dynamically changing pragmatic factors resulting in different processes running at different speeds (which themselves vary over time, as the pragmatic factors vary).

Volume 2, Part II—Similarity and Analogical Mapping

The chapters in this part contain more general investigations into particular analogical mapping techniques and constraints, the role of mapping in similarity judgments, and connectionist support for analogical mapping. (See also Barnden's chapter in Volume 3 on this last point.)

Goldstone and Medin's chapter (Chapter 6) addresses human judgments of the similarity of visual figures. The authors claim that there is more to similarity than property listing and matching. Comparing scenes and objects requires a more structured representation than a feature list, and requires a more sophisticated process than counting up matches and mismatches. Features are organized into objects; objects are organized into relations; relations are organized into scenes. The parts of a scene are mapped onto the parts of the scene with which it is compared, and this process of finding corresponding parts has an important influence on the perceived similarity. The purposes of the chapter are: (a) to demonstrate the process of mapping in human scene comparison, (b) to present new experimental findings implicating mapping in similarity assessment, and (c) to organize and interpret these results with a connectionist model of mapping and similarity (SIAM). This system is hybrid in the same way that ACME is. (See also earlier description of Chapter 2.)

The chapter by Halford, Wilson, Guo, Gayler, Wiles, and Stewart (Chapter 7) presents a parallel distributed processing model of the structure-mapping component of analogical reasoning. The model is designed to make realistic demands on processing capacity. The cognitive processing capacity literature is reviewed, and it is suggested that approximately four chunks (independent items of arbitrary size) can be processed in parallel. After noting similarities between chunks and attributes on dimensions, it is predicted that adult humans can process four dimensions in parallel. Empirical evidence on this proposition is presented. A conceptual complexity metric, which defines concepts based on from one to four dimensions, is presented, together with empirical evidence that concepts of higher dimensionality impose higher processing loads. The predicate-argument binding problem is handled by representing a predicate and its arguments each as a single vector, with the binding being represented as the tensor product of the vectors (following the approach of Smolensky, 1991). This representation is used in a mathematical and computer simulation model of analogical reasoning called the Structured Tensor Analogical Reasoning (STAR) model. Analogies of the form $A:B::C:?$ can be solved by entering A and B into the tensor product as arguments of an unknown predicate, and solving for the predicate. The predicate and the argument C are then entered into the tensor product, and the remaining argument, D, is found. Analogical reasoning tasks are categorized into six basic types, all of which can be handled in principle by the proposed model. The complexity of computing tensor products of high rank provides a natural explanation for processing loads imposed by concepts of high dimensionality. Concepts with a dimensionality that exceeds processing capacity are either recoded into fewer dimensions (conceptual chunking) or are decomposed into components that are processed serially (segmentation). The model as presented is entirely connectionist, although the possible extensions that are described are not given in connectionist form.

The chapter by Hummel, Burns, and Holyoak (Chapter 8) considers the possibility that some of the limitations of ACME with respect to psychological and neural plausibility might be alleviated by adapting connectionist techniques for dynamic binding by synchrony of firing. These techniques have proved useful in modeling visual object recognition and in implementing rapid logical inference in connectionism. As a preliminary exploration of the roles that synchrony may play in analogical mapping, the authors describe two variants of mapping models, both in early stages of development, that provide examples of the approach. One variant permits dynamic link creation and is to that extent hybrid, but the second variant is entirely connectionist.

Stenning and Oberlander's chapter (Chapter 9) focuses on the analogy between spatial inclusion and set membership, as a case study of the way in which mental processing is aided by analogical mappings. In the case of the chosen analogy, this comes down to the question of how graphical representations aid processing. The chapter sketches a general theory (developed more fully elsewhere) that rests on the observation that graphical representation systems limit abstraction and thereby purchase computational tractability. In applying this general theory to the case of graphical methods of syllogism solution, the authors sketch a way of using Euler's Circles, and then use the Euler's Circle method as a guide to connectionist implementation of corresponding internal representations. Stenning and Oberlander maintain that graphical representations share some general computational properties with connectionist systems. In the domain of the syllogism, the central issue is the implementation of the binding of attributes into type descriptions. Various proposals for connectionist variable binding in the literature are assessed as partial implementations. As noted above, the authors' own view is that people's mental bindings are based on experience with particular content areas and that some bindings are therefore more easily maintained than others.

Volume 3, Part III—Analogy, Metaphor, and Reminding

Here the chapters focus on some connections between analogy and language, on metaphor, and on the question of the retrieval of source analogs in either analogy-based reasoning or case-based reasoning (CBR).

Lange and Wharton's chapter (Chapter 1) is based on the observation that most AI research on natural language has modeled memory retrieval separately from language understanding, even though both activities seem to use many of the same processes. The chapter describes REMIND (Retrieval from Episodic Memory through INferencing and Disambiguation), a localist connectionist model of integrated text comprehension and episodic reminding. In REMIND, activation is spread through a semantic network that performs dynamic inferencing and disambiguation to infer a conceptual representation of an input cue. Because stored episodes are associated with concepts used to understand them, the spreading-activation process also activates any memory episodes in the network that share features or knowledge structures with the cue. Since the inferences made from a cue often include actors' plans and goals only implied in a cue's text, REMIND is able to get abstract, analogical remindings that would not be possible without an integrated understanding and retrieval model. Because the remindings are affected by plans and goals inferred from the text, REMIND goes some way towards incorporating into analogical processing the high-level planning and thematic knowledge structures used as retrieval indices in CBR. The authors also make the interesting observation about the role of elaborative inferencing in retrieval that was noted in Section 5.

The REMIND system is almost entirely connectionist. The semantic network described in the chapter and the processing it supports are fully cashed out in connectionist terms. However, the overall approach is currently hybrid in that the insertion of new episodes into the network is done by hand, and not by the net itself, although the authors ultimately intend that the net be able to do it. An interesting connectionist feature of REMIND is that it achieves dynamic binding by means of "signatures," which are activation patterns that name specific concept-representing subnetworks. Signatures are therefore pointers is the very general sense implied in Section 5, above. (Inferences are not like pointers in a computer.)

Seifert's chapter (Chapter 2) points out that most feature-based memory models assume that retrieval of cases is an automatic process where an input is matched to the contents of memory and an episode is activated based on overall similarity. However, when there are many instances that overlap in similarity, or when the similarities are abstract in nature, it appears that retrieval based on similarity alone will often fail to result in case access. Seifert argues that the context of processing goals must affect the retrieval of cases: the same input, the presence of different processing goals such as explanation or planning, appears to result in retrieval of different cases from memory. The evidence for this claim consists of a series of experiments demonstrating that activation of cases does not occur automatically, but is dependent on strategic processing goals. Reminding protocols and examples of case-based reasoning programs are also examined to determine if similar processing goal effects might be evident. Finally, a hybrid model of retrieval is proposed that incorporates the content-addressable character of connectionist models with a controlling mechanism that uses goal context to select relevant features. A weighting scheme is proposed to override features that prevent a match in favor of features that are related to the current goals of the processor. The role of processing-goal context is particularly important for case retrieval in computer models, where the nature of the strategic task processes is often left implicit.

Domeshek's chapter (Chapter 3) argues that retrieval of cases from memory in a CBR system can reasonably be conceptualized as a massively parallel matching process and may be a good application for a connectionist network. Domeshek maintains, however, that for the foreseeable future, knowledge engineering will remain a hard problem and that people must do the work of inventing appropriate encodings for retrieval cues. Domeshek does this work for the specific task domain of providing advice about personal-relationship problems by retrieving episodes centered on similar problems. The encodings Domeshek constructs are flat feature-vector encodings of complex symbolic structures describing the states, themes, events, causal connections, and so on that are involved in the personal-relationship domain. The system presented in the chapter is realizable in fully connectionist terms, but is to be considered part of a larger imagined system that is not given a connectionist description by the author.

Bonissone, Rau, and Berg's chapter (Chapter 4) also addresses retrieval in CBR systems, and rests on the claim that CBR systems need to exhibit associative retrieval and partial matching. The conventional wisdom holds that the distributed representations of connectionist models of the parallel distributed processing variety are unsurpassed when it comes to these qualities. The chapter argues that for practical CBR systems this may not be the case. The retrieval method for the authors' CBR system, which is called CARS, uses a localist representation scheme combined with marker passing and intersection search. It has all of the relevant desirable qualities of a parallel distributed processing system, namely, associative retrieval, pattern completion, and approximate matching. (Notice the similarity to some of the arguments in Barnden's chapter, see below.) On the other hand, CARS does not have the drawbacks of parallel distributed processing systems, in particular, the need for protracted training, and the lack of mechanisms for retrieval of more than one answer.

Lakoff's chapter (Chapter 5) presents the claim that the study of metaphor is of special interest to connectionist cognitive scientists. The bulk of the chapter goes to surveying previous findings that basic concepts like time, state, attribute, cause, purpose, and means are metaphorical, and that, in general, abstract concepts are metaphorically understood in terms of more concrete, typically spatial, concepts. Lakoff, therefore, maintains that an account of metaphor will go a long way towards a characterization of human concepts, and a connectionist theory of metaphor will correspondingly go a long way toward providing a connectionist theory of the human conceptual system. However, the chapter, when put together with our comments above on difficulties faced by connectionism, makes it apparent that there are major disparities between the various kinds of things that connectionist models of metaphor must eventually be able to do and the current capacities of existing connectionist models. Lakoff argues nevertheless that a connectionist approach is appropriate. One reason is that connectionism could naturally support the simultaneous activation of several metaphorical mappings, a phenomenon that seems to occur in some types of metaphor. (Lakoff also maintains that so-called image schemas—see Lakoff, 1990—are important in metaphor, but that symbol-manipulation systems cannot handle them. However, it remains to be seen whether connectionism is good at handling them.)

Weber's chapter (Chapter 6) presents an implemented, localist (or "structured") connectionist model whose capabilities include the understanding of (initially) unfamiliar figurative adjective-noun combinations, such as "green recruit," where the meaning of an adjective needs to be metaphorically extended away from its initially encoded meanings. Weber's model, which is entirely connectionist, features a unified account of literal and metaphoric interpretation. The model is built on mechanisms for dynamic conceptual attribute retrieval, where attributes primed by context will be retrieved in preference to those which are contextually irrelevant. The model uses property abstraction and scalar value transference as interpretive mechanisms for novel metaphoric usages, and uses a frequency-based word sense acquisition mechanism common to both literal and figurative usages.

Harris (Chapter 7) adopts the hypothesis that natural language displays organizational principles which are fundamental to human cognition. The chapter integrates the ideas of modern analogy theorists with language data—in particular, with data relevant to the systems of rules and partial regularities holding between linguistic expressions and their conventional interpretations. Harris argues that the continuum from abstract rules to analogical relations to similarity of properties observed for both conceptual and linguistic processing arises from a common substrate, the cognitive microstructure, as described by researchers working in the parallel distributed processing framework. The ideas are illustrated by two implementations of parallel distributed processing models of polysemy. The specific problem to be solved is identifying the relationship among entities in expressions containing the polysemous prepositions "over," "across," "through," "around," "above," and "below." The hidden units of the trained network can be analyzed to see how linguistic information is represented, but the analysis also sheds light on questions of interest to the modern analogy theorists, such as whether novel patterns are processed "on analogy" to patterns which share similar features, similar relations, or similar systems of corresponding features. In addition, examples such as "talk over a problem" and "around $100" might be construed as exhibiting metaphor. The model presented in the chapter is entirely connectionist.

Barnden's chapter (Chapter 8) pursues two related themes, both concerned with largely unexplored connections between analogy and connectionism. The first theme is that analogy-based reasoning provides a bridge over the gap between traditional AI and connectionism. This claim rests mainly on the observation that analogy-based reasoning, even when given a traditional symbolic implementation, overcomes much of the rigidity for which traditional AI is criticized by connectionists. (The chapters by Nelson et al. [Sections 2 & 4] and Bonissone et al. make related observations.) Implementing analogy-based reasoning in connectionism then confers further advantages, such as the possibility of doing efficient structural indexing of source analogs by means of connectionist reduced representations (see Section 5). The chapter sketches ABR-Conposit, an entirely connectionist analogy-based reasoning system that is being implemented, and which is a descendant of the connectionist rule-based reasoning system described by Barnden (1991). ABR-Conposit uses the same basic techniques for implementing complex, temporary data structures as the older system did, namely "relative-position encoding" and "pattern-similarity association" (neither of which had previously been used in connectionism).

The second theme of Barnden's chapter is to do with the types of structural matching that human-like cognition requires. Barnden claims that it requires WM/WM matching—the construction of a mapping between two data structures in working memory, where neither need have been brought down from long-term memory. This type of matching is of course unexceptional in the traditional symbolic framework, but presents a problem for styles of connectionism that seek to avoid the mere implementation of traditional symbolic processing.

7. SUMMARY

We hope that this book and its companion will serve to stimulate further research on connecting connectionism to analogy, metaphor, similarity, reminding, and case-based reasoning, whether such research focuses on special benefits or illumination that connectionism might bring to these topics, or on challenges and goals that these topics might present to connectionism. In addition, we hope that future research will delve more deeply into the perceptual metaphor for thought, and explore to what extent connectionism may or may not provide a basis for the metaphor. We need to understand why and how thought is, in fact, similar to perception (if indeed it is), and also why it is that the human mind is so constructed that, rightly or wrongly, it perceives a similarity here. We also hope that research on connectionist approaches to metaphor will catch up with work on applying connectionism to analogy. Given the strong links between metaphor and analogy and the not inconsiderable body of computational work that has been done on metaphor within symbolic AI, there is a solid basis for more research on developing computationally detailed connectionist approaches to at least some aspects of metaphor.

Finally, we note that most connectionist models bear merely an analogical or metaphorical relationship to biological neural networks. Whether work such as that represented in these volumes will indirectly throw light on biology, and whether biological neural nets have extra features that might help support analogical or metaphorical processing, are other matters for future pondering.

REFERENCES

Aizawa, K. (1992). Biology and sufficiency in connectionist theory. In J. Dinsmore, (Ed.), *The symbolic and connectionist paradigms: Closing the gap* (pp. 69–88). Hillsdale, NJ: Erlbaum.

Barnden, J.A. (1984). On short-term information processing in connectionist theories. *Cognition and Brain Theory, 7*(1), 25–59.
Barnden, J.A. (1991). Encoding complex symbolic data structures with some unusual connectionist techniques. In J.A. Barnden & J.B. Pollack (Eds.), *Advances in connectionist and neural computation theory, Vol. 1: High-level connectionist models* (pp. 180–240). Norwood, NJ: Ablex.
Barnden, J.A. (1992). *Connectionist, structure-sensitivity, and systematicity: Refining the task requirements* (Memoranda in Computer and Cognitive Science, No. MCCS-92-227). Las Cruces, NM: Computing Research Laboratory, New Mexico State University.
Barnden, J.A., & Pollack, J.B. (Eds.). (1991a). *Advances in connectionist and neural computation theory, Vol. 1: High-level connectionist models*. Norwood, NJ: Ablex.
Barnden, J.A., & Pollack, J.B. (1991b). Introduction: Problems for high-level connectionism. In J.A. Barnden & J.B. Pollack (Eds.), *Advances in connectionist and neural computation theory, Vol. 1: High-level connectionist models* (pp. 1–16). Norwood, NJ: Ablex.
Barnden, J.A., & Srinivas, K. (1991). Encoding techniques for complex information structures in connectionist systems. *Connection Science, 3*(3), 263–309.
Blank, D.S., Meeden, L.A., & Marshall, J.B. (1992). Exploring the symbolic/subsymbolic continuum: A case study of RAAM. In J. Dinsmore (Ed.), *The symbolic and connectionist paradigms: Closing the gap* (pp. 113–148). Hillsdale, NJ: Erlbaum.
Carbonell, J.G. (1983). Learning by analogy: Formulating and generalizing plans from past experience. In R.S. Michalski, J.G. Carbonell, & T.M. Mitchell (Eds.), *Machine learning: An artificial intelligence approach* (pp. 137–161). Palo Alto, CA: Tioga.
Chalmers, D.J. (1990). Syntactic transformations on distributed representations. *Connection Science, 2*(1 & 2), 53–62.
Chandler, S.R. (1991). Metaphor comprehension: A connectionist approach to implications for the mental lexicon. *Metaphor and Symbolic Activity, 6*(4), 227–258.
Dinsmore, J. (Ed.). (1992). *The symbolic and connectionist paradigms: Closing the gap*. Hillsdale, NJ: Erlbaum.
Feldman, J.A., & Ballard, D.H. (1982). Connectionist models and their properties. *Cognitive Science, 6*, 205–254.
Fodor, J.A., & Pylyshyn, Z.W. (1988). Connectionism and cognitive architecture: A critical analysis. In S. Pinker & J. Mehler (Eds.), *Connections and symbols*. (pp. 3–71). Cambridge, MA: MIT Press, and Amsterdam: Elsevier. (Reprinted from *Cognition*, 1988, *28*.)
Gentner, D. (1983). Structure-mapping: A theoretical framework. *Cognitive Science, 7*, 155–170.
Gick, M.L., & Holyoak, K.J. (1980). Analogical problem solving. *Cognitive Psychology, 12*, 306–355.
Hall, R.P. (1989). Computational approaches to analogical reasoning: A comparative analysis. *Artificial Intelligence, 39*, 39–120.
Helmholtz, H.L.F. von. (1962). *Helmholtz's treatise on physiological optics* (Translated from the 3rd German edition; J.P.C. Southall, ed.). New York: Dover Publications.
Hinton, G.E. (1986). Learning distributed representations of concepts. *Proceedings of the Eighth Annual Conference of the Cognitive Science Society* (pp. 1–12). Hillsdale, NJ: Erlbaum.

Hinton, G.E. (1988). Representing part-whole hierarchies in connectionist networks. *Proceedings of the Tenth Annual Conference of the Cognitive Science Society* (pp. 48–54). Hillsdale, NJ: Erlbaum.

Hinton, G.E. (1991a). *Connectionist symbol processing*. Cambridge, MA: MIT Press.

Hinton, G.E. (1991b). Mapping part-whole hierarchies into connectionist networks. In G.E. Hinton (Ed.), *Connectionist symbol processing* (pp. 47–75). Cambridge, MA: MIT Press.

Holyoak, K.J., & Thagard, P. (1989). Analogical mapping by constraint satisfaction. *Cognitive Science, 13*, 295–355.

Indurkhya, B. (1991). Modes of metaphor. *Metaphor and Symbolic Activity, 6*(1), 1–27.

Lakoff, G. (1990). The Invariance Hypothesis: Is abstract reason based on image-schemas? *Cognitive Linguistics, 1*(1), 39–74.

Lakoff, G., & Johnson, M. (1980). *Metaphors we live by*. Chicago: University of Chicago Press.

Maier, N.R.F. (1930). Reasoning in humans. I. On direction. *Journal of Comparative Psychology, 10*, 115–143.

Marr, D., & Poggio, T. (1976). Cooperative computation of stereo disparity. *Science, 194*, pp. 283–287.

Plate, T. (1991). Holographic reduced representations: convolution algebra for compositional distributed representations. *Proceedings of the Twelfth International Joint Conference on Artificial Intelligence* (pp. 30–35). San Mateo, CA: Morgan Kaufmann.

Pollack, J.B. (1987). Cascaded back-propagation on dynamic connectionist networks. *Proceedings of the Ninth Annual Conference of the Cognitive Science Society*. Hillsdale, NJ: Erlbaum.

Pollack, J.B. (1991). Recursive distributed representations. In G.E. Hinton (Ed.), *Connectionist symbol processing* (pp. 77–105). Cambridge, MA: MIT Press.

Richards, G. (1989). *On psychological language and the physiomorphic basis of human nature*. London: Routledge.

Rumelhardt, D.E., Smolensky, P., McClelland, J.L., & Hinton, G.E. (1986). Schemata and sequential thought processes in PDP models. In J.L. McClelland, D.E. Rumelhart, & the PDP Research Group (Eds.), *Parallel distributed processing* (Vol. 2). Cambridge, MA: MIT Press.

Shastri, L. (1991). The relevance of connectionism to AI: A representation and reasoning perspective. In J.A. Barnden & J.B. Pollack (Eds.), *Advances in connectionist and neural computation theory, Vol. 1* (pp. 259–283). Norwood, NJ: Ablex.

Smolensky, P. (1991). Tensor product variable binding and the representation of symbolic structures in connectionist systems. In G.E. Hinton (Ed.), *Connectionist symbol processing* (pp. 159–216). Cambridge, MA: MIT Press.

Spellman, B.A., & Holyoak, K.J. (1992). If Saddam is Hitler then who is George Bush? Analogical mapping between systems of social roles. *Journal of Personality and Social Psychology, 62*, 913–933.

Stolcke, A., & Wu, D. (1992). *Tree matching with recursive distributed representations* (Tech. Rep. No. 92-025). University of California, Berkeley, CA: Computer Science Division.

Sumida, R.A., & Dyer, M.G. (1989). Storing and generalizing multiple instances while maintaining knowledge-level parallelism. *Proceedings of the Eleventh Interna-*

tional Joint Conference on Artificial Intelligence. San Mateo, CA: Morgan Kaufmann.

Sweetser, E.E. (1990). *From etymology to pragmatics: Metaphorical and cultural aspects of semantic structure.* Cambridge, United Kingdom: Cambridge University Press.

van Gelder, T. (1991). What is the "D" in "PDP"? A survey of the concept of distribution. In W. Ramsey, S.P. Stich, & D.E. Rumelhart (Eds.). *Philosophy and connectionist theory* (pp. 33–59). Hillsdale, NJ: Erlbaum.

1
REMIND: Retrieval From Episodic Memory by Inferencing and Disambiguation*

Trent E. Lange
Charles M. Wharton

1. INTRODUCTION

The most parsimonious account of language comprehension and episodic reminding is that they "amount to different views of the same mechanism" (Schank, 1982, p. 23). Consider the following:

> There were sightings of great whites off Newport, but Jeff wasn't concerned. The surfer was eaten by the fish. They found his board with a big chunk cut out. (**Killer Shark**)

When reading this passage, we may be reminded of analogous stories of people being eaten by sharks, or, more abstractly, of others who knowingly ventured into mortal danger and suffered the consequences (e.g., skiers being buried under avalanches they were warned about). Why do these remindings occur? To comprehend this passage, a reader must find structures in memory that will provide important inferred information such as the goals and plans of story characters and the characteristic features of events and locations. Thus, in the process of constructing the meaning of a text passage, we may be reminded of similar episodes because these episodes were understood with (and have became associated with) the same knowledge structures.

---

* This research was supported by NSF Grant DIR-9024251, Army Research Institute Contract MDA 903-89-K-0179, and by a grant from the Keck Foundation. We would like to thank John Barnden, Michael Dyer, Keith Holyoak, Eric Melz, and John Reeves for their helpful comments on the model and on earlier drafts of this chapter.

In spite of the apparent connectedness of comprehension and memory, artificial intelligence simulations of memory retrieval have usually modeled reminding separately from story and language understanding. While this approach may make accounts of each phenomena more manageable, it is undeniable that real-world retrieval cues are the product of the comprehension process. Further, the manner in which a fully elaborated scene interpretation, or discourse model (Kintsch, 1988), is constructed from an explicit textual representation will influence what is retrieved from memory. Thus, we believe that a model that integrates the process by which a cue is understood with the process by which it is used to recall information from memory can make an important contribution to the understanding of episodic memory retrieval.

In this chapter we describe REMIND (Retrieval from Episodic Memory through INferencing and Disambiguation), a structured connectionist spreading-activation model that integrates language understanding and memory retrieval. We start by giving an overview of the comprehension and reminding processes that REMIND models. We then summarize relevant psychological and artificial intelligence (AI) investigations of sentential comprehension, word sense selection, inference generation, and episodic reminding. Next, we describe and demonstrate how the model performs language understanding and memory retrieval. We conclude by showing several examples to illustrate REMIND's inferencing and reminding abilities and compare them with those of other AI and psychological models of episodic reminding.

1.1. Aspects of Reminding

All researchers agree that people tend to be reminded of episodes from memory that are somehow similar to a cue story or thought, as opposed to being reminded of episodes that are completely dissimilar. Much debate has concerned whether memory retrieval is affected by surface similarity, thematic similarity, or a combination of both (cf. Seifert, this volume). Surface, or *superficial*, similarity between a cue story and an episode occurs when both share similar features, such as similar actors, places, or actions. Thematic, or *analogical*, similarity occurs when episode representations mostly share the same abstract goals, plans, roles, causal structures, beliefs, and attitudes. It is generally assumed that thematic remindings are more useful than surface remindings for a problem solver because thematically similar remindings are likely to contain information most relevant to the problem at hand. Different computational models of memory retrieval have made use of surface and abstract similarities to varying degrees, but empirical evidence from cognitive psychology indicates that both types of similarities have an important effect on the episodes of which people are reminded.

There is overwhelming psychological evidence that human memory retrieval is highly sensitive to the degree of surface feature overlap between the cue and long-term memory episodes (Gentner & Landers, 1985; Ratterman & Gentner, 1987; see discussion in Gentner, 1989, pp. 226-233). In the case of **Killer Shark**, a person would likely be reminded of other stories that also involve great whites, surfers, surf boards, Newport, or eating, because these stories contain concepts that are semantically associated to individual lexical items in this story. In general, people tend to recall stories that have a large semantic overlap with what they are currently thinking about.

While the influence of surface similarity on remindings has generally been agreed upon, the effect of thematic similarity on memory retrieval is still a matter for debate. The most robust finding in the analogy literature is that people often fail to retrieve analogous, but superficially dissimilar, targets (e.g., Gick & Holyoak, 1980; Seifert, McKoon, Abelson, & Ratcliff, 1986). Gentner and her associates (Gentner & Landers, 1985; Ratterman & Gentner, 1987) have found reliable retrieval advantages for cue/target story pairs that shared similar concrete nouns but no analogical similarity in comparison with story pairs that, conversely, were analogically similar but shared no similar concrete nouns. In the context of their SME model of analogical mapping, these findings led Falkenhainer, Forbus, and Gentner (1989, p. 35) to propose that memory access is determined by object-attribute similarity ("mere-appearance rules"), but not the relational similarity between cues and targets.

Intuitively, however, using only the surface features of a text does not seem to tell the whole story of memory retrieval. In fact, it misses most of the story—the actual meaning that a person infers to understand the surface features. Using only the surface features for memory retrieval in **Killer Shark**, for example, would miss the important inferences that the surfer took his surfboard out into the waters off Newport, that he did so despite being warned of the danger, and that he was therefore killed in a vicious fashion by a shark. These inferences would seem to be at least as important cues as surface features such as "sightings," "great white," and "eaten." Even more valuable, from a planning perspective, is the ability to access episodes by more abstract features inferred from the text, so that the memories can be useful in other contexts. For example, recall of the planning failure caused by ignoring the danger warning in **Killer Shark** could literally be life saving to a person who was about to ignore another life-threatening situation (such as warning of avalanches).

Such as approach is taken by many AI models of episodic reminding (e.g., Kolodner, 1984) and case-based reasoning (e.g., Hammond, 1989; Kolodner, Simpson, & Sycara, 1985; Owens, 1989; Schank & Leake, 1989). Because of their problem-solving orientation, such models generally attempt to retrieve the episode from memory that is most likely to help them in their current task. To do this, they search memory using intelligent indexing methods for the best matching episodes that share an analogous structure of goals, plans, enablements, or failures with the current problem situation, depending on the reasoning task. Almost all case-based reasoning models use highly structured representations of episodes (or cases) that include not only their surface features, but also abstract features and structures that allow them to be retrieved at useful times.

Case-based reasoning models have received indirect support from several psychological experiments. For example, the notion that inferred explanations for the reason something failed will cause people to think of other episodes with similar failures was tested by Read and Cesa (1990). These authors found that when subjects were asked to give reasons for unexpected events in stories, they were reminded of previously read stories that had analogous outcomes. Similarly, in contrast to the claims of Falkenhainer et al. (1989), several empirical studies have shown that reminding is sensitive to cue/target analogical or thematic similarity at least in some cases (Gentner & Landers, 1985; Holyoak & Koh, 1987; Ross, 1989; Wharton, Holyoak, Downing, Lange, & Wickens, 1991; Gick & McGarry, 1992). In two experiments in Wharton et al. (1991), subjects studied a number of pairs of two competing passages, such as **Killer Shark** and the following:

> Larry had never had sushi before. His friends bet $20 he couldn't eat everything on the plate, but they lost. The sailor consumed the fish.

The individual words of the competing passages were equally associated with the reminding cues (e.g., *The diver devoured the eel*), but only one of the competing passages shared an analogous sentence with the cue (e.g., *The sailor consumed the fish.*) Wharton et al. (1991) found that analogous passages were recalled more frequently than disanalogous passages when surface similarities were equated, especially when there was more than one related story in memory. In an experiment having a similar competitive design, Wharton, Holyoak, Downing, Lange, and Wickens (1992) found that target stories sharing the same abstract theme with a cue were more likely to be retrieved than competing stories having equivalent surface similarities but which were not thematically related to the cue.

In general, psychological evidence seems to support a theory of reminding in which surface similarities between a cue and the target episodes in memory form a major basis for retrieval, but for which deeper structural similarities and abstract meanings inferred during the understanding and planning process also play an important part.

1.2. The Need For Integrating Reminding and Understanding

As mentioned previously, most psychological and artificial intelligence models of memory retrieval and language understanding have looked at the processes of comprehension and retrieval in isolation. Due to the enormous complexity of human memory retrieval and language comprehension and the limited understanding that we have of them, such an approach has been necessary to make any progress at all. Models of analogical retrieval and case-based retrieval are usually given a complete representation of the input cues, a representation that is either explicitly or implicitly assumed to be the result of general comprehension or reasoning processes. Similarly, models of language understanding (cf. Schank & Abelson, 1977; Dyer, 1983; Kintsch, 1988; Norvig, 1989) have generally performed only language understanding, and not episodic retrieval. The exceptions that perform both (e.g., Lebowitz, 1980; Kolodner, 1984) have generally implemented the understanding and reminding processes as relatively separate modules using a "conventional" language parser to understand the story and passing its output representation to the reminding as a cue.

We believe that building an *integrated* model of language understanding and episodic memory retrieval will allow insights into the processes of both that cannot be gained by modeling them separately. The relationship between language comprehension and episodic reminding is neither simple nor unidirectional. Not only does reading or hearing something occasionally cause one to be reminded of similar episodes, but those remindings themselves can have an important effect on subsequent reasoning and comprehension. An integrated model is perhaps the only way to successfully model some of the more subtle aspects of this interaction. One example is that almost all English language words have multiple senses (e.g., river *bank*, money *bank*). Given the previously noted importance of cue/target lexical similarity, accounting for how individual words are semantically disambiguated is important for a theory of reminding. If the ambiguous sentence *John shot some bucks* is used in a context in which a forest is being talked about, a likely interpretation is that John shot a few deer with a gun (Waltz & Pollack, 1985). However, if the same sentence is read in a context involving casinos, a more likely interpretations is that John lost some money while gambling. Although it has yet to be demonstrated empirically, the different interpretations reached by language understanders in different contexts should also affect what episodes they recall. In the first context, one would be likely to be reminded of episodes involving gambling—an obvious effect of the understanding process on reminding. More telling, however, is that the stories one is reminded of themselves affect the context in which subsequent sentences are read. For example, the context of "the forest" itself could have been activated by having just recalled a particular trip to a national forest after a discussion about vacations. Such priming effects could only be explained by an integrated model in which the understanding and reminding processes interact with and directly affect each other.

Finally, modeling episodic reminding and discourse understanding within an integrated model imposes important constraints on the types of processing and knowledge that can be used in either mechanism. If reminding cues are the direct results of the language comprehension process, then the type of indices that those cues contain is limited to the information that the normal understanding process can (and does) infer. Without modeling this integration and thereby constraining the representations used as recall cues, reminding models are in danger of using information (or input) that might not normally be available for retrieval. For example, some case-based reasoning models routinely assume that the representations of cue stories contain high-level thematic inferences. This is because such inferences are necessary for getting the cross-contextual remindings that these models need for analogical transfer and problem solving to take place. However, it is not necessarily reasonable to assume that people always recognize the high-level themes in the stories they read. This seemed to have been the case in a study by Seifert et al. (1986) in which subjects read two stories that were either superficially dissimilar instantiations of the same theme (such as "closing the barn door after the horse has gotten out"), or instantiations of two different themes. When subjects simply read these stories, there was no evidence for cross-contextual reminding in a speeded recognition task. However, when the subjects were instructed to pay special attention to the thematic structure of the target stories (and therefore were presumably more likely to recognize or infer their abstract themes), an effect of the similar thematic structure on reminding was found. Only by building an integrated model of language comprehension and reminding can one expect to model the specific circumstances under which understanders infer and can use thematic information in probing memory.

1.3. Overview of REMIND

To explore how comprehension and reminding processes interact, we have developed REMIND, a spreading-activation model that integrates language understanding and memory retrieval. REMIND is initially given a syntactic representation of a short input text as a memory cue. Using general knowledge stored in its long-term memory, REMIND constructs an elaborated interpretation of the cue, and then retrieves the sentence or episode that is most similar to the surface and inferred features of that interpretation. REMIND is a model of the type of deliberate, nonaccidental reminding that would occur when one intentionally uses a cue to probe memory, as in attempting to remember an analogous solution to a current problem. While REMIND does not currently model unintentional memory reminding, we are optimistic that much of what we have developed will generalize to such a theory.

REMIND's structured spreading-activation networks encode world knowledge about concepts and general knowledge rules for inferencing in the same way as ROBIN (Lange & Dyer, 1989; Lange, 1992), a structured connectionist model that performs some of the high-level inferencing and disambiguation processes needed for natural language understanding. REMIND's networks also contain representations of prior episodes, such as *Fred put his car in the car wash before his date with Wilma* (**Car Wash**) and *Billy put his Playboy under the bed so his mother wouldn't see it and spank him* (**Dirty Magazine**). The representations of these episodes are the actual plan/goal analysis (or discourse model) that was inferred by the network when input for them was first presented to the network to be understood. These prior episodes are indexed into the semantic comprehension network through connections with all the knowledge structures with which they were understood.

To perform retrieval, REMIND is given a short text passage to use as a deliberate memory cue, such as *John put the pot inside the dishwasher because company was coming* (**Dinner Party**). Units in the network representing the cue and its syntactic bindings are clamped to high levels of activation, which then spreads through the network. By propagating *signature* activation, the network makes the different possible inferences that might explain the input (Lange & Dyer, 1989; see Section 3 below). For example, one of the multiple interpretation paths that gets inferred as a possible explanation for John putting the pot inside the dishwasher in **Dinner Party** is that John was trying to clean the pot to satisfy his goal of having everything ready for entertaining his guests. Other interpretations concurrently activated include the possibilities that he was trying to store the pot or hide it. Activation spreads until the network settles and the units representing the most plausible set of inferences has the most activation. The final most highly-activated chain of inferences represents the network's disambiguated plan/goal interpretation of the cue.

Because the units representing long-term memory episodes are connected within the network, an important side effect of the understanding process is that episodes having concepts related to the elaborated cue also become highly activated. This includes episodes related because there is superficial semantic overlap with the cue (e.g., episodes involving other kitchen appliances or guests) and episodes related abstractly because they share similar inferred plans and goals of their actors (e.g., the **Car Wash** episode becomes activated after receiving the **Dinner Party** cue because both share the inferences that a person was trying to Clean something in preparation for an Entertainment act). After the network settles, the episode that received the most activation from the cue's interpretation and surrounding context becomes the most highly activated, and is therefore retrieved as the best match for the cue.

REMIND is thus an integrated model in which a single mechanism drives both the language understanding and memory retrieval processes. The same spreading-activation mechanism that infers a single coherent interpretation of a cue also activates the episodes the model retrieves from memory. Activation of these episodes combines evidence from both the surface semantics of the input (i.e., different possible word and phrase meanings) and the deeper thematic inferences made from the input, so that the recalled episodes depend on both surface and analogical similarities with the cue. Further, because all representations of the cue and target episodes used in memory retrieval are constructed from inferences made by the language understanding portion of the model, REMIND predicts that the ability to recall analogous episodes directly depends on the context and level of processing when the input was originally understood. And finally, because both inferencing and memory retrieval occur within a single integrated network, the context in which interpretations are formed affects the episodes that are retrieved, which in turn influence the context in which disambiguation and interpretation of input cues takes place. Thus, text comprehension and memory retrieval processes are tightly coupled and strongly effect each other.

1.4. Language Understanding and High-Level Inferencing

The part of the natural-language understanding process that REMIND concentrates on is the problem of *high-level inferencing* (Lange & Dyer, 1989). Because everything that REMIND infers becomes part of the representation of the cue, high-level inferencing is also the basis of its ability to recall analogous memory episodes. High-level inferencing is the use of knowledge and rules about the world to build new beliefs about what is true. To understand a text, a reader must often make multiple inferences to understand the motives of actors and to causally connect actions that are unrelated on the basis of surface semantics alone. Complicating the inference process is the fact that language is often both lexically and conceptually ambiguous. A sentence that serves as a good example of many of the problems of high-level inferencing is the following:

> *John put the pot inside the dishwasher because the police were coming.* (**Hiding Pot**)

Contrast this with the **Dinner Party** example mentioned earlier (*John put the pot inside the dishwasher because company was coming*). In **Dinner Party**, most people would infer that John transferred a Cooking-Pot inside a dishwasher to get the Cooking-Pot clean. In **Hiding Pot**, however, it seems more likely that John was trying to hide his Marijuana from the police. In this case, there are conflicts in the interpretation suggested by the first clause by itself (that John was cleaning a cooking pot) and the final interpretation suggested by the first clause combined with the second clause (that John was hiding marijuana). This reinterpretation requires inferences like those shown in Table 1.1 to understand the most probable causal relationship between the actions in **Hiding Pot**.

To understand episodes such as **Dinner Party** and **Hiding Pot**, a system must be able to dynamically make chains of inferences and temporarily maintain them with a variable-binding mechanism. For example, a system must know about the general concept (or frame) of an actor transferring himself to a location (*coming*). To initially represent the phrase *police were coming* in **Hiding Pot**, the system must be able to temporarily maintain a particular instantiation of this Transfer-Self frame in which the Actor role (a variable) is bound to Police and the location role is bound to some unknown location (which should later be

Table 1.1.
Types of Inferences Needed to Understand the Sentence *John put the pot inside the dishwasher because the police were coming* **(Hiding Pot).**

> I1: If the police see John's marijuana, then they will know that he possesses an illegal object (since marijuana is an illegal substance).
> I2: If the police know that John is in possession of an illegal object, then they will arrest him, since possessing an illegal object is a crime.
> I3: John does not want to get arrested.
> I4: John has the goal of stopping the police from seeing his marijuana.
> I5: The police coming results in them being in the proximity of John and his marijuana.
> I6: The police being in the proximity of John's marijuana enables them to see it.
> I7: John's putting the marijuana inside the dishwasher results in the marijuana being inside the dishwasher.
> I8: The marijuana is inside an opaque object (the dishwasher).
> I9: Since the marijuana is inside an opaque object, the police cannot see it, thus satisfying John's goal.

inferred to be the location of **John**). The system must also have the general knowledge that when an actor transfers himself to a location, he ends up in the proximity of that location, which might be represented as the rule:

R1: (Actor X **Transfer-Self** Location Y)
$==$ results-in $==>$ (Actor X **Proximity-Of** Object Y)

Applying this rule to the instantiation of the police **Transfer Self** would allow the system to make Inference I5 in Table 1.1, that the police will be in the proximity of John and his marijuana. Another rule the system must have to understand **Hiding Pot** is that an actor must be in the proximity of an object in order to see it:

R2: (Actor X **Proximity-Of** Object Y)
$==$ precondition-for $==>$ (Actor X **See-Object** Object Y)

If Rule R2 is applied to the new knowledge that the **Police** will be in the proximity of **John**, then the system infers that there is the potential for the **Police** to see John and his marijuana (I6). The rest of the inferences in Table 1.1 required to understand **Hiding Pot** are the result of the application of similar knowledge rules about the world.

Even the ability to maintain variable bindings and apply general knowledge rules of the above sort is often insufficient for language understanding and other high-level cognitive tasks. This is because language is often ambiguous, as

Hiding Pot illustrates, with several possible interpretations that must be discriminated. One of the fundamental problems in high-level inferencing is thus that of *frame selection* (Lytinen, 1984; Lange & Dyer, 1989). When should a system make inferences from a given frame instantiation? And when conflicting rules apply to a given frame instantiation, which should be selected? Only a system that can handle these problems will be able to address the following critical subparts of the frame selection problem:

> *Word-Sense Disambiguation*—choosing the contextually appropriate meaning of a word. In **Dinner Party**, the word *pot* refers to a Cooking-Pot, but when **Hiding Pot** is presented, the evidence is that the interpretation should change to Marijuana.
>
> *Inferencing*—applying causal knowledge to understand the results of actions and the motives of actors. There is nothing in **Hiding Pot** that explicitly states that the police might see the pot (I6), or even that the police will be in proximity of it and John (I5). Nor is it explicitly stated what the police will do if they see he possesses Marijuana (I1, I2). Each of these assumptions must be inferred from the facts specified in the text.
>
> *Concept Refinement*—instantiating a more appropriate specific frame from a general one. In **Dinner Party**, the fact that the pot was put inside a dishwasher tells us more than the simple knowledge that it was put inside a container. In contrast, the salient point in **Hiding Pot** is the it is inside of an opaque object (I8), which allows us to infer that the police will not be able to see it (I9).
>
> *Plan/Goal Analysis*—recognizing the plan an actor is using to fulfill his goals. In **Dinner Party**, John has put the pot into the dishwasher as part of the $Dishwashing-Cleaning script (a stereotypical sequences of actions) to satisfy his goal of getting the pot clean, perhaps itself serving as part of his plan to prepare for company coming over. In **Hiding Pot**, however, it appears that John has put the pot into the dishwasher to satisfy his subgoal of hiding the pot from the police (I4), which is part of his overall goal of avoiding arrest (I3).

High-level inferencing is complicated by the effect of additional context, which often causes a *reinterpretation* to competing frames. For example, the interpretation of **Hiding Pot** can change again if the next sentence is:

P3: *They were coming over for dinner.*

P3 provides more evidence for the possibility that John was trying to clean the pot to prepare for dinner, perhaps causing the word *pot* to be reinterpreted back to Cooking-Pot, as in **Dinner Party**. These examples clearly point out two subproblems of frame selection, those of *frame commitment* and *reinterpretation*. When should a system commit to one interpretation over another? And if it does commit to one interpretation, how does new context cause that interpretation to change?

The issues of word-sense disambiguation and inferencing have been relatively well explored in psychological experiments. Experiments have shown that many potential meanings of a word (e.g., **Cooking-Pot**, **Marijuana**, and **Planting Pot** for the word *pot*) are "primed" immediately after the word is read—causing subjects, for example, to respond more quickly to words closely related to each of the meanings than to nonprimed words (Swinney, 1979; Till, Mross, & Kintsch, 1988). However, after no more than a second, the contextually appropriate meaning of the word becomes significantly more primed than the nonappropriate meanings. The meaning of the ambiguous word becomes constrained by the lexical environment in which it appears, which is crucial to the selection of its contextually appropriate sense (Glucksberg, Kreuz, & Rho, 1986; Till, Mross, & Kintsch, 1988).

Semantic reinterpretation is necessary when an old lexical interpretation is no longer appropriate to a new linguistic context. While there have been very few studies of this phenomenon, it would seem reasonable that previously activated word meanings would not immediately decay to baseline activation. This residual activation might play a role in the ability to reinterpret word meanings when new linguistic contexts are encountered, as in **Hiding Pot**.

2. RELATED MODELS OF COMPREHENSION AND MEMORY RETRIEVAL

In REMIND, the understanding mechanism constructs an elaborated interpretation of its input that not only serves as the model's representation of the meaning of the text, but is also used as a cue for episodic memory retrieval. The language-understanding component of the system must be able to (a) perform the high-level inferencing necessary to create a causal plan/goal analysis of the cue, (b) dynamically store the complex structured cue representation, and (c) to perform lexical disambiguation (and possible reinterpretation) to select the most contextually appropriate representation. Thus, the brunt of the work in an integrated language understanding and memory retrieval system falls upon the language understanding part of the mode. In this section we discuss several related symbolic and connectionist approaches to these language understanding problems and give a brief overview of previous models of memory retrieval.

2.1. Symbolic Rule-Based Systems

Symbolic rule-based systems have been the most successful AI models at performing the high-level inferencing necessary for natural language understanding. A good example is BORIS (Dyer, 1983), a program for modeling in-depth understanding of relatively long and complex stories. BORIS has a symbolic knowledge base containing knowledge structures representing various actions, plans, goals, emotional affects, and methods for avoiding planning failures. When a story is read in, BORIS fires rules from its knowledge base to infer additional story information. This allows BORIS to form an elaborated representation of the story, about which it can then answer questions. Other models that have successfully approached complex parts of the language understanding process have all had similar types of knowledge representation and rule-firing capabilities (cf. Schank & Abelson, 1977; Lebowitz, 1980; Wilensky, 1983; Lytinen, 1984; Reeves, 1991).

While traditional symbolic models have demonstrated an ability to understand relatively complex stories (albeit in limited domains), these models encounter difficulty when trying to resolve and reinterpret ambiguous input. One solution has been to use expectation-based conceptual analyzers, as in such models as CA and BORIS (Dyer, 1983). These systems use bottom-up or top-down *requests* or *demons* that are activated as words are read in. A word is disambiguated when one of the request rules fires. An example of a bottom-up request that might be used to disambiguate the word *pot* would be:

"If the context involves **cleaning**
then interpret 'pot' as a **cooking pot**."

Once such a request is fired, the interpretation chosen is generally used throughout the rest of the inferencing process, and the word is thrown away. However, this makes it impossible to reinterpret the word if the context changes, such as in **Hiding Pot**. A partial answer might be to keep words around in case a new context causes another disambiguation request to fire. However, this solution creates a different problem—how to decide between conflicting disambiguation rules. For example, one cannot simply specify that the *pot* disambiguation request involving the *police* context always has a higher priority than the request involving the *cleaning* context, because police can be in the same place as cooking pots (e.g., if **Hiding Pot** was followed by *They were coming over for dinner in half an hour.*). As the amount of knowledge stored in the system grows, the number of disambiguation requests needed grows with them, producing even more conflicts. Moreover, because rule application in traditional symbolic models is fundamentally serial, these systems dramatically slow down as the number of inferencing and disambiguation rules increases.

Partially because they avoid such problems, connectionist networks have significant potential advantages over traditional symbolic approaches to language understanding. Their conceptual knowledge is stored entirely in an interconnected network of units whose states are computed in parallel. The activation of these units is calculated solely by local update functions that are based on their previous state and the other units to which they are connected. As a result, a major portion of the understanding process is potentially controlled by a relatively simple, local spreading-activation mechanism, instead of by a large collection of brittle and possibly ad hoc rules.

2.2. Marker-Passing Networks

Marker-passing models operate by spreading symbolic markers in parallel across labeled semantic networks in which concepts are represented by individual nodes. Possible interpretations of the input are formed when marker propagation results in a path of units connecting words and concepts from the input text. Like rule-based systems, marker-passing systems are able to perform much of the high-level inferencing necessary for language understanding because of the symbolic information held in their markers and networks (cf. Charniak, 1986; Riesbeck & Martin, 1986; Granger, Eiselt, & Holbrook, 1986; Norvig, 1989; Kitano, Tomabechi, & Levin, 1989). The primary advantage of marker-passing networks over traditional symbolic, rule-based systems is that their massively parallel marker-passing process allows them to generate all of the different possible interpretations of a text in parallel. This is a tremendous advantage for ambiguous texts such as **Hiding Pot** and for more complex stories.

Marker-passing systems have many of the same problems as traditional symbolic systems in performing disambiguation and reinterpretation. Because of the generally all-or-none symbolic nature of the inference paths generated by the marker-passing process, these systems have problems choosing the most contextually sensible interpretation out of all the paths that they generate. Most marker-passing models attempt to deal with this problem by using a separate symbolic path evaluation mechanism to select the best interpretation. Unfortunately, the marker-passing process generally creates an extremely large number of *spurious* (i.e., unimportant or logically impossible) inference paths, which often represent over 90% of the paths generated even for small networks (Charniak, 1986). As network size increases to include more world knowledge, there is a corresponding explosion in the number of paths generated. Because path evaluation mechanisms work serially, marker-passing systems' advantage of generating inference paths in parallel is substantially diminished. This explosion of generated connections and the generally all-or-none nature of marker-passing inference paths become especially difficult problems when applying marker-passing systems to ambiguous natural language texts (Lange, 1992).[1]

---

[1] Partial solutions to these problems have been proposed by several researchers using *hybrid* marker-passing networks that include some of the aspects of spreading activation (cf. Hendler, 1989; Kitano et al., 1989).

2.3. Distributed Connectionist Networks

Distributed connectionist (or PDP) models represent knowledge as patterns of activation within massively parallel networks of simple processing elements. Distributed connectionist models have many desirable properties, such as learning rules that allow stochastic category generalization, noise-resistant associative retrieval, and robustness against damage (cf. Rumelhart, Hinton, & McClelland, 1986).

A good example of how distributed connectionist models have been used to model language understanding is provided by the case-role assignment model of McClelland and Kawamoto (1986). The main task of their model is to learn to assign proper semantic case roles for sentences. For example, given the syntactic surface form of the sentence *The boy broke the window*, their network is trained to place the semantic microfeature representation of **Boy** in the units representing the agent role on the output layer, whereas given *The rock broke the window*, it is trained to place the representation of **Rock** in the instrument role. Their network is also trained to perform lexical disambiguation, for example, mapping the pattern for the word *bat* to a **Baseball-Bat** for sentences such as *The boy hit the ball with the bat*, and to a **Flying-Bat** for sentences such as *the bat flew*. Once the input/output pairs have been learned, the network exhibits a certain amount of generalization by mapping the cases roles and performing lexical disambiguation for new inputs that are similar to the training sentences.

One of the main limitations of McClelland and Kawamato's model for language understanding is that it can only successfully analyze direct, one-step mappings from the input to the output. This limits the model to sentences that can be understood and disambiguated based solely upon the surface semantics of the input. Two distributed connectionist models that get around this limitation are those of Mikkulaninen and Dyer (1991) and St. John (1992). Both models use *recurrent networks* with a hidden layer of units whose activation pattern essentially stores the state (or "gestalt") of the stories being understood. This allows them to learn to process more complex texts based on stereotypical scripts and script-like stories (Schank & Abelson, 1977). Both models have the lexical disambiguation abilities of McClelland and Kawamoto's model, but are able to infer unmentioned story events and role-fillers from the script that has been recognized by the hidden layer.

Unfortunately, there may be significant problems in scaling distributed connectionist models to handle more complex language. Both the Miikkulainen--Dyer and the St. John model work by resolving constraints from the context of the input to recognize one of their trained scripts and to instantiate it with the bindings of the particular input story. However, much of language understanding involves the inference of causal relationships between events for completely novel stories in which no script or previously trained input/output pair can be recognized. This requires *dynamic inferencing*—producing chains of inferences over simple known rules, with each inference resulting in a potentially novel intermediate state (Touretzky, 1990). Most importantly, the problem of ambiguity and the exponential number of potential causal connections between two or more events requires that multiple paths be explored in parallel (the forte of marker-passing networks). It remains to be seen whether a single blended activation pattern across the bank of hidden units in a recurrent network can solve this problem by simultaneously holding and making dynamic inferences for multiple, never-before encountered interpretation chains.

Other distributed models explicitly encode variables and rules, such as the models of Touretzky and Hinton (1988) and Dolan and Smolensky (1989). Consequently, such *rule-implementing* distributed models are able to perform some of the dynamic inferencing necessary for language understanding. However, the types of rules they can currently encode are generally limited. More importantly, like traditional rule-based systems, they are *serial at the knowledge level* (i.e., they can fire only one rule at a time). As previously mentioned, this is a serious drawback for natural-language understanding, particularly for ambiguous text, in which the often large number of multiple alternative inference paths must be explored in parallel (Lange, 1992).

2.4. Structured Spreading-Activation Models

Structured (or localist) spreading-activation models are connectionist models that represent knowledge in semantic networks like those of marker-passing networks, but in which the nodes are simple numeric units with weighted interconnections. The activation on each conceptual node generally represents the amount of *evidence* available for its concept in a given context. As in marker-passing networks, structured connectionist networks have the potential to pursue multiple candidate interpretations of a story in parallel as each interpretation is represented by activation in different local areas of the network. Unlike pure marker-passing networks, however, the evidential nature of structured spreading-activation networks make them ideally suited to perform lexical disambiguation. Disambiguation is achieved automatically as related concepts under consideration provide graded activation evidence and feedback to one another in a form of constraint relaxation (cf. Cottrell & Small, 1982; Kintsch, 1988; Waltz & Pollack, 1985).

As an example of how structured connectionist models process language and perform disambiguation, consider the sentence:

The astronomer married the star. (**Star Marriage**)

The word *star* could easily be disambiguated to **Movie-Star** by a symbolic rule-based system having selectional restrictions (even astronomers cannot marry celestial bodies, except perhaps metaphorically). However, many readers report this and similar sentences as "cognitive doubletakes" because *astronomer* initially primes the **Celestial-Body** interpretation. Figure 1.1 shows an extended version of the semantic portion of the structured network Waltz and Pollack (1985) built to process *star marriage* and illustrate this effect. After the input units for *star marriage* are clamped to a high level of activation, the **Celestial-Body** interpretation of *star* initially acquires more activation than the *movie star* interpretation because of priming from **Astronomer** through **Astronomy** (Figure 1.2). However, **Movie-Star** eventually wins out because activation feedback over the semantic connections from the **Marry** unit to **Movie-Star** outweighs that spreading from **Astronomer** to **Celestial-Body**.

Until recently, the applicability of structured connectionist models to natural language understanding has been severely hampered because of their difficulties representing dynamic role bindings and performing inferencing. The basic problem is that the evidential activation on structured networks' conceptual units gives no clue as to *where* that evidence came from. For example, the network of Figure 1.1 has no way to distinguish between the sentences *The astronomer saw the star* and *The star saw the astronomer*, despite the crucial difference that the role bindings make in their interpretation. More importantly, without a mechanism to represent such dynamic bindings, they cannot propagate bindings to make the chains of inferences necessary for understanding more complex texts. Thus, unlike marker-passing systems, most structured connectionist models have been limited to simple language processing tasks that can be resolved solely on the surface semantics of the input.

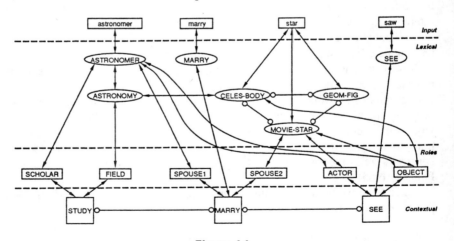

Figure 1.1.
Localist Spreading-Activation Network based on Waltz and Pollack (1985). Lines with arrows are excitatory connections; lines ending with open circles are inhibitory.

Figure 1.2.
Activations of Meaning of Word *star* **after** *astronomer married star* **is Clamped for Network in Figure 1.1.**

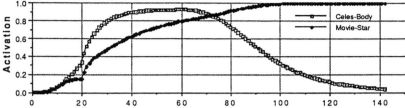

A way of compensating for the lack of dynamic inferencing abilities in spreading-activation networks is to use a symbolic processing mechanism external to the spreading-activation networks themselves to perform the variable binding and inferencing necessary for language understanding. Such a spreading-activation/symbolic hybrid has been used in Kintsch's (1988) construction-integration model of language comprehension. This system uses a traditional symbolic production system to build symbolic representations of the alternative interpretations of a text. These representations are then used to construct a spreading-activation network in which the different interpretations compete to integrate contextual constraints. The integration of constraints with spreading activation in the network allow Kintsch's model to correctly disambiguate and interpret input sentences. A somewhat similar approach is taken by ACT* (Anderson, 1983), a psychologically based spreading-activation model of language understanding, fact encoding and retrieval, and procedure encoding and retrieval. Kintsch's and Anderson's models both illustrate many of the impressive emergent properties of spreading-activation networks for modeling realistic language understanding, such as their ability to model the time course of lexical disambiguation in a way consistent with psychological evidence (e.g., Swinney, 1979). However, if a mechanism internal to the networks (instead of an external symbolic production system) could be found to construct text inferences, the psychological realism of structured spreading-activation networks would be greatly increased.

Recently, a number of researchers have shown how structured connectionist models can handle some variable binding and inferencing abilities within the networks themselves (e.g., Barnden, 1991; Hölldobler, 1990; Shastri & Ajjanagadde, 1993; Sun, in press). Most of these models, however, have not been applied to language understanding and have no mechanisms for handling ambiguity. An exception is ROBIN (Lange & Dyer, 1989), a structured spreading-activation model that propagates *signatures* (activation patterns that identify the concept bound to a role) in order to generate all possible interpretations of an input text in parallel. At the same time, ROBIN uses the network's evidential constraint satisfaction to perform lexical disambiguation and selection of the contextually most plausible interpretation. Thus, ROBIN is able to perform high-level inferencing and disambiguation within the structure of a single network, without the need for external symbolic processing. Given these abilities, such a structured spreading-activation model seems a promising place to start for building an integrated language understanding and memory retrieval model.

2.5. Memory Retrieval Models

The process of memory retrieval has generally been explored in isolation from the process of language understanding. Storage and retrieval of complex episodes requires many of the same abilities to represent and handle structural relationships and variable bindings that natural language understanding does. Because connectionist models have had difficulties handling complex structural relationships in general, few attempts have been made to build connectionist retrieval models for the type of high-level episodes discussed in this chapter. Nonetheless, a few models have shown the potential value of connectionist models for memory storage and retrieval. For example, COPYCAT (Hofstadter & Mitchell, 1994) uses connectionist constraint-satisfaction in solving letter-string analogy problems. Although the retrieval portion of COPYCAT only retrieves simple concepts and not memory episodes, it seems to exhibit some of the fluidity of concepts and perception apparent in human analogical reasoning. Miikkulainen (1993) shows how a variety of distributed connectionist topological feature maps (Kohonen, 1984) can be used to store and retrieve the script-based stories that it has understood using recurrent distributed networks. Besides showing how purely distributed connectionist models can store and retrieve multiple-sentence episodes, Miikkulainen's model exhibits a number of features of human episodic memory, such as certain kinds of memory confusions and recency effects. Although connectionist models such as COPYCAT and Miikkulainen's DISCERN are currently able to store only relatively simple or stereotypical episodes, they do illustrate their promise for psychologically plausible memory retrieval.

As for natural-language understanding, symbolic models have had the greatest success in modeling retrieval of complex, high-level memory episodes. Case-based reasoning (CBR) models (cf. Hammond, 1989; Riesbeck & Schank, 1989) form the largest class of symbolic memory retrieval models. In CBR models, memory access is performed by recognition of meaningful *index patterns* in the input that allow retrieval of the episodes (or cases) most likely to help them solve their current problem. An analysis phase is usually performed to determine the indices that are most important for finding relevant cases for a particular problem, such as cases that share similar plans, goals, enabling preconditions, or explanation failures. In addition, CBR models are usually careful to retrieve *only* those cases that will help find a solution, explicitly rejecting cases that do not. CBR models are therefore generally models of expert reasoning within a given domain of expertise, rather than models of general human reminding. It is quite possible that expert memory retrieval may be satisfactorily modeled by such methods. However, general reminding seems to be substantially "messier," being affected by not only by the sort of useful abstract indices used in CBR models, but also by superficial semantic similarities that often lead to quite *inexpert* remindings. Further, the problem of selecting and recognizing appropriate indices becomes substantially more difficult when reading ambiguous texts outside of limited expert domains.

General, nonexpert reminding has been modeled in systems such as ARCS (Thagard, Holyoak, Nelson, & Gochfeld, 1990) and MAC/FAC (Gentner & Forbus, 1991). These systems model retrieval without using specific indexing methods. Instead they retrieve episodes whose representations share superficial semantic similarities with retrieval cues, with varying degrees of preference towards retrieval of episodes that are also analogically similar or structurally consistent. However, unlike most CBR models, these systems do not specify how they construct the representation of retrieval cues from a source input or text, and so cannot explain how inferences and comprehension affect reminding.

Theoretically, REMIND lies somewhere between case-based reasoning models and general analogical retrieval models such as ARCS and MAC/FAC. Like ARCS and MAC/FAC, REMIND is meant to be a psychologically plausible model of general human reminding. However, we believe that many of the types of high-level planning and thematic knowledge structures used as indices in case-based reasoning systems also have an important effect on reminding. REMIND is thus partially an attempt to bridge the gap between case-based and analogical retrieval models. As it turns out, this gap is naturally bridged when the same spreading-activation mechanism is used to both understand cues and to retrieve episodes from memory. Using the same mechanism for both processes causes retrieval to be affected by all levels that a text was understood with, as hypothesized by Schank (1982). This is the case in REMIND, in which the understanding mechanism is given the superficial features and actions of a text and attempts to explain them by inferring the plans and goals being used—causing long-term memory episodes to be activated by both.

3. LANGUAGE UNDERSTANDING IN REMIND

REMIND is a structured spreading-activation model that integrates language understanding and memory retrieval. REMIND is an extension of ROBIN (Lange, 1992; Lange & Dyer, 1989), a structured connectionist model that performs high-level inferencing and disambiguation to build interpretations of syntactically parsed input for short texts such as **Hiding Pot** and **Dirty Magazine**. These interpretations are then added to the network to encode the model's long-term memory episodes.

In REMIND, memory retrieval is a natural side effect of using spreading activation to perform language understanding. The knowledge structures used to understand an input cue activate similar episodes that were understood and stored in the network earlier. For example, **Dirty Magazine** becomes active when **Hiding Pot** is being understood because both involve hiding to avoid punishment. An episode is retrieved from memory when there are enough similarities between it and a cue's interpretation to cause it to become the most highly active episode in the network. Because both inferencing and memory retrieval occur within a single spreading-activation network, these processes strongly interact and affect each other, as appears to be the case in human memory. In this section, we give an overview of how REMIND performs high-level text inferencing and disambiguation. A more detailed description is provided in Lange and Dyer (1989).

3.1. Knowledge Given to REMIND

REMIND, like ROBIN, uses structured networks of simple connectionist units to encode semantic networks of frames representing world knowledge. Each frame has one or more roles, with each role having expectations and selectional restrictions on its fillers. General knowledge rules used for inferencing are encoded as interconnected pathways between corresponding roles. The knowledge base of frames and rules consist of the causal dependencies relating actions, plans, goals, and scripts (Schank & Abelson, 1977) necessary for understanding stories in a limited domain. The knowledge base is hand-built, as in most structured connectionist models. However, there is no information in the knowledge base about specific episodes (such as **Hiding Pot, Dinner Party**, and **Dirty Magazine**) that the networks will be used to understand.

Table 1.2 gives an example of how knowledge is defined in REMIND. It defines the conceptual frame **Inside-Of**, which represents the general state of one object being inside of another. **Inside-Of** has three roles: an object that is inside of something (which must be a **Physical-Object**), a location that the object is inside of (which must be a **Container-Object**), and a planner that may have caused the state to be reached (which must be a **Human**). The rest of Table 1.2 define **Inside-Ofs relations** to other frame. The knowledge represented here is that it is (a) *directly* accessed by the phrase <S_"is inside of"_DO> (as in *The fork is inside of the dishwasher*), (b) a **Result-Of** the action **Transfer-Inside**, and (c) has several possible concept **Refinement** frames: **Inside-Of-Dishwasher, Inside-Of-Opaque**, and **Inside-Of-Carwash**.

Refinements (short for concept refinements, an inverse of the *is-a* relation) of frames are useful because they allow more specific inferences to be made when role bindings are known (Lytinen, 1984). For example, if the network has inferred that a cooking utensil is inside of a dishwasher (**Inside-Of-Dishwasher**), a likely inference is that it is about to be cleaned. If the network has

Table 1.2.
Simplified Definition of the Frame Representing the State *Inside-Of*

(FRAME Inside-Of
  State
  :Roles (Object (Physical-Object 0.05))
       (Location (Container-Object 0.30))
       Planner (Human 0.05))
  :Phrase
             (<S_"is inside of"_DO> 1.0 (Object Subject) (Location Direct-Object))
  :Result-Of   (Transfer-Inside 1.0 (Object Object) (Location Location) (Planner Actor))
  :Refinements (Inside-Of-Dishwasher 1.0 (Object Object) (Location Location) (Planner Planner))
             (Inside-Of-Opaque 1.0 (Object Object) (Location Location) (Planner Planner))
             (Inside-Of-Carwash 1.0 (Object Object) (Location Location) (Planner Planner))

inferred that any object is inside of an opaque object (**Inside-Of-Opaque**), the network can infer that the object is blocked from sight.

When multiple frames are defined as alternatives for a given relation to a frame, as in the multiple **Refinements** of **Inside-Of**, they are defined as *mutually exclusive* relations which compete for selection as the relation's instantiation at any given time. For example, although there are multiple possible **Plans-For** the goal of **Satisfy-Hunger** (e.g., $Restaurant, $Eat-At-Home, etc.), generally only one will be used as the plan for a *given* instance of somebody wanting to satisfy his hunger in a particular story.

The relations and their role correspondences shown in Table 1.2 also define the network's general knowledge rules, such as the following:

R3: (Subject X <S—"is inside of"—DO> Direct-Obj Y)
== phrase ==>
(Object X *Inside-Of* Location Y)
(The phrase "X is inside of Y" means that object X is inside of object Y).

R4: (Actor X *Transfer-Inside* Object Y Location Z)
== results-in ==>
(Object Y *Inside-Of* Location Z Planner X)
(When an actor X transfers an object Y into a location Z, then object Y is inside of location Z).

Finally, the numbers in Table 1.2 represent the connection weights (ranging from 0 to 1) from each of the related concepts to **Inside-Of**, and are chosen on the basis of how much evidence they provide. For example, if an object has just been transferred inside of something else (**Transfer-Inside**), then the network can definitely infer that the object is **Inside-Of** it. Therefore, the weight from **Transfer-Inside** to **Inside-Of** is maximal (1.0). If something that is a container (**Container-Obj**) has been mentioned in a story, then there is some, though not certain, evidence that something is inside of it, so a corresponding "middling" weight of 0.3 from **Container-Obj** to **Inside-Of**'s location role is given. On the other hand, a very small weight (0.05) is given from **Physical-Object** to **Inside-Of**'s object role, since mere mention of any particular physical object does not very strongly imply **Inside-Of**. The actual weights chosen are clearly arbitrary. What is important is that they be in a *range* reflecting the amount of evidence the concepts provide for their related concepts in a certain knowledge base.

3.2. Structure of REMIND

The knowledge given to REMIND is used to *construct* the network before any processing begins. As with other structured connectionist models, a single node in the network represents each frame or role. Relations between concepts are represented by weighted connections between the nodes. Activation on frame and role nodes is *evidential*, corresponding to the amount of evidence available from the current context for that concept. However, as described earlier, simply representing the amount of evidence available for a concept is not sufficient for complex inferencing tasks. Solving the variable binding problem requires a way to *identify* the concept that is dynamically bound to a role. Furthermore, the network's structure must allow such role bindings to propagate across the network to dynamically instantiate inference paths and form an elaborated representation of the input.

3.3 Variable Binding With Signatures

Representation of variables and role bindings is performed in REMIND by network structure that processes signatures—activation patterns that uniquely identify the concept bound to a role (Lange & Dyer, 1989). Every concept in the network has a set of *signature units* that output its signature, a constant activation pattern different from all other signatures. A dynamic binding exists when a role or variable's *binding units* have an activation pattern matching the activation pattern of the bound concept's signature.

An example of signatures is shown in Figure 1.3, which shows the concept nodes for the concepts **Police**, **John**, and **Dishwasher** (on the lower plane) and their associated signature units (banks of units on the top plane). Here signatures are shown as unique six-unit distributed patterns, with different levels of activation being represented by different levels of gray. The figure also shows some of the units for the frame **Transfer-Inside** and their activation values when its actor is bound to John. The *virtual binding* of **Transfer-Inside**'s actor role to

Figure 1.3.
Examples of Signature Patterns (banks of units on top plane) for Concepts (ovals on lower plan). Actor and location roles and of the Transfer-Inside frame and their binding units are also shown.

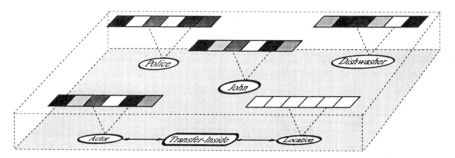

John is represented by the fact that its binding units have the same activation pattern as John's signature. The binding banks for the location role have no activation because this role is currently unbound. The complete Transfer-Inside frame is represented in the network by the group of units that include the conceptual unit Transfer-Inside, a conceptual unit for each of its roles (the object role not shown), and the binding units for each of its roles. The same binding units could, at another time, hold a different virtual binding, simply by having the activation pattern of another concept's signature.

In general, signatures can be uniquely identifying activation patterns of any size. Ideally, signatures are distributed activation patterns (e.g., made up of semantic microfeatures) that are themselves reduced semantic representations of the concept for which they stand (Figure 1.3). Having the signatures represented as distributed activation patterns carrying semantic information may allow their future use as inputs for local distributed learning mechanisms after they have been propagated for inferencing (Lange & Dyer, 1989). For simplicity, however, REMIND's simulations are currently run with signatures simply being unique arbitrarily generated scalor values (e.g., 6.8 for Marijuana and 9.2 for Cooking-Pot).

3.4. Propagation of Signatures for Inferencing

The most important feature of signatures is that they can be propagated without change across long paths of binding units to dynamically instantiate candidate inference paths. Figure 1.4 shows how the network's structure accomplishes this and automatically propagates signatures to fire rules (such as R4). Evidential activation for disambiguation is spread through the paths between conceptual units on the bottom plane (e.g., Transfer-Inside and its object role). Signature

Figure 1.4.

Simplified ROBIN/REMIND Network Segment Showing Parallel Paths over Which Evidential Activation (bottom/plane) and Signature Activation (top plane) are Spread for Making Inferences. The figure shows the initial activation and clamping for the first phrase of **Hiding Pot** (*John put the pot inside the dishwasher*). Signature nodes (outlined rectangles) and binding nodes (solid black circles) are in the top plane. Thickness of conceptual node boundaries (ovals) in the bottom plane represents their levels of evidential activation. Node names do not affect the spread of activation in any way. They are used only to initially set up the network's structure and to aid in analysis.

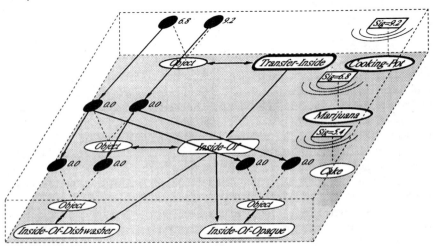

activation for dynamic role bindings is spread across the parallel paths of corresponding binding units (solid black circles) on the top plane. For simplicity, the signatures in the figure are uniquely identifying scalar values. Units and connections for the actor, planner, and location roles are not shown. As shown here, there are actually multiple binding units per role to allow simultaneous propagation of ambiguous bindings, such as the multiple meanings of the word *pot*. In general, this requires that there be as many binding units per role as there are possible meanings of the most ambiguous word in the network.

Initially there is no activation on any of the conceptual or binding units in the network. When input for a phrase such as *John put the pot inside the dishwasher* (**P1**) is presented, the lexical concept nodes for each of the words in the phrase are clamped to a high level of evidential activation. This directly provides activation for the concepts **John**, **Transfer-Inside**, **Cooking-Pot**, **Marijuana**, and **Dishwasher**. To represent the role bindings given by phrase **P1**, the binding units of each of **Transfer-Inside**'s roles are clamped to the signatures of the concepts bound to them. For example, the binding units of **Transfer-Inside**'s object are clamped to the signature activations (6.8 and 9.2) of **Marijuana** and

Figure 1.5.
Simplified ROBIN/REMIND Network Segment Showing Activation Midway through Processing Hiding Pot. At this time, Cooking-Pot and Inside-of-Dishwasher have higher evidential activations than Marijuana and Inside-Of-Opaque, as is illustrated by their thicker ovals.

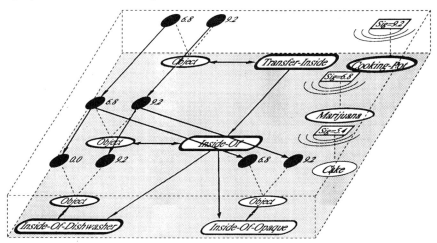

Cooking-Pot, representing the candidate bindings from the word *pot* (Figure 1.4).[2] An alternative input, such as *George put the cake inside the oven*, would be represented by clamping the signatures of its bindings (i.e., **George, Cake,** and **oven**) instead. A completely different set of inferences would then ensue.

The activation of the network's conceptual units is equal to the weighted sum of their inputs plus their previous activation times a decay rate, similar to the activation function of previous structured networks. However, the activation of the binding units is equal to the maximum of their unit-weighted inputs so that signatures can be propagated without alteration. Binding units calculate their activation as the maximum of their inputs because this preserves their signature input value even when the signature can be inferred from more than one direction. The actual relative signature activation values do not matter, because gated connections (not shown) ensure that two different signatures do not reach the same binding node.

As activation starts to spread after the initial clamped activation values in Figure 1.4, **Inside-Of** receives evidential activation from **Transfer-Inside**, representing the strong evidence that something is now inside of something else. Concurrently, the signature activations on the binding units of **Transfer-Inside's** object propagate to the corresponding binding units of **Inside-Of's** object (Figure 1.5), because each of the binding units calculates its activation as the

---
[2] REMIND and ROBIN do not currently address the problem of deciding upon the original syntactic bindings, that is that *pot* is bound to the object role of phrase **P1**. Rather, their networks are initially given these bindings and then use them for high-level inferencing.

maximum of its inputs. For example, Inside-Of's left object binding unit has only one input connection, that from the corresponding left object binding unit of Transfer-Inside has an activation of 6.8. Inside-Of's left object binding unit also becomes 6.8 (Marijuana's signature), because 6.8 is its maximum (and in this case only) input. The potential binding of Cooking-Pot (signature 9.2) to Inside-Of's right object binding unit propagates at the same time, as do the bindings of Inside-Of's planner role to the signature of John and its location role to the signature of Dishwasher.

By propagating signature activations from the binding nodes of Transfer-Inside to the binding nodes of Inside-Of, the network has made its first inference. Because of the signatures now on Inside-Of's binding nodes, the network not only represents that something is inside of something else, but also represents exactly which thing is inside the other. REMIND continues to make subsequent inferences from the activations of this new knowledge. Evidential and signature activation spreads, in parallel, from Inside-Of to its Refinements Inside-Of-Dishwasher and Inside-Of-Opaque and their corresponding binding units (see Figure 1.5), on through the rest of the network.[3] Figure 1.6 shows an overview of the signature bindings in a portion of the network after presentation of the input for the rest of **Hiding Pot** (*because the police were coming*) is presented and the network eventually settles. The network has made inferences I1-I9 of Table 1.1, with most being shown in the figure.

3.6. Disambiguation and Reinterpretation

REMIND's propagation of signature activations dynamically instantiates candidate inference paths in parallel in much the same way as marker-passing systems and the structured connectionist bindings mechanisms of Shastri and Ajjanagadde (1993) and Sun (in press). However, as described earlier, natural-language understanding requires more than simple basic variable binding and rule-firing capabilities—it also requires the ability to resolve ambiguities and select between the large number of candidate inference paths instantiated by rule firing. This is handled in REMIND by the evidential activation that spreads in parallel with signature bindings.

If this were a marker-passing system constructing an internal representation of **Hiding Pot**, an external symbolic path evaluator would have to be used to select between the dishwasher cleaning path and the longer hiding path

---

[3] The reader may note that the signature for marijuana did not reach the binding nodes of inside-of-dishwasher in Figure 1.5. This is due to additional structure of gated links that encode knowledge about what kind of concepts can be bound to the roles of particular frames—such that only concepts that are refinements of cooking-utensils are prototypically cleaned as the objects in inside-of-dishwasher. These *selectional restrictions* and their importance are described further in Section 3.7.

Figure 1.6.
Overview of a Small Portion of a ROBIN/REMIND Network Showing Inferences Made after Clamping of Inputs for Phrases P1 and P2 of Hiding Pot. Thickness of frame boundaries shows the amount of evidential activation on the frames' conceptual nodes. Role fillers shown are the ones dynamically instantiated by propagation of signature activation over the role's binding nodes (as in Figure 1.5). Darkly shaded area indicates the most highly activated path of frames representing the network's interpretation of the input. Dashed area shows the discarded dishwasher-cleaning interpretation. Frames outside of both areas show a small portion of the rest of the network that received no evidential or signature activation.

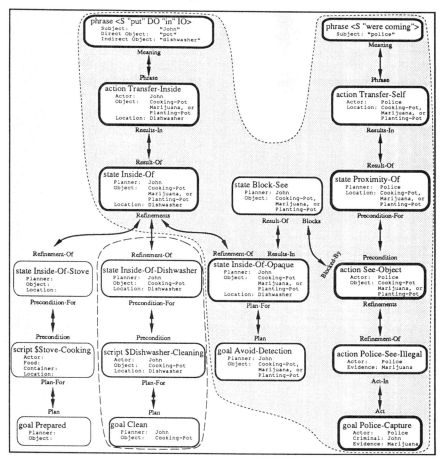

connecting **John's Transfer-Inside** to the **Police's Transfer-Self**. At the end of processing, the path evaluator would also have to recognize that **Marijuana** should be selected over the **Cooking-Pot** and **Planting-Pot** bindings throughout the network.

Such disambiguation is performed entirely within REMIND's network without resorting to a separate path-evaluation module. Instead, the evidential portion of the network decides between the competing inference paths that have been instantiated by signature activation (see Figure 1.5). The activations of the conceptual frame nodes are always approximately proportional to the amount of evidence available for them in the current context from their bindings and related frames. REMIND's interpretation of its input is the most highly activated path of frame units and their bindings when the network settles.[4]

Often there are multiple possible competing interpretations for a given frame. This occurs when there are multiple plans to achieve a goal or multiple **refinements** for a frame (e.g., the **Inside-Of-Dishwasher** and **Inside-Of-Opaque refinements** of **Inside-Of**). In these cases, the most highly activated interpretation that has been instantiated with compatible signature role bindings is chosen as part of the inference path. Similarly, when there are multiple possible bindings for a role, the binding chosen at any given time is the one whose concept has the highest level of evidential activation.

Figure 1.7 illustrates how evidential activation works through constraint satisfaction to disambiguate meanings and interpretations. The evidential activations of the competing meanings of *pot* and **Refinements of Inside-Of** change during the processing of **Hiding Pot**. Initially there is more evidence for the interpretation that John was trying to clean a cooking pot. This is shown by the fact that after **Inside-Of-Dishwasher** becomes activated at about cycle 60, **Cooking-Pot** becomes more highly activated than **Marijuana** or **Planting-Pot**. Input for the second phase of **Hiding Pot** (*because the police were coming*) is presented at cycles 51 through 61. The evidential activation levels shown by the thickness of conceptual node boundaries in Figure 1.5 correspond to the activations at cycle 90. The inferences about the police propagate through **Transfer-Self, Proximity-Of, See-Object,** and **Block-See**, until they reach **Inside-Of-Opaque** (see Figure 1.6). This occurs at about cycle 95. By about cycle 160, reinforcement from the **Block-See/Police-Capture** path causes **Inside-Of-Opaque** to become more activated than **Inside-Of-Dishwasher**, and **Marijuana** to become more highly activated than **Cooking-Pot**. Thus, REMIND's interpretation of **Hiding Pot** is that John was trying to avoid detection of his **Marijuana** from the police by hiding it inside of an opaque dishwasher. The final inference path interpretation is shown in the darkly shaded area of Figure 1.6.

---

[4] The network's "decision" or "selection" is actually simply the interpretation that the human modeler gives to the levels of activation present in it, as in all connectionist models.

RETRIEVAL FROM EPISODIC MEMORY   57

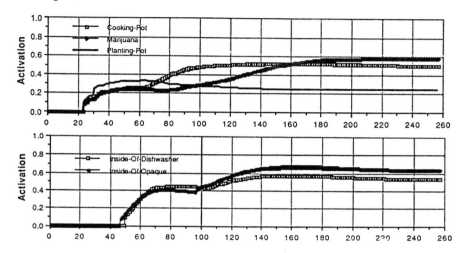

Figure 1.7.
Evidential Activations for Meanings of Pot and of Competing *Refinements* of *Inside-Of* After Presentation of *John put the pot inside the dishwasher* (P1) at Cycles 1 Through 31 and the *police were coming* (P2) at Cycles 51 Through 61.

3.7. Activation Control

A major issue for all structured connectionist networks is controlling the spread of activation. Other spreading-activation models have usually addressed this problem by using direct inhibitory connections between competing concepts (e.g., between meanings of "*star*" in Waltz & Pollack's network in Figure 1.2). For inferencing tasks, however, the inhibitory connections that these networks use are usually semantically unjustifiable and combinatorially explosive. The biggest problem, however, is that they are *winner-take-all networks*, acting to kill the activations of input interpretations that do not win the competition. This becomes a problem when a new context arises that makes an alternative interpretation more plausible. With the activations of the alternative interpretations killed by the inhibition from the false winner, it is exceedingly difficult for the activation from the new context to revive the correct one. The automatic reinterpretation capabilities of the networks are thus sabotaged.

In contrast, REMIND, like ROBIN, has no inhibitory links between competing concepts. It instead uses a group of units which act as a global inhibition mechanism. These *global inhibition* units serve to inhibit by equal proportions (normalize) all concepts in the network when their average activation becomes too high. The concepts in the network are thus free to keep an activation level relative to the amount of evidence in their favor. Global inhibition nodes are similar to the "regulator units" of Touretzky and Hinton (1988), except that regulator units are *subtractive inhibitory*, subtracting a constant amount of activation from all nodes and implementing a winner-take-all network, while REMIND's global inhibition nodes are *short-circuiting inhibitory*, controlling the spread of activation, but leaving *relative* values of evidential activation unchanged.

As opposed to driving the "losers" activations down to zero using winner-take-all networks, REMIND's short-circuiting global inhibition mechanism allows all concepts in the network to hold a level of evidential activation relative to the amount of evidence in their favor. Letting losing interpretations keep activation proportional to their evidence enables REMIND to easily perform reinterpretation. When new context enters the network that favors an alternative interpretation over a previous one, it boosts the new interpretation's relative levels of evidential activation—often being enough to cause the new interpretation to become most highly activated. This occurs in **Hiding Pot**, in which the evidence from **P1** (*"John put the pot inside the dishwasher"*) initially favors **Cooking-Pot**. However, after evidence from the inferences of **P2** (*"the police were coming"*) is introduced, **Marijuana**'s activation increases enough so that the network reinterprets *pot* and **Marijuana**.

3.8. Elimination of Crosstalk: Interaction of Signature and Evidential Activation

The use of signatures and evidential activation is a partial solution to the variable binding and inferencing problems of structured connectionist networks. However, the highly complex, overlapping, and ambiguous knowledge needed for language understanding (and eventual memory retrieval) requires more than simple integration of a variable binding mechanism and a standard evidential spreading-activation network. In particular, the problem of *crosstalk* inherent to all spreading-activation networks makes it crucial that the two paths of activation interact so that the dynamic variable bindings in the network control and channel the spread of activation (Lange, 1992). This section gives a brief overview of some of the problems of crosstalk for language understanding and how REMIND solves them. The reader interested mainly in memory retrieval may skip to the next section.

Crosstalk occurs when activation spreads from one area of a network into another area when it should not. This often provides unsupported activation evidence to a subset of network nodes and therefore disrupts the contextual disambiguation of the network. This can especially become a problem as networks get bigger and begin to have larger areas activated from inferences, as in REMIND. As an example, consider the following sentence:

John ate some rice before he went to church on Sunday morning. (**Church Service**)

The most probable interpretation of **Church Service** is that John had rice for breakfast before he went to attend services at church ($Church-Service). However, in a normal spreading-activation network, crosstalk from the combined activity of Rice and Church can cause $Wedding to become more highly activated than $Church-Service, since $Church-Service would only receive evidence from Church. This is an example of crosstalk from *logically unrelated inferences*. In general, Rice in the context of a Church should provide evidence for $Wedding. However, in the case of **church service,** Rice should not lead to the inference that a $Wedding is occurring, because the Rice is being eaten and not thrown.

One of the main potential sources of crosstalk in spreading-activation networks is that of *spurious*, or *logically impossible* inferences, which is also a problem in many marker-passing systems. In **Church Service**, an inference path connecting the Ingesting of the Rice to $Wedding would be spurious, because the actions of eating and going to church are not causally related. As another example, consider the sentence:

After Bill put the omelet on the stove, he put the bowl inside the dishwasher. (**Cook and Clean**)

The most likely interpretation of **Cook and Clean** is that after Bill cooked his omelet, he put the bowl in the dishwasher so that he could clean it. Inside-Of-Dishwasher with Bill as the actor and Bowl as the object should be the winning Refinement of Inside-Of. However, if Inside-Of-Stove (a refinement of Inside-Of leading to cooking inferences) is allowed to combine activation from Inside-Of with that from Stove, then Inside-of-Stove could become more activated than Inside-Of-Dishwasher. The network might then might make the impossible inference that Bill was trying to cook something in the bowl even though he put in the dishwasher.

REMIND's network structure controls such spurious, logically impossible inferences by enforcing *selectional restrictions*, or binding constraints, on role fillers. Selectional restrictions on role fillers are defined in the knowledge base, and encode knowledge such as that only Cooking-Utensils and Eating-Utensils are typically cleaned in dishwashers. However, the network calculates that Cooking-Pot (9.2) does match the selectional restrictions. Cooking-Pot is allowed to propagate as a possible object of Inside-Of-Dishwasher (Figure 1.5). Though not shown, the network recognizes selectional restriction violations basically by having units that compare the bindings' signatures to those of the expected signatures.

In other cases, the role-filler's selectional restrictions on a frame are completely violated. For instance, Inside-Of-Stove and Inside-Of-Car-Wash are impossible interpretations for **Hiding Pot** and **cook and clean**, because the pot was put inside of a dishwasher and not a stove or car wash. In these cases, signature bindings interact with evidential activation so that the violated frames are completely stopped from receiving activation. Thus, selectional restrictions dramatically reduce the number the spurious, logically impossible inference paths generated by the propagation of signatures—and thereby allows REMIND to avoid one of the major pitfalls of marker-passing systems.

Another basic problem of structured connectionist networks is using the dynamic bindings of case role information to perform lexical disambiguation. For example, normal structured network cannot distinguish between the sentences *The astronomer saw the star* and *The star saw the astronomer*. Signatures partially solve this problem by allowing the network to represent the bindings of the two sentences differently and keep track of who is seeing whom. However, if these bindings do not have an effect on the spread of evidential activation, then they do not help disambiguate between the meanings of *star*. For example, the extended Waltz and Pollack (1985) network of Figure 1.1 disambiguates the word *star* in *The astronomer saw the star* to a **Celestial-Body**, because **Celestial-Body** receives activation through hard-coded connections from both the network does almost exactly the same thing. **Celestial-Body** again ends up with more activation than **Movie-Star**, because it is still receiving activation from the hard-coded connection from **See**'s object. This occurs even though **Celestial-Body** is not bound to **See**'s object in this story (see analysis in Lange, 1992). This is an example where the default, hard-coded case role connections that work in the general case can fail catastrophically in specific instances where the actual variable bindings are known.

ROBIN and REMIND solve this problem and use dynamic role-binding information to perform lexical disambiguation by using gated connections that give them a temporary *virtual structure* specific to the network's current dynamic bindings. These connections feed evidential activation back from frames *only* to concepts that are actually bound to their roles with signature activation. For example, in the case of *The star saw the astronomer*, only the signature of **Movie-Star** reaches the actor role of **See**. **Celestial-Body** does not, because it violates **See**'s selectional restrictions (celestial bodies have no eyes, and cannot see). Because frames only feed evidential activation back to the objects that are bound to their roles, **Movie-Star** therefore receives evidential activation from **See**'s object. **Celestial-Body** does not, and so **Movie-Star** wins as the interpretation of *star*.

The combination of selection restrictions and the channeling of evidential activation through the virtual role-binding structure solve the problems of crosstalk exemplified by **cook and clean** and **church service**. In **cook and clean**, the **Inside-Of-Stove** and stove cooking frames that might otherwise have won do not receive signature or evidential activation because their selectional restrictions are violated. In **church service**, the evidential activation from **Rice** goes to the eating frame that it is bound to and to the breakfast frames those bindings reach, and not (aside from a small amount of biasing activation) to the

$Wedding frames. In both cases REMIND's structure avoids normal spreading-activation network's crosstalk problems and allows it to arrive at the most plausible interpretation. REMIND's virtual structure is also often key to disambiguating more complex stories such as **Hiding Pot**. As shown in Figure 1.6, only **Cooking-Pot** reaches the receives $Dishwasher-Cleaning frames and receives evidential activation from them. Similarly, only **Marijuana** reaches and receives evidential activation from the Police-Capture frames. Thus, frames supported by contextual evidence of the network's inferences and bindings become more activated than their competitors, and so are more likely to be chosen as part of REMIND's interpretation of its input.

Finally, it is important to note that the evidential activation of the network also affects the spread of signatures. Signatures stop spreading to frames when the frames' evidential activation drops below threshold. This stops the network from making an infinite number of inferences—forward inferences are made, but only as far as there is support from context. For example, when input for *John put the pot inside the dishwasher* (**P1**) is presented to the network, evidential and signature activation reaches the Clean frame, but then drops below threshold and stops spreading. While **P1** provides enough evidence to infer that John might have to put the pot inside the dishwasher to clean it, there is not enough evidence to make any further inferences as to why he would want to clean it. Further inferences, such as that John might have wanted to clean the pot to get ready for a **Dinner-Party** (as in **Dinner Party**), require additional evidential activation from the input, such as the convergent evidence from inferences for *company was coming*.

In summary, REMIND is able to avoid most crosstalk problems because of its structure of units and gated connections that allow signature bindings to control the spread of activation. Spurious inferences are avoided because activation only spreads to inference paths that are logically possible interpretations of the input. Highly unlikely inferences are not made because signatures spread only to concepts that have evidential activation. And most importantly, the virtual structure created by signatures allows it to combine evidence as if the network was hand-built for the current bindings. Because of these interactions between evidential and signature activation, crosstalk is avoided, and REMIND is influenced only by contextually appropriate evidence. Thus, the interpretation REMIND constructs of its cues is influenced only by its input activation, the biases of its connection weights, and its inferences.

4. MEMORY RETRIEVAL

In REMIND, memory retrieval occurs automatically as a side effect of the spreading-activation understanding process. Representations of previously understood episodes are connected directly to the same semantic network that understood them in the first place. This direct form of indexing causes episodes that share conceptual similarities with the cue to become active as REMIND interprets the cue.

4.1. Representation of Long-Term Episodes

Whereas the general world knowledge and inference rules used to initially build REMIND's networks are hand-coded, REMIND is not given any information about the particular episodes it is going to understand and store in long-term memory. The representations used for these target episodes are created entirely by REMIND's spreading-activation understanding process. Input for each episode's text is presented to the network, which then infers an interpretation of it by the spread of signature and evidential activation. Next, units and connections are added (by hand) to store the episode's entire resulting interpretation in REMIND's long-term memory. Accordingly, each episode's representation includes all aspects of its interpretation, from its disambiguated surface features (such as the actors and objects in the story) to the plans and goals that REMIND inferred that the actors were using.

To determine the symbolic representation used to store an episode in memory, the state of the network is examined by hand to determine the interpretation it has settled on. As described previously, the network's interpretation is the most highly activated path of frames and their role-bindings. For example, the representation of **Hiding Pot** that the network would store in long-term memory would include all of the instantiated frames and their disambiguated role bindings in the dark gray area of Figure 1.6, representing the inferred interpretations of John hiding his *marijuana* from the police to avoid being arrested.

As a complete example, consider how **Dirty Magazine** (*Billy put the Playboy under his bed so his mother wouldn't see it and spank him*) is processed and stored in the network as a memory episode. First, signature and evidential activations representing its phrasally analyzed input are clamped to the network to start the understanding process. The actual phrasally analyzed input given to the network for **Dirty Magazine** is the following:

(Phrase <Subject "put" Direct-Object "under" Indirect-Object>
  (Subject "Billy") (Direct-Object "Playboy") (Indirect-Object "bed"))
(Phrase <Subject "see" Direct-Object>
  (Subject "Mother") (Direct-Object "Playboy"))
(Phrase <Subject "spank" Direct-Object>
  (Subject ?) (Direct-Object "Billy"))

Possessives (*his*), connectives (*so, would*), and negations (*not*) are not included in the phrasally analyzed input given to REMIND. The above input for **Dirty**

Magazine could therefore be more accurately be described as *Billy put Playboy under bed. Mother see Playboy <Somebody unmentioned> spank Billy.* REMIND is left to infer the relations between the actions described by the individual phrases itself.

As described earlier for **Hiding Pot**, the input is presented to the network by clamping the evidential activations of the input's phrase and word nodes to one and clamping the binding units of the phrases' roles to the signatures of their bindings' word meanings. Activation then spreads through the network to infer and disambiguate an interpretation of the input. As in **Hiding Pot**, the network infers that somebody is hiding something (*avoid detection*) and that it is blocked from sight (**Block-See**). Here, however, the inferred signatures show that it is Billy hiding a Playboy-Magazine rather than John hiding Marijuana.

The entire representation inferred for **Dirty Magazine** is shown in Figure 1.8. The ".1" after each frame name (e.g., Transfer-Under.1 and Bed.1) indicate that they are specific instantiations of concepts in the first episode processed by the network. For example, **Dirty Magazine's** interpretation includes a surface action inferred directly from the first phrase (*Billy put the Playboy under the bed*) (i.e., that an instance of Transfer-Under, Transfer-Under.1, had occurred. The actor of this Transfer-Under.1 is Billy.1, the object is Playboy-Magazine.1, and the location is Bed.1. The inferred representation also includes instantiations of more distant frames used by the network to understand **Dirty Magazine**, such as Avoid-Detection.1 and Block-See.1. As in **Hiding Pot**, the network's representation of **Dirty Magazine** also includes the possibility of a Punishment taking place, as it inferred for **Hiding Pot** (not shown in Figure 1.6)—though in this case the Refinement of Punishment.1 is a Spank rather than an In-Jail. These similarities make **Dirty Magazine** a likely candidate for reminding when the network is presented with **Hiding Pot** as a cue.

It is important to note that each episode's representation also includes all of the simple bridging inferences that were necessary to make the plan/goal analysis. Here the bridging inferences for **Dirty Magazine** include that the Playboy was Under.1 the bed, that Billy possessed the Playboy (Possess-Obj.1), that the salient refinement of this possession was that it was possession of a "naughty" object (Possess-Naughty Obj.1), and so on.

Once the full interpretation for an episode has been determined, units and connections representing this interpretation are hand-coded into the network's long-term memory. For **Dirty Magazine**, the units added include (a) nodes representing each instantiated frame of its interpretation in Figure 1.8 (e.g., Billy.1, Playboy-Magazine.1, avoid-Detection.1, and Possess-Obj.1), (b) units to represent their roles, and (c) a unit to stand as a placeholder for the entire episode (e.g., Episode.1). These units are then connected to their corresponding local elements in the normal evidential semantic network. They are also interconnected to encode their role bindings and which episode they are part of.

Figure 1.9 shows an example of the units and connections that are added to the network to represent episodes. The figure shows a simplified part of the

Figure 1.8.
Interpretation Inferred by Spread of Signature and Evidential Activation Through the Network for *Billy put the Playboy under his bed so his mother wouldn't see it and spank him* **(Dirty Magazine).** Frame names are followed by ".1" (e.g., Transfer-Under.1) to indicate that they are instantiations of concepts inferred in the first episode stored in the network. Numbers following instance names are final evidential activations of the frame.

```
(Instance Transfer-Under.1     0.57          (Instance Parent-See-Naughty.1
    :Roles (Actor Billy.1)                       :Roles (Actor Mother.1)
           (Object Playboy.1)                           (Evidence Playboy.1)
           (Location Bed.1)                      :Refinement-Of     See-Object.1
    :Phrase <S "put" DO "under" IO>.1            :Plan-For          Parent-Know-Naughty.1)
    :Refinement-Of    Do-Action-To-Obj.1    (Instance Parent-Know-Naughty.1
    :Results-In       Under.1)                   :Roles (Actor Mother.1)
(Instance Under.1              0.37                     (Object Billy.1)
    :Roles (Planner Billy.1)                            (Evidence Playboy.1)
           (Object Playboy.1)                    :Plan              Parent-See-Naughty.1
           (Location Bed.1)                      :Precondition      Naughty-Committed.1
    :Refinement       Under-Opaque.1             :Precondition-For  Child-Punishment.1)
    :Result-of        Transfer-Under.1)     (Instance Child-Punishment.1
(Instance Under-Opaque.1       0.27              :Roles (Actor Mother.1)
    :Roles (Planner Billy.1)                            (Object Billy.1)
           (Object Playboy.1)                           (Evidence Playboy.1)
           (Location Bed.1)                      :Precondition      Parent-Know-Naughty.1
    :Refinement-Of    Under.1                    :Results-In        Spank.1)
    :Results-In       Block-See.1            (Instance Spank.1
    :Plan-For         Avoid-Detection.1)         :Roles (Actor Mother.1) (Object Billy.1)
(Instance Avoid-Detection.1    0.10              :Phrase            <S "spank" DO>.1
    :Roles (Planner Billy.1)                     :Result-Of         Child-Punishment.1
           (Object Playboy.1)                    :Refinement-Of     Punishment.1)
    :Plan             Under-Opaque.1)       (Instance Punishment.1     0.28
(Instance Block-See.1          0.24              :Roles (Actor Mother.1) (Object Billy.1)
    :Roles (Planner Billy.1)                     :Refinement        Spank.1)
           (Object Playboy.1)                (Instance Naughty-Committed.1
    :Result-Of        Under-Opaque.1             :Roles (Actor Billy.1)
    :Refinement       Inside-Of-Carwash                  (Evidence Playboy.1)
    :Blocks           See-Object.1)               :Precondition-For  Parent-Know-Naughty.1
(Instance See-Object.1                           :Refinement-Of     Possess-Naughty-Obj.1
    :Roles (Actor Mother.1) (Object Playboy.1) (Instance Possess-Naughty-Obj.1
    :Phrase           <S "see" DO>                :Roles (Actor Billy.1) (Object Playboy.1)
    :Precondition     Proximity-Of.1              :Refinement        Naughty-Committed.1
    :Blocked-By       Block-See.1                 :Refinement-Of     Possess-Obj.1)
    :Refinement       Parent-See-Naughty)   (Instance Possess-Obj.1
(Instance Proximity-Of.1                         :Roles (Actor Billy.1) (Object Playboy.1)
    :Roles (Actor Mother.1) (Object Playboy.1)   :Refinement        Possess-Naughty-Obj.1
    :Precondition-For  See-Object.1                :Implied-By        Do-Action-To-Obj.1)
    :Result-Of        Transfer-Self.1)       (Instance Do-Action-To-Obj.1  0.34
(Instance Transfer-Self.1                        :Roles (Actor Billy.1) (Object Playboy.1)
    :Roles (Actor Mother.1) (Object Playboy.1)   :Refinement        Transfer-Under.1
    :Results-In       Proximity-Of.1)             :Implies           Possess-Obj.1)
```

network's evidential layer after several episodes have been understood and added to long-term memory. The gray units in the figure are the normal semantic conceptual units originally in the network, including the conceptual units for frames **Possess-Obj** and **Possess-Naughty Obj** and units in part of the physical object refinement (is-a) hierarchy. At this stage, two episodes have been processed that include **Possess-Obj** or **Possess-Naughty-Obj** as part of their interpretation—**Dirty Magazine** (**Episode.1**), and *Betty wanted to smoke a*

RETRIEVAL FROM EPISODIC MEMORY   65

Figure 1.9.
Encoding of *Possess Obj* and *Possess-Naughty-Obj* instances for *episode.1* (Dirty Magazine) and *Episode.4* (Cigarette Lighting). Gray units are pre-existing conceptual nodes. White units are nodes added to represent the episodes.

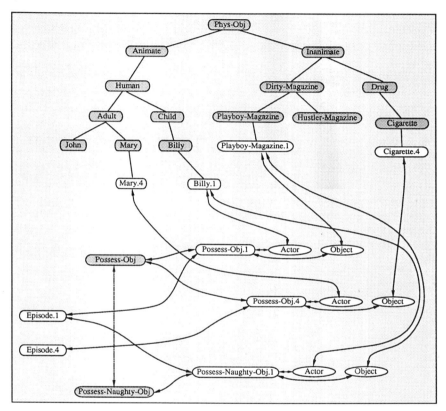

cigarette, so she put it on top of the stove and lit it (**Cigarette Lighting**; **Episode.4**). **Cigarette Lighting**'s interpretation includes an instance of Possess-Obj because the network inferred that Betty must have possessed the cigarette to light it.

The white units in Figure 1.9 show some of the units added to the network to encode **Dirty Magazine** and **Cigarette Lighting**. For each episode, there is a single *episode unit* serving to represent and group all of its elements together, such as **Episode.1** and **Episode.4** in Figure 1.9. In addition, there is an *episode instance unit* representing each element of the episode's interpretation. For **Dirty Magazine**, there is an episode instance unit for Billy.1, Playboy-Magazine.1,

Possess Obj.1, and **Possess-Naughty Obj.1**, along with units (not shown) representing all of the other elements of its representation. These episode instance units are connected both to the general semantic concept of which they are an instantiation (e.g., **Billy.1** is connected to **Billy**) and to the episode unit of which they are part (e.g., **Episode.1** for **Dirty Magazine**'s elements). Furthermore, each episode instance is connected to units representing its roles (e.g., the actor and object unit for **Possess-Obj.1**), which are in turn connected to the concepts that were bound to them (e.g., **Possess-Obj.1**'s actor is connected to **Billy.1**, and its object is connected to **Playboy-Magazine.1**). The rest of the interpretation of each episode (e.g., in Figure 1.8) is encoded similarly with units and connections that represent all of its other instantiated frames and elements.

As can be seen, REMIND's method of encoding its episodes is different from that of many memory retrieval and case-based reasoning models. Episodes in REMIND are not indexed under any one knowledge structure or important groups of knowledge structures. They are instead "indexed" under every concept that was an aspect in understanding them in the first place. These concepts include both the surface features of the text (such as its direct disambiguated word and phrase meanings) and the abstract inferences that make up the plan/goal analysis of the episode. As will be discussed later, this fully dispersed form of indexing has important implications for the kinds of remindings that the model produces.

4.2. Detailed Connectivity of Episodic Units

Unlike the inferencing and understanding portion of the network, the units and connections representing long-term memory episodes reside entirely on the evidential layer of the network. Because the bindings of each individual long-term memory episode are fixed once an episode has been understood and remembered, the bindings can be encoded by direct connections between role units and the elements that are bound to them. Thus, long-term memory episodes do not need the more complex inferencing structure that holds and propagates dynamic signature bindings.

An example of the full set of units and connections used to encode each frame instance in an episode is shown in Figure 1.10. As in the normal conceptual units of REMIND, each incoming connection to a concept unit from other concepts goes through an *input branch unit*. Input branch units are analogous to the *input sites* described by Cottrell and Small (1982). They serve both to specify the relationships concepts hold to each other and to control the spread of evidential activation.

Episode instance units have four input branches: an **Instance-Of** branch, an **Element-In** branch, a **Roles** branch, and a **Bound-To** branch. For example, **Possess-Obj.1** has three input branch units in Figure 1.10, (a) an **Instance-Of** input branch that receives activation from **Possess-Obj**, the concept it is an

Figure 1.10.
Detailed View of Units added to Represent *Possess-Obj.1* of *Episode.1*.
Labels next to nodes (e.g., Instances, Instance-Of) represent their input branch units.

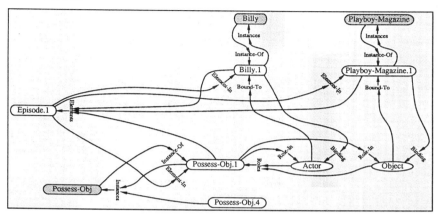

long-term instance of, (b) an Element-In input branch that receives activation from the episode it is a part of (i.e., Episode.1), and (c) a Roles input branch that receives activation from each of its role units (i.e., its actor and object units). The Instance-Of and Element-In branch units calculate their activation as the sum of their single input, since any one instance can only be an instantiation of one general semantic frame. Likewise, any one instance can only be an element in one episode. The Roles input branch, on the other hand, calculates its activation as the *average* of its role unit inputs, so that frames with multiple roles do not become the most active simply because they have more role bindings than simpler frames. Episode instance units also have a Bound-To input branch that has connections from any of the episode roles they are bound to. For example, Billy.1 is bound to the actor roles of Possess-Obj.1 and Possess-Naughty Obj.1 (amongst others), and so receives activation from those roles through its Bound-To branch. Bound-To input branches calculate their activation as the *maximum* of their inputs, so that they receive activation from the most active role they are bound to.

Episode role units, such as Possess-Obj.1's actor and object roles, have two input branches a Role-In branch and a Binding branch. Role-In branches receive activation from the episode instance unit of which the episodic role is part. In Figure 1.10, Possess-Obj.1's actor and object roles therefore both have Role-In branches that receive activation from Possess-Obj.1. In contrast, Binding branches have a connection from the element that is bound to their role to represent its long-term role-binding. Since Possess-Obj.1's actor role is bound to Billy.1, it therefore receives activation from Billy.1 through its Binding branch.

Similarly, the **Binding** branch of **Possess-Obj.1**'s object role receives activation from **Playboy-Magazine.1**.

The episode units themselves have a single **Elements** branch that receives and sums up the activation of all elements that make up the episode. For example, **Episode.1**'s elements branch receives activation from **Billy.1, Playboy-Magazine.1, Possess Obj.1**, and all the other episode instance elements of its interpretation. This serves two functions: to keep track of all the elements in each episode, and to cause episode units to become active when their elements are active.

Finally, all of the concept units in the normal evidential semantic network have an **Instances** input branch that is used to activate them from each of their instantiations in long-term memory. For instance, **Possess-Obj** has an **Instances** branch that receives activation from **Possess-Obj.1, Possess-Obj.4** and all of its other episode instances (not shown). This is in addition to the normal conceptual input branches of the network (see Lange & Dyer, 1989). An **Instances** branch unit calculates its activation as the *maximum* of its inputs, because, in general, REMIND can only be reminded of one instantiation of a given frame at a time. An important effect of this activation function is that it also stops concepts that have been seen in many stories before (and therefore have a lot of instances) from dominating concepts that may have more unique (and therefore fewer) instantiations in memory.

All connections in Figure 1.10 have unit weight, with the exception of the connections from the episode units (e.g., **Episode.1**) to the **Element-In** branches of their episode instances, which have a weight of 0.05. The unit weights from semantic concepts to each of their episode instances make episode instances likely to become active when related concepts are active. On the other hand, the small weights from episode units to the **Element-In** branches of episode instance units cause their elements to become moderately primed when their episode is active, without becoming too active unless they share other similarities with the reminding cue.

4.3. The Process of Episodic Reminding

Retrieval in REMIND begins with presentation of an input cue to the network to be understood. Because episode instance units are connected directly to their corresponding concept units, they become active when the concepts they are instantiations of become activated by the understanding process. The more similarities an episode shares with the inferred interpretation of a cue, the more of the episode's instance units will become active. Episodes having a number of elements in common with the cue's interpretation therefore tend to become highly active. After the network settles, the episode with the most highly activated episode unit is retrieved.

Figure 1.11 shows an overview of part of the network after it has understood and encoded the eight different episodes shown in Table 1.3. The circled numbers above frame nodes in the figure indicate instantiations in different episodes that are connected to the frames. For example, the episode instance units for **Possess-Obj.1** and **Possess-Naughty Obj.1** of **Episode.1** (**Dirty Magazine**) shown in Figure 1.9 are indicated by the circled "1"'s above **Possess-Obj** and **Possess-Naughty-Obj** in Figure 1.11.

Notice that more specific frames tend to have fewer episode instances than less specific frames. This is to be expected, since specific knowledge structures pertaining to certain situations (such as a police search or a parent disciplining a child) represent events that are less frequently encountered than general knowledge structures about simple actions and states (such as being inside of something, or possessing an object). As an example, five of the episodes in Table 1.3 and Figure 1.11 (1,2,4,6, and 7) inferred a **Possess-Obj** as part of their interpretation, but only one episode (1) involved a **Possess-Naughty-Obj** or **Avoid-Detection**. An important consequence of specific frames providing activation evidence for a smaller number of instances is that specific, contentful knowledge structures tend to be stronger reminding indices than general ones.

Now consider what happens when input for **Hiding Pot** is presented as a cue to the network. Evidential and signature activation spread through the network, dynamically instantiating the competing inference paths as described earlier. Figure 1.12 shows the activation levels of the eight episodes as activation spreads through the network. As can be seen, **Episode.6** (*Barney put the flower in the pot, and then watered it*) initially becomes highly active because it shares a number of surface features with **Hiding Pot**—for example, both involve a **Transfer-Inside**, both have humans, and **Planting-Pot** receives activation from the word *pot*. Similarly, **Episode.2** (**Car Wash**) initially becomes active because of shared surface features with **Hiding Pot**. Episode 2's activation continues to climb when the **Clean** frame is inferred, since a **Clean** is part of **Car Wash's** interpretation. However, as REMIND continues to process **Hiding Pot**, the hiding and punishment frames are inferred and become active. Eventually, **Episode.1**'s (**Dirty Magazine**) activation climbs and wins because it shares the most surface *and* abstract features of any episode with **Hiding Pot's** interpretation (see Figure 1.11). **Dirty Magazine** is therefore retrieved as the episode most similar to **Hiding Pot**.

An explanation for why **Dirty Magazine** becomes the most highly activated of the eight episodes can be seen in Figure 1.11. The gray boxes around nodes in Figure 1.11 indicate the final levels of evidential activation of the frames inferred for **Hiding Pot**. Of the eight episodes stored in the network, **Dirty Magazine** has the most instances of its interpretation shared with **Hiding Pot's** final active interpretation (e.g., instantiations **Avoid-Detection.1**, **Block-See.1**, **Punishment.1**, and **Possess-Obj.1**). It therefore eventually becomes the most activated of the episodes.

Figure 1.11.
Overview of Part of the Network after Activation has Settled in Processing of Hiding Pot. Gray boxes around nodes represent the level of evidential activation on the frame concept nodes (darker = higher activation, no box = no activation). Circles above frames indicate long-term instances connected to them. Numbers within circles indicate which episode the instance is part of in Table 1.3.

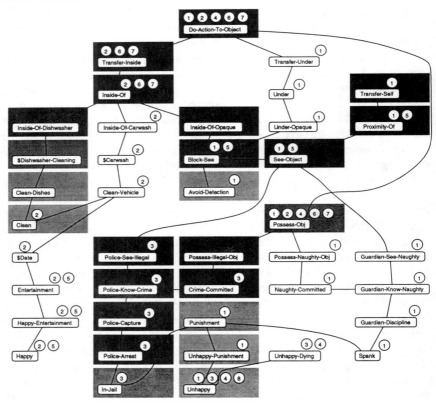

Figures 1.13 and 1.14 show the activation levels of the different elements in **Flower Planting** (Episode.6) and **Dirty Magazine** (Episode.1) as **Hiding Pot** is being understood. **Flower Planting** initially becomes the most active of the episodes because it shares a number of superficial similarities with the undisambiguated phrase *John put the pot inside the dishwasher*. As shown in Figure 1.13, it quickly receives activation when its element **Planting-Pot.6** becomes activated from the **Planting-Pot** meaning of *pot* at about cycle 25. Additional activation is received when **Transfer-Inside.6** becomes activated from **Transfer-Inside** at about cycle 40. The activation of **Episode.6** continues

Table 1.3.
Episodes for Which Input was Understood and Stored in the Network of Figure 1.10.

	Episode Text	Phrasally-Parsed Input Given the Network	
1	Billy put the Playboy under his bed so his mother wouldn't see it and spank him. (**Dirty Magazine**)	(<S "put" DO "under" IO> <S "see" DO> (S "Mother") <S "spank" DO>	(S "Billy") (DO "Playboy") (IO "bed") (D) "Playboy") (DO "Billy")
2	Fred put his car inside the car wash before his date with Wilma. (**Car Wash**)	(<S "put" DO "inside" IO> <S "date" DO>	(S "Fred") (DO "car") (IO "carwash") (S "Fred") (DO "Wilma")
3	Jane shot Mark with a Colt-45. He died.	(<S "shot" DO "with" IO> <S "died">	(S "Jane") (DO "Mark") (IO "Colt-45") (S "Mark")
4	Betty wanted to smoke a cigarette, so she put it on top of the stove and lit it.	(<S "smoke" DO> <S "put" DO "on top of" IO> <S "lit" DO>	(S "Betty") (DO "cigarette") (S "Betty") (DO "cigarette") (IO "stove") (DO "cigarette")
5	The pleasure boat followed the whales to watch them.	(<S "followed" DO> <S "watch" DO>	(S "pleasure-boat") (DO "whales") (DO "whales")
6	Barney put the flower in the pot, and then watered it. (**Flower Planting**)	(<S "put" DO "inside" IO> <S "watered" DO>	(S "Barney") (DO "flower") (IO "pot") (DO "flower")
7	Mike was hungry. He ate some fish.	(<S "was hungry"> <S "ate" DO>	S "Mike") (S "Mike") (DO "fish")
8	Suzie loved George, but he died. Then Bill proposed to her. She became sad. (**Sad Proposal**)	(<S "loved" DO> <S "died"> <S "proposed to" DO> <S "became sad">	(S "Suzie") (DO "George") (S "George") (S "Bill") (DO "Suzie") (S "Suzie")

Figure 1.12.
Evidential Activations of Episode Units for Eight Episodes of Table 1.3 after Presentation of Hiding Pot.

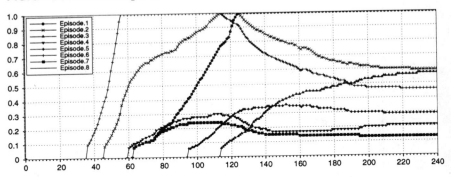

to climb along with Planting-Pot.6 and Transfer-Inside.6, and gets even more activation when the network infers that the pot is Inside-Of the dishwasher, directly activating Inside-Of.6 at about cycle 50. That, however, is where **Flower Planting's** similarities with **Hiding Pot's** inferences end, except for a couple of other shared elements (Do-Action-To-Object.6 and Possess-Obj.6). For example, Inside-Of-Planting Pot.6, part of **Flower Planting's** interpretation, does not become significantly active because Inside-Of-Planting pot is never

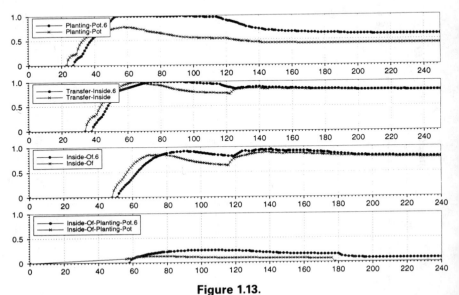

Figure 1.13.
Evidential Activation of Elements of *Episode.6* (Flower Planting) after Presentation of Hiding Pot.

Figure 1.14.
Evidential Activation of Elements of *Episode.1* (Dirty Magazine) after Presentations of Hiding Pot.

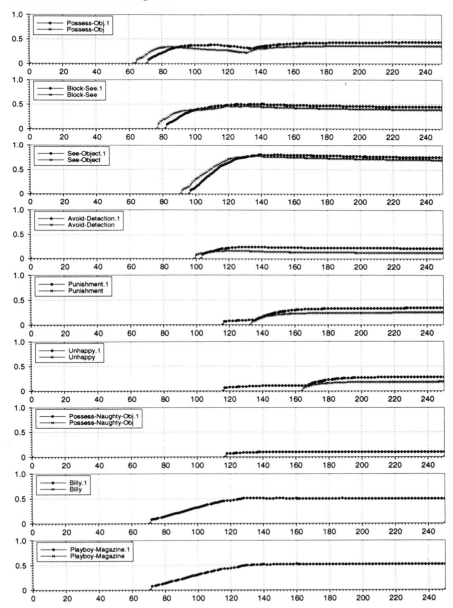

inferred by the network (because a pot inside a dishwasher violates its selectional restrictions).

Figure 1.14 shows the activation levels of **Dirty Magazine's** elements as the network eventually infers the plans and goals of **Hiding Pot** that the two episodes share. One of the first similarities activated is the **Possess-Obj.1** instantiation of **Episode.1** (see Figure 1.9) after about cycle 60. This causes **Episode.1**'s activation to climb above threshold, though its activation is still much lower than that of **Episode.6** or **Episode.2**. However, as time goes on, **Block-See, See-Object, Avoid-Detection, Punishment**, and the other shared knowledge structures of **Dirty Magazine** are inferred by the spread of signatures and evidential activation for **Hiding Pot**, so that eventually the cumulative evidence from all the shared inferences causes **Episode.1** to become the most highly activated episode at around cycle 170 (Figure 1.12).

Besides serving as an example of retrieval in , this example illustrates a number of important points about the model. The first point to notice is that even when the network settles, the "losing" episodes retain a level of evidential activation relative to the amount of evidence available for them, rather than being driven down to zero. As in the normal evidential semantic network, this is the result of controlling episodes' activation through REMIND's global inhibition rather than normal mutual inhibition.

A second point of interest is that elements and episodes that are superficially similar to the cue tend to become activated *before* elements and episodes that are only abstractly related to the cue (through inferences). This is a direct result of the spreading-activation process, since activation and signature inferences reach closely related concepts before they reach more distant concepts. An example of this was seen in Figure 1.12, where the superficially related **episode.6** became activated before the more abstractly related **Dirty Magazine**. As seen, however, the early activation of superficially similar episodes does not stop thematically similar episodes from winning if the thematically similar episodes ultimately share more features and activation with the cue. Because all episodes retain their relative supported levels of activation, thematically similar episodes such as **Dirty Magazine** can climb as inferences reach them and end up with the highest level of activation when the network settles.

Another important thing to note is that retrieval in REMIND is not all-or-nothing. As in human recall, REMIND often gets *partial* recall in which only subparts of the retrieved episode are activated. Parts of the retrieved episode distant from the current context of inferences may not become activated initially. **Possess-Naughty-Obj.1**, for example, only becomes partially primed (from its element in and roles branches), because **Possess-Naughty-Obj** was never activated from the inferences made for **Hiding Pot**. The same is true for most of the other parts of **Dirty Magazine** that differ significantly from **Hiding Pot**'s interpretation (such as the **Guardian-Discipline** and **Spank** structures, which are relatively distant from anything in **Hiding Pot**). However, the primary actors and objects in episodes, such as **Billy.1** and **Playboy-Magazine.1** in **Dirty Magazine**, do tend to become active because they play a part in so many of its roles.

5. EXPERIMENTS AND DISCUSSION

REMIND has been implemented and tested in the DESCARTES connectionist simulator (Lange, Hodges, Fuenmayor, & Belyaev, 1989). The knowledge base used for the examples in this chapter currently includes 206 distinct conceptual frames (e.g., **Inside-Of, Avoid-Detection, Cooking-Pot**) and 333 inference rules (e.g., **R1, R2**). It has understood and retrieved the examples presented here (including **Hiding Pot, Dinner Part,** and the episodes of Table 1.3) and a number of other episodes of similar length and complexity.

In this section we discuss three simulations that illustrate (1) the importance of inferences and disambiguation on retrieval in REMIND, (2) the strong influence of superficial feature similarities on retrieval, and (3) the affect of episodic recall on the understanding process. We then compare REMIND to the ARCS and MAC/FAC models of general reminding. Finally, we discuss several directions we are exploring to extend the model.

5.1. Importance of Inferences

The retrieval of **Dirty Magazine** when **Hiding Pot** was presented as a cue to REMIND illustrates the importance of inferencing and disambiguation in the retrieval process. **Dirty Magazine** was retrieved over the more superficially similar **Flower Planting** and **Car Wash** episodes because **Dirty Magazine** and **Hiding Pot** were more thematically similar, since both involved somebody hiding something to avoid punishment. Without being able to infer these similarities, the model would not have been able to retrieve the most analogous episode.

Another example of how text comprehension affects REMIND's retrieval process is shown when two superficially similar cues that have entirely different interpretations are presented to the network. On the surface, the cue *John put the pot inside the dishwasher because company was coming* (**Dinner Party**) is nearly the same as **Hiding Pot**. The only difference is that *company* is coming rather than *the police*. Analogical retrieval models such as ARCS (Thagard et al., 1990) and MAC/FAC (Gentner & Forbus, 1991) that do not have inferencing mechanisms would therefore have to predict that the same episode would be retrieved for both cues from amongst those shown in Table 1.3. This would occur for two reasons. First, the only surface feature difference between the two cues does not make a difference in overall surface similarity to all objects in these episodes. Second, the isomorphic structure (structural consistency) of the two cues is the same.

In contrast to ARCS and MAC/FAC, REMIND retrieves different episodes for **Dinner Party** and **Hiding Pot**. This is because REMIND interprets the two cues very differently. Whereas in **Hiding Pot** it appears John is trying to hide marijuana from the police, in **Dinner Party** it appears that he is trying to clean a cooking pot in preparation for company coming over. As such, **Dinner Party** is not likely to cause a reminding of **Dirty Magazine** and its hiding event. It seems more likely that **Dinner Party** would cause reminding of another episode involving somebody cleaning something in preparation for entertaining, such as the **Car Wash** episode (*Fred put his car in the car wash before his date with Wilma*).

This is exactly what happens in REMIND when episodic memory contains **Dirty Magazine, Car Wash**, and the other six episodes of Table 1.3. Figure 1.15 shows the evidential activations of the meanings of *pot* and some of the competing Refinements of Inside-Of after REMIND is given input for **Dinner Party**. As when **Hiding Pot** is presented, Planting-Pot initially becomes highly activated because the input for *John put the pot inside the dishwasher* (**P1**) contains the word *pot*. After about cycle 60, REMIND infers Inside-Of-Dishwasher and Inside-Of-Opaque. Cooking pot's activation therefore starts to climb because of its unmatched activation from Inside-Of-Dishwasher and the other $Dishwasher-Cleaning frames. Input for *company was coming* is

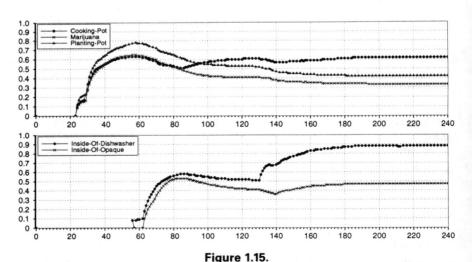

Figure 1.15.
Evidential Activations for Meanings of *Pot* and of Competing *refinements* of Inside-Of after Presentation of *John put the pot inside the dishwasher* (P1) at Cycles 1 Through 31 and *company was coming* (P2) at Cycles 51 Through 61 (Dinner Party).

presented to REMIND at cycles 51–61. Spreading signature and evidential activation makes candidate inferences for *company was coming* starting from Transfer-Self, through Proximity-Of and then the Dinner-Party frames (representing somebody making dinner for somebody else). Activation eventually reaches the Clean-Dishes frame (a *precondition* for Dinner-Party). The cleaning frames were already active after the initial inferences from **P1**, so activation continues to spread and provide added support for the Inside-Of-Dishwasher refinement of Inside-Of at about cycle 130. Inside-Of-Opaque also gets added evidence at about cycle 140 from inferences through the Block-See frames from *company was coming* (since John could still have been hiding the pot). However, Inside-Of-Opaque does not receive enough activation to compete with Inside-Of-Dishwasher. Similarly, Marijuana never seriously competes with Cooking-Pot, because the Police-Capture and Police-See-Illegal frames that gave it unique activation in **Hiding Pot** are not inferred here (since Company does not match their selectional restrictions). The network's final interpretation of **Dinner Party** is therefore that John was trying to clean a Cooking-Pot to prepare for a Dinner-Party he was giving for company.

Figure 1.16 shows the activation of the eight episodes and of two of **Car Wash's** elements as **Dinner Party** is processed. As when **Hiding Pot** is

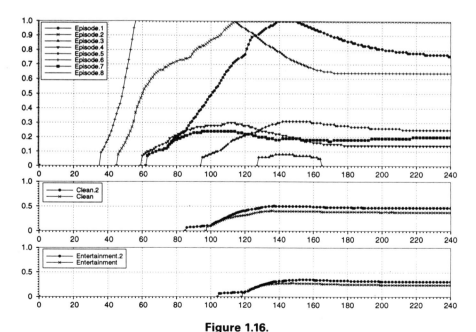

Figure 1.16.
Activations of Eight Episodes of Table 1.3 and Two of the Elements of Winning *Episode.2* (Car Wash) after Presentation of Dinner Party.

presented, **Episode.6** (*Mike put the flower in the pot, and then watered it*) is the first episode to become activated because of its surface similarities with *John put the pot inside the dishwasher*. **Episode.2** (**Car Wash**) gets activated after about cycle 45 because of the shared inferences of transfer-inside and inside-of, and continues to gain more activation when Clean is inferred at around cycle 100. The activation of **Episode.1** (**Dirty Magazine**) also starts climbing at around cycle 100 because the network is also activating the hiding and seeing structures as possible inferences for **Dinner Party**.

At about cycle 120, the network infers that an entertainment is being planned (the dinner party). This activates entertainment.2 and provides more evidence for **Car Wash**. At about the same time, the cleaning frames (including inside of dishwasher) get reinforcement from the *company was coming* inferences (cycles 100-140). This boosts the activations of many of the remaining elements of **Car Wash**, such as clean.2. Accordingly, episode.2's activation begins to dominate over episode.1's (**Dirty Magazine**), which gradually loses support starting about cycle 150. Thus, REMIND retrieves the **Car Wash** episode when **Dinner Party** is presented as a cue. This demonstrates that even changing a single word in the cue (from *police* to *company*) can completely change the inferences and interpretations REMIND makes, and, consequently, the episode REMIND retrieves.

5.2. Superficial Similarities

As mentioned earlier, human reminding seems to be affected strongly by superficial feature overlap between cues and memory episodes. Even when episodes exist in memory that are highly analogous to a cue (and hence useful for problem solving), people may instead get reminded of nonanalogous episodes simply because they are more superficially similar. For example, stories about sharks eating people, such as **Killer Shark**, may remind people of other stories about sharks or other man-eaters devouring people, rather than thematically similar stories that do not happen to involve sharks. Superficial remindings therefore often come at the expense of perhaps more valuable cross-contextual remindings.

This characteristic of reminding can be explained quite readily if episodes are remembered by storing all aspects of their interpretation, as in REMIND. Because REMIND stores all of the knowledge structures used in building an interpretation of the episode, from surface features to abstract inferences, it predicts that episodes that share many surface features with a cue are indeed likely candidates for reminding. For example, consider the sentence:

Cheech put the grass inside the bong because Chong was coming. (**Cheech and Chong**)

Cheech and Chong is an example of a superficially similar episode that can prevent retrieval of an analogous episode. Although **Cheech and Chong** is not analogous to **Hiding Pot**, the two episodes share a number of surface features. Both involving marijuana, marijuana being put inside of something, and somebody coming near. The plans and goals in the two episodes are completely different, however. In **Cheech and Chong**, the most probable interpretation is that Cheech was readying the marijuana to be smoked with his friend Chong. In **Hiding Pot**, of course, the network's interpretation was that John was hiding the marijuana so he would not be punished. So if **Cheech and Chong** is understood and stored in memory along with the eight episodes of Table 1.3, then **Dirty Magazine** is still the most *analogous* story in memory to **Hiding Pot**. **Cheech and Chong**, however, shares far more *total* features with **Hiding Pot's** interpretation, and is therefore more likely to be retrieved by the model when **Hiding Pot** is presented as a cue.

To test this, input for **Cheech and Chong** was presented to the network to be understood and then remembered. The network disambiguated *grass* to **marijuana** (instead of **lawn grass**), and inferred an interpretation that Cheech put the marijuana inside a **marijuana bong** to light it for the **pot party** that Chong was transferring himself to. **Cheech and Chong's** interpretation was then added (as **episode.9**) to the eight episodes already stored in the network.

Figure 1.17 shows the evidential activations as **Hiding Pot** is being understood in the network containing **Cheech and Chong** and the eight other episodes of Table 1.3. Both **Cheech and Chong** (episode.9) and **Flower Planting** (episode.6) quickly become activated because of their surface similarities with the undisambiguated *John put the pot inside the dishwasher*. However, **episode.9's** activation starts to dominate and **episode.6's** starts to fall after the *police were coming* is presented to the network. This occurs because *the police were coming*

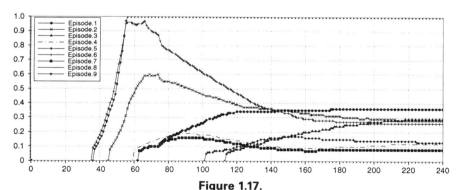

Figure 1.17.
Activations of Eight Episodes of Table 1.3 and Cheech and Chong after Presentation of Hiding Pot.

adds more superficially similar activation to **episode.9's Chong was coming**. **Episode.6's** activation drops further when **planting pot's** activation falls as the network disambiguates *pot* to **cooking pot** (the cleaning inferences) or **marijuana** (the hiding and police capture inferences). **Episode.9's** activation, on the other hand, remains at its maximum (1.0) until the network settles. **Cheech and Chong** is therefore the episode retrieved for **Hiding Pot**. The other eight episodes end up with relatively little activation, since **Cheech and Chong** is so (superficially) similar to **Hiding Pot** relative to them. As might be expected, **Dirty Magazine** is the most highly activated of the remaining eight episodes, since it was the episode most similar to **Hiding POt** before **Cheech and Chong** was remembered.

5.3. Effect of Reminding on Interpretation

REMIND only models how cues are understood and how episodes are consequently retrieved from memory. Unlike case-based reasoning models, it does not model how the information in those episodes can be used for analogical transfer or applied for problem solving. One of the reasons this would be difficult for REMIND is that the *analogical inferences* that are made by case-based reasoning models are essentially equivalent to applying *novel* rules (e.g., applying a newly mapped rule from a previous case to the bindings of the new case). Structured connectionist networks such as REMIND cannot currently represent such completely novel "rules," because rules connecting concepts are hard coded with units and links that cannot themselves be dynamically recruited. The possible extensions to signatures' representational and inferencing capabilities discussed in Lange (1992) might solve some of these problems. Eskridge (this volume) and Barnden and Srinivas (1992) show that *hybrid* connectionist models that use complex symbolic abilities can perform analogical and case-based transfer from the cases they retrieve.

Though it does not reason from the episodes it recalls, REMIND's integration of the reminding and understanding processes shows that memory retrieval can have pragmatically interesting and useful effects on the understanding process. Episodes that become active during the understanding process feed activation back into the inferencing part of the network. This, in effect, can prime and bias the interpretation REMIND settles on for a given input. For example, consider the following example:

The star loved the plumber, but he was shot by a thief. Then the astronomer proposed to her. She started to cry. (**Astronomer Proposal**).

There are two possible reasons for the movie star starting to cry after the astronomer proposed to her: either the proposal made her extremely happy, or the proposal made her extremely sad. Perhaps the most likely reason for her crying was that the proposal reminded her of murdered lover, therefore making her upset and sad. REMIND, however, does not have the complex knowledge about memories and how they affect people's emotions that would be necessary to make that interpretation. However, REMIND is given the knowledge that a person will become sad when someone they loves dies (**unhappy dead friend**). The network is also knows that marriage proposals can be either happy events (**happy proposal**) or sad events (**unhappy proposal**), as in ATLAST (Eiselt, 1987).

When the network is presented with input for **Astronomer Proposal**, the word *star* is quickly disambiguated to **movie star** because of the selectional restrictions that only **humans** can be the actors of **love** (Figure 1.18). REMIND then infers that the $shooting causes the plumber to be **dead**, and that the **movie star** that **loved** him will therefore be sad (**unhappy dead friend** leading to **unhappy**). After input for the phrase *the astronomer proposed to her* is presented, the network infers at about cycle 120 that there are two possible results from this **marriage proposal**: that she will consider it a **happy proposal** or an **unhappy proposal**. These inferences then instantiate the more general **happy** and **unhappy** frames, respectively, both of which connect to the **movie star's crying**, because **crying** can be the **result-of** states **happy** or **unhappy**.

As shown in Figure 1.18, **happy proposal** initially becomes more highly activated than **unhappy proposal**. This is a result of the network being biased to normally consider **marriage proposals** to be **happy proposals**—the weight from **marriage proposal** to **happy proposal** is 0.6, but the weight from **marriage proposal** to **unhappy proposal** is only 0.4. The gap in **happy**

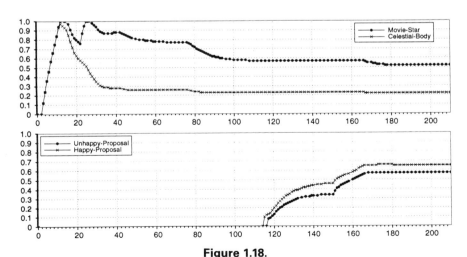

Figure 1.18.
Activations of Ambiguous Meanings of Word *star* and of *Happy-Proposal* and *Unhappy-Proposal* Interpretations of *Propose-Marriage* after activation is presented for Astronomer Proposal.

proposal and unhappy proposal's activations begins to narrow at about cycle 150 when both begin to receive feedback from crying *(she started to cry).* This narrowing occurs because (a) crying has a higher weight to unhappy than to happy, and (b) unhappy is already highly active from unhappy dead friend. However, REMIND's bias towards marriage proposals being happy proposals is too great, and happy proposal finishes with more activation than unhappy proposal. The final interpretation of **Astronomer Proposal** is therefore that (1) the movie star was made happy by the astronomer's proposal and started to cry "tears of joy," and (2) she was also sad because her lover the plumber was killed (an active inference path for which REMIND could find no causal connection to the crying of the marriage proposal).

As **Astronomer Proposal** illustrates, REMIND often comes up with counter intuitive interpretations of stories when the biases of its connection weights are too strong or when it does not have enough knowledge to make the needed inferences for the right interpretation. However, when there is a highly analogous episode (or case) in memory, the influence of episodic retrieval upon text understanding can lead REMIND to a correct interpretation of its input. For example, consider:

Suzie loved George, but he died. Then Bill proposed to her. She became sad. (**Sad Proposal**)

Sad Proposal is quite similar to **Astronomer Proposal**, except that in **Sad Proposal** the input made it explicit that Suzie became unhappy after Bill proposed to her. This essentially forces the network to make the "correct" interpretation, that the marriage proposal after the death of her lover was an unhappy proposal. This interpretation, including the inference unhappy proposal.8, is stored in memory as episode.8 in Table 1.3.

Figure 1.19 shows the activation levels of **Sad Proposal** (episode.8) and the other episodes as **Astronomer Proposal** is being understood by REMIND. As expected, **Sad Proposal** quickly dominates most of the other episodes because it is so similar to **Astronomer Proposal**. Episode.3 becomes temporarily active because it also involves somebody shooting somebody to death. However, **Sad Proposal** eventually wins and is retrieved.

The most interesting result shown in Figure 1.19 is the activation levels of the competing happy proposal and unhappy proposal frames. As when **Astronomer Proposal** was presented to the network without any episodes in memory, happy proposal initially has more activation than unhappy proposal because of its higher weight from propose marriage. In this case, however, episode.8 is highly active, and with it unhappy.8 and unhappy proposal.8 As described in Section 4, these episode instances feed activation back into their concepts in the understanding network. Unhappy proposal therefore gets significant activation from unhappy proposal.8. This added evidence allows its activation to climb over that of happy proposal, which gets no added evidence from any of the episodes in memory. When the network settles, unhappy proposal wins over happy proposal, so REMIND's interpretation is that the astronomer's marriage proposal made the movie star unhappy. The network therefore selects the correct interpretation of **Astronomer Proposal** because of activation feedback from an analogous case in memory, **Sad Proposal**.

REMIND's use of the same spreading-activation mechanism for both language understanding and episodic memory retrieval demonstrates one way memory retrieval can subtly affect the interpretation process. When stored episodes share conceptual similarity with a cue that REMIND is comprehending, these episodes feed evidential activation back into the inferencing network. This feedback can bias REMIND's interpretation to be consistent with the active episodes, a limited form of case-based reasoning. These effects emerge entirely from the integration of language understanding and retrieval within a single spreading-activation network.

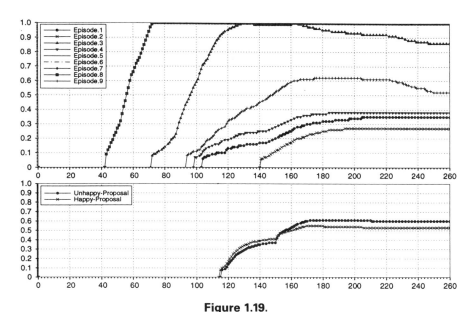

Figure 1.19.
Activations of Episodes and of *Happy-Proposal* and *Unhappy-Proposal* Interpretations of *Propose-Marriage* after Activation is Presented for Astronomer Proposal in Network Containing Sad Proposal Episode.

5.4. Comparison to General Models of Reminding

It is difficult to compare REMIND to most case-based reasoning models because they were developed with different goals in mind. As described previously, CBR models are usually models of expert reminding or models built to demonstrate how certain kinds of abstract remindings can occur. Unlike REMIND, they are not meant to be models of general, nonexpert human reminding. An advantage of case-based reasoning models over REMIND is that their use of symbolic processing abilities allow them to handle longer and more complex episodes than REMIND (and connectionist models in general) can currently handle. On the other hand, as a model of comprehension and general reminding, REMIND is better able to explain psychological results such as the relatively high prevalence of remindings based on superficial similarities and on how the reminding and language understanding processes interact and effect each other.

The models that REMIND is most directly comparable to are ARCS (Thagard et al., 1990) and MAC/FAC (Gentner & Forbus, 1991), two other simulations of general, nonexpert reminding. All three models were built to take into account psychological evidence showing that episodic memory retrieval is strongly influenced by surface feature similarities between a cue and the target episodes in memory, but that deeper analogical or thematic similarities sometimes play an important role. However, there are two important differences between how REMIND explains this evidence compared to ARCS and MAC/FAC.

The most obvious difference is that REMIND is an inferencing-based theory of reminding. Memory retrieval in REMIND results directly from the inferencing and disambiguation process used to understand and form elaborated interpretations of REMIND's cue. ARCS and MAC/FAC, on the other hand, are stand-alone memory retrieval models that are given complete propositional representations of their cues and memory episodes. An advantage of this approach is that it allows ARCS and MAC/FAC to deal with retrieval of much more complicated episodes than does REMIND. ARCS, for example, performed memory retrieval using complex, hand-coded predicate calculate representations of synopses of 24 Shakespearean plays. On the other hand, a major criticism of ARCS and MAC/FAC is that neither model specifies exactly how the representation of its input cues and episodes is formed. More importantly, neither model specifies what kinds of knowledge those representations should generally include. Should the cue representations include only the surface propositions directly stated in phrases of a cue's text? Or should they include a fully elaborated interpretation of the cue, including a complete causal plan/goal analysis of the text and any abstract themes it involves?

We believe that many types of memory retrieval cannot be performed without such inferences, as illustrated by some of the examples in this chapter (e.g., Section 4.3 and 5.1) and some of the examples of case-based reasoning systems.

However, even if stand-alone retrieval models such as ARCS and MAC/FAC used fully elaborated interpretations of their cues, we believe that not without modeling the *process* by which these interpretations are formed misses an important factor in reminding. People read texts with widely different levels of analysis, ranging from simply skimming the text to reading it carefully and thinking deeply about its ramifications. While there are circumstances under which it is reasonable to assume that subjects make relatively deep thematic inferences, it is misleading to think that this is always the case (e.g., Seifert et al., 1986). Thus, when the process by which the retrieval cue is constructed itself is not modeled, there is no way to simulate the specific circumstances under which understanders infer and can use planning or thematic information in probing memory. In contrast, REMIND explicitly models the cue interpretation process, and so can potentially explain when elaborated abstract inferences are available to affect reminding.

Another major difference between REMIND and ARCS and MAC/FAC is in how they theorize that analogical similarity exerts an influence on memory retrieval. Both ARCS and MAC/FAC perform memory retrieval in two stages. In their first stage, both search memory to find the episodes in memory sharing the most surface semantic commonalities with the cue. In their second stage, they compute which of the contacted episodes best match the cue and should be retrieved. In addition to counting surface similarities, they calculate the degree of *structural isomorphism* (or *related consistency*) as an explicit factor in their computation of which episode best matches the cue. Eskridge (this volume) describes a hybrid connectionist model of analogical retrieval and transfer that acts in a similar way.

Isomorphism can best be explained by an example from Thagard et al. (1990) for the cue *The dog bit the boy and the boy ran away from the dog* (**Boy Run**). Compare this to the analogs *Fido bit John and John ran away from Fido* (**John Run**) and *Rover bit Fred and Rover ran away from Fred* (**Rover Run**). **John Run** is structurally isomorphic with **Boy Run**, because mapped objects play the same roles in mapped predicates. In both cases, the dog did the biting and the person it bit did the running. In **Rover Run**, however, it was the dog that ran from the person it bit. **John Run** is therefore more isomorphic, in a purely syntactic sense, to **Boy Run** than **Rover Run**, and is therefore a better analog.

Both ARCS and MAC/FAC explicitly compute the level of isomorphism between a cue and episodes that share surface semantic overlap with the cue. The degree of cue/target isomorphic match is factored into their second stage's matching process. Analogical similarity is hypothesized by these models to exert its effect on memory retrieval as a direct result of this specifically computed degree of syntactic relational consistency between cues and memory episodes. REMIND, on the other hand, never explicitly computes the degree of isomorphism between a cue and memory episodes. In REMIND, the influence of such relational consistency is entirely the result of the inferencing process. Relationally consistent targets are retrieved over relationally inconsistent targets in REMIND only when the different syntactic structure of each input *leads to different inferences*. For example, if presented with **John Run**, REMIND would infer that the boy ran away because he was afraid that the dog would continue its attack. However, if presented with **Rover Run**, REMIND would infer that the dog ran away because it feared retaliation in the form of anger or a kick from the boy. Because of the different inferences and interpretation of the two episodes, REMIND, like ARCS and MAC/FAC, would therefore retrieve **John Run** when presented with **Boy Run** as a cue. Unlike ARCS and MAC/FAC, however, REMIND does so without having to go through a separate stage to explicitly compute the degree of syntactic isomorphism.

Like ARCS, our earlier model of integrated language understanding and memory retrieval, SAARCS (Lange, Melz, Wharton, & Holyoak, 1990), included relational consistency as an explicit factor in reminding. SAARCS was a hybrid connectionist model that combined ROBIN (Lange & Dyer, 1989) with aspects of ARCS. Like REMIND, SAARCS used the ROBIN portion of the network to infer and disambiguate an interpretation of a cue. Unlike REMIND, SAARCS then explicitly calculated relational consistency to build a constraint satisfaction mapping network like ARCS' to determine which episode was retrieved. Oftentimes SAARCS would not have enough knowledge to make different inferences between cues with cross-mapped bindings, such as for *The boat followed the dolphins* versus *The dolphins followed the boat*. In those cases, SAARCS's use of ARCS' explicit influence of relational consistency between cues and targets led SAARCS to retrieve the right analog (Lange et al., 1990). However, when SAARCS had enough knowledge to build a different interpretation for cross-mapped cues (such as for *The surfer ate the shark* versus *The shark ate the surfer*), the explicit effect of relational consistency turned out to be unneeded. As in REMIND, the different shared inferences in SAARCS were enough to activate the analogous episode enough to win. It turned out that in every case that we built enough knowledge into the network for it to build different interpretations for disanalogous episodes, the degree of syntactic isomorphism only boosted (confirmed) the analogous episode that had already won due to those different interpretations. This was a primary motivating factor for simplifying the model and moving to REMIND, a purely inferencing-based model of episodic reminding.

We therefore believe that the noted effects of syntactic isomorphism and relational consistency on memory retrieval can be fully explained by the understanding process. Relationally consistent episodes tend to have similar inferences, interpretations, and themes, while relationally inconsistent episodes tend to have different inferences, interpretations, and themes. In REMIND, relationally based reminding occurs as a natural side effect of interpreting and disambiguating an input text. Relational consistency only affects reminding to the degree that it changes those inferences.

5.5. Future Work

In the future, there are three main areas that we would like to explore: (1) improved inferencing abilities, (2) the ability to determine the initial surface role-bindings with additional lexical information in the networks, and (3) automatic learning of the episodes the network has understood.

5.5.1. Improved Inferencing.
REMIND's propagation of signature activations dynamically instantiates candidate inference paths in parallel, in much the same way as marker-passing systems. The use of ROBIN's signatures therefore allows REMIND to perform dynamic inferencing difficult for most connectionist models, while using its evidential activation allows it to perform disambiguation and reinterpretation difficult for most symbolic models. However, REMIND's representation and rule-firing abilities are currently limited relative to those of traditional symbolic models, limiting the length and complexity of the texts the model can understand and therefore remember.

One of the main restrictions of the model as described is that there can be only one dynamic instance of each frame at any given time, since binding units can only hold one signature activation at once. Because of this, REMIND cannot yet represent or interpret texts involving two different seeing or eating events, for instance. Another limitation is that REMIND currently only propagates signatures of *pre-existing* concepts, such as of cooking pot, marijuana, or John. REMIND does not propagate signatures of the *dynamically* instantiated frames inferred by signatures, such as the dynamic instance of cooking pot or marijuana being inside of a dishwasher in Figure 1.5. Not being able to propagate signatures of dynamically instantiated frames makes it impossible for REMIND to encode most rules for *general* planning knowledge or complex interactions of goals, which generally require the ability to reason over any dynamic plan or goal instance the system might have. These type of rules are needed to understand many complex texts, such as those involving abstract planning failures or themes (cf. Dyer, 1983; Schank, 1982).

These and other restrictions on the types of inferencing REMIND performs limit the complexity of the episodes REMIND can currently understand and retrieve relative to many symbolic language understanding and case-based reasoning models. We are currently exploring solutions to some of these problems to allow multiple dynamic instantiations of individual frames and to allow rules that propagate signatures of the novel concepts inferred by the network. A number of different ways to approach these problems and handle more complex text are discussed in Lange (1992). Ajjanagadde (1990) discusses an analogous solution for structured networks that do not perform disambiguation.

5.5.4. Lexical Information and Initial Role Bindings.
ROBIN does not currently address the problem of deciding upon the original syntactic bindings (e.g., that "*pot*" is bound to the object role of a phrase). Rather, ROBIN's networks are given these initial bindings and use them for high-level inferencing.

To handle natural language input entered as text, the network must somehow contain and use syntactic and phrasal information to create the initial role bindings that ROBIN is currently given by hand.

5.5.3. Automatic Learning of Episode Units. The representations that REMIND uses for its memory episodes are created entirely by REMIND's spreading-activation understanding process. To store those representations in the network, however, the units and connections used to encode them must be added by hand. It would be desirable to have those episode units be learned automatically by the network itself. We are currently exploring a mechanism to *recruit* units (cf. Diederich, 1991) to encode the interpretation held by signature and evidential activation in the network and therefore allow episode learning to proceed without intervention.

Another area to explore will be gradual decay of the weights between episode units and the semantic network. Episodes that are not retrieved for a long time should gradually have their weights decay so that they become more difficult to become reminded of as time goes on. This is also a potential solution to the problem of "indexing" too many episodes under general concepts, such as **possess obj** and **inside of**, since connections from them to old episodes could gradually decay away and become available for new ones.

CONCLUSIONS

The process of memory retrieval has generally been explored in isolation from the process of language understanding, even though both activities seem to share many of the same processes. One of the reasons for this is that building an integrated model of language understanding and retrieval requires not only solving the important aspects of each of the processes individually—a difficult enough problem separately—but also finding a parsimonious way to integrate the two processes that can explain the effect they have on each other. Because of their simple processing mechanism and demonstrated abilities to perform disambiguation and model the psychological effects of priming and context, structured spreading-activation networks seem to have a great deal of potential for building such an integrated model.

A number of difficult problems for spreading-activation networks have to be solved to use them for language understanding and memory retrieval. First, language understanding requires the ability to represent variable bindings within the network and to perform dynamic inferencing to explain the plans and goals of actors. Second, problems of disambiguation and frame selection require the ability to combine evidential domain knowledge with the contextual evidence of the network's inferences to select the best interpretation of a text from multiple possible interpretations. In addition, ambiguous texts requiring many inferences make the problems of controlling crosstalk between unrelated concepts and inferences especially important to solve. And finally, a method for representing episodes in the network's long-term memory that allows them to be influenced and retrieved by the spreading-activation understanding process must be developed.

This chapter described REMIND, a structured spreading-activation model that solves most of these problems in an integrated model of language understanding and episodic reminding. In REMIND, activation is spread through a semantic network that performs dynamic inferencing and disambiguation to infer a conceptual representation of an input cue. Because stored episodes are associated with concepts used to understand them, the spreading-activation process also activates any memory episodes in the network that share features or knowledge structures with the cue. After the cue's conceptual representation is formed, the network recalls the memory episode having the highest activation. Since the inferences made from a cue often include actors' plans and goals only implied in a cue's text, REMIND is able to get abstract, analogical remindings that would not be possible without an integrated understanding and retrieval model.

Theoretically, REMIND lies somewhere between case-based reasoning models and general analogical retrieval models such as ARCS and MAC/FAC. Like ARCS and MAC/FAC, REMIND is meant to be a psychologically plausible model of general human reminding, and therefore takes into account the prevalence of superficial feature similarities in remindings. However, we believe that many of the types of high-level planning and thematic knowledge structures used as indices in case-based reasoning systems also have an important effect on reminding. REMIND is thus partially an attempt to bridge the gap between case-based and analogical retrieval models. As it turns out, this gap is naturally bridged when the same spreading-activation mechanism is used to both understand cues and to retrieve episodes from memory. Using the same mechanism for both processes causes retrieval to be affected by all levels that a text was understood with. This is the case in REMIND, in which the understanding mechanism is given the superficial features and actions of a text and attempts to explain them by inferring the plans and goals being used—causing long-term memory episodes to be activated by both.

Although being an integrated comprehension and retrieval model makes REMIND more complex than the retrieval mechanisms of case-based reasoning models and ARCS and MAC/FAC, it also allows REMIND to be simpler than them in a couple of significant respects. A large amount of the research in case-based reasoning models is devoted towards discovering the best indices to store cases under (the *indexing problem*). In REMIND, however, episodes are simply stored (indexed) under all of the concepts that played a part in understanding them. When combined with the comprehension part of the model, this simple connectionist approach to indexing avoids the indexing problem altogether, while still giving the effect of having chosen the "proper" indices since the most salient and unique features of an episode in a given context naturally become highly activated as part of the understanding process.

ARCS and MAC/FAC also avoid the indexing problem of CBR models because they both make contact with episodes that share any feature similarities with the cue, in effect using all features as indices. Where REMIND differs from ARCS and MAC/FAC is that both ARCS and MAC/FAC use separate mechanisms to explicitly factor the degree of syntactic relational consistency (analogical similarity) into retrieval. We believe that psychological effects of analogical similarity on memory retrieval that their separate syntactic mechanisms are meant to model can be fully explained by the understanding process. Relationally consistent episodes tend to have similar inferences, interpretations, and themes, while relationally inconsistent episodes do not. In REMIND, analogically based reminding therefore occurs as a natural side effect of understanding an input text, rather than as a result of a separate process that explicitly computes it, as in ARCS and MAC/FAC.

A final aspect to note about REMIND concerns how language understanding and retrieval processes come full circle. The episode retrieved depends crucially on the interpretation of the cue from the spreading-activation network's inferences. Once an episode is retrieved, it in turn primes the activation of the evidential spreading-activation network, perhaps leading to a different disambiguation and therefore interpretation of the next cue. Thus, we believe that REMIND is able to uniquely provide insights which other current reminding models are not able to show. As such, REMIND represents an entirely new class of reminding models.

REFERENCES

Ajjanagadde, V. (1990). Reasoning with function symbols in a connectionist system. *Proceedings of the Twelfth Annual Meeting of the Cognitive Science Society.* Hillsdale, NJ: Erlbaum.

Anderson, J.R. (1983). *The architecture of cognition.* Cambridge, MA: Harvard University Press.

Barnden, J. (1991). The power of some unusual connectionist data-structuring techniques. In J.A. Barnden & J.B. Pollack (Eds.), *Advances in connectionist and neural computation theory* (Vol. 1). Norwood, NJ: Ablex.

Barnden, J., & Srinivas, K. (1992). Overcoming rule-based rigidity and connectionist limitations through massively-parallel case-based reasoning. *International Journal of Man-Machine Studies, 36,* 221–246.

Charniak, E. (1986). A neat theory of marker passing. *Proceedings of the Fifth National Conference on Artificial Intelligence* (pp. 584–588). Los Altos, CA: Morgan Kaufmann.

Cottrell, G., & Small, S. (1982). A connectionist scheme for modeling word-sense disambiguation. *Cognition and Brian Theory, 6,* 89–120.

Diederich, J. (1991). Steps toward knowledge-intensive connectionist learning. In J.A. Barnden & J.B. Pollack (Eds.), *Advances in connectionist and neural computation theory (Vol. 1)*, (pp. 284–304). Norwood, NJ: Ablex.
Dolan, C.P., & Smolensky, P. (1989). Tensor product production system: A modular architecture and representation. *Connection Science, 1*(1), 53–68.
Dyer, M.G. (1983). *In-depth understanding: A computer model of integrated processing for narrative comprehension.* Cambridge, MA: MIT Press.
Falkenhainer, B., Forbus, K.D., & Gentner, D. (1989). The structure-mapping engine: Algorithm and examples. *Artificial Intelligence, 41*, 1–63.
Gentner, D. (1989). The mechanisms of analogical learning. In S. Vosniadou & A. Ortony (Eds.), *Similarity and analogical reasoning* (pp. 199–241). New York: Cambridge University Press.
Gentner, D., & Forbus, K.D. (1991). MAC/FAC: A model of similarity-based retrieval. *Proceedings of the Thirteenth Annual Conference of the Cognitive Science Society* (pp. 504–509). Hillsdale, NJ: Erlbaum.
Gentner, D., & Landers, R. (1985). Analogical reminding: A good match is hard to find. *Proceedings of the International Conference on Systems, Man and Cybernetics* (pp. 607–613). Tucson, AZ.
Gick, M., & Holyoak, K.J. (1980). Analogical problem solving. *Cognitive Psychology, 12*, 306–355.
Gick, M.L., & McGarry, S.J. (1992). Learning from mistakes: Inducing analogous failures to a source problem produces later successes in analogical transfer. *Journal of Experimental Psychology: Learning, Memory, and Cognition, 18*, 623–639.
Glucksberg, S., Kreuz, R.J., & Rho, S.H. (1986). Context can constrain lexical access: Implications for models of language comprehension. *Journal of Experimental Psychology: Learning, Memory, and Cognition, 12*, 323–335.
Granger, R.H., Eiselt, K.P., & Holbrook, J.K. (1986). Parsing with parallelism: A spreading-activation model of inferencing processing during text understanding. In J. Kolodner & C. Riesbeck (Eds.), *Experience, memory, and reasoning* (pp. 227–246). Hillsdale, NJ: Erlbaum.
Hammond, K. (1989). *Case-based planning.* Boston: Academic Press.
Hendler, J. (1989). Marker-passing over microfeatures: Towards a hybrid symbolic/connectionist model. *Cognitive Science, 13*, 79–106.
Hofstadter, D.R., & Mitchell, M. (1994). An overview of the copycat project. In K.J. Holyoak & J.A. Barnden (Eds.), *Advances in connectionist and neural computation theory (Vol. 2)*, (pp. 31–110). Norwood, NJ: Ablex.
Hölldobler, S. (1990). A structured connectionist unification algorithm. *Proceedings of the Eighth National Conference on Artificial Intelligence* (pp. 589–593). Menlo Park, CA: AAAI Press/MIT Press.
Holyoak, K.J., & Koh, K. (1987). Surface and structural similarity in analogical transfer. *Memory & Cognition, 15*, 332–340.
Keane, M. (1988). *Analogical problem solving.* Chichester, England: Ellis Horwood.
Kintsch, W. (1988). The role of knowledge in discourse comprehension: A construction-integration model. *Psychological Review, 95*, 163–182.
Kitano, H., Tomabechi, H., & Levin, L. (1989). Ambiguity resolution in DMTRANS PLUS. *Proceedings of the Fourth Conference of the European Chapter of the Association of Computational Linguistics.* New York: Manchester University Press.

Kohonen, T. (1984). *Self-organization and associative memory*. New York: Springer Verlag.

Kolodner, J. (1984). *Retrieval and organizational strategies in conceptual memory: A computer model*. Hillsdale, NJ: Erlbaum.

Kolodner, J., Simpson, R., & Sycara, K. (1985). A process model of case-based reasoning in problem solving. *Proceedings of the Ninth International Joint Conference on Artificial Intelligence* (pp. 284–290). Los Altos, CA: Morgan Kaufmann.

Lange, T. (1992). Lexical and pragmatic disambiguation and reinterpretation in connectionist networks. *International Journal of Man-Machine Studies, 36*, 191–220.

Lange, T., & Dyer, M.G. (1989). High-level inferencing in a connectionist network. *Connection Science, 1*(2), 181–217.

Lange, T., Hodges, J., Fuenmayor, M., & Belyaev, L. (1989): DESCARTES: Development Environment For Simulating Hybrid Connectionist Architectures. *Proceedings of the Eleventh Annual Meeting of the Cognitive Science Society* (pp. 698–705). Hillsdale, NJ: Erlbaum.

Lange, T., Melz, E., Wharton, C., & Holyoak, K. (1990). Analogical retrieval within a hybrid spreading-activation network. In D.S. Touretzky, J.L. Elman, T.J. Sejnowski, & G.E. Hinton (Eds.), *Proceedings of the 1990 Connectionist Models Summer School* (pp. 265–276). San Mateo, CA: Morgan Kaufmann.

Lebowitz (1990). *Generalization and memory in an integrated understanding system*. Doctoral dissertation, Research Report #186, Yale University, Department of Computer Science, New Haven, CT.

Lytinen, S. (1984). *The organization of knowledge in a multi-lingual integrated parser*. Doctoral dissertation, Research Report #340, Yale University, Department of Computer Science, New Haven, CT.

McClelland, J.L., & Kawamoto, A.H. (1986): Mechanisms of sentence processing: Assigning roles to constituents of sentences. In J.L. McClelland & D.E. Rumelhart (Eds.), *Parallel distributed processing* (Vol. 2, pp. 272–325). Cambridge, MA: MIT Press.

Miikkulainen, R. (1993). *Towards subsymbolic natural language processing: An integrated model of scripts, lexicon, and memory*. Cambridge, MA: MIT Press.

Miikkuleinen, R., & Dyer, M.G. (1991). Natural language processing with modular PDP networks and distributed lexicon. *Cognitive Science, 15*, 343–399.

Norvig, P. (1989). Marker passing as a weak method for text inferencing. *Cognitive Science, 13*, 569–620.

Owens, C. (1989). Integrating feature extraction and memory search. *Proceedings of the Eleventh Annual Conference of the Cognitive Science Society* (pp. 163–170). Hillsdale, NJ: Erlbaum.

Ratterman, M.J., & Gentner, D. (1987). Analogy and similarity: Determinants of accessibility and inferential soundness. *Proceedings of the Ninth Annual Meeting of the Cognitive Science Society* (pp. 22–34). Hillsdale, NJ: Erlbaum.

Read, S.J., & Cesa, I.L. (1991). This reminds me of the time when: Expectation failures in reminding and explanation. *Journal of Experimental Social Psychology, 27*, 1–25.

Reeves, J.F. (1991). *Computational morality: A process model of belief conflict and resolution for story understanding*. Unpublished doctoral dissertation, Computer Science Department, University of California, Los Angeles.

Riesbeck, C.K. (1975). Conceptual analysis. In R.C. Schank (Ed.), *Conceptual information processing* (pp. 83–156). New York: American Eisener.
Riesbeck, C.K., & Schank, R.C. (1989). *Inside case-based reasoning*. Hillsdale, NJ: Erlbaum.
Riesbeck, C.K., & Martin, C.E. (1986). Direct memory access parsing. In J. Kolodner & C. Riesbeck (Eds.), *Experience, memory, and reasoning* (pp. 209–226). Hillsdale, NJ: Erlbaum.
Ross, B.H. (1987). This is like that: The use of earlier problems and the separation of similarity effects. *Journal of Experimental Psychology: Learning, Memory, and Cognition, 13*, 629–639.
Ross, B.H. (1989). Distinguishing types of superficial similarities: Different effects on the access and use of earlier problems. *Journal of Experimental Psychology: Learning, Memory, and Cognition, 15*, 456–468.
Rumelhart, D.E., Hinton, G.E., & McClelland, J.L. (1986). A general framework for parallel distributed processing. In D.E. Rumelhart & J.L. McClelland (Eds.), *Parallel processing* (Vol. 1, pp. 45–76). Cambridge, MA: MIT Press.
Schank, R.C. (1982). *Dynamic memory*. New York: Cambridge University Press.
Schank, R.C., & Abelson, R. (1977). *Scripts, plans, goals and understanding*. Hillsdale, NJ: Erlbaum.
Schank, R.C., & Leake, D.B. (1989). Creativity and learning in a case-based explainer. *Artificial Intelligence, 40*, 353–385.
Seifert, C.M., McKoon, G., Abelson, R.P. & Ratcliff, R. (1986). Memory connections between thematically similar episodes. *Journal of Experimental Psychology: Human Learning and Memory, 12*, 220–231.
Shastri, L., & Ajjanagadde, V. (1993). From simple associations to systematic reasoning. A connectionist representation of rules, variables, and dynamic bindings using temporal synchrony. *Behavioral and Brain Sciences, 16*(3), 417–494.
Spencer, R.M., & Weisberg, R.W. (1986). Context-dependent effects on analogical transfer. *Memory and Cognition, 14*, 442–449.
St. John, M. (1992). The story gestalt: A model of knowledge intensive processes in text comprehension. *Cognitive Science, 16*, 271–306.
Sun, R. (in press). Beyond associative memories: Logics and variables in connectionist models. *Information Sciences*.
Swinney, D.A. (1979). Lexical access during sentence comprehension: (Re)consideration of context effects. *Journal of Verbal Learning and Verbal Behavior, 15*, 681–689.
Thagard, P., Holyoak, K.J., Nelson, G., & Gochfeld, D. (1990). Analog retrieval by constraint satisfaction. *Artificial Intelligence, 46*, 259–310.
Till, R.E., Mross, E.F., & Kintsch, W. (1988). Time course of priming for associate and inference words in a discourse context. *Memory & Cognition, 16*, 283–298.
Touretzky, D. (1990). Connectionism and compositional semantics. In J.A. Barnden & J.B. Pollack (Eds.), *Advances in connectionist and neural computation theory* (Vol. 1). Norwood, NJ: Ablex.
Touretzky, D., & Hinton, G. (1988). A distributed connectionist production system. *Cognitive Science, 12*, 423–466.
Waltz, D., & Pollack, J. (1985). Massively parallel parsing: A strongly interactive model of natural language interpretation. *Cognitive Science, 9*, 51–74.
Wharton, C.M., Holyoak, K.J., Downing, P.E., Lange, T.E., & Wickens, T.D. (1991). Retrieval competition in memory for analogies. *Proceedings of the Thirteenth*

Annual Conference of the Cognitive Science Society (pp. 528–533). Hillsdale, NJ: Erlbaum.

Wharton, C.M., Holyoak, K.J., Downing, P.E., Lange, T.E., & Wickens, T.D. (1992). The story with reminding: Memory retrieval is influenced by analogical similarity. *Proceedings of the Fourteenth Annual Conference of the Cognitive Science Society* (pp. 588–593). Hillsdale, NJ: Erlbaum.

Wilensky, R. (1983). *Planning and understanding.* Reading, MA: Addison-Wesley.

2
The Role of Goals in Retrieving Analogical Cases*

Colleen M. Seifert

1. THE PROBLEM OF CASE RETRIEVAL

A central problem in analogical reasoning is the successful retrieval of appropriate cases from memory. In many reasoning tasks, prior experience could be successfully applied to improve plans and decisions. Particularly when learning a new domain, learning a generalization, or applying old rules within new contexts, reasoning from past cases is a functional method for successful performance. In addition, there is evidence for successful case retrieval in some task contexts from human experimental data. Therefore, a desirable feature of memory models is a high rate of successful retrieval of analogical cases in some processing conditions. Two common approaches to models of memory retrieval are *featural similarity* and *case-based reasoning* models. These two approaches offer advantages that must ultimately be combined in order to achieve consistent access to relevant analogical cases in memory.

1.1. Feature Similarity Models

Retrieval in feature models is often assumed to be an automatic process that is dependent solely on the similarity of an input to a case in memory (Rumelhart, 1989). In such models, the features of the input case are compared to the features of the stored cases, and the match with the most features in common, and fewest distinctions, "wins" (Tversky, 1977). Under certain circumstances, a similarity

---

* This work was supported by ONR Contract N0014-91-1128 to the University of Michigan. Special thanks to David Rumelhart, who collaborated with me on the distributed memory model implementation. Thanks also to Michael Mozer and Kristian Hammond for helpful conversations about this work, and to Steven Sloman, John Barnden, Keith Holyoak, and two anonymous reviewers for comments on earlier drafts.

metric alone may be sufficient to identify a single prior case in memory. For example, if an input case has a great many features in common with a particular case in memory (high similarity to target), and both cases share little with other cases in memory (high distinctiveness of target), then similarity alone may be enough to account for the spontaneous retrieval of the case from memory. Recent schemes have attempted to encode semantic similarity within a feature-based system (Thagard & Holyoak, 1989).

Representations for cases in these featural similarity models tend to be fairly simple. Typically, the input features are included as a flat representation of case content; for example, to encode President Bush into memory, a feature set might contain feature vectors representing "president, Bush, George, approval ratings, thyroid, foreign policy, Millie." The input features can be at any level of description, and the associations between features are the degree to which the stated features are correlated. Thus, in connectionist models, the selection of which features to use in representing a particular domain is left to the programmer. Innovations in this approach lie instead in the methods for *implementing* the matching process (Rumelhart, 1989). Content-addressable memory retrieval, emergence of prototypes, and activation schemes are advantages of this approach (Rumelhart, McClelland, & the PDP Research Group, 1986). There is also some indication that practical constraints on the number of features utilized in the match may be removed by highly parallel machine architectures, so that the number of features utilized in the match can be increased at little computational cost. Therefore, the success of this approach is due in part to its simple assumptions about representations: Matching algorithms that compute large numbers of similarity comparisons are feasible because of the simple representations employed.

However, there are some circumstances where feature matching based on similarities will not successfully identify a unique, appropriate episode in memory. For example, when cases share many features, then there will be high overlap and low distinctiveness of target retrieval cases. In addition, when the similarities between the input and the target case vary in the level of generality, then the overall number of similarities may not be an adequate metric for identifying the target case. That is, there may be other cases in memory that have *more* overlapping specific features, but not the particular abstract, analogical features of interest in the match. Therefore, retrieval based on a simple count of common features may be unsuccessful in promoting case access in some circumstances.

1.2. Case-Based Reasoning Models

In contrast, the main contribution of the case-based reasoning approach (Hammond, 1989; Riesbeck & Schank, 1989) lies in *knowledge representation*, or the nature of the features describing the content of the case information. Rather than simple feature descriptions, Schank (1982) argued on the basis of reminding protocols that the similarities between cases often consist of complex, abstract descriptions. Without including such abstract features within the match process, Schank argues, it will be impossible to retrieve the rich and interesting remindings that are the signature of human analogical reasoning.

Consider this example of cross-contextual reminding from Schank (1982):

> X described how his spouse would never make his steak as rare as he liked it. When this was told to Y, it reminded Y of a time, 30 years earlier, when he tried to get his hair cut in a short style in England, and the barber would not cut it as short as he wanted it.

What features might be encoded into memory to represent this case? Besides the obvious ones either scheme might use (i.e., steak, haircut, England), Schank argues that there are abstract relationships in the story that must be encoded in order to say one has "understood" the story. These abstractions are revealed by the commonalities in the reminding: "Providing service" seems to capture what is common to the two episodes. In both cases, an unusual request (raw steak, very short hair) is responded to by the server with more usual service. The case-based reasoning approach argues that a rich representational scheme is necessary to describe the similarities in cases as revealed by remindings. In contrast to the feature similarity models, the case-based reasoning approach focuses on representing features, yet provides few specific process innovations about retrieval. Most models of case-based reasoning assume automatic retrieval of prior episodes based on the overlap of the input features with the features of a particular case indexed in memory (Kolodner, 1983, 1984). The input features are passed off to a discrimination net representation of features and cases, and the resulting match is output as the closest related case in memory (Riesbeck & Schank, 1989).

Schank (1982) also argues that retrieval of cases falls out during the comprehension of an episode—that the process of reminding is *mediated* by knowledge structures used to understand the original input. In reminding, characteristic memory organizations are set up such that attempting to encode a new case with a particular knowledge structure will call to mind a prior case encoded with that structure. So, this approach is also based on similarity, but with two differences: (a) that the representation includes relevant input features including abstract relationships, and (b) that retrieval falls out of other comprehension processing.

1.3. Goals in Retrieval

Goals have already been identified as an important aspect of analogy (Burstein, 1986; Burstein & Adelson, 1987; Seifert, 1989). However, neither of the two approaches presented above has addressed the variable role that processing goals play in analogical access. By processing goals, I mean the subtasks within reasoning processes, such as to verify a plan, justify a decision, explain an anomaly, or illustrate a method. In this chapter, I argue that strategic processing goals can act to focus attention on features so as to promote access to prior cases. The role of goals in case access may lie in guiding retrieval towards particularly relevant remindings. This requires incorporating the strengths of feature similarity approaches with the representational power of case-based systems.

In the next sections, I present evidence from experimental investigations that goals are a critical influence on access to prior cases. Then, examples of protocols and case-based reasoning programs are considered. A final section presents a proposal for incorporating processing goals into the case retrieval process.

2. AUTOMATIC VS. STRATEGIC RETRIEVAL OF PRIOR CASES

The colloquial use of "reminding" refers to cases where one is conscious of the result of the retrieval process, but not necessarily aware of the features responsible for the match. However, one may also be unaware of the retrieval of cases, yet show effects from the *activation* of cases in memory. Perhaps cases, like concepts, are activated in memory by accessing their shared features in a manner similar to semantic priming. This strong version of memory retrieval and indexing theory argues that the presence of featural commonalities alone is sufficient to produce activation of prior cases in memory (Schank, 1982).

An alternative possibility is that, even though commonalities exist between cases, the representations stored in memory and the utilization of the connections between cases may depend upon the use of some *goal* to connect and later access cases in memory. Consequently, the presence of commonalities between cases would not be sufficient to result in retrieval of cases; instead, the presence of some processing strategy in retrieval would be necessary to facilitate the recall of cases. Under this hypothesis, some processing goal utilized by subjects, in addition to the common features of the cases, would be necessary to promote the retrieval of cases.

The question of whether memory organization alone will result in the automatic memory activation of cases has been investigated experimentally. In this section, several experiments addressing automatic, nonstrategic access to cases are summarized, which test both abstract commonalities and more concrete features shared by cases. Then, some experiments are presented where the goal to be reminded is made explicit to the subjects.

2.1. Abstract Similarities

Many studies have identified the failure to spontaneously utilize past analogical cases in current problem solving (Gick & Holyoak, 1980, 1983; Holyoak, 1985;

Holyoak & Koh, 1987). However, when such analogical remindings *do* occur in the experimental context (Gentner, 1983; Gentner & Landers, 1985; Rattermann & Gentner, 1987;) it is usually the case that subjects were explicitly aware of the goal to retrieve the prior exemplar. For example, the instructions given to subjects sometimes direct them to "write down any prior examples that this new story reminds you of" (Rattermann & Gentner, 1987). Other studies, such as Ross's work on analogies during learning (Ross, 1989b) and Reiser and Faries's (1988) study of case retrieval during tutoring do not include an explicit request for reminding; however, both task contexts naturally promote the use of prior cases during testing on new cases. Consequently, these studies do not address the question of whether reminding will occur in the *absence* of such a processing goal.

However, several studies have been conducted that attempt to examine whether analogical case access will occur when the subject is *unaware* of the relevance of past cases (McKoon, Ratcliff, & Seifert, 1989; Seifert, McKoon, Abelson, & Ratcliff, 1986). The question of interest is, do subjects in fact build characteristic memory organizations such that prior cases are *automatically* activated as a result of normal comprehension processes? The strong version of Schank's (1982) theory of reminding is that prior cases are automatically reactivated when new cases involve the same abstract features. Therefore, a similar new case should activate the same structures in memory as prior similar cases, and result in a semantic priming effect (Meyer & Schvaneveldt, 1971).

Alternatively, some additional factor, such as goal-based influences, may be necessary to facilitate case access. The studies discussed in this section address this question by utilizing experimental tasks where subjects are unaware of the goal to be reminded. To the subject, the experiment appears to be a story reading and question-answering task, and subjects have no awareness of access to prior stories as the dependent variable of interest.

The basic paradigm in these studies is a story understanding paradigm, used to present cases sharing controlled types of similarities. New cases are provided for subjects to learn as reference instances in memory. The experimental context functions as a bounded memory set for the comparison of cases, so that subjects are not likely to utilize other memories when considering the relative similarity of the stories. Thus, new examples can be presented, and their ability to retrieve related target instances already encoded into memory can be systematically measured. The studies (see Seifert, McKoon, Abelson, & Ratcliff, 1986) involved presenting pairs of stories that either share or do not share an abstract knowledge structure, and then testing whether the memory organization that results causes differing activation properties. Semantic priming has been shown in a variety of tasks to provide a sensitive measure of differences in accessibility of information (e.g., Gibbs, 1984). In the current studies, time to answer a question about a previously read story is used to measure the accessibility of the story in memory. Activation of the test story may occur when answering a question about a related story (the prime) immediately prior to answering the test item. If the two stories are connected by the organizing structure in memory, then answering a question from one story should activate the other story in memory, resulting in faster responses to a question from that story.

The materials chosen for the experiments on abstract commonalities (Seifert, McKoon, Abelson, & Ratcliff, 1986) included similarities based on the types of goal and plan interactions that occur as themes in common adages (Dyer, 1983; Lehnert, 1980; Schank, 1982; Seifert, Dyer, & Black, 1986). For example, the adage "closing the barn door after the horse is gone" can be characterized as a planning failure, where one knows a plan to prevent goal failure, but delays execution to avoid the cost until the goal is failing; then, the plan is executed, but fails because it is "too late" (Dyer, 1983). Here are two stories used in the experiments that represent this thematic pattern:

Story 1: Academia
Dr. Popoff knew that his graduate student Mike was unhappy with the research facilities available in his department. Mike had requested new equipment on several occasions, but Dr. Popoff always denied Mike's requests. One day, Dr. Popoff found out that Mike had been accepted to study at a rival university. Not wanting to lose a good student, Dr. Popoff hurriedly offered Mike lots of new research equipment. But by then, Mike had already decided to transfer.

Story 2: Wedding Bells
Phil was in love with his secretary and was well aware that she wanted to marry him. However, Phil was afraid of responsibility, so he kept dating others and made up excuses to postpone the wedding. Finally, his secretary got fed up, began dating, and fell in love with an accountant. When Phil found out, he went to her and proposed marriage, showing her the ring he had bought. But by that time, his secretary was already planning her honeymoon with the accountant.

Both stories are encoded with the same thematic structure, consisting of information about failing to prevent a goal failure by failing to perform a sure fix to the problem until it is too late. Most of the stories capturing this theme also include the notion of a resulting "proximity violation," as the goal failure may cause the desired person (or horse) to leave. In addition, the two stories presented above each contain a failed expectation (an agreement that was not fulfilled (e.g., that "graduate students expect support from their advisors" and that "lovers expect commitment")). This notion (called "contract violation" by Dyer, 1983) is not present in the example depicted in the adage "closing the barn door after the horse has gone" (that is, the horse does not expect or desire to stay in the barn). Therefore, based on these thematic similarities, understanding these two same-theme stories is predicted to result in the memory representation (Dyer, 1983) shown in Figure 2.1.

If such a characteristic reminding structure is set up during the understanding process, reference to the academia story should result in automatic activation of the wedding-bells story.

Figure 2.1.
Discrimination Net Representation of Case Storage in Memory Based on Abstract Commonalities (from Dyer, 1983).

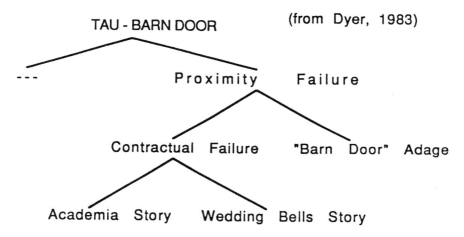

In the experiment, pairs of stories sometimes shared the same theme or did not, and were followed by a test list of items to respond to. On each trial, subjects read a pair of stories which either shared or did not share a theme. Then, subjects' responses to a series of eight test sentences about the two stories were measured. These test items included foils requiring a negative recognition response (i.e., "Mike decided to buy his own research equipment") and the two test items of interest:

Prime: by then, Mike had already decided to transfer

Target: his secretary fell in love with an accountant

If the stories are in fact connected in memory based upon the similar themes, then activation from answering an item about the first should facilitate responding to an item from the second story. The automaticity hypothesis suggests that if two concepts are connected in memory, responding to an item from one should speed the time to respond to an item from the other (Meyer & Schvaneveldt, 1971). This same-theme response time is compared to one where the preceding item refers to a story that does not share the same theme, and therefore should have no connection in memory between the two stories. For example, if one story was based on the "pot calling the kettle black" theme, and the other on the barn door theme, no priming of the target item would be expected.

An alternative model is that, though not automatic, access to related cases may still occur under certain *strategic* conditions. That is, successful case access may result when there is an explicit goal context that facilitates access to relevant cases. In this condition, subjects were instructed to think about the theme as they read, and to rate the similarity of the story pair after the test list. In every other way, this condition was identical to the first.

The results revealed a significant effect of thematic similarity on response times, but only when *strategic* processing goals were included in the task (instructions to think about thematic similarity). Under these task goal conditions, responses were faster for test items when the story pair shared the same thematic organizing structure, while with no goal context, there was no difference in response time to related items. The only difference between the two experiments was the instruction to strategically attend to thematic similarity. Because the shared knowledge structure did not affect the ease of access of the episodes in memory, the strong hypothesis that similar features *alone* result in automatic activation of related episodes (Schank, 1982) was not supported. We conclude, then, that sharing common thematic features alone does not *automatically* provide access to cases in memory; instead, some strategic purpose is necessary to promote activation of prior episodes. This strategic basis for the ability to utilize connections between episodes to access cases has been replicated in later experiments (Seifert, McKoon, Abelson, & Ratcliff, 1986).

2.2. Content-Based Similarities

For abstract similarities, strategic processing was required to promote access to related cases. Is this type of case access dependent on a goal-based strategy only for abstract feature commonalities, or will this principle hold true for more content-based features? To answer this question, we examined the effects of more surface-level commonalities on access to prior cases (McKoon, Ratcliff, & Seifert, 1989). Pairs of stories were written to instantiate the same memory organization packets (MOPs) (Schank, 1982), similar to "scripts" (Schank & Abelson, 1976). Each pair of stories had different characters participate in a sequence of typical activities (such as "going to the beach"). The stories were written so as to avoid overlapping lexical items in the description of the shared MOP actions. As in the theme experiments, these experiments involved testing for activation between test items from two stories when the stories shared the same MOP compared to when they did not. Subjects again had no knowledge of the role of case access within the experiment.

The results of these experiments showed that, first, when the priming items were story-specific and did not include any features of the shared MOP, no case activation was observed. Second, when the priming items were based on the shared MOP features, then target case activation was demonstrated. This was true no matter which of the two stories the priming items were from; for example, "spreading out her towel in a dry place" from one story and "found an empty space for her blanket" from another story were equally good primes for the target item ("slowly strolled into the cool ocean"). Thus, the activation of the MOP structure could occur from cues within a single story or from cues related to different stories.

This result suggests that MOP features are utilized to encode and recall information, lending support to the notion of memory structures proposed by Schank (1982). The semantic relationship between items that result in priming can be characterized as related to the items' roles within a MOP structure. For example, "towel" and "blanket" activate "ocean" due to their relationship through the MOP structure, such as the same items might activate "heavy load" in the context of a laundry MOP. Therefore, facilitation from semantic associates includes the possibility of connections between examples based on MOPs.

The priming benefits appear to come from the memory structures and *not* from case-to-case activation, as shown by the failure of case-specific, non-MOP-based items (such as "noticed a bird flying overhead") to produce activation. Consequently, the results of these experiments support the failure of automatic access to cases based on common features, both when the features are based on content, surface-level information and when based on more abstract commonalities. When there is no strategy or goal driving the processing, no evidence was found for spontaneous case retrieval. In conclusion, from this experimental evidence on automatic activation of cases in memory, it can be concluded that even though commonalities exist between cases, memory organization and retrieval processes do not appear to promote access alone. However, with the presence of a processing strategy, subjects were shown to form memory connections and to reliably access prior cases in memory.

2.3. Goal-Based Retrieval of Prior Cases

Based on the experiments where subjects were given a strategy (to think about and compare the story themes) that enhanced case access, a goal-based process appears to be involved in the activation of cases. A next step is to look at reminding within *strategy*-based tasks, where the goal to be reminded is an explicit and natural part of the subject's task. In the experiments presented in the last section, the testing procedure left the subject unaware of the intent of the experiment, and we tested for activation of cases in memory rather than conscious reminding experiences. Given the conclusion that activation appears dependent upon strategic processing, reminding can be examined within paradigms where subjects are aware of the goal to access a prior case.

In these experiments (Seifert, Abelson, & McKoon, 1984; Seifert, McKoon, Abelson, & Ratcliff, 1986), subjects were asked to study a set of stories, which served as the reference cases in memory. Next, a new set of test stories was presented on a computer screen. Following each test story, a phrase from one of the studied stories was presented on the screen. This target item was always from a studied story, and subjects were told this. The test stories had either the same theme (as described in the earlier experiments) or a different theme than the target story. In one experiment, the subjects had to respond by pressing a key according to whether the target item was true in the story it was from; in a second experiment, they pressed a key as soon as they remembered which story it was from, and then wrote a short description to allow a test of the accuracy of their memory.

The results for both tasks showed a large facilitation effect for same-theme pairs. When the test story shared the same theme as the target item's reference story, response times to the item were faster than when the test story had a different theme from the reference story. Thus, the new story appeared to activate the reference story based on its thematic similarity, resulting in response facilitation to the target item from the reference story. Two pieces of evidence suggest that subjects did not systematically search through the set of reference stories. First, the test stories were presented word by word at a normal reading speed, requiring ongoing processing. Second, the subjects were not able to recall the full reference set even given unlimited free recall time, so successful search *during* the task was even less likely. This experimental method has several advantages: it requires a response of short duration (less than two seconds reaction time per item); it minimizes strategic search through the reference set; and finally, it minimizes variability introduced by untimed free recall methods. Because the reading rate presentation of the test story keeps the subject engaged in comprehension, the reminding is more likely to occur during "natural" understanding processes rather than through a deliberate attempt to match cases among the reference set.

This methodology was the first to examine reminding of prior cases and to show that, under conditions where subjects are aware of the goal to be reminded, they can successfully access prior cases based on abstract similarities. Other robust methodologies have since been developed; for example, Gentner and Landers (1985) and Rattermann and Gentner (1987) developed a reminding paradigm where subjects study a reference set of stories and return a week later for testing. When given each test story, subjects are told to "write down the study story that it reminds them of." The results show that subjects were able to reliably access prior cases based on commonalities to new test cases. Evidence was also found in these studies for remindings based on "true analogy," similar to the thematic commonalities presented above. Further, these studies showed that other types of similarities, such as common surface features (animal characters, goals of the characters) play a large role in reliable access to past cases. These studies provide evidence that, when the processing goal of retrieving prior episodes is consciously guiding processing, subjects are able to utilize many different types of similarities in order to successfully access prior cases.

Other work on instruction and analogy more directly supports the role of goals in accessing prior instances. In these paradigms, subjects are taught with examples, and retrieve examples and transfer information to new cases. The learning strategies studied show strong utilization of prior cases in acquiring new principles (Pirolli & Anderson, 1985; Reiser & Faries, 1988). These models mainly focus on analogy within a particular processing task (Carbonell, 1986). Other studies of analogical access, such as Ross's (1987, 1989a) studies of reminding during statistics instruction, demonstrate successful access and utilization of past cases in solving current problems. The robust use of remindings in this paradigm supports the access and use of prior cases when engaged in strategic learning.

A remaining question is how to reconcile lack of transfer results with the goal-based processing hypothesis (Gick & Holyoak, 1980, 1983; Holyoak, 1985; Holyoak & Koh, 1987). In these studies, extensively replicated, the spontaneous use of a prior problem solution for a new, analogical problem was fairly rare. In these studies, when no intention to utilize prior cases is present, subjects do not frequently retrieve the prior case and use it in solving a new problem; however, when subjects were instructed to think about the earlier case, many more subjects were able to access and apply the prior solution. It is not clear whether the stated task goals in the transfer paradigm (reference case presented as "story understanding," test case as "problem solving") are viewed as similar strategic goals by the subjects (Holyoak, 1989) or whether other factors may contribute to lack of spontaneous transfer (Hammond, Seifert, & Gray, 1991).

3. TYPES OF FEATURES IN GOAL-BASED RETRIEVAL

Research on the types of features useful in retrieving analogies again points to the possible role of processing goals in retrieval of prior episodes. In this research, the types of features in cases that seem to promote more frequent remindings are examined (Brooks, Allen, & Norman, 1989; Gentner & Landers, 1985; Rattermann & Gentner, 1987; Ross, 1987, 1989a). The main result of these studies is the demonstrated advantage for "surface" or content-related features (i.e., squirrels) over more abstract or "structural" features (i.e., giving a gift that is turned against the giver) in retrieving prior related cases. The power of surface-level features in retrieval is an important finding that has been incorporated into computational models of analogy (Falkenhainer, Forbus, & Gentner, 1986; Hall, 1988; Holyoak & Thagard, 1989b).

However, this surface feature advantage may depend on particular aspects of domain contents. For example, in the Gentner and Landers (1985) studies, the surface similarities shown to be very useful in access are quite distinctive among the set of prior stories (i.e., only one pair of "squirrel" stories appear in the set). Therefore, the set of cases used in the experiment would allow the use of surface features as distinctive identifiers. However, in some analogies, the domain features may overlap a great deal (a squirrel expert), or require cross-textual features. Of course, the thematic story pairs were also distinctive within the story set, while sharing some abstract features such as "loss" or negative outcome across themes. The point is that the surface feature advantage may rely in part on the ability to distinctively identify a past case, a role they are unlikely to play in real-world domains where the surface features overlap in many cases (Hammond, Seifert, & Gray, 1991). This suggests that abstract remindings are extremely important when they *do* occur, as they provide information in the face of non-distinctive and overlapping surface features.

A second question regarding the interpretation of the surface feature advantage in retrieval is whether any aspect of the goal context may be favoring surface features more heavily compared to the other available features. Two of the conditions in Gentner and Landers (1985) and Rattermann and Gentner (1987) involved Mere Appearance (MA) matches, where relations between objects are preserved between target and base (first-order relations), and True Analogy (TA) matches, which also preserve relations between relations (higher order relations). Here are example stories of each of these two similarity types:

Mere Appearance:
Once there was an eagle named Zerdia who donated a few of her tail feathers to a sportsman so he would promise never to attack eagles. One day Zerdia was nesting high on a rocky cliff when she saw the sportsman coming with a crossbow. Zerdia flew down to meet the man, but he attacked and felled her with a single bolt. As she fluttered to the ground, Zerdia realized that the bolt had her own tail feathers on it.

True Analogy:
Once there was a small country called Zerdia that learned to make the world's smartest computer. One day Zerdia was attacked by its warlike neighbor, Gagrach. But the missiles were badly aimed and the attack failed. The Zerdian government realized that Gagrach wanted Zerdian computers so it offered to sell some of its computers to the country. The government of Gagrach was very pleased. It promised never to attack Zerdia again.

Test Story:
Karla, an old hawk, lived at the top of a tall oak tree. One afternoon, she saw a hunter on the ground with a bow and some crude arrows that had no feathers. Karla knew the hunter wanted her feathers so she glided down to the hunter and offered to give him a few. The hunter was so grateful that he pledged never to shoot at a hawk again. He went off and shot deer instead.

Studies by Rattermann and Gentner (1987) and Gentner and Landers (1985) found that more remindings occurred for mere appearance matches, attributable to the surface features, than for true analogy matches. They concluded that surface feature correspondence is more important than higher order structure correspondence for access of similarity matches, while higher order structure is more important in determining the soundness of those same matches. Of note, the studies did find significant occurrences of remindings based on structural similarities only; however, they were not as frequent as remindings based on surface similarities. Surface feature matches appear to be a fast and easy way to gain access to distinctive prior cases in memory, and thus serve as an important source of remindings (Rattermann & Gentner, 1987).

However, the results of these studies also fit the notion of focus on features related to processing goals. Specifically, the shallow processing goals within the task context may have biased subjects towards attending to surface features. Surface features by definition require less inferential processing to identify and extract them from text. Therefore, one might expect surface features to have an advantage in processing contexts where the understanding is accomplished at a shallow level of processing. The instructions in these experiments may have encouraged subjects to marginally comprehend the stories by directing subjects towards "the names of the characters, their motives and what happened" as opposed to why the events took place or what meaning they have. Further, the remindings appear anecdotally to occur very early in reading the test story, before the full set of relation-based features could be understood or encoded. Therefore, it is possible that surface features may dominate structural features in these studies due to the greater accessibility of surface features under relatively shallow processing goal conditions.

An experiment reported in Hammond, Seifert, and Gray (1991) supports this interpretation of the Gentner and Landers (1985) studies. This experiment manipulated the type of processing subjects were able to perform on the test cases. In one condition, subjects read stories from Gentner and Landers (1985) where the story word order was scrambled (in random order), which presumably allowed no access to relational or abstract features and limited comprehension to surface features.

The results showed the same *pattern* of retrieval for the scrambled word order condition as in the intact version. This replicates the original Rattermann and Gentner (1987) and Gentner and Landers (1985) finding that surface features are more useful than structural in retrieving a particular target, and the ordering of conditions (literal similarity with the most remindings, mere appearance, true analogy, and false analogy with the fewest). The fact that this same pattern of results is obtained when subjects were unable to use thematic features suggests that the dominance of surface features in these results must be more subtly interpreted. That is, surface features may not dominate abstract features in retrieval when both are equally available; instead, the surface features, being more readily available (as shown in the scrambled word order condition), may produce comparatively higher retrieval rates. Of course, thematic reminding did occur in the Gentner and Landers (1985) studies, showing detection of and retrieval based on abstract features in those studies; however, the main finding of the comparative utility of the two cue types may reflect the more readily available surface feature matches pre-empting possible thematic remindings requiring deeper comprehension.

A third line of evidence on the types of features used in retrieving cases and their relationship to processing goals compares goal-related features to descriptive features (Johnson & Seifert, 1990, 1991). In these experiments, a single session reminding paradigm patterned after Gentner and Landers (1985) was used, where subjects studied a set of base stories, and then after a distractor task, were given a set of cue stories and asked to write down any base stories that come to mind. The stories consisted of common failures in planning, such as "counting your chickens," where one plan is presumed successful and other actions are taken based on it without guarantee of its success. Presumably, subjects adopted processing goals in story comprehension that involved thinking about the characters' choices and how the characters could avoid these errors. One set of cues contained thematically matching features up to the point of a planning decision (predict-theme cues); the other set included the thematically matching features from the point of decision through the outcome (outcome-theme cues). For example, given this target story in memory about "counting your chickens," either of these two cues would be presented:

Target story:
Judy was overjoyed about the fact that she was pregnant. She looked forward to having a baby boy, and wanted one so badly she felt absolutely certain it would be male. As a result, she bought all kinds of toy cars, trucks, miniature army soldiers, and even arranged an extravagant "it's a boy" party. Finally, the big moment came, and she was rushed to the hospital. Everything went smoothly in the delivery room, and at last she knew. Judy's lively bouncing baby was actually a girl.

Predict-theme test story:
Harrison disliked his small apartment and shabby furniture. His rich Aunt Agatha was near death, and although he hadn't seen or spoken to her in 15 years, he felt assured of inheriting a great fortune very shortly because he was her only living relative. He had already thought of plenty of ways to spend a lot of money fixing his place up.

Outcome-theme test story:
Confident of his pending inheritance, Harrison began charging everything from color televisions to cars to gourmet groceries. When Aunt Agatha finally died and her will was read, she had left all her millions to the butler. Now Harrison was in debt with no way to pay for all of his recent purchases.

The results showed that, while both sets of cues resulted in reliable retrieval of base stories, the partial cue set that included features *predictive* of a planning decision were better cues than the outcomes of those decisions. This retrieval advantage is not due to differences in similarity to the target, as the features in the two sets were rated as equally similar in both overall and thematic similarity.

It appears that the features related to planning decisions are more *distinctly* related to the target stories because they provide information about how to *avoid* planning failures. Features related to when and how to make a particular decision were more useful in retrieving past cases than equally similar information. Therefore, presuming subjects were monitoring the planning activities in the stories, the results support the notion that processing goals can determine the relevance of available features.

The experiments presented in these two sections argue for the necessity of a processing goal in the successful access and transfer of past case information. Intention, in terms of processing goals, appears to play an even larger role in case-based reasoning than had been identified in Schank's (1982) theory. The retrieval or activation of prior instances has been empirically demonstrated only in the presence of processing goals. Further, the types of features useful in retrieving past episodes also appear to depend on the type of processing context. In the next section, the processing goals inherent in natural examples of remindings and in case-based reasoning models are examined.

4. PROCESSING GOALS IN CASE-BASED REASONING MODELS

The evidence presented above for the influence of processing goals on retrieval consists of a series of experiments demonstrating that activation of cases does not occur automatically, but is dependent on strategic task processing goals. This strategic aspect of retrieval points out the importance of domain-independent processing goals such as "explaining" and "planning"; apparently, such goals may act as a level of processing or constraint on retrieval, in that activation occurs that would not without such goals. In this sense, cognitive goals appear to form a context within which retrieval operates, and the nature of this context determines whether and what remindings will occur.

With this in mind, we can return to the "steak and the haircut" protocol (Schank, 1982). What was the goal context that may have mediated retrieval of the haircut case? Y may have the goal of *explaining* why the steak was underdone to X. He may have been motivated to help X understand why his spouse performed such unusual service behavior, so that X could understand the situation and respond appropriately. Y is saying to X "sometimes the server can't *believe* the extremity of the request as stated, and so they do the more normal thing"—in other words, "she just can't believe you want it so raw." Y's reminding addresses disparity in the belief state of the server and recipient, and ultimately redirects X's attention away from the idea that the behavior was intended to dissatisfy. The goal to generate such an explanation may facilitate retrieval of a specific case from memory.

The goal-based context for reminding can be demonstrated in this example by assuming that some goal other than explanation is mediating processing. Suppose *Y* was instead attempting to create a plan to prevent the failure—to preserve the service but arrange to avoid the overcooked steak. *Y* might have instead been reminded of the recipe for steak tartare, which would obviate the need for any cooking and avoid the negative outcome. Being reminded of this recipe would accomplish the goal of *planning* to avoid the failure, but would not serve to *explain* the failure, as the haircut example does. Therefore, the content of these two distinct remindings accomplishes different purposes, suggesting that different cognitive goals may be a mediating factor in whether and which prior cases are accessed. While protocols have been used extensively in developing case-based reasoning (Hammond, 1989; Kolodner, 1984; Schank, 1982), little attention has been paid to the context of processing goals.

Some cognitive functions that may foster natural remindings in humans are *explanation, planning, argumentation, decision making,* and *conversation* (Seifert, 1988a). For example, the understander seeks, in his processing of new input in conversation, to be reminded of a memory that relates to what he heard and provides extension to the topic of discussion. For example, Schank (1990) discusses the role of remindings in preserving and presenting stories of life events. Remindings can serve to explain the meaning of an episode, illustrate why reasoning is valid, justify, support, or defend a claim, provide planning information, or simply verify interpretation (Hammond, 1989; Schank, 1982; Seifert, 1988). Processing subtasks within higher order cognitive tasks have begun to be identified (Chandrasekaran, 1987), and reminding phenomena may be useful in studying commonalities between processing goals. Thus, accessing a reminding appears to be a much more active, inference-intensive, and goal-directed process than what results from simple parsing to generic semantic representations (Schank, 1982).

The need to identify goals in processing subtasks and their role in information access is critical for computer models that may utilize cases within a single task. In these programs, processing goals are often left implicit in the model, the memory base for cases, and case representation system. Including an implicit processing goal will limit the generality of the system by not providing a role for alternative goals operating within the same case domain. For example, the JUDGE program (Bain, 1984) encoded new cases and determined an appropriate sentence for a convicted offender. However, no other goals can be used to retrieve cases within this system, as a judge might when reviewing prior cases he has seen within a variety of goal contexts (such as assessing probabilities, deriving categories of sentence types, telling stories, giving advice, and providing summaries). The cost of not explicitly including goals in the model is a loss of generality in potential use of the case base.

There are some tasks where access to a specific case is desirable; even with an available organizing schema, it may be necessary to retrieve a case for support, justification, or verification of information. Some early CBR programs assumed reminding of a past case would occur with every new input case. For example, in the CYRUS program (Kolodner, 1983, 1984), the goal was to retrieve a particular episode in memory given an input set of features. Reconstructive strategies were applied to generate enough indices to retrieve an episode whenever enough features distinguished it from its organizing structure. In human reasoning, access to prior cases appears neither necessary nor constant; organizing schemas serve to provide information needed in many cases, while the need for explicit case access may be relatively infrequent in routine processing (see Alba & Hasher, 1983; Jacoby, 1978). Within a domain, the utility of high similarity between an input and a past case in memory, and the high distinctiveness of the set of cases in memory, are washed out by the high volume of overlapping cases within the domain. Therefore, the role of strategic processing is even more important in fostering retrieval of individual cases in single-domain models. Strategic goals within reasoning processes that make use of remindings may increase the retrieval of experiences from memory.

Frequent access to past cases is achieved in some case-based reasoning models when researchers select tasks that incorporate a purpose for retrieval of past cases. For example, in the CHEF program (Hammond, 1983, 1989), the goal of creating a new recipe guides the search of memory for useful past information. Modifying past recipes is an important method for generating new recipes, and therefore the need to examine past cases is built into the program as a processing goal. In this type of task, strategic reminding is used in the creation of new plans from past successes and failures (Hammond, 1989). Other case-based reasoning tasks that promote remindings take advantage of domain properties such as the encapsulation of information within cases. For example, in the legal domain (Rissland & Ashley, 1986), cases stand as precedents for decisions, and lawyers need to utilize cases as exemplars to formulate arguments. In complex diagnosis tasks, where detailed reasoning is required, remindings can aid in thinking through the factors involved in a problem. For example, in the domain of psychiatric diagnosis, where complex information is available to be considered, recall of previous cases may suggest correlations not previously noted (Kolodner & Simpson, 1984). Finally, in examining alternative conceptualizations or scenarios, possible solutions can be used as memory indices to find past instances where the solutions were tried, and the resulting episodes can be compared to the current instance (Hammond, 1989).

I have argued from experimental results that strategic goals mediate automatic processes like memory retrieval. In addition, CBR models (i.e., Bareiss, 1989) that are considered successful include built-in processing goals by selecting narrow tasks and case representations that facilitate retrieval of cases. Strategic processing goals may assist in formulating internal "questions" or information goals that promote remindings. The role of such informational goals in generating explanations has been supported (Hunter, 1989; Kass, Leake, & Owens, 1986; Ram, 1987; Schank, 1986); however, the notion of a reminding as an answer to an internally posited question may be more general. Owens (1990a, 1990b) argued for the integration of index generation and memory search as a way to use both current input and memory to generate possible features for retrieval. One difficult question is where intentionality arises within this process. From the experimental results presented above, I suggest that the context of processing goals may serve as the driving force behind the strategic manipulation of memory search to retrieve cases. In the next section, a method is proposed to model the processing goal context and its effects on case access.

5. MODELING GOALS IN RETRIEVAL

Processing goals may play a role in case retrieval by affecting which features are attended to most within a similarity match process. A hybrid model of retrieval could incorporate the properties of content-addressable distributed memory models with processing goals as a controlling mechanism to favor features that will bias towards relevant remindings. This ability to select the features most important in the current context is supported by the experimental results presented in earlier sections. In addition, the idea of weighting features within a similarity metric has been proposed (Kruschke, 1992; Mozer & Smolensky, 1989; Rumelhart, 1989; Sloman & Rumelhart, 1992; Tversky, 1977) and may be necessary for case retrieval within a distributed memory model. The proposal here is to use the processing goal context as the determinant of feature weightings, rather than a static abstraction or feature-preference scheme.

5.1. Distributed Models of Memory Retrieval

Memory retrieval of cases has been modeled in a completion network within a parallel distributed processing model of memory (McClelland & Rumelhart, 1985). The "distributed memory" constitutes a feature space, plus an encoding algorithm and a retrieval algorithm, where prior episodes are encoded. Memory access is then determined by the similarity between input features and stored patterns, where the process finds the activation pattern that best fits the stored connection constraints. This type of network maximizes goodness of fit to find the most related pattern in memory. This pattern can consist of features comprising a single instance or a prototype structure. While such networks have the desirable feature of blending examples into generalizations and compound instances, accurate retrieval of prior encoded episodes is another performance goal. Because of the built-in capacity for generalization in connectionist models, there is some question as to whether such models can accurately preserve memory for instances.

Rumelhart (1988, 1989) has investigated whether such networks are capable of reliably recording and reproducing individual cases. One implementation took input data consisting of 200 descriptions of individuals rated on 250 social features (such as traits, behavior, and appearance) and autoencoded into an 80 by 80 unit memory network (Rumelhart, 1988; Seifert, 1988b). The input feature vectors contained no structural information, but simply provided associations between an individual and a set of characteristics. First, the network was trained under noise for robust learning, and utilized the entire corpus as the learning set to avoid interference effects. Then, the network was tested and found to reliably retrieve each instance of an individual vector pattern given a partial segment of the input pattern. Therefore, a distributed memory model that produces a blended memory association network can capture a large number of individual cases and successfully retrieve each input pattern. A similar mechanism proposed by Sloman and Rumelhart (1992) successfully allows retrieval of both exemplars and prototypes.

5.2. Mechanisms for Feature Selection

The next question is whether these individual cases can be accessed on the basis of a small set of features given that they are correlated with many other cases in memory. Using an overall similarity metric, the standard match procedure in such a network involves clamping the input features on to one, and waiting until the network's pattern of activation resolves to a stable best fit pattern of activation that includes the input feature set (Rumelhart, 1989). For example, setting the input features "athlete, male, blond" each to one may result in a variety of retrieval results containing these three features.

A good fit may occur when a specific case is retrieved from the network, such as "athlete, male, blond, fast, gymnast, Bart." Presumably, the retrieved case is the best match in memory with those input features present, compared to other patterns in memory. However, a generalized schematic pattern may be activated instead, such as "athlete, male, blond, strong." Another possibility is that no recognizable conceptual combination will match well enough for a stable pattern containing the input features to be achieved. The types of match results can be characterized in terms of maximizing goodness of fit: a good fit may be an episode reminding, an adequate fit may be a generalization or a moderately similar case, and a low fit may mean no close matches could be found (Rumelhart, 1989).

However, this standard approach of finding the "most similar" pattern may miss opportunities for good analogies. It would be most useful to be able to force a fit to a prior episode using strategic methods, so that interesting case comparisons could be retrieved. Along with others (see Thagard, Holyoak, Nelson, & Gochfield, 1990), Rumelhart (1989) proposed that the matching process can operate by relaxing constraints on the match. This *relaxed match* process provides a potential mechanism for overriding features that are preventing a match while giving increased importance to features that may be helpful in

Figure 2.2.
Standard Match Procedure for Retrieval, Where the Input Features are Clamped on to "1" and the Network Resolves to a "Best Fit" Pattern of Activation.

STANDARD MATCH PROCESS

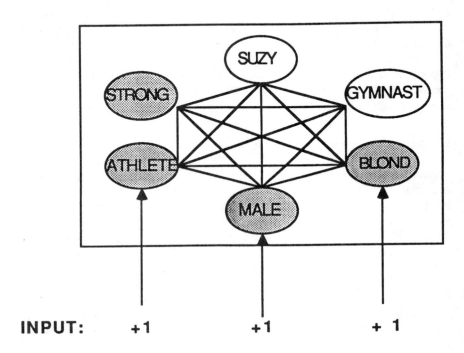

analogical transfer to other episodes. Such a scheme has been implemented in a variety of ways, such as presetting values on the input nodes to reflect relative preferences, or Rumelhart's (1989) "soft clamping" procedure which results in the dynamic adjustment of individual input feature strengths as required to promote matches (as opposed to simply lowering the criterion for any matches). An example where the input values are changed during the matching process so as to avoid requiring all input features to be present in the resulting retrieval pattern (i.e., "athlete, blond, skier, Suzy") is presented in Figure 2.3.

Relaxed matching may result in an analogy being retrieved in situations where no distinct pattern could have been retrieved based on strict similarity to the input pattern. The notion that constraints on a match may be progressively relaxed to result in analogical access has been demonstrated by Holyoak and Thagard (1989b; Thagard et al., 1990). This general approach of feature weighting has been incorporated into many recent approaches (Hanson & Burr, 1990; Kruschke, 1992; Mozer & Smolensky, 1989; Sloman & Rumelhart, 1992).

Figure 2.3.
Relaxed Match Procedure (Rumelhart, 1989), Where Input Feature Values are "Soft Clamped" with Variable Strengths, and the Network Can Relax Constraints by Turning Down the Preset Input Values.

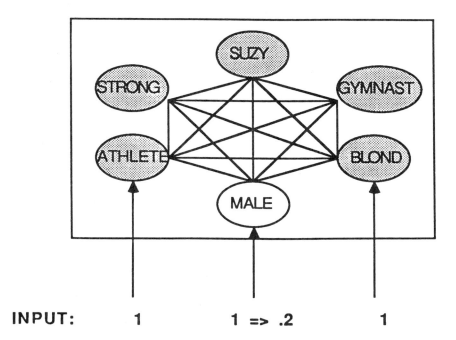

The selection of which features to weigh heavily is central to the solution of the relaxed match procedure. While these models show that such selective attention is possible in principle, no basis for feature selection across domains and tasks has been determined. The next step is to find a method for feature selection that will assist in biasing feature weighting toward case retrieval, as the experimental data have suggested is desirable.

One possibility would be to select the biases assigned to each input feature at random. This could be expected to generate a lot of episode remindings with varied content, including nonrelevant similarities. From the example above, a random feature-weighting on the input features might retrieve "male, blond, actor, Robert." A random weighting scheme in memory retrieval does not appear likely to produce coherent similarities or inferable relevance to the input case. Such a random weighting scheme may be of interest for some applications, but may not provide the focus on relevant features observed in the psychological data on reminding presented in the earlier sections.

Analogies of interest usually share a subset of abstract features. Therefore, another method of assigning values to the input features is to order all the features along an abstraction hierarchy (Rumelhart, 1988). By weakening constraints on concrete features first, and then progressing to more abstract features until reaching a match, greater weight is given to abstract features, and more abstract analogies will result from the relaxed match process. This approach seems plausible given the need to generate remindings based on abstract feature commonalities; however, there are several problems with an intrinsic ordering on features. First, "abstract" is hard to define, as even thematic patterns like "closing the barn door after the horse has gone" can have surface features (i.e., being "too late"). It would be difficult to generate a set of universal abstractions useful in memory. A second problem is that the relative importance of features may change dynamically, or with interactions of features. For example, in choosing a car, color, size, and speed may be given a particular ordering of importance; in selecting a mode of transportation, these same features may be given a different ordering. Finally, it is not always the most abstract features that are responsible for a reminding (Gentner & Landers, 1985; Rattermann & Gentner, 1987; Ross, 1989b); therefore, following a strict abstractness metric may not always be desirable. In any case, a strict preference for abstract features does not appear to fit current experimental findings.

5.3. Selecting Features Based on Goal Context

Processing goal context has been presented as a possible explanation for access to cases during certain tasks. The same input features, in the presence of different goal contexts, will produce retrieval of different cases. The context of the current goals being pursued can be incorporated into distributed memory models as a method of weighting features for a match (Seifert, 1989). Remindings appear to have more to do with what a person is attending to than to any a priori notions about abstractness. It is these processing goals that can be used to provide more weight to particular features and allow others to be relaxed from the match.

Here's an example of how processing goals may act to select features:

> *Input*: Teletrack (Connecticut's off-track betting auditorium) has a "no smoking" policy which means, in effect, that every section is a smoking section. The rule is disregarded often enough that no section can be guaranteed to be smoke-free. You argue that the management should allow smoking in some sections, if only to be sure that some sections can actually be nonsmoking.

Suppose that you are engaged in an argument about this comment. Your goal is to buttress your claim that "control is better than abolishment when disobedience is common." Supporting your claim involves retrieving another instance with this pattern; based on the abstract characterization of the claim, an analogous situation is recalled. You may then be reminded of the legalization of heroin in England. This case supports the claim by serving as a known instance (in England) where control (of heroin use) was thought to have had fewer bad effects on nonparticipants than the outright banning of the substance. Within the argument, you buttress your claim with an example of the "control is better than prohibition" principle.

Suppose instead that your goal is to plan a way to get your idea implemented. You need to figure out a way to get Teletrack to recognize that their control problem is worse now than it would be under the smoking section plan. Planning for implementing your solution selects out problem features that are relevant to the management of the policy. That is, what features are most relevant to the need to invoke the "control rather than prohibit" solution? You may then be reminded of how abuse of the pet policy in student housing resulted in a rule change. Pets were officially banned, but a minority of students got pets anyway, causing quite a bit of disturbance. In an attempt to manage this, the housing office declared several buildings "pets allowed" to ensure at least some buildings would be pet-free. This suggests a plan for getting the smoking policy changed at Teletrack: increase the level of violation to an unmanageable point. Therefore, you should smoke as much as possible, and encourage others to, in a way that exacerbates the problem for nonsmokers, and therefore the management. They will then be more likely then to see the benefit of control rather than prohibition. The feature selection leading to reminding may be guided by goals such as argumentation and planning, which serve to focus on particular features in the match process.

The point is that the "goodness" of an analogy depends on what you are interested in. Therefore, the relevance of features will change dynamically as a result of the goals of a system. One way to incorporate the influence of processing goals within a distributed memory model is through connections that "gate" the activation of the input features. The use of gating in networks has been demonstrated (Mozer & Smolensky, 1989). In this case, the processing goal connections can multiplicatively or additively influence the strength of the input features within the match. The processing goals function to "turn down" unrelated and "turn up" related features in the match, resulting in the features relevant to the goal being the focus of the relaxed match process discussed above. This gating technique will provide activation based on information about what is relevant to the goals in the current processing context, dynamically changing with the context of active processing goals.

In this scheme, goals are not treated simply as additional input features that connect to other features in the network; instead, goals are treated as a separate source of information that *acts on* the features input to the match. One motivation is that if goals are included as additional features, then the retrieval algorithm must include all possible processing goals as input features. In addition, the current goal context may be different than the originally encoded goals. Remindings often serve to explain or highlight information in a prior case that was not perceived in the same way at encoding; for example, an experience where a traffic ticket was received may later be recalled as an instance of antagonistic behavior. In this sense, the goal relevance is not equivalent to a feature like other input features; instead, it may act upon patterns of features to draw new comparisons not present in initial encodings of cases. Thus, the goal context can be modeled as *influences* on the input connections, as shown in Figure 2.4.

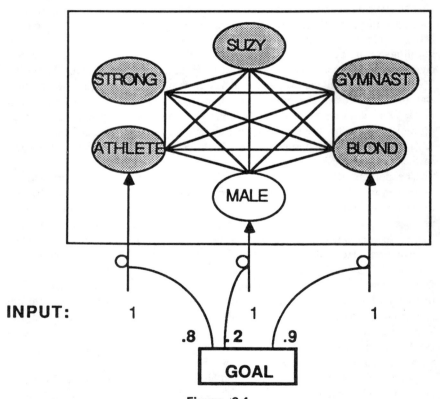

Figure 2.4.
Schematic Depiction of Goal Connections to Input Feature Lines in the Proposed Retrieval Model, Where Goals Gate Activation Through Multiplicative Links.

By separating the gating function of the goals, they operate as an independent source of weightings apart from the input lines established for the retrieval network. On a theoretical level, this is important for several reasons. First, the goal context may be independent of the match process that utilizes it; therefore, the model should avoid equating goals with regular input features. Second, these goal weightings are also influencing other processes at the same time that they are contributing to retrieval. For example, active goals are affecting the search for further perceptual information in a top-down fashion. Because their influence within the cognitive system may be much broader than the role they play in retrieval, a separation of goal influence from input features maintains the genesis and function of goals as external to the match process. The goal context will be generated from and operate within other cognitive processes, so identifying them as separate from the input case may help to understand how perception is affected by expectation. Finally, an external source of goal influence makes it clear that goals can change at retrieval time, resulting in variable remindings. Alternative architectures may also provide these properties, allowing a broader role for goals within the cognitive system beyond the matching process.

5.4. Extensions to Goal-Based Learning

The tendency to treat all features as equal, without regard to how particular features may be attended to in certain cognitive contexts, is a major problem in models of learning. For example, distributed models of learning often consider all features present as potentially equally important to the rule being learned (Mozer & Smolensky, 1989). Consequently, it takes many trials to determine which features are actually predictive of what is to be learned. This approach hurts learning rates mathematically because some features will take many trials to be ruled out, and information available as a priori notions of what features are likely to be related to the rule is ignored.

In a learning system, treating all features equally will mean a lot of effort spent examining features that have no importance. With the addition of a mechanism to select the features most likely to be relevant to the rule, one can save time by focusing on features that will pay off more quickly. A particular method to control learning might be to reduce focus on input values which have small outgoing weights, in a sense betting that the information to be learned will have to do with the features already shown to be relevant in previous learning. Mozer (1988) studied this approach using a bootstrapping learning procedure that attenuates input values with small weights. The results suggest that, with noisy input, the network decides to ignore the noise inputs before solving the mapping, and in the case of redundant inputs, the attentional mechanism selects one and shuts out the redundant feature. Of course, when the same network is used for other tasks, then a gating method will be required as proposed for the retrieval model, to allow the current system goals to directly impact which features are attended to (Mozer & Smolensky, 1989).

Obviously, feature selection and weighting can be of great utility in learning. For similar tasks, different goals can make a huge difference to feature importance. Consequently, by utilizing prior knowledge, one can shut off features that are not a priori relevant to learning. It seems that people often have notions of what features may be important to learning in a particular domain (Pazzani, 1991). For example, in learning a new video game, the actions effective in killing enemies tend to be predictable from common-sense notions of physical causality (e.g., a linear position to a target to shoot it). However, in learning as in retrieval, which features are most relevant in a domain cannot be set a priori for all learning contexts. One needs a mechanism to affect the attention at the connections depending upon the processing context.

Some evidence of processing goals producing biases in learning is that, to the extent that the actual game mechanics violate prior notions, they may be more difficult for people to learn. In fact, the less face validity to the rule, the more often people may fail to perceive its presence among the possible factors. So, using prior knowledge and processing goal context to bias feature learning has the advantage of speeding learning when the world is consistent with expectations. However, when those expectations are violated, their presence will slow learning of unexpected or random associations. This is a drawback to the process of using default expectations for the relevancy of features; however, it may be compensated for by the ability to quickly detect the operation of common factors. By attending to features differentially, the learning process may be faster, at the cost of failing to discover nonintuitive or novel connections in the data. Within human systems at least, the gain from attention in speed of learning may more than make up for missing counterintuitive or unusual patterns. Utilizing cognitive goals to affect the attention paid to features based upon their inferable connections seems a promising approach to improve speed of learning as well as case retrieval.

6. CONCLUSION

Processing goals have been shown to be an important factor in retrieval of prior cases in memory; however, the importance of these goals, and their role in processing, has often been overlooked or left implicit within models of analogy. Results from experiments on strategic factors in remindings and from protocols point to the importance of goal processing context in retrieval of cases. The same input, in the presence of differing processing goals, will lead to different case remindings. Therefore, in models of case retrieval, the role of task-based goals in affecting whether and what type of reminding occurs must be incorporated. The processing goal context must be explicitly identified in order to make claims about the generality of any access model of cases. As proposed here, the goal context may act in feature selection, mediating similarity-based retrieval by controlling the degree of influence particular features have in the match. The effect of the model is to allow a similarity metric to produce varied remindings based on the relative importance of particular features to the current processing context.

Other approaches to feature matching processes have begun to incorporate goals, or pragmatics, as part of the retrieval process. In particular, Holyoak (1985), Holland, Holyoak, Nisbett, and Thagard (1986), and Holyoak and Thagard (1989a, 1989b) incorporated goal relevance as part of the retrieval and mapping processes. Pazzani (1989) proposed using goals in indexing cases in memory, and Kedar-Cabelli (1988) incorporated task purpose into derivational analogy. Part of the value of goal-related features is the ability to distinguish among many similar cases (Johnson & Seifert, 1991). In general, the domain specificity of CBR programs has allowed the role of goals in access to cases to remain implicit in models. As domains expand to include cases in a variety of goal contexts, the explicit modeling of these goal-derived selection processes may be of great assistance in the retrieval of relevant cases from memory.

Frequent remindings of prior cases will benefit any cognitive system by bringing to mind information not captured in basic generalizations. Cases serve as an opportunity to learn new generalizations not previously anticipated, and as models of past experience to aid in understanding novel situations. Because frequent case access is desirable for an analogical system, factors which promote retrieval are critical to successful systems. The influence of processing goals on feature-based retrieval suggests a method to generate remindings and to maximize the relevance of remindings that do occur.

REFERENCES

Alba, J.W., & Hasher, L. (1983). Is memory schematic? *Psychological Bulletin, 93*, 203–231.
Bain, W.M. (1984). *Toward a model of subjective understanding* (Tech. Rep. No. 324). New Haven, CT: Computer Science Program, Yale University
Bareiss, R. (1989). *Exemplar-based knowledge acquisition: A unified approach to concept representation.* New York: Academic Press.
Brooks, L.R., Allen, S.W., & Norman, G. (1989). The multiple and variable availability of familiar cases. *Proceedings of the Second DARPA workshop on Case-Based Reasoning.* Pensacola Beach, FL.
Burstein, M. (1986). Concept formation by incremental analogical reasoning and debugging. In R.S. Michalski, J.G. Carbonell, & T.M. Mitchell (Eds.), *Machine learning* (Vol. II). Los Altos, CA: Morgan Kaufmann.

Burstein, M., & Adelson, B. (1987). Analogical learning: Mapping and integrating partial mental models. *Proceedings of the 1987 Conference of the Cognitive Science Society.* Hillsdale, NJ: Erlbaum.

Carbonell, J. (1986). Derivational analogy: A theory of reconstructive problem solving and experience acquisition. In R.S. Michalski, J.G. Carbonell, & T.M. Mitchell (Eds.), *Machine learning* (Vol. II). Los Altos, CA: Morgan Kaufman.

Chandrasekaran, B. (1987). Towards a functional architecture for intelligence based on generic information processing tasks. *Proceedings of the Tenth International Joint Conference on Artificial Intelligence.* Milan, Italy.

Dyer, M.G. (1983). *In-depth understanding: A computer model of integrated processing for narrative comprehension.* Cambridge, MA: MIT Press.

Falkenhainer, B., Forbus, K.D., & Gentner, D. (1986). *The structure mapping engine* (Tech. Rep. No. UIUCDCS-R-86-1275). Urbana: University of Illinois at Urbana-Champaign.

Gentner, D. (1983). Structure-mapping: A theoretical framework for analogy. *Cognitive Science, 7,* 155–170.

Gentner, D., & Landers, R. (1985). Analogical reminding: A good match is hard to find. *Proceedings of the International Conference on Systems, Man, and Cybernetics.* Tucson, AZ.

Gibbs, R.W. (1984). Literal meaning and psychological theory. *Cognitive Science, 8,* 275–304.

Gick, M., & Holyoak, K. (1980). Analogical problem solving. *Cognitive Psychology, 12,* 306–355.

Gick, M., & Holyoak, K. (1983). Schema induction and analogical transfer. *Cognitive Psychology, 15,* 1–38.

Hall, R.P. (1988). Computational approaches to analogical reasoning: A comparative analysis. *Artificial Intelligence, 39,* 39–120.

Hammond, K.J. (1983). Planning and goal interaction: The use of past solutions in present situations. *Proceedings of the National Conference on Artificial Intelligence, AAAI.* Washington, DC.

Hammond, K.J. (1989). *Case-based planning: Viewing planning as a memory task.* San Diego, CA: Academic Press.

Hammond, K.J., Seifert, C.M., & Gray, K.C. (1991). Functionality in analogical transfer: A hard match is good to find. *Journal of the Learning Sciences, 1*(2), 111–152.

Hanson, S.J., & Burr, D.J. (1990). What connectionist models learn: Learning and representation in connectionist networks. *Behavioral and Brain Sciences, 13,* 471–489.

Holland, J., Holyoak, K., Nisbett, R., & Thagard, P. (1986). *Induction.* Cambridge, MA: MIT Press.

Holyoak, K.J. (1985). The pragmatics of analogical transfer. In G.H. Bower (Ed.), *The psychology of learning and motivation* (Vol. 19, pp. 59–87). New York: Academic Press.

Holyoak, K., & Koh, K. (1987). Surface and structural similarity in analogical transfer. *Memory and Cognition, 15*(4), 332–340.

Holyoak, K., & Thagard, P. (1989a). A computational model of analogical problem solving. In S. Vosniadou & A. Ortony (Eds.), *Similarity and analogical reasoning.* New York: Cambridge Univ. Press.

Holyoak, K., & Thagard, P. (1989b). Analogical mapping by constraint satisfaction. *Cognitive Science, 13*, 295–355.

Hunter, L. (1989). *Knowledge acquisition planning: Gaining expertise through experience.* Unpublished doctoral dissertation, Yale University, New Haven, CT.

Jacoby, L.L. (1978). On interpreting the effects of repetition: Solving a problem versus remembering a solution. *Journal of Verbal Learning and Verbal Behavior, 17*, 649–667.

Johnson, H.M., & Seifert, C.M. (1990). Predictive utility in case-based memory retrieval. *Proceedings of the Twelfth Annual Cognitive Science Society.* Cambridge, MA.

Johnson, H.M., & Seifert, C.M. (1991). Predictive features in analogical access. *Journal of Memory and Language, 31*, 648–667.

Kass, A., Leake, D., & Owens, C. (1986). Programming the theory: SWALE, a program that explains. In R. Schank (Ed.), *Explanation patterns: Understanding mechanically and creatively.* Hillsdale, NJ: Erlbaum.

Kedar-Cabelli, S. (1988). Toward a computational model of purpose-directed analogy. In A. Prieditis (Ed.), *Analogica.* London: Pitman.

Kolodner, J.L. (1983). Reconstructive memory: A computer model. *Cognitive Science, 7*, 281–328.

Kolodner, J.L. (1984). *Retrieval and organizational strategies in conceptual memory: A computer model.* Hillsdale, NJ: Erlbaum.

Kolodner, J.L., & Simpson, R.L. (1984). Experience and problem solving: A framework. *Proceedings of the Sixth Annual Conference of the Cognitive Science Society.* Boulder, CO.

Kruschke, J.K. (1992). ALCOVE: An exemplar-based connectionist model of category learning. *Psychological Review, 99*, 22–44.

Lehnert, W.G. (1980). Plot units and narrative summarization. *Cognitive Science, 5*, 293–331.

McClelland, J.L., & Rumelhart, D.E. (1985). Distributed memory and the representation of general and specific information. *Journal of Experimental Psychology: General, 114*, 159–188.

McKoon, G., Ratcliff, R., & Seifert, C.M. (1989). Making the connection: Generalized knowledge structures in story understanding. *Journal of Memory and Language, 28*, 711–734.

Meyer, D.E., & Schvaneveldt, R.W. (1971). Facilitation in recognizing pairs of words: Evidence of a dependence between retrieval operations. *Journal of Experimental Psychology, 10*, 227–234.

Mozer, M.C., & Smolensky, P. (1989). *Skeletonization: A technique for trimming the fat from a network via relevance assessment* (Tech. Rep. No. CU-CS-421-89). Boulder, CO: University of Colorado.

Owens, C. (1990a). *Indexing and retrieving abstract planning knowledge.* Unpublished doctoral dissertation, Department of Computer Science, Yale University, New Haven, CT.

Owens, C. (1990b). Functional Criteria for Indices and Labels. *Working Notes of the AAAI Spring Symposium Series.* Palo Alto, CA.

Pazzani, M.J. (1989). Indexing strategies for goal specific retrieval of cases. *Proceedings of the Case-Based Reasoning Workshop.* Pensacola Beach, FL.

Pazzani, M.J. (1991). Influence of prior knowledge on concept acquisition: Experimental and computational results. *Journal of Experimental Psychology: Learning, Memory, and Cognition, 17*(3), 416–432.

Pirolli, P.L., & Anderson, J.R. (1985). The role of learning from examples in the acquisition of recursive programming skills. *Canadian Journal of Psychology, 39*, 240–272.

Ram, A. (1987). AQUA: Asking questions and understanding answers. *Proceedings of the Sixth Annual National Conference on Artificial Intelligence* (pp. 312–316). Seattle, WA.

Rattermann, M., & Gentner, D. (1987). Analogy and similarity: Determinants of accessibility and inferential soundness. *Proceedings of the 9th Annual Conference of the Cognitive Science Society*. Hillsdale, NJ: Erlbaum.

Reiser, B.J., & Faries, J.M. (1988). Access and use of previous solutions in a problem solving situation (Tech. Rep. No. 29). Princeton, NJ: Princeton University, Cognitive Science Laboratory.

Riesbeck, C.K., & Schank, R.C. (1989). *Inside case-based reasoning*. Hillsdale, NJ: Erlbaum.

Rissland, E., & Ashley, K. (1986). Hypotheticals as heuristic device. *The Proceedings of the Fifth Annual Conference on Artificial Intelligence*. Philadelphia, PA.

Ross, B.H. (1987). This is like that: The use of earlier problems and the separation of similarity effects. *Journal of Experimental Psychology: Learning, Memory, and Cognition, 13*, 629–639.

Ross, B.H. (1989). Distinguishing types of superficial similarities: Different effects on the access and use of earlier problems. *Journal of Experimental Psychology: Learning, Memory, and Cognition, 15*, 456–468.

Ross, B.H. (1989). Remindings in learning and instruction. In S. Vosniadou & A. Ortony (Eds.), *Similarity and analogical reasoning*. Cambridge, MA: Cambridge University Press.

Rumelhart, D.E. (1989). Towards a microstructural account of human reasoning. In S. Vosniadou & A. Ortony (Eds.), *Similarity and analogical reasoning*. Cambridge, MA: Cambridge University Press.

Rumelhart, D., McClelland, J., & PDP Research Group. (1986). *Parallel distributed processing, vol. 1: Foundations*. Cambridge, MA: MIT Press.

Schank, R.C. (1982). *Dynamic memory: A theory of reminding and learning in computers and people*. New York: Cambridge University Press.

Schank, R. (1986). *Explanation patterns: Understanding mechanically and creatively*. Hillsdale, NJ: Erlbaum.

Schank, R.C. (1990). *Tell me a story*. New York: Scribner's.

Schank, R.C., & Abelson, R.P. (1976). *Scripts, plans, goals, and understanding*. Hillsdale, NJ: Erlbaum.

Seifert, C.M. (1988a). Goals in Reminding. *Proceedings of the DARPA Workshop on Case-based Reasoning in AI*. Clearwater Beach, FL.

Seifert, C.M. (1989a). A retrieval model of feature selection. *Proceedings of the Sixth International Workshop on Machine Learning*. Cornell, NY.

Seifert, C.M. (1988b). A retrieval model of case-based memory. *Proceedings of the AAAI Workshop on Case-Based Reasoning*. Minneapolis, MN.

Seifert, C.M., Abelson, R.P., & McKoon, G. (1984). Being reminded of thematically similar episodes. *Proceedings of the Sixth Conference of the Cognitive Science Society*. Boulder, Colorado.

Seifert, C.M., Dyer, M.G., & Black, J.B. (1986). Thematic knowledge in story understanding. *TEXT, 6*(4), 393–426.

Seifert, C.M., McKoon, G., Abelson, R.P., & Ratcliff, R. (1986). Memory connections between thematically similar episodes. *Journal of Experimental Psychology: Learning, Memory, and Cognition, 12*, 220–231.

Sloman, S.A., & Rumelhart, D.E. (in press). Reducing interference in distributed memories through episodic gating. In A. Healey, S. Kosslyn, & R. Shiffrin (Eds.), *Essays in honor of W.K. Estes*.

Thagard, P., & Holyoak, K. (1989). How to compute semantic similarity. *Proceedings of the DARPA Workshop on Case-based Reasoning in AI*. Pensacola Beach, FL.

Thagard, P., Holyoak, K., Nelson, G., & Gochfield, D. (1990). Analog retrieval by constraint satisfaction. *Artificial Intelligence, 46*, 259–310.

Tversky, A. (1977). Features of similarity. *Psychological Review, 84*, 327–352.

3
A Case Study of Case Indexing: Designing Index Feature Sets to Suit Task Demands and Support Parallelism*

Eric A. Domeshek

1. INTRODUCTION

Case-based reasoning (CBR) (Hammond, 1989; Kolodner, Simpson, & Sycara-Cyranski, 1985) is a framework for cognitive models claiming that intelligent behavior in the present is generated from memories of specific events in the past. Accordingly, CBR requires, as a bare minimum, that a system be able to store and retrieve cases in a memory. The work reported here argues that retrieval of cases from memory can reasonably be conceptualized as a massively parallel matching process and may be a good application for a connectionist network; the work assumes, however, that for the foreseeable future, knowledge engineering will remain a hard problem and that people must do the work of inventing appropriate encodings for retrieval cues. The hope is that the presented approach to case retrieval will encourage interaction between the CBR and connectionist communities.

In CBR, the reduction of case retrieval (*reminding*) to the calculation of some sort of distance metric between feature vectors has never been popular. This

---

*This work was largely prepared while the author was a student in Yale University's Department of Computer Science, visiting at Northwestern University's Institute for the Learning Sciences. The work was supported in part by the Department of Defense, specifically by the Defense Advanced Research Projects Agency, the Air Force Office of Scientific Research, and the Office of Naval Research. The Institute for the Learning Sciences was established in 1989 with the support of Andersen Consulting, part of the Arthur Andersen Worldwide Organization. The institute receives additional funding from Ameritech (an institute partner) and IBM. Eric Jones and Mathew Brand read and commented on an early draft of this chapter; the encouragement of this volume's editors and the comments of several anonymous reviewers are also gratefully acknowledged.

chapter, however, argues in favor of using feature vectors as the basis for retrieval, and describes an example system that does so. Arguments point out expected benefits of such a format; the implementation shows that vectors need not be composed of surface features whose similarity indicates little about a case's applicability. The system to be discussed shows how feature vectors can encode detailed representations of a domain's content, incorporating not just property knowledge, but also taxonomic and relational knowledge typically represented in structured descriptions. Using such encodings, this system produces reasonable behavior on the sample task of generating lovelorn advice (i.e., advice about how to resolve problems in romantic relationships).

Connectionists, for their part, while recognizing the importance of choosing appropriate input and output representations, tend to deemphasize that aspect of their work in favor of learning algorithms and training regimens designed to coax the systems into building appropriate internal encodings linking input to output. I argue that for many AI problems, there are practical, methodological, and theoretical reasons to deemphasize learning. On the positive side, by developing a detailed feature set for a particular domain and demonstrating its implementation in a system with a clear mapping to a connectionist network, I bolster claims that connectionist mechanisms are adequate for efficiently performing interesting tasks most often tackled with conventional symbolic systems.

Although this chapter does not address connectionist issues such as learning or activation functions, it is relevant to connectionism in that it appeals to connectionist-style massive parallelism (with many simple processors communicating simple messages over fixed pathways) and microfeature vectors (Hinton, 1981). As a result, the mechanisms discussed could be implemented in connectionist networks. What this chapter offers to connectionism is an argument, by example, that building a system to tackle traditional high-level real-world AI tasks requires committing seriously to the particular content being encoded in the networks. The representations used in the system discussed here are justified by their ability to capture distinctions relevant to choosing remindings for the system's particular task and domain. It is difficult to imagine this representational content being learned by a tabula rasa network; the proposals developed here are also more detailed than representations typically considered by researchers focused on improvements in connectionist techniques.

The remainder of this chapter is composed of five sections followed by a summary. Section 2 is devoted to a discussion of CBR in general, the issue of case retrieval (the *indexing problem*) in particular, and, most specifically, my own approach to indexing. The three sections that follow present a particular indexing system designed for the task of giving advice in the domain of lovelorn problems: Section 3 justifies representative details of the index components used in the **Abby** lovelorn advising system; Section 4 explains how such indices can be compiled into a feature vector; Section 5 briefly sketches how a collection of such feature vectors can be interpreted as a network that computes similarity. Section 6 is a discussion touching on the performance of this indexing system, and its relationship to connectionism and CBR.

2. CASE RETRIEVAL: INDEXING AND PARALLELISM

This section has four purposes: (a) to motivate CBR and, in particular, the case retrieval problem; (b) to propose lovelorn advising as a task well suited to exploring retrieval in isolation; (c) to define the *indexing hypothesis*—the most prevalent approach to case retrieval; and (d) to justify my particular version of indexing, a version intended to allow a massively parallel implementation.

2.1. A Focus on Retrieval

Long familiar with student life and travel, when I want breakfast on the road, I will probably try walking to the inevitable "family restaurant" next to my motel (unless I am going to a conference, in which case I may wait for the coffee break); walking next door will get me fed about every time. Why argue with success? Faced with a common situation and a recurring goal, simply do what worked last time.

One way of looking at life is as a continuous sequence of situations, each one potentially an occasion for action that protects or promotes some of your goals. At any point, you have to assess the situation, notice threats and opportunities it presents, and decide what, if anything, to do about them. Now assume that any action you take will be chosen from a repertoire of possible responses accumulated through experience and often tied to records of particular experiences. Suddenly, deciding what to do starts to look like the classification task of fitting situations into categories defined by your remembered situations and responses. CBR can be read as the claim that this classification view of situated decision making is primary: the first line of reasoning, problem solving, or planning is to try doing something you have done before.

Of course life is not always so simple or behavior so regular. Most practical instantiations of CBR add steps to the process that allow for novel behaviors to arise by evaluating and tweaking past cases. At a large conference, it can be hard to find where they have hidden the coffee. I am flexible enough to generate subgoals like looking for signs that direct me to coffee; I can tweak my plan and look for signs directing me to an information booth instead of directly to the coffee; if time is running short, I can switch plans and try the hotel coffee shop or campus union.

A complete CBR theory must account both for retrieval of past cases and for the effective use of what is retrieved. That is a tall order, equivalent to a complete theory of analogy that accounts for everything from access to base domains through appropriate mapping of concepts and transfer of inferences. The methodology of AI is to build working models to illustrate cognitive theories. But when we try to model a partial theory—part of a complex process like CBR—we run up against a standard problem: building a working model requires implementing the *entire* process and thus requires commitment to all sorts of atheoretical details. The result is that it becomes hard or impossible to sort out the necessity of the claimed theoretical features.

I am interested in the contents of memory and in the retrieval phase of CBR. CBR needs a detailed theory of retrieval. Until we know what we can expect to get from memory, we do not really know how much work remains for the rest of the system. The point of CBR is that, ideally, there should be relatively little work left over.

When I set out, then, the appropriate research strategy was to build a small focused model—to build what might be called a *retrieve and respond* system. The trick was to balance the demand that a demonstration system *do* something (ideally, something that people actually do or that someone wants done) with the restriction that the task could be performed adequately without appeal to the later stages of the CBR process.

2.2. The Value of Stories

Perhaps surprisingly, *purposeful conversation* is an example of a behavior well suited to a retrieve and respond system. Schank (1991) observed that people's everyday conversations are often dominated by storytelling and that the stories told are often chosen from a repertoire of old favorites. A story can be seen as a frozen response behavior; much of conversation can be modeled as simply following your interlocutor's ramblings well enough to decide which of your stories to choose as a response. Given a good collection of stories, you can carry on an engaging conversation without ever doing anything new.

For example, what do you say when someone tells you the long sad story of their latest break-up? Most likely, if you say more than, "Gee, tough break," what you say is something like, "Well, I had a friend once who went out with this woman for a month..." and then you tell a story that comes to mind and strikes you at the moment as relevant to what you just heard.

This kind of storytelling satisfies a purpose. When you tell such a story in response to someone else's problems, you effectively offer reassurance, consolation, empathy, or advice. Here then is a task worth modeling. Telling stories to give advice is in fact something that people do. People love to offer advice. If it is offered the right way, people may even appreciate receiving advice. If it fits what they already believe, they may occasionally follow other people's advice. In any case, when you tell a story to a person, they are expected to be clever enough to interpret it and evaluate their interpretation, effectively carrying out the later steps of the CBR process for you.

Telling a story is a good way to give advice for several reasons. A story communicates more than the surface facts of a situation and also more than a generalization or rule. Unlike raw experience, stories include explicit interpretation and causal attributions; by editing experience, a story can insinuate causal relationships or highlight them as needed to reach the hearer. Stories can capitalize on the hearer's identity and interests. Particular characters or events can capture the hearer's attention. Playing on character identification may get across different points of view. Telling an analogous story in another domain may circumvent biases or misunderstandings. Compared to a rule, a specific instance gives substance and shape to a generalization—the specifics help to determine the extent of a generalization's applicability. Finally, when it comes to influencing someone else's behavior or beliefs, stories make strong arguments because they usually purport to describe something that actually happened.

As an example of the value of a good story, consider the classic driver's education film *The Last Prom*. Why do they show films like this? The answer should be clear: A movie about happy teenagers ending up as puddles of blood and gore smeared across the road is more effective then simple rules packaged in limp slogans like "Don't drink and drive." The story of *The Last Prom* makes sure teenagers understand that this rule applies to them, and that, for instance, a special occasion is not grounds for making an exception. This film may not be great art, but it is still a good story in the sense that it reaches its intended audience, makes them see its point, and then tends to stick with them.

2.3. Abby: The Lovelorn Advisor

I have designed and built a computerized lovelorn advising system named **Abby** as a way of studying memory. The system's behavior was, of course, chosen to allow a tight focus on memory while still producing recognizable and evaluable task-directed behavior: given a problem description, the system tells a story in return. For example, when presented with the problem "*an old man regrets that he put off settling down and never married,*" **Abby** responds by telling the following story:

> Whenever I have something that I'm going to have to make a choice or a decision about—where whatever I decide will commit me to something for a long period of time and really change the rest of my life—my reaction is to procrastinate and avoid the decision. For example, when I was applying to graduate schools, I found there were several schools I wanted to apply to, but I knew once I applied I'd have this decision to make about which one to go to. I just didn't like to think about it, so I kept putting it off and putting it off.
>
> Really the only thing that made me eventually send out the applications and end up in graduate school was the fact that there was this deadline: all the applications had to be in by December 15. So December 14 I spent a lot of time at the typewriter

typing up those applications; and the existence of that deadline forced me to make my decisions about which graduate schools were more interesting than others.

In no way is this a direct solution to the old man's problem; it is not really a solution to anything. Instead, it is a story of a problem and an outcome: *procrastination overcome in response to an external deadline*. Interestingly, this story is not even directly concerned with love and marriage. Nonetheless, it can readily be interpreted as advice to the old man because of the underlying similarity: both men avoided making a commitment. A straightforward mapping would suggest that the old man could resolve his problem if conditions forced him to choose someone for a wife. In keeping with its focus on retrieval **Abby** leaves it up to a human user to suggest this mapping.

The many mismatches between these situations mean the advice may not in fact apply very well. Does the old man have a list of potential wives? Exactly what sort of external pressure could be arranged? Is it still possible for the old man to correct this problem from long ago? The story retrieved was not a perfect match by any means, but it is not an unreasonable story to tell. We would understand what was meant if a person told us this story in response to this problem. It might stir the old man to set himself a personal deadline to go out, meet women, and choose a wife.

Abby contains stories and gives advice about lovelorn problems. These are problems that affect goals or arise from situations dependent on a broad range of social relationships. For the most part these include romantic and familial relationships, but many stories also touch on other domestic, social, educational, professional, religious, or civic affiliations. For example, **Abby** can offer advice on the following sorts of problems:

- *A young woman feels neglected because her boyfriend spends time with his friends,*
- *A man wants to continue being housemates with a woman and would also like to become romantically involved with her, but the household breaks up,*
- *A young man in a long-distance relationship is losing touch with his girlfriend because she is not communicating,*
- *A man and woman set up a date at his request, but she does not show, and*
- *A young man sleeps around though his girlfriend wants him to be loyal; this leads her to have some affairs which leaves him feeling that she has been disloyal.*

The system's exact behavior in each case is to take a formalized problem description as input and to tell a story as output. The story is picked out of a memory containing 500 such stories describing 250 different situations collected through interviews and from newspaper columns. In order to build **Abby** I had to concentrate on answering the questions: What should problem descriptions look like and what should they contain so that they efficiently retrieve relevant cases from a large memory of stories?

2.4. The Indexing Problem

When using CBR to find a solution, getting appropriate cases out of memory becomes half the problem. Within the CBR community, the standard way to frame retrieval issues is in terms of *indexing*. A term borrowed from computer science (borrowed still earlier from library science), "indexing" implies a general model of how you find an appropriate memory item: starting with a compact description of what you are interested in, you match against the elements of an organized collection containing many such descriptions, and when a match succeeds you get immediate access to a stored item.

For example, the back of a book often includes an alphabetized list of keywords meant as short descriptions of concepts in which a reader might be interested; these are paired with page numbers serving as pointers into the text where those concepts are discussed. This is a prototypical indexing system and we will continue to refer to this bookish model. The analogy, of course, is not perfect. For one thing, there is the obvious terminological confusion: though we typically refer to this entire section of a book as "the index," in CBR terminology each keyword entry would be "an index" giving access to a particular part of the text.

To eliminate potential confusion, it is worth introducing a distinction between *probe* and *label* indices. Probes are the descriptions a searcher invents when trying to find something in the memory (the picky reader's guess at a good keyword); labels are the descriptions that have been assigned to the contents of memory and organized for efficient search (the alphabetized list of keywords in the back of the book).

The appeal of treating case retrieval as an indexing problem, then, is that it provides a simple understandable model that focuses attention on a series of subproblems.

What are indices?
1. *General content:* In general, what sorts of descriptions can function as indices?
2. *Specific content:* For any particular memory item, what situation descriptions would indicate it was appropriate to retrieve that item?
3. *Structure:* What is an appropriate format for representing indices?

How do indices work?
4. *Organization:* What is an appropriate organization for our collection of labels?

5. *Search algorithm:* What sort of search algorithm will work with our chosen structure and organization to make retrieval efficient?
6. *Match criterion:* What will count as a match between a probe and a label?

Where do indices come from?
7. *Probe generation:* When faced with a situation, how are probes generated?
8. *Label generation:* When storing (or restoring) a case in memory, how are labels assigned?
9. *Feature reification:* When should new features be added for coding indices?

These research-focusing questions strongly determine what a theory of index-based case retrieval will look like. Questions 1 and 2, for example, demand that an indexing theory explicitly specify the possible and actual content of indices. The more specific we can be about this, the better our theory. We may start out claiming that indices ought to be goal-relevant situation descriptions, but we will have done better once we can say exactly how detailed our language of situation descriptions needs to be, what can be said in the language, and why those sorts of things are worth saying.

These questions do not completely determine their answers. When we set about our research, we have to keep in mind some additional constraints that any theory of indexing ought to satisfy. I consider two here.

First, our method of searching through the available indices must work efficiently when there are large numbers of indices. A system's apparent intelligence is going to be strongly determined by how many cases it can appropriately choose among (particularly if it is a limited retrieve and respond system like **Abby** that gets by without the ability to mutate old cases into new behaviors). Imagine an old man who insists on telling one of his favorite five stories no matter what you say; what are the chances that he will say something very on point? You say, "My girlfriend just left me." The old man replies, "Well, when I was fighting in France we holed up for a week in an old chateau and lived off their wine cellar."

Having a large memory stocked with potentially relevant items is crucial. It is not worth building an elaborate index for the back of a Dr. Seuss beginner's book. It is not worth consulting the index of your favorite cookbook if you are looking for advice on car repair. Once you have got your hands on the right auto manual though, its alphabetized keyword index can work reasonably efficiently; if you do something approximating binary search, you can find the matching heading in time proportional to the logarithm of the number of entries.

The catch of course is that you have to have guessed the right keyword when you started your search. Though book indices perform relatively well in terms of efficient scaling, they do not fare well judged by our second constraint: book indices fail to be forgiving about matching fragmentary or partially misstated probes to the available labels. You have to guess *exactly* right about what labels have been assigned to the items you are hoping to find.[1] Requiring exact match becomes untenable when the number of items in the memory gets large, when the user is unfamiliar with the memory contents or its labeling system, or when the user is in fact a rather dim nonhuman probe-generating algorithm.[2]

Prior research in CBR suggests that if you need to find a case that will help you accomplish a task, the most effective indices will be descriptions of task-related goals and features of the world causally relevant to the status of those goals (Hammond, 1989). If you are a cooking advisor, then you ought to index cases on desired properties of dishes and features of ingredients that affect those properties; if you are a lovelorn advisor then you ought to index cases on social goals that can run into difficulties and on features of social situations that lead to such difficulties. When you must cover a large domain and discriminate among many memories, such indices become rather elaborate. It becomes almost as unlikely that the system will form *exactly* the same index on more than one occasion as that the state of the world will *exactly* repeat itself from time to time. Again, partial matching is a necessity.

I focus on these two constraints—large memories and partial index matching—because they speak to the process of retrieval. In the context of discussing connections to connectionist theory, the *structure* of indices and the *processes* that manipulate them (Questions 3–6 above) come to the fore. Nonetheless, when constructing an indexing system that will accomplish a particular task in a particular domain, the bulk of the work must go into specifying the *content* of indices (Questions 1 & 2) (Schank & Brand, 1990). It turns out that the claims I make for the structure of **Abby**'s indices are mainly novel when considered in concert with the detail and breadth of the claims about content.

I aim to demonstrate that it is both possible and useful to implement complex structured descriptions as feature vectors. Obviously, what I mean by feature vector here is not simply a collection of surface features. Rather I mean to emphasize the rigid fixed format of a vector—the lack of internal structure typically implemented in declarative representations by variable bindings or pointers.

---

[1] This is not precisely true. You might stumble over a more apt keyword choice in the course of your search (but that is hardly very dependable). The index might offer you a forward reference from your guess to *its* idea of the right keyword (but then in some sense you really did guess a right keyword). You might guess a relevant root or prefix without knowing exactly how the word ends (but this is fairly unlikely and of limited applicability).

[2] One possible approach is to have the set of available labels influence the probe-generating algorithm so that it only generates probes that are known to match some existing label. Weaker versions of this idea are being pursued by Burke (1989), and have been implemented by Owens (1988), but it remains unclear how the strong form of this proposal could be realized. We will still need partial matching.

2.5. Why Feature Vectors?

Given that the first questions to be answered concern the *content* of index representations, you might wonder why anyone would want to convert structured descriptions into flat feature vectors. Composable, inspectable, declarative representations have a long and honorable history in AI; they are, after all, multipurpose, and constructs that serve more purposes are presumably better than those that serve fewer. Standard declarative representations can also be arbitrarily detailed, and you never know what information might turn out to be useful in judging relevance (Ashley & Rissland, 1988; Kolodner, 1989).

Adopting feature vectors as the framework for our answer to Question 3 above (what is the structure of indices?) turns out to have many advantages: it provides a way to address the two constraints of large memories and partial matching; it helps ensure that answers to Questions 1 and 2 (what is the general and specific content of indices?) will be clear, complete, and explicit; it suggests simple answers to Questions 4–6 (how do indices work?); it may contribute to answering Questions 7–9 (where do indices come from?).

The argument for feature vector indices is largely the argument for a particular massively parallel implementation of case retrieval—a style of parallelism that assumes only very simple processors. The initial motivation for this approach is found in the first constraint suggested in the previous section: a case retrieval system should scale up and work efficiently with large memories. Now the very idea of an indexing system implies the existence of a finite number of distinct labels, so *any* indexing system could be implemented by assigning each label an individual processor devoted to matching that label against a broadcast probe. But matching a complete index—particularly a structured description—seems to require complex communication and processing: encoding, transmitting, and decoding the description; walking over its parts; verifying variable binding constraints; accumulating an overall rating for the match.

With feature vectors, we can imagine a system where we assign a processor to each feature of each label.[3] In this scheme, not only are all labels matched in parallel, but all features of all labels are matched in parallel. This of course requires many more processors, but each one does much less, and accordingly, can be much simpler. With the right choice of combination function and implementation technology, accumulating the partial results into a final match rating need not be a bottleneck. With enough hardware of the right type, the result is a retrieval process that takes only a constant amount of time no matter how many items there are in memory. There is reason to hope that we will see

---

[3] Actually, in a network implementation, we would probably assign one *link* (rather than one *node*) to each feature of each label.

technologies develop in which matching vectors this way will be both fast and scalable.[4]

Feature-vectors also provide a clear way to think about addressing the second constraint from the previous section: handling inexact and partial matching. Any nonatomic index format—simply by virtue of having parts—can support partial matching, but feature vectors have some advantages when it comes to clarity of process formulation. First, when the parts to be matched are features arranged in a vector, the fixed positional encoding enforced by the vector helps keep distinct the problem of establishing correspondences between the parts of two indices, from the problem of verifying or rating equivalence of corresponding parts. Second, feature vectors encourage clarity about what the possible parts of a partial match can be; if you want something to affect the match, you must name it and explicitly include it in the vector. Finally, feature vectors suggest a simple way for the parts to contribute to an overall match rating—through linear combination (i.e., by formation of a weighted sum). A linear combination rule in turn constrains what ought to count as a part in the first place; nonlinear effects call for the reification of a new feature. Connectionist learning schemes suggest ways to individually tweak the importance of matching each part of each label's description, and may even be able to propose useful higher order features built from nonlinear combinations of base features.

Thinking of indices as feature vectors is a good way to push our formulation of an indexing theory towards clear and specific answers to the first two questions such theories must answer: what is the possible content of some class of indices in general, and what is the actual content of any index in particular? By the time you have finished listing the features of your vector, you have said exactly what can be an index; only features that you have explicitly listed can affect retrieval. This is not to say that you can really write down the list of features sufficient for indexing once and for all, or that a system ought not in the long run learn new features to which it should attend. It simply means that at any one time, it is easy to tell what you are claiming indices are.

This specificity of commitment is harder to come by when using more standard recursively composable declarative representations (the sort of frame structures commonly used to describe case contents in memory). While a set of such representational items with their syntax for combination might compactly characterize an indexing language, most existing systems would result in *infinite*

---

[4] For example, researchers in optical computing have proposed adapting existing optical disk technologies to produce a system capable of matching 16,384-bit patterns, finding the closest match to a probe from a corpus of 14,500 labels in just 25 msec (Marchand, Krishnamoorthy, Ambs, & Esener, 1990). The particular system mentioned is actually largely serial, and was justified by its designers as a stopgap measure; systems that can handle patterns with 10^8 or 10^9 bits are considered a real possibility. As such systems are developed and improved, the question will become how to put such capacity to good use.

indexing languages. Maybe that is not a problem (though it certainly seems less of a commitment than the finite structure of a feature vector) since any particular index instance will be finite (at least if you make sure to avoid forming cycles in the resulting graph structures, or if you adopt assumptions about how such cycles will be cut).

But then simply being finite is not much of a restriction on an index instance; what we really want is for indices to constitute clear and interesting statements about the grounds for case retrieval. When indices are built from structured components this implies you must avoid the temptation to reuse the components already serving as parts of the case representation. Pieces of the case representation are somehow linked to all the other pieces describing details of the case; an index which contains such components either obscures, or worse, makes no interesting claims about the basis for retrieving the case (other than saying that any detail of our knowledge of the case may have an effect on whether or not the case is retrieved).[5]

To see the final advantage of feature vectors, we have to take a slightly broader view of the retrieval problem and ask where indices come from. The answer must include *inference* (since the world will not present all index features on a silver platter), and along with the need to infer index features will come the need to *control* inference. Control of inference is one of the perennial thorny problems of AI. With his ANON system, however, Owens (1988) showed how a system performing inference in the service of discriminating among a set of possible retrieval targets, could apply massive parallelism to control inference; the system approximated an optimal discrimination network (d-net) no matter the order in which information became available, and did this without incurring the exponential space costs that make such d-nets a practical impossibility. One requirement of ANON's algorithm was that all potentially inferable features could be referenced unambiguously from any label, so that the system could determine how many labels contained any particular feature; a feature vector format meets this condition trivially.

Feature vectors also have their problems, but among commonly stated objections, some are more serious than others. For example, the complaint that feature vectors are insufficiently expressive, because, being flat and unstructured, they cannot encode structural information, is simply wrong. If structural features are needed then they can simply be reified and encoded as features in the feature vector. Continuing concern over this issue usually centers on the *efficiency* of such encodings, a more serious issue which I discuss below.

---

[5] In this context, it is worth noting that I am not proposing that all representation be cast as feature vectors; I am concerned here with indices. The assumption is that there ought to be some larger structured description of stored cases and current situations from which indices are constructed through a process of analysis and selection focused by the goals of the system as it performs some task (Seifert, 1988).

A more justified complaint about the expressivity of feature vectors is that they place restrictions on the composition of novel meanings. But even this objection holds in an absolute sense only if you insist on the need for *infinite* expressivity (and if you disallow incremental growth of the feature vector). Otherwise, this also is basically an efficiency concern: at what point will the combinatorics of the encoding make further expressivity impractical? The call for infinite expressivity arises in modeling open-ended learning systems (as people are usually taken to be) or unrestricted text understanders (which ought to be equivalent to open-ended learners). But many interesting and useful models and performance systems have been built that are not so powerful. Earlier I suggested that for purposes of understanding index content, we would rather *not* presuppose an infinite indexing language. In short, I believe that for many practical purposes we need not worry about the limits feature vectors may impose on composition of novel meanings.

I take efficiency problems to be the most serious objection to feature vector encodings; these will determine what is practical. **Abby** is, in fact, straining against the limits of what is practical using its approach on present-day workstations. Further, it is straining despite the fact that as a serial implementation it can take advantage of efficient encodings for its sparse feature vectors using tricks that might not be available in a truly parallel system. This seems particularly damning given that **Abby** need only concern itself with a single task and domain (though social problems is a rather large domain); if, for instance, it also had to worry about detailed descriptions of the physical world, its feature vector encodings would become still larger and still sparser.

While extreme sparseness of a coding scheme (which may require devoting resources to many irrelevant features that must then be ignored) is a valid concern, I do not see it as knock-down argument against the proposal to use feature vectors either as a way to explore index content or as a way to implement indexing systems. A system that did a good job of case retrieval, even if only in one domain, could be a useful system. A system that serves as a model (defining a methodology and spawning a supporting tool set) for building domain specific retrieval systems would be useful. On such a base, multifunction systems might be constructed simply by partitioning their understanding of the world into several disjoint domains. In any case, we have become accustomed in this field to living a bit in the future because as technology advances, this year's strain is next year's easy fit.

I am not against more efficient encodings, so long as there is some way to understand what they are representing and how they are representing it. When explicit feature vectors are proposed, connectionists start worrying about where the features come from, how to find the "best" set of features, how to modify the set over time. Defining a useful feature vector looks worryingly like a serious knowledge engineering problem. That is the point: it *is* a serious knowledge engineering problem, and it is not likely to go away any time soon. What this suggests to me is that concern over feature set efficiency (really over automatically approximating optimality) is premature; we do not yet need the best set of features, we need some set that seems to work.

Abby is not alone in proposing that tasks that might seem to require arbitrary amounts of processing over open-ended representations can be adequately performed by networks quickly combining fixed inputs. This orientation links **Abby** to situated action systems like Pengi (Agre & Chapman, 1987). In both, restricting possible inputs to a fixed vector allows the use of a network to implement the behavior choice procedure. Just as Pengi's input can be interpreted as a restricted form of situation calculus descriptions (Subramanian & Woodfill, 1990), so too **Abby**'s indices can be mapped onto more standard representations for its domain.

In the case of **Abby**, system development *started* with standard content theorizing—representations were proposed based on analysis of the particular task, and logical argument from contrasting instances found in data. Only in later stages did the emphasis shift towards the definition of restricted encodings of that representational content. In what follows, I largely follow this historical (and methodological) path. The next three sections, which constitute the bulk of this chapter, discuss in some detail what **Abby**'s representations look like, demonstrate how they are mapped into a fixed format feature vector, and then describe how collections of such vectors can be interpreted as networks.

3. THE CONTENT OF ABBY'S INDICES

We know what indices are supposed to do: indicate the conditions under which it would be useful to retrieve a particular case. Now the question is how are they to do this: what sorts of features reliably describe relevance conditions for lovelorn advice? The purpose of this section is to specify and to justify the content of **Abby**'s indices so that in the following sections we can describe the mapping of this index content into a feature vector format. The specifics of this representational system and the methodology underlying its development constitute the core of my work on **Abby** (both are described in greater detail in (Domeshek, 1992). Both the effort to specify index content and the form of the resulting indices are most closely related to work previously reported in (Schank, Brand, et al., 1990; Schank, Osgood, et al., 1990) aimed at defining a universal indexing frame (UIF). Though it may not be as obvious, the design of **Abby**'s indices was also strongly influenced by the description of plot units in (Lehnert, 1981).

In defining the content of **Abby**'s indices we start from the observation, noted earlier, that effective indices are likely to include task-relevant goals and situational features that determine the status of those goals (Hammond, 1989). We also build upon the body of representation theory developed by Schank's school of natural language processing (NLP) during the last two decades for describing everyday goals, plans and actions, and states (Schank, 1982, 1986; Schank & Abelson, 1977).

A need for advice implies the existence (at least potentially) of a problem. The point of the advice is to contribute towards correcting (or avoiding, or at least explaining) the problem. Conceptually then, indices to advice ought to be problem descriptions. What would a problem description look like? A problem is defined as a negative impact on some goal held by an agent involved in the current situation. At the very least, a problem/index ought to contain a description of the suffering goal. This very least, though, is clearly much too little; if an index were merely something like "desire to be married" (implicitly indicating the problem, "failure to be married"), there would be no basis for choosing among the hundreds, or even thousands, of stories about people who wanted to be married (but for some reason were not) that the average adult could reasonably be expected to know from personal experience, from the lives of friends and family members, from second-hand stories, and from imaginative works like novels, TV soap operas, plays, and movies.

3.1. Mutant Intentional Chains

We need to elaborate the index by including a causal account saying something about exactly *why* there was a failure to be married. The *mechanism* of failure will give us the additional information we need to choose a more specifically appropriate story. The old man of our opening example wasn't married (though he wanted to be) because (so our probe said) he deferred carrying out the normal plan to get married—he never seriously looked around, chose someone, and asked her to marry. With this additional detail included in the index, **Abby** could retrieve the "procrastinating applicant" story told earlier.

In order to be sure you can represent the possible range of failure mechanisms for a goal like **being-married**, you need a model of how someone would normally come to be married (Hammond, 1989). The NLP literature gives us some guidance as to what a model of normal everyday goal-directed action might look like. Schank and Abelson (1977), and later Schank (1986) suggested a useful formalism for representing the causation of states under the influence of agents. The *intentional chain* is a standardized sort of explanation (an intentional explanation) for observed **facts** (either **actions** or **states**, which may include thematic, emotional, and belief states); it is a fixed grouping of representational components describing how a **state** resulted from an **action** that was performed as part of a **plan** in service of a **goal** that stemmed from some longer term **theme** held by an **agent**. The intentional chain is a way to encode pieces of our model of how someone would normally come to be married.

Consider part of that model: a normal adult in our society (THEME), wants to become someone's spouse (GOAL) and goes about finding a partner (PLAN)

Figure 3.1.
The Generic Intentional Chain and an Example

Slot-Names	Chain-Contents	Slot-Names	Chain-Contents
Theme	theme (state)	*Theme*	be-adult
Goal	goal (state)	*Goal*	achieve-spouse-of
Plan	plan (event)	*Plan*	find-partner
Action	action (event)	*Action*	marry
Effect	state	*Effect*	spouse-of

culminating eventually in their getting married (ACTION) which results in their being married (EFFECT). Figure 3.1 shows, side-by-side, the general template for an intentional chain and how that template might be filled out to represent this standard marriage explanation. In both diagrams, the left-hand column names the five pieces of the intentional chain: THEME, GOAL, PLAN, ACTION, and EFFECT. In the diagram of the generic intentional chain, the right-hand column specifies the generic class of filler allowed for each slot (usually noting in parenthesis a more general category to indicate commonalities). The right-hand column in the diagram of the marriage chain is filled with particular items of the appropriate classes.

Consider now how we might encode the old man's problem as an intentional chain. The left diagram in Figure 3.2 shows the interpretation I suggested, whereby the old man had the goal to have a wife and knew how to go about finding a partner; the DEFER annotation on the plan indicates that he simply put his quest for a mate on the back-burner so that he did not marry and therefore did not have a wife. Notice that this is not a standard intentional chain; that the man is *not* married is hardly explained by the fact that he is an adult and wanted to get married. A problem description is going to hinge on some fault in the normal mechanism.

In this example we really have something like two interacting causal sequences: (1) being a man he wanted a wife and he planned to find one; and (2) for some unknown reason he deferred finding a mate, did not marry, and therefore failed to have a wife. The advantage of packaging both strains in this format is that it helps us understand the *impact* of the fact that the man is not married—that it is in fact a failure of one of his goals.

Slot-Names	Chain-Contents	Slot-Names	Chain-Contents
Theme	be-man	*Theme*	be-successful
Goal	achieve-husband-of	*Goal*	achieve-student-in
Plan	find-partner /defer	*Plan*	find-group / defer
Action	not-marry	*Action*	not-apply
Effect	not-husband-of	*Effect*	not-student-in

Figure 3.2.
Intentional Chains for "Old Bachelor" and "Procrastinating Graduate-Student"

In order to represent problems, we need to be able to talk about situations where an action (intentionally or not) leads to a state that has a *negative* impact on a goal. In such a mutant intentional chain, one (or more) of the normally assumed causal links is abrogated: the plan does not address the goal, the action does not follow from the plan, or the EFFECT state produced by the action was not the one intended to address the goal.

The right diagram in Figure 3.2 shows a possible representation for the label of the retrieved story: *"A young man wants to go to graduate school but puts off doing his applications."* Notice the forms and contents of these two problems are quite similar. Both can be coded as single mutant intentional chains; in both, a failure to carry through on a reasonable plan leads to the failure of the goal.

There are many other ways in which observed and inferred groupings of theme, goal, plan, action, and effect might fail to meet the standard intentional chain format. For instance, an inappropriate plan might be chosen (perhaps as part of the pursuit of some other goal), the plan might be incorrectly implemented in ways other than deferring execution (choosing an inappropriate specific action), an action might produce effects other than those desired.

These two problem descriptions, packaged as mutant intentional chains, indicate the sorts of information that must be included in an index if we hope to retrieve relevant advice. In the next three subsections, consideration of more complex problems will lead us to expand the sorts of problem descriptions we use as indices. The intentional chain, however, will remain a convenient conceptual building block. Expansion will take the form of introducing additional ways in which such chains can fail to cohere, and of relating several intentional chains.

3.2. Chain Interactions

A single intentional chain is very limited in what it can express. For instance, one thing we will want to be able to represent is situations where an action fits into one intentional chain normally, while simultaneously making a mess of another intentional chain. The observation that an action can have more than one effect, one good and another bad, leads to the notion of a *tradeoff* (similar to Wilensky's (1983) notion of *goal interaction*). Whenever we find a negative impact we have to suspect that it is probably not part of the main-line intentional chain that accounts for the action; somehow the action probably has some positive effect which led to its performance. Unless an agent is just plain stupid or callous, we expect tradeoffs to be involved in most problems. Advice aimed at alleviating negative effects must take positive effects into account.

Consider the problem: *"A young woman feels neglected because her boyfriend spends time with his friends."* The boyfriend's spending time with his friends is a problem for this woman. Yet he probably is not doing it just to spite her; spending time with the gang satisfies a goal of his to enjoy their companionship. We can fit his spending time with friends into two different intentional chains:

Figure 3.3.
Chain Interaction Probe for "Neglected Girlfriend"

Theme	friend-of	Theme	lover-of
Goal	satisfy-companionship	Goal	satisfy-companionship
Plan	act-as-partner	Plan	
Action	socialize		
Effect	high-companionship	Effect	low-companionship

(1) a normal account explaining the action in terms of his goal to enjoy his friends' companionship, and (2) a mutant chain where the action serves to interfere with the woman's goal that he spend his time with her.

In order to capture tradeoffs, we introduce the notion of a *chain interaction*: two intentional chains grouped together because they share a common action. Figure 3.3 shows our analysis of this sample problem as a chain interaction. We will adopt the convention that when, as will often happen, a chain interaction contains one chain with a positive impact and another with a negative impact, we will place the one with the positive impact (the normal intentional chain) in the left column.

Using an elaborated version of the probe index in Figure 3.3 the **Abby** system matched a label index in its memory that can be paraphrased as "*A young man feels neglected because his girlfriend is constantly working;*" Figure 3.4 shows a sketch of this label. In response then, **Abby** told the following story:

There was a guy whose girlfriend was into being a superprofessional. She was working a million hours a week, making it as a star at her company, but he was just hanging out wishing she was around more often. He eventually got tired of her not being around or being too burnt out to do anything, so he started doing things on his own.

One weekend, he went out to a party alone; she of course was too tired to go along. He didn't get home until early the next morning, and that, it turned out, was what it took to get her attention. She never did ask him what he'd been up to that night, but from then on, she started working less and being there to do things with him more. It made him wish he'd gone ahead and done something like that to force her to pay attention earlier.

Theme	be-successful	Theme	lover-of
Goal	achieve-status	Goal	satisfy-companionship
Plan	act-as-member	Plan	
Action	work		
Effect	high-status	Effect	low-companionship

Figure 3.4.
Chain Interaction Label Matching "Neglected Girlfriend" Probe

In this reminding story, the conflicting demand is different (work vs. play), but the result is the same (failure to spend enough time with lover). The story can be read as suggesting that the woman take drastic threatening action to force her boyfriend to realize his behavior is risky. Part of what makes this probe and label a good match is their agreement on the pattern of relationships (if not always their exact content). In both cases, the sufferer is the lover of the actor and the suffering goal stems from their relationship; also in both cases the actor has chosen the action in support of one of their own goals.

There are many such relationships that can be extracted from a chain interaction. The most interesting ones, for our purposes, concern the relationships between the agents involved in the themes, goals, and actions. A tradeoff can be characterized according to the relationship between the HOLDER of the benefiting goal (the BENEFICIARY), the HOLDER of the suffering goal (the SUFFERER), and the ACTOR of the action. When all three are the same individual, we have an instance of something like a *preference*; when the ACTOR and SUFFERER are the same and the BENEFICIARY is someone else, we may have an instance of *selflessness*; when the ACTOR and the BENEFICIARY are the same but the SUFFERER is someone else, as in this case, we have something like *selfishness*.

While preference, selflessness, and selfishness are useful assessments of the tradeoffs involved—useful enough to suggest some simple strategies like invoking self-interest or guilt—the recognition conditions as stated are much too impoverished to live up to these labels. Justifying a label like "selfishness" requires **Abby** to represent features like *volition, prediction,* and *intention*. Discussion of how **Abby** represents these features is beyond the scope of this chapter.[6]

3.3. Compound Chains

Intentional chains are restricted as to how long a story they can tell; they provide an explanation for a *single* action or state. The chain interactions just introduced basically suffer the same limitation (though they can account for two states provided they both result from the same action). Most interesting stories however involve more than the simple motives for a single action and its effects. In the social world, a typical story may hinge on some additional background to an action (often on some prior action), or, looked at another way, on some later response to an initial provocation.

Consider the problem: "*A young man in a long-distance relationship is losing touch with his girlfriend because she is not communicating.*" This example could

---

[6] But see Domeshek (1990) for a short discussion of the representation of volition, and Domeshek (1992) for a more complete discussion of **Abby**'s entire indexing system.

A CASE STUDY OF CASE INDEXING   145

almost be handled by a single mutant chain: their theme of being lovers suggests a goal to maintain empathy, but the normal plan is aborted when they fail to communicate leading to the deterioration of their mutual understanding. What is missing in this representation is the crucial fact that *the physical distance between them made communication harder.*

Or consider the problem: "*A man and woman set up a date at his request, but she does not show.*" The problem that arises when the woman fails to show up for their date is really only understandable in light of her prior commitment to meet him; the background is an action setting up the expectation for successful completion of a plan. In the couple's problem, the background is simply a fact about the world—the couple is separated by significant distance; we don't know how that came to be or why.

In both cases, what we need is a way to achieve a wider field of view, one that takes in not only the motivation for a single action, but also prior conditions which might shape that motivation, the choice of plan and action, or the eventual outcome. One way to do this is to concatenate intentional chains together, such that we can describe how facts from an earlier chain influence the course of a temporally later chain; a *compound chain* is defined as such a concatenation of intentional chains. Figure 3.5 sketches compound chains that represent the "long-distance romance" and "stood-up date" problems described here. For brevity we skip **Abby**'s remindings and their indices.

Abby's indices are restricted to compounds built out of two intentional chains, though in principle longer sequences might prove useful. Two-step compounds are sufficient to capture common sequences like a provocation followed by a response. Given the number of stories in **Abby**'s memory, this amount of discrimination seems sufficient. So the content of a compound chain is just that of two basic chains, with the single addition of a LINK field specifying the relationship between those two chains.

Theme	
Goal	
Plan	
Action	
Effect	diff-location
Link	effect-sustains-action
Theme	lover-of
Goal	maintain-empathy
Plan	act-as-partner / abort
Action	not-communicate
Effect	low-empathy

Theme	date-of
Goal	satisfy-companionship
Plan	act-as-partner
Action	commit-to-socialize
Effect	high-confidence
Link	plan-sequence
Theme	date-of
Goal	satisfy-companionship
Plan	act-as-partner / abort
Action	not-socialize
Effect	low-companionship

Figure 3.5.
Compound Chain Probes for "Long-Distance Romance" and "Stood-Up Date"

3.3.1. Chains are Linked with Links Not in Chains. The existence of some causal linkage between an element of the first chain and some element of the second is what makes a pair of intentional chains cohere as a compound chain. In the examples just considered, the distance separating the lovers is described as a sustaining condition of their not communicating, and the commitment to socialize and the socializing are supposed to follow one another as steps in a plan.

The link connecting intentional chains into a compound ought not to be one that could be part of a normal intentional chain. For instance, there is no point linking two intentional chains by pointing out that the GOAL of the first one can be addressed by the PLAN of the second; better to simply package each plan into a separate intentional chain including the same goal.

If you then want to say something about the relationship between those intentional chains—for instance, that first one plan was tried and then the other—then the linkage ought to express that relationship. We might build a compound chain using the simple temporal link **after** between Plan 2 and Plan 1.

Alternately, and more informatively, we might imagine that an attempt to carry out Plan 1, (in part by execution of some Action 1 which led to an Effect 1) failed to satisfy the goal; this failure could be identified as the reason Plan 2 was adopted to address the same goal in the second intentional chain. Note that this more detailed representation subsumes the simple temporal linkage, since the intentional chains include implicit causal links, at least some of which include temporal succession in their meaning. In effect, we admit simple temporal relationships as a subset of the causal relationships. Put another way, an interesting causal relationship asserts both some temporal relationship and some claim to mechanism which makes the relationship more dependable and informative than mere co-occurrence.

The sorts of links that have so far proven useful in **Abby** include EFFECT to GOAL, EFFECT to PLAN, EFFECT TO ACTION, and ACTION to ACTION. This last form generally captures simple temporal succession or plan sequencing, as in the representation of the "stood-up date" index. The more common situation is that the end of one intentional chain (the EFFECT state or its interpretation as an impact) influences some part of the second intentional chain.

3.4. Compound Chain Interactions

Compound chains and chain interactions are both useful problem representations; not surprisingly however, many problems require that we combine these formats. This becomes necessary when, for instance, we need to represent the background to an action that is usefully described as a tradeoff, or to indicate that one tradeoff led to another. *Compound chain interactions* are simply the combination of compound chains and chain interactions. The best way to think about them is as a pair of chain interactions where there is some causal linkage

A CASE STUDY OF CASE INDEXING 147

Figure 3.6.
Compound Chain Interaction Probe for "Tit-For-Tat Affairs"

Theme	be-young-man	Theme	lover-of
Goal	satisfy-sex	Goal	maintain-loyalty
Plan	cheat-partner	Plan	
Action	have-sex		
Effect	satisfied-sex	Effect	low-loyalty

| Link | effect╱-initiates-goal╱ |

Theme	be-young-woman	Theme	lover-of
Goal	satisfy-sex	Goal	maintain-loyalty
Plan	cheat-partner	Plan	
Action	have-sex		
Effect	satisfied-sex	Effect	low-loyalty

(fitting the constraints of a compound chain) between an element of the first and an element of the second.

Situations that require this more elaborate representation arise frequently in the social domain. For example, the problem: *"A young man sleeps around though his girlfriend wants him to be loyal; this leads her to have some affairs which leaves him feeling that she has been disloyal,"* requires this treatment. Figure 3.6 sketches a compound chain interaction to represent this problem, while Figure 3.7 sketches one that represents a label we can paraphrase as: *"A young woman starts school far from her lover and while there, has a series of affairs jeopardizing the relationship."* The story **Abby** tells is as follows:

> A good friend of mine had been going out with a guy starting from about the first day freshman year in college. They'd gone out together for their four undergraduate years. They had originally planned that they would go to grad school in the same city, but then she got into Harvard Law, while his best choice was a school in New York. So they ended up in different towns.

Theme	be-successful	Theme	lover-of
Goal	achieve-status	Goal	maintain-relationship
Plan	find-group	Plan	
Action	join-school		
Effect	advance-status	Effect	diff-location

| Link | effect╱-biases-plan╱ |

Theme	be-young-woman	Theme	lover-of
Goal	satisfy-sex	Goal	maintain-relationship
Plan	cheat-partner	Plan	
Action	have-sex		
Effect	satisfied-sex	Effect	low-loyalty

Figure 3.7.
Compound Chain Interaction Label Matching "Tit-For-Tat Affairs" Probe

> *Her first year at law school something happened—I don't really know what—and she just decided that she was going to go out with different people. She went out with a whole crew of people. He wasn't crazy about it, but her boyfriend just bided his time. After her year of sowing her wild oats, they got back together and they just recently got married. I'm not sure that always works out, but it certainly did this time. I really think the two of them are right for each other.*

The major defect in this reminding is that it misses out on the provocation/response structure (in particular a "tit-for-tat" pattern [Seifert, 1987]) of the input problem. In the probe, the woman's affair is a response to her boyfriend's affair; in the retrieved label, the woman's affair follows from her own decision to relocate for school. Unlike the case of the constantly working girlfriend, **Abby**'s sensitivity to the difference between who first caused harm to whom (the background to the final infidelity) was not sufficient to override the strong similarity between the final problem of infidelity. This could have been due to a dearth of infidelity stories in the memory, or a lack of infidelity stories with causal background specified; it could have been due to insufficient weight having been placed on the pattern of agent relationships.

Lacking an adaptation and application component to the system, we cannot know precisely how well or how poorly this reminding would serve a full CBR system. Instead, we have to imagine what sort of advice might be implied by this story. Taking the story as a whole, the most straightforward advice is simply, stop fooling around and try to make things work out. But a system can sometimes make better use of a case by playing with several partial and possibly inconsistent mappings. The story suggests thinking about the following sorts of issues: did the girlfriend do something (prior to her infidelity) that led to this problem, did she do something that led to her boyfriend's initial infidelity, how long and strong a history did they have together before the infidelities began, and, is either of them interested in trying to make things work out? In some situations, these sorts of questions may be all a more constructive system needs from a reminding; Jones (1990), with his *Brainstormer* program, demonstrates how cases can contribute to ongoing problem solving by focusing attention and suggesting specific answers.

3.5. What's in a Field?

Compound chain interactions are the format **Abby** uses for representing indices. That is to say, this is the maximum complexity allowed for an index (we do not require that all the pieces be filled in for any one index). It may seem arbitrary to restrict indices to two-way interactions and two-step sequences; in fact it is. Nonetheless, going from one to two and stopping is methodologically sound. It was the need to appropriately index and discriminate among examples that drove us to consider indices composed of more than a single chain; similarly, we will require examples to drive us beyond the current limit. It is technically easy to build larger indices, but it adds (at this point, unnecessarily) to the burden of the human index coder and the memory requirements for index storage. For now, it is a working hypothesis that this is as much detail as needs to be considered as the basis for indexing.

Adopting compound chain interactions as the framework for indices puts one sort of limit on indices—in effect I have framed the sides of a box into which indices must fit. The job of specifying what can be in an index is not complete yet because I have not said what information you are allowed to specify about a THEME, GOAL, PLAN, ACTION, or EFFECT—I have so far neglected to provide a bottom for my index box. An expanded specification of these fields' possible contents is needed, but a clear answer to the question, "what can be in an index" and the feature vector formalism, both demand that such expansion be precise and limited. Each field may expand into a fixed number of subfields (and so on, through limited recursion), and each of those subfields may take a filler of some fixed complexity. Once we are done with this expansion, we can make a list of every potential feature of every broken-down field of each intentional chain in our index structure and call that our index vector.

I do not have space to discuss, in detail, **Abby**'s expansion for each of the primary fields introduced so far. Instead, only the expansion of the THEME component of our indices' intentional chains will be presented as a way to illustrate this process. When an index includes a theme, it cannot include an arbitrary amount of information about that theme; here we lay out what the important attributes of a theme might be, and design a set of subfields that can encode a fixed set of theme attributes.

Schank and Abelson's (1977) initial proposal of themes as representational constructs to provide ultimate justifications for people's goals and plans distinguished PERSONAL and INTERPERSONAL themes. A theme always has a HOLDER (the agent whose theme it is), but only interpersonal themes also have a PARTNER (another agent to whom the HOLDER is related in a way described by the theme). Interpersonal themes, they suggested, could be classified along three dimensions: *polarity*—the degree to which the relationship is positive or negative; *closeness*—how intimate or distant the relationship is; and *power*— whether the parties are equally balanced, or whether there is a clear pattern of dominance and submission. Locating a relationship on each of these scales captures many interesting general inferences. In keeping with Carbonell's (1979) work on goal trees, it also seems reasonable to rate themes by their strength and by their importance relative to other themes. Finally, as a shorthand way to capture commonalities amongst themes that belong to the same domain, address related sets of needs, and sort themselves into recognizable temporal patterns, **Abby** often assigns themes to a *thread* (something like a MOP (Schank, 1982) composed of themes).

In order to capture all these attributes of themes, we end up with a picture of themes like that shown in Figure 3.8. Here, again, the left column is a sequence of field names and the right column gives the corresponding filler classes for each field. There are a couple of things to notice about this format.

First, note how the encoding of a theme's relative importance appears here in the REL-VALUE and VS-THEME subfields: a REL-VALUE filler describes how the theme compares in importance to some other theme; VS-THEME (with its associated HOLDER and PARTNER sub-subfields) provides a way to identify the other theme that is being compared. Conceptually, a theme may have relative importance ratings with respect to many other themes, but in **Abby**'s limited index language we allow a set of fields sufficient to partially specify only *one* other related theme and one relationship. Furthermore, filling these fields is not really equivalent to linking one instance of a theme to another in a graph structure; such linkages effectively give a match routine access to any information about the linked theme (including, potentially, any information about any theme *it* is linked to). **Abby**'s more restricted format only encodes the related theme's type and its agents, plus some variable binding information about these entities. Exactly what binding information is available and how it gets encoded is discussed in the next section.

Second, several of the attributes ascribed to themes are not yet in evidence in these specified fields. In particular, the three dimensions of polarity, closeness, and power do not appear. That is because they are hidden in the encoding of potential fillers of the THEME fields. Here is another sort of incompleteness in our description of indices; we are only part way towards nailing a bottom on our index box. The remaining step will be taken in the next section when we discuss the encoding of field fillers into binary feature vectors. Once we have described how field fillers are specified and revealed all the hidden features, such as variable binding information, there will be no more room for uncertainty about what is in an index.

Slot-Names	Field-Contents
Theme	theme (state)
Holder	agent
Partner	agent
Value	degree
Vs-Theme	theme (state)
Holder	agent
Partner	agent
Rel-Value	comparison
Thread	thread

**Figure 3.8.
The Expansion of a Theme**

A CASE STUDY OF CASE INDEXING   151

4. FROM CONTENT TO FEATURE VECTORS

4.1. Fields and Fillers

What can go in an index's THEME fields (or VS-THEME subfields)? For the convenience of the human designer, we would like to be able to use meaningful type names like those that have appeared in the preceding examples: **lover-of**, **friend-of**, and so on. Internally, these should be defined so they encode their important attributes such as polarity, closeness, and power. Standard AI representations define types, associate properties with them, and usually link the types into an inheritance graph that propagates such properties. **Abby** takes an approach more like that suggested by Hinton (1981) defining these recognizable types as sets of microfeatures from some underlying universe of distinctions that matter for the class.

Abby encodes each of the three theme scales so as to distinguish up to five possible values on each. The encoding is intended to ensure both that different values have different encodings, and that related values share some part of their encoding to capture the commonality. As a simple example, two of the five points on each scale are taken to represent positive values, so these share the microfeature of being **positive**; any inferences that follow from the positive polarity of a relationship, such as a tendency to act in service of the PARTNER's goals, can be made sensitive to this microfeature of the polarity scale. Likewise the two negative values share a microfeature. The remaining neutral value does not contain either the **positive** or **negative** microfeature. As another example, the two **extreme** values on a scale are noted as sharing the property of being **extreme**; feeling either very positive about someone or very negative may share in common the inference that the relationship is a good place to look for explanations of affect.

Abby uses the following seven microfeatures to encode polarity: polarity--, polarity-, polarity0, polarity+, polarity++, polarity-mid, and polarity-extreme. The definitions of the five points on the polarity scale are listed below; on each line, the polarity rating appears to the left of the = sign, and the right side lists the conjunction of microfeatures defining that rating.

very-positive	= polarity-extreme	polarity+	polarity++
positive	= polarity-mid	polarity+	
neutral	= polarity-mid	polarity0	
negative	= polarity-mid	polarity-	
very-negative	= polarity-extreme	polarity-	polarity--

The same sorts of encoding are used for the closeness and power scales. If these three dimensions were all that defined an interpersonal theme, then we could represent such themes using 21 microfeatures. **Abby**, however, uses a richer encoding of themes than just these three dimensions. For instance, themes encode features describing their *entry conditions*, noting which agents exercised consent or control in setting up the relationship.[7] They specify expectations about their stability, and how many comparable themes an individual is likely to hold at a given time or throughout their life. Themes also contain features reflecting classification in terms of broad and specific types of social conventions that govern the relationship. Some themes are distinguished by properties of the agents or by relations between properties of the agents. One of the more complex examples would be **child-of**, which is coded as the microfeatures[8]:

Distinguishing Major Theme Categories
   scaled mental thematic
   relation social from-agent to-agent

Polarity, Intimacy, and Power Scales
   polarity-extreme polarity+ polarity+ +
   intimacy-mid intimacy+
   power-extreme power- power--

Entry, Exit, and Enforcement Power
   self-consent- self-control- partner-consent+ partner-control+

Idiosyncratic Functional/Definitional Features
   younger family same-nuclear-family same-bloodline
   diff-generation younger-generation -1-generation

The first seven microfeatures included in the definition of CHILD-OF—**scaled mental thematic relation social from-agent to-agent**—are there to distinguish interpersonal themes from states in general and from other types of themes: **scaled** indicates that a theme is not an absolute state, but can be a matter of degree; **relation** indicates that this theme describes a relationship between two entities (in this case, those entities are agents as indicated by the microfeatures **from-agent** and **to-agent**; **mental**, **social** and **thematic** further characterize what sort of state a theme is. The other groups of microfeatures ought to be more self-explanatory.

Themes are one of the most complicated filler classes, with about 200 microfeatures available for their specification; but then thematic relationships are central to making sense of problems in the social world. Note that the features listed above encode just the default **child-of** relationship. If you wanted to talk about a child who did not like his or her parents, or who never confided in them, it would be easy to invent a new type that encoded those variations from

---

[7] This set of distinctions was suggested by work done jointly with Robin Burke.
[8] Actually, the list given here is a somewhat simplified version of **Abby**'s, full encoding of this theme.

the norm. To simplify hand coding of indices, **Abby** does not currently provide anything like the potentially huge inventory of idiosyncratic theme variants that are expressible using the underlying microfeatures, or that might prove useful.

4.2. Encoding Relationships

We are in the middle of detailing how the content of a problem description can be mapped into a feature vector representation. Effectively, we are making explicit what we think the significant features of a problem description are. So far, we have for the most part discussed the encoding of *type* information; the features of the **child-of** theme describe that theme whenever it holds between any two agents. But a problem description must also include *token* information, that is, part of the description must be relational information linking entities referred to in the description.

Some such relational information is already implicitly encoded by the position of fields in the vector. Consider the decomposition of the original THEME part of a chain into a whole series of fields including a new decomposed THEME field (defined to contain **theme** patterns), and a HOLDER field (defined to contain **agent** patterns). The definition of these fields implies there is a relationship between whatever fills the new THEME fields and whatever fills the HOLDER field—the HOLDER pattern describes an agent who holds the theme. Or on a larger scale, consider the relationship between the THEME and GOAL of any intentional chain; packaging these in an intentional chain normally asserts the relationship that the goal stems from the theme. This relationship information only makes sense if you consider the filler of a field to be not just its type pattern, but to stand for some instance of that type (a token).

There are many other potential relationships in a problem description. Basically any field filler reasonably conceptualized as a token can potentially be related to any other token filler. Of course the move to a feature vector was intended precisely to avoid the ability to have our index include arbitrary amounts of information (relational or otherwise). What we want to do is pick out some limited classes of relationships worth including in limited numbers (and not already included in the privileged set encoded by position.

4.2.1. The Identity Relationship (Variable Binding). One obvious candidate class of relationships to consider is the *identity* relationship normally expressed as variable binding constraints in other AI formalisms. Very simply, this is the relationship of two things being the *same* thing. With a finite number of base fields to be related, there are a finite number of such relationships possible (with N fields there are $\binom{N}{2}$ potential variable binding relationships). The index feature vector then must be expanded by introducing one microfeature for each possible binding relationship.

We need only consider potential identity relationships between fields of the same class, and for field classes that are reasonably conceptualized as tokens.

For instance, **themes** are reasonable tokens; the same theme may account for several goals and the fact that those goals stem from a single theme may be a significant point in analyzing a problem. On the other hand, the **degree** fillers stored in the VALUE fields of a theme are not good candidates for tokenhood. Degree ratings are simply attributes, in this case describing the strength of a theme; where the theme is an entity which might play several roles or about which there might be several things to say, in the current system, the degree has no such independent existence.

4.2.2 Thematic Relationships. The social world is characterized by the rich relationships amongst agents. Including social relationship information in the index might be expected to pay off because like other themes, these relationships can usefully be viewed as the root causes of people's intentional behavior—they generate social goals that motivate social plans and actions. Thus, when features of thematic relations between agents present in the current situation are found in a label, this will often indicate that the actions and outcomes described in the label's story would apply in the current situation. For example, if a story describes a situation where a man caused a problem for someone who had **power++** over him, and he ended up getting squashed, the lesson of that story might apply in any situation where the sufferer of a negative impact had **power++** over the actor who caused the problem.

Where instances of classes like **states** and **actions** appearing in an index are noted as either being the **same** or **different** (by the variable binding microfeatures), instances of **agents** can usefully be described as being **child-of**, **parent-of**, or whatever their thematic relationship might actually be. The only problem with this proposal is, that if done indiscriminately as in **Abby**, this leads to the addition of a staggering number of new features. Remember, the encoding of themes is already the most elaborate domain in **Abby**'s representations, using about 200 microfeatures. It turns out that agents are the most common sort of fillers in this index format with 132 agent fields. This means that the index feature vector must be expanded to include 132^2 (or 17,424) sets of these 200 microfeatures to encode the possible thematic relationships between pairs of agents in the index. I have found that in the current serial implementation, the cost of carrying these 3.5 million relationship microfeatures is not prohibitive, and that their inclusion contributes to the system's performance. If an order of magnitude difference in feature vector size would make a difference in whether or not the system could be implemented as a network, it would of course be worth the effort to severely prune this combinatoric explosion and attempt to include only those pairwise relationships that seemed to matter.

4.2.3. Not Encoding Comparisons. It may be worth mentioning one set of features which seemed *not* to make much difference in what the system retrieved. I had hypothesized that in addition to encoding relationships between tokens filling index fields, it would also be useful to encode comparisons between the fillers' types. The obvious way to encode such comparisons would be to calculate the set overlap and differences between the features used to encode the fillers.[9]

For instance, in the probe index describing the problem of the "neglected girlfriend" the system would have calculated comparisons between the **friend-of** and **lover-of** themes effectively adding many higher order features to the index: both the theme that benefited and the theme that suffered were **interpersonal-themes** (set overlap); the theme that benefited, but not the theme that suffered was an aspect of **social-life** (set difference of **benefited-suffered**); the theme that suffered, but not the theme that benefited was an aspect of **love-life** (set difference of **suffered-benefited**).

At one tine, **Abby** actually calculated and used such features, but analysis of the system's remindings with and without those features revealed that there was not very much difference. The features were dropped with a consequent saving of many millions of bits per label. Perhaps with a larger corpus or the need to make finer distinctions such higher order features would come into their own. Picking out some subset of all possible comparison features and the circumstances under which they were relevant might be a reasonable task for a connectionist learning system with an intermediate layer of initially uncommitted units.

5. FROM FEATURE VECTORS TO NETWORKS

From the start, my stated goal has been to design indices that can be mapped into simple unstructured feature vectors thereby allowing fast parallel matching using massively parallel hardware. This section sketches the translation from feature vectors to a network that can match a probe against a set of labels. The section has three parts: the first describes the intended semantics of partial match between feature vectors; the second casts such matching as the multiplication of the probe vector by a matrix formed from the labels; finally, the mapping to a network model follows standard techniques.

5.1. Partial Matching

Ideally, each bit in an index represents some distinction that makes a difference—the distinction serves to help license or prohibit some set of inferences. A one bit in a *probe* is interpreted as the belief that the corresponding feature holds in the current situation and is relevant to the choice of response. A one bit

---

[9] Such an encoding echoes a proposal by Tversky (1988) about assessing similarity for the purposes of classification.

in a *label* represents the expectation that the label's story is more likely to be worth telling in situations where the corresponding feature holds. Under this interpretation, an overlapping bit between a probe and a label means that the system believes the feature currently holds and expects that the label's case will be worth retrieving because the feature holds.

As an idealization, if all the diagnostic features specified by a label are present in a probe, we should be certain that the accompanying story is relevant. This is an idealization because there may not, in fact, be sufficient conditions under which it is always worth telling a particular story, and because even if there were, we may have missed some of them in cropping our indices so they fit the fixed format. And, of course, we do not expect to get complete matches often.

There are, in fact, two types of incompleteness in matching. We could be concerned that the entire contents of a label has not been matched, and thus that some of the conditions believed to support the case's relevance are not satisfied (or are not known to be satisfied). Alternately, we could be concerned that the entire contents of the probe has not been matched indicating that the matching label's case probably does not address some of the issues that the probe generator took to be important about the current situation. This suggests a match-scoring scheme that rates matches as a function not just of the overlap between the probe and label, but also taking into consideration the differences between the probe and label (both those features in the label but not in the probe, and those features in the probe but not in the label). Again, this is compatible with Tversky's (1988) proposal for a theory of similarity assessment; **Abby** uses a simple version of this similarity function built from a linear combination of the cardinality of the overlap and difference sets. If P is the set of probe features and L is the set of label features, then **Abby**'s formula for similarity is just $a|P \cap L| - b|L-P| - c|P-L|$ where a, b, and c are constants (in the current implementation, $a=2$, $b=1$, and $c=1$).

To see what is going on here, consider the following example. What if there are two stories in memory: the first one is simply "Gee, tough break," and is indexed under the very sparse label **negative-impact**; the second is some longer story about divorce proceedings following a husband catching his wife in bed with another man, and is indexed under a complex label like **the-couple-was-married-and-she-had-a-lover-and-the-husband-saw-her-having-sex-with-him-and-this-generated-a-negative-impact-to-his-goal-that-she-be-faithful-to-him**. Now you can be quite certain that you will be saying something *relevant* by saying "Gee, tough break," any time you get a probe that includes a negative impact; unfortunately, "Gee, tough break" will never by a very *specific* response. On the other hand, it would take quite a specific probe for you to be certain that it was worth telling your long divorce story, but if you saw a probe that made you reasonably certain the story was relevant, you would also have reason to believe it would offer more specific information than the story attached to the **negative-impact** label which only matched a minute fraction of the probe.

Abby increases the match rating as the amount of overlap increases and deducts from the match score for unmatched features in either probe or label. The question arises: how much influence should any feature match or mismatch have on the overall rating of a partial match? Despite its ability to directly represent fine grain distinctions **Abby** has a rather coarse follow-through: it assumes that all distinctions make the same amount of difference in all situations. As mentioned earlier, in the first discussion of feature vectors, it might be possible to use real-numbered weights to indicate how strongly each feature ought to be considered as evidence for or against a match, using standard gradient descent weight tuning algorithms to make adjustments based on feedback from past performance.

Even without fiddling with individual feature weights, there are some adjustments that might pay off. Depending on the situation or the provenance of probes and labels, we might care more or less about unmatched features in the probe or in the label. For instance, if a probe is hand constructed by a user of the system, we might figure that the features included are all there for a reason, and we really ought not to ignore many of them if we can help it. Alternately, if we have less faith in the focusing ability of our probe generator and more faith in the selection of features included in labels, we might adjust our scoring so that mismatches on the label were across-the-board considered more damaging than mismatches on the probe. Either type of mismatch might be considered more or less negative than matches are counted positive.

Another possibility is that we might arrange for the weights of some features to vary depending on whether other features were matched. Reflecting the hierarchical structure present in our external conception of these situation descriptions (e.g., that the VS-THEME is part of the THEME description), matches on dominant features might gate whether or not we count matches on subordinate features (only count matches on VS-THEMEs if the dominant THEMEs match). This kind of context-sensitive weighting could produce effects similar to what many structured matchers might do in similar circumstances

It is possible to get indefinitely fancy about weighting schemes and scoring formulas. In all cases, **Abby** sticks to the simplest methods that proved successful. Currently, **Abby** uses no per-feature weights at all. In the current scoring formula, overlapping features count twice as much as features missing from either the probe or label; features missing from either index carry the same amount of negative influence.

5.2. From Labels to Matrix

The counting of shared and differing features between probe and label needs to be carried out for each label. Simply treating these binary feature vectors as numeric vectors and calculating the scalar product of a probe and a label yields a count of the number of features in the overlap. Multiplying corresponding elements results in a one only where both vectors contain a one, and zero everywhere else; summing these one and zero elements counts the number of positions where an overlap was found.

The same scalar product trick can be used to count overlap (positively) and difference in each direction (negatively) if we create expanded versions of each label and probe vector, composed from three modified copies of the originals. The three blocks of the new labels could be composed as follows: the first block would be just the original vector; the second block would be a negated version of the original label, with all ones flipped to minus ones and all zeros left as they were; the third block would be the negated complement of the original label, with all ones flipped to zeros and all zeros flipped to minus one. We can, if we wish, scale the entries in each of these three blocks by constants representing the relative importance of matches, missed label features, and missed probe features. The blocks of the tripled probe vector are even easier to describe: the first block would also be just the original probe vector; the second block would be the complement of the original, with ones replaced by zeros and zeros by ones; the third would again be just the original vector.

The scalar product of these tripled label and probe vectors would calculate their similarity rating as described earlier. We can consider a simple example based on a pair of binary vectors with five elements; imagine using this system to calculate a similarity rating for a label 11,001 and a probe 10,101, where each overlapping feature counts $+a$, each feature of the label not in the probe counts $-b$, and each feature of the probe not in the label counts $-c$:

```
Label:    a  a  0  0  a  ||  -b -b  0  0 -b  ||   0  0 -c -c  0
Probe:    1  0  1  0  1  ||   0  1  0  1  0  ||   1  0  1  0  1
          -- -- -- -- --     -- -- -- -- --      -- -- -- -- --
Product:  a  0  0  0  a  ||   0 -b  0  0  0  ||   0  0 -c  0  0   = 2a-b-c
```

At this point we simply take our set of labels and stack them up so that we get a matrix representing the entire memory. In this matrix, the rows represent labeled stories in memory, the columns (broken up into three groups) represent the features of our indices. Multiplying this memory matrix by a probe vector is equivalent to calculating the scalar product of the probe with each label; the result is a new vector containing the match scores for each label. The best matching label is simply the one whose entry is the maximum element of this output vector. **Abby** tells the story associated with the high-scoring label.

5.3. From Matrix to Network

There is a trivial construction (discussed, for instance, in Jordan, 1986) that maps either binary or real-numbered matrices and the operation of multiplying

Figure 3.9.
Sketch of a Possible Network Implementation for Reminding

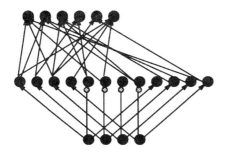

All Labeled Stories

Expanded Probe Feature Encoding
[Input/Complement/Input]

Probe Input Feature Encoding

such a matrix by a vector onto a two layer feedforward network like those described in Kohonen (1988). The first layer has one unit for each feature in our (tripled) feature vector.[10] The second layer has one unit for each label in memory. Connections between feature units and label units are set to mimic the entries of the matrix described above (using the feature's column and label's row). Positive numbers are excitatory links; negative numbers are inhibitory links. This system requires one node for each label, three nodes for each feature of our original index, and, potentially, links from each feature node to each label node. Figure 3.9 sketches this network with the extra preprocessing layer up front.

The decision procedure following the similarity rating is the only non-linearity in this network; winner-take-all competition (see, e.g., Feldman & Ballard, 1982) among the nodes of the final layer, representing the labels would handle the decision if we simply wanted the label with the highest similarity rating. This introduces the need for another set of links, still growing only as the square of the number of labels, at most.

6. DISCUSSION

6.1. Evaluating Abby

6.1.1. Implementation. **Abby** is implemented in CommonLisp using graphics extensions peculiar to SUN Sparcstations on which it currently runs. The program is a collection of tools that support the definition and comparison of indices; the memory constructed using these tools currently contains 500

---

[10] Of course we can introduce another layer to preprocess the input; with one input node per feature, it could feed normal and complement signals to the input layer described in the text.

label indices describing over 250 different situations; each label points to a story (a piece of text that can be displayed for the user). The ultimate target for **Abby**'s memory is 1,000 stories. **Abby** can currently process an average probe against its 500 labels in less than a minute.

There is one fixed format defined for all indices and it currently contains 340 basic fields (that is, fields other than variable binding and relationship encodings). Each field may either be empty, or contain a single filler of a fixed class. Each of these field/filler classes is defined in terms of some fixed set of discriminations; thus each basic field defined for the index format requires some fixed number of bits. The total number of bits in all the basic fields is currently 46,967. The number of possible variable binding bits is 11,020. The number of possible relational bits is about 3.5 million (most of these are always zero and so could obviously be pruned). The average index currently specifies about 22,000 bits. Clearly, viewed as a matrix, **Abby**'s memory is very sparse.

As mentioned earlier, **Abby** sticks to the simple one/zero present/absent representation of each discrimination. It completely eschews weight tuning. It is encouraging that getting reasonable performance from **Abby** does not depend critically on the exact setting of billions of individual weight parameters. On the other hand, I would still expect that were the necessary hardware support and training regimen available, the system's performance could be improved gradually (but only within the limits of represented distinctions) by an automatic weight tuning algorithm.

6.1.2. Performance. I am interested in gauging how well **Abby** does at its task of offering lovelorn advice. This seems to me a more appropriate question than worrying about the system's speed or testing how well its responses correspond to human behavior. Unfortunately, rating this kind of performance is not a simple task, and I do not have solid detailed results to report.

The first problem is, how do you judge the quality of lovelorn advice—particularly when it comes in the form of stories? I have adopted the following standard for judging the appropriateness of a story as advice for a particular problem: with the problem in mind, I allow one minute to read the story and write down, in English, as specific a problem-relevant action recommendation as can be extracted by trying to see the story as advice. I then rate the specificity and quality of that extracted recommendation on a scale ranging from 1 to 7.

I carried out a preliminary review of the system's performance at a time when its memory contained 100 labels. I used labels chosen at random from the corpus as probes to the balance of memory; I set my threshold for acceptable stories as those suggesting specific responses rated 4 or above on the 7-point scale. At that time, sampling indicated that about 20% of the stories in the corpus would serve as acceptable advice for the average probe. In contrast, 80% of the program's three top scoring remindings for each probe (above a threshold) were judged to be acceptable remindings by the same criterion.

I do not claim that this is a rigorous validation of **Abby**'s design. I am however confident that the system was in fact performing well above chance, and that at its current size it continues to do so. Regrettably, this form of evaluation—essentially running psychological tests on a computer program—is too time consuming to be practical on a regular basis and perhaps insufficiently convincing to repay the investment in any case. Nonetheless, lacking any realistic alternative, I plan a final formal evaluation, using independent raters and sample sizes of known statistical validity, once **Abby**'s memory reaches its target size.

Along the way I have also performed some tests to verify that proposed features were having the expected effect. This too is a time consuming effort with sparse payback. It appears that you can eliminate many subsets of the proposed index features without catastrophically degrading performance; there is a lot of redundancy in this feature set (which, to some extent, is a positive attribute). On the other hand, the evidence suggests that broad classes of features (thematic relationship information, variable binding information, various novel social features included in encodings of fillers such as themes), all contribute something to the system's performance. The exception mentioned in earlier discussion was the comparison features which clearly were not, as a class, pulling their weight.

As the memory grows, the chances that the corpus contains a more relevant story for any problem within its domain should increase. So long as the index formalism is sufficiently expressive and the particular indices in memory are coded appropriately **Abby** should continue to improve as its memory grows. So long as the system continues to demonstrate acceptable average performance, we can concentrate on the more useful task of analyzing particular failures. Where the system fails to find relevant stories that are actually in its memory, we can learn something about the shortcomings of the index representations: the need for more detail or nested structure, distinctions we have missed, unrepresented higher order features, major differences in the relative importance of features.

6.2. Why Design Representations by Hand?

Connectionism and neural modeling attract attention for many reasons. They offer practical computational advantages such as expected scalable performance (should appropriate hardware materialize). They have theoretical attractions such as a more obvious mapping to the biological systems we seek to model. The most outstanding feature of networks combines practical advantage with theoretical allure: networks have been demonstrated capable of learning interesting generalizations about their environment—of building recognizably useful and economical representations of their domains. The appeal of getting the programmer out of the loop on this task is obvious.

The question arises then, why have I placed so much emphasis on the design of an index vocabulary and the coding of indices by hand? Why, if I intended to use a connectionist flavored retrieval algorithm in the end, did I not go all the way and have the system learn its own indexing system? There are many reasons why I did not take the learning approach, but they fall into three broad (if slightly fuzzy) categories: the practical, the methodological, and the theoretical.

The main practical objection should be plain. If I had not selected a fixed problem description format and defined a mapping to a fixed feature vector, what would I have used as input to my learning network? All isolated networks (that is to say, all partial experimental systems) require some encoding to map inputs onto the nodes of their input layer. English texts simply will not do. The work reported in Miikkulainen and Dyer (1989) indicates how much training is required to get a network to extract one small set of conceptual regularities from one highly constrained set of texts; further, achieving this level of performance depended on breaking the problem up hierarchically, using internal representations borrowed from earlier representational theorizing. The bulk of the work for **Abby**'s task is actually in the analysis required to map from texts to indices; detailing a target encoding was the major thrust of my research.

An additional practical problem is that the system is simply too large for convenient implementation in connectionist form on current hardware. Most well-known demonstration networks seem to have on the order of from a hundred to a thousand nodes (Rumelhart & McClelland, 1986; Sejnowski & Rosenberg, 1986). **Abby** is supposed to have on the order of a thousand stories and the index vector has about 58,000 base and binding microfeatures (leaving aside the thematic relations, which bring the total up to around 3.5 million microfeatures).

The methodological problems start with the fact that if I had built **Abby** as a learning system, then this would be research on learning rather than on indexing. By that I mean simply that learning mechanisms for networks are still experimental. I was not out to prove that any particular learning mechanism was capable of learning to choose cases appropriately, or worse, that some mechanism I happened to choose turned out to be incapable of doing so.

The next problem is that an undecipherable network that somehow was producing good remindings would not have answered the original questions of index content. The point of this exercise was, from the start, to determine what features were worth attending to in analyzing social situations—to contribute to our understanding of what people know about social situations, and what a computer ought to know too. Again, the point was not to discover an optimal set of features, but to compile some set that would work.

Abby is part of a larger research program with theoretical commitments other than connectionism; the distinctions captured in its representations ought to contribute to other tasks and make contact with other representation theories. Only by explicitly defining the vocabulary of indices is there hope of being able to talk about the inferences that bind index features into a larger conceptual network. In the not-so-long run, there must be some way to construct indices. This will demand mappings among the representations designed specifically for **Abby**, and linkages to other representation theories. Eventually all these representations must make contact with symbolic input (lexical items).

In the end, it is unreasonable to expect a system to learn the sorts of concepts people use in understanding the social world, because no system—certainly no current trainable connectionist network—can have the sorts of experiences people go through to acquire those concepts. At this point we stand a better chance of capturing the distinctions we want through introspection, experimentation, and logical argument, than through automatic data analysis by network. It may well be that we have to figure out what people know before we can figure out how they come to know it.

It is not novel to propose use of semantic feature encoding; but while the technique is well known, applying it can hardly be counted a solved problem. I expect the moral for connectionists ought to be the following: at this stage of the game, for any complex domain and task, someone still as to sit down and do the work of inventing an appropriate set of features to use as a starting point. The need for such knowledge engineering efforts is unlikely to disappear for some time. The work on **Abby** exemplifies that kind of effort, and the methodology underlying it needs to be codified and supported by appropriate tools.

6.3. Connectionism vs. Connection Machinism

There is another style of massively parallel computation that might seem better suited to a style of AI preoccupied with the content of representations. In contrast to connectionism, McDermott (1986) dubbed systems that depend on the communication of structured information among a very large number of nodes as *connection machinism*. In the Connection Machine™ model each node is a complex processor capable of manipulating symbols and sharing them with other processors. The core of the idea is not that you use a particular brand of computer, but that nodes tend to represent recognizable semantic units of a larger grain size than is typical in connectionist systems and these nodes are therefore called upon to do more complex and varied processing and communication.

I alluded to a connection machinist implementation of probe-to-label matching when motivating the use of feature vectors; I described a parallel model with one processor for each label. It is worth examining this option in more detail, and comparing it to **Abby**'s approach because it turns out that at least one researcher has implemented a system with something of this connection machinist spirit to solve the problem of case retrieval for CBR. Kolodner (1989) made two major claims for the PARADYME system: first, that PARADYME's use of heuristics to *select* cases from memory is more flexible than the normal

CBR process of using available information to *restrict* possible remindings; second, that the information PARADYME uses to do its selecting leads to the retrieval of more appropriate (more useful) cases.

Abby turns out to share both these properties to a large extent (and when it does not, it is usually a failing of the implementation, not the paradigm). Consider the six classes of heuristics PARADYME uses to guide selection. Two of those heuristics—preference for matching on salient feature sets, and preference for more specific cases—are automatically implemented by **Abby**'s use of indices, by the chosen encoding of index features, and by the metric for closeness of match. Two others—preference for cases accessed with higher frequency in the past, and preference for cases more recently accessed—depend on simple numeric ratings which can easily be coded in feature vectors; though, as in PARADYME, they would not participate directly in similarity ratings, they could influence the final selection decision.

The final two heuristics—preference for cases that address the system's current goals, and preference for cases that are more easily adaptable—are the most interesting, directly implementing PARADYME's bias towards retrieving more *useful* cases. **Abby** addresses only a limited range of goals (i.e., avoid the described problem, correct the problem, warn about the problem, explain the problem), and has had the freedom to assume the human user will do the adaptation. Still, **Abby** effectively implements something like the goal-directed preference through the choice of features included in its indices. Kolodner, herself, includes a discussion of the systematic variation in the content of salient-feature sets (indices) she has found useful for particular classes of tasks such as finding solutions, evaluating proposed solutions, and explaining outcomes. A reasonable way to express the ease-of-adaptation preference is by manipulating the weights of the features; remember, feature weights are supposed to reflect how relevant a case is, and a case is more relevant when it is easier to adapt into usefulness, less relevant when a lot of work will be required to make it contribute to the current situation.

PARADYME, with its six heuristics, does at least as good a job as serial indexing schemes when it comes to elaborating a set of issues to which case retrieval should be sensitive. The bottom line, then, is that **Abby**'s retrieval mechanism, based on similarity between feature vector indices, can provide most of the desired sensitivity; feature vector indexing and the type of parallelism it allows need not suffer the problems associated with case retrieval based on similarity between surface descriptions of raw cases. The search for an in-principle performance difference between **Abby**'s and PARADYME's models of parallelism must turn to the distinction Kolodner draws between heuristics that *select* and heuristics that *restrict*. The idea is that a system will be better off if it uses its knowledge and heuristics to propose and rate potential remindings (selecting) than it is uses this knowledge to ruthlessly rule out potential remindings (restricting).

Even here, indices, as used in **Abby**, exhibit only part of the restricting effect Kolodner fears. Failure of a label to include some feature specified by the probe will not rule that label out.[11] Restriction only occurs in the sense that the existence of some feature in the case attached to a label, but not actually mentioned as part of the label, will not contribute towards causing the case to be retrieved. This use of indices is in fact more limiting than Kolodner's use of salient feature sets; where **Abby** will only draw cases into consideration based on the content of its indices, PARADYME's retrieval mechanism includes an extra phase prior to invocation of the heuristics (meaning, prior to preference by salient feature sets) that apparently has access to the entire content of the case.

The justification offered for allowing such unrestricted access to whole cases is that it would be unreasonable to expect the system to have correctly guessed, in advance, all the possible indices that could be assigned to a case that might some day turn out to be useful. PARADYME's concession to this reality however is equivalent to ceding a significant piece of the indexing hypothesis. Instead, I would prefer, in the spirit of Kolodner's (1984) earlier work on *Cyrus*, to handle such hard retrieval problems by postulating an explicit inference process that recasts the probe until it succeeds in matching an existing label in memory. The need for such a memory search might serve as a warrant for reindexing the case under a new label.

To summarize: what differences there are between **Abby** and PARADYME seem to hinge less on what sorts of heuristics guide reminding, than on a fundamental disagreement over the extent to which case retrieval is usefully thought of as being based on indices. Underlying this disagreement are fundamentally different assumptions about what sorts of computations can be carried out efficiently; connection machinism assumes that any information can be broadcast to any node and matched against the appropriate part of an arbitrary description, while connectionism suggests such flexibility is not cheap. It is not clear that we need this extra flexibility in the retrieval phase since there are many other processes—probe elaboration, retrieval evaluation, directed interpretation, application tweaking—that might make up for suboptimal retrievals.

7. SUMMARY

Massively parallel implementation suits CBR case retrieval for many reasons. The most obvious is the necessity that the retrieval process scale up to handle efficiently a very large number of cases. The kind of parallelism suggested by connectionism not only meets this criterion, but offers other advantages such as a

---

[11] This fear seems to be based on experience with discrimination networks; here, parallelism per se seems to be the liberating influence.

clean definition of partial match and efficient inference control. At the same time, the discipline of fitting indices into a fixed format contributes towards clarity in specifying the content of indices.

Abby demonstrates not only that this approach will work, but that it works at little cost. The mapping from structured index format into a feature vector is straightforward. We continue to reap the benefits and bear the burden of theorizing appropriate representations for the content of our indices. We do not lose the ability to make retrieval sensitive to the sorts of heuristic influences identified by researchers like Kolodner. The main cost is an acceptable amount of inefficiency in implementation of the representation system.

Beyond that, all that is sacrificed is the ability to compose old elements into arbitrary novel representations on the fly; from the perspective of this study of indexing, that hardly seems like a sacrifice of either theoretical elegance or practical capability. Remember the picture we started with: the agent with a limited repertoire categorizing each situation in terms of a reasonable response. At any time there are only so many things the agent might do, so many indices it could have in its memory. If each index is finite, then a generalized index that subsumes all current indices must exist at any time.

The only question then, is whether this overall structure will have any interesting regularities or comprehensible structure. It is worth assuming that the union of all indices will meet this criteria, or more accurately, that as in the case of **Abby**'s indices, a designer's fiat can usefully invent regularity. At this point, as we try to understand what an index might be and as we code indices by hand or imagine algorithms to generate indices automatically, we can use all the regularity we can invent.

REFERENCES

Agre, P., & Chapman, D. (1987). Pengi: An implementation of a theory of activity. *Proceedings of the Sixth National Conference on Artificial Intelligence* (pp. 268–272). Los Altos, CA: Morgan Kaufmann.

Ashley, K., & Rissland, E. (1988). Waiting on weighting: A symbolic least commitment approach. *Proceedings of the Seventh National Conference on Artificial Intelligence* (pp. 239–244). San Mateo, CA: Morgan Kaufmann.

Burke, R. (1989). Understanding and responding in conversation: Case retrieval with natural language. *Proceedings of the Second Case-Based Reasoning Workshop* (pp. 230–234). San Mateo, CA: Morgan Kaufmann.

Carbonell, J. (1979). *Subjective understanding: Computer models of belief systems.* Unpublished doctoral dissertation, Yale University.

Domeshek, E. (1990). Volition and advice: Suggesting strategies for fixing problems in social situations. *Proceedings of the Twelfth Annual Conference of the Cognitive Science Society* (pp. 844–851). Hillsdale, NJ: Erlbaum.

Domeshek, E. (1992). *Do the right thing: A component theory for indexing stories as social advice.* Unpublished doctoral dissertation, Yale University.

Feldman, J.A., & Ballard, D.H. (1982). Connectionist models and their properties *Cognitive Science*, 6, 205–254.
Hammond, K. (1989). *Case-based planning: Viewing planning as a memory task.* Boston: Academic Press.
Hinton, G. (1981). Implementing semantic networks in parallel hardware. In G. Hinton & J. Anderson (Eds.) *Parallel models of associative memory* (pp. 161–187). Hillsdale, NJ: Erlbaum.
Jones, E. (1990). Brainstormer: A model of advice taking. *Proceedings of the Twelfth Annual Conference of the Cognitive Science Society* (pp. 269–276). Hillsdale, NJ: Erlbaum.
Jordan, M. (1986). An introduction to linear algebra in parallel distributed processing. In D. Rumelhart & J. McClelland (Eds.), *Paralleled distributed processing: Explorations in the microstructure of cognition* (Vol. 1, pp. 365–422). Cambridge, MA: Bradford, MIT Press.
Kohonen, T. (1988). Correlation matrix memories. In J. Anderson & E. Rosenfeld (Eds.), *Neurocomputing: Foundations of research* (pp. 174–180). Cambridge, MA: MIT Press.
Kolodner, J. (1984). *Retrieval and organizational strategies in conceptual memory: A computer model.* Hillsdale, NJ: Erlbaum.
Kolodner, J. (1989). Selecting the best case for a case-based reasoner. *Proceedings of the Eleventh Annual Conference of the Cognitive Sciences Society* (pp. 155–162). Hillsdale, NJ. Erlbaum.
Kolodner, J., Simpson, R., & Sycara-Cyranski, K. (1985). A process model of case-based reasoning in problem-solving. *Proceedings of the Ninth International Joint Conference on Artificial Intelligence* (pp. 284–290). Los Altos, CA: Morgan Kaufmann.
Lehnert, W. (1981). Plot units and narrative summarization. *Cognitive Science*, 4 293–331.
Marchand, P., Krishnamoorthy, A., Ambs, P., & Esener, S. (1990). Optoelectronic associative recall using motionless-head parallel readout optical disk. In B. Javidi (Ed.), *Optical information processing systems and architectures II* (Vol. 1347, pp. 86–97). Bellingham, WA: International Society for Optical engineering.
McDermott, D. (1986). Comments during a panel discussion on connectionism. *The Fifth National Conference on Artificial Intelligence.*
Miikkulainen, R., & Dyer, M. (1989). A modular neural network architecture for sequential paraphrasing of script-base stories. *Proceedings in the 1989 IEEE INNS International Joint Conference On Neural Networks* (Vol. 2, pp. II–47 - II–56). Piscataway, NJ: IEEE TAB Neural Network Committee.
Owens, C. (1988). Domain-independent prototype cases for planning. *Proceedings of the First Workshop on Case based Reasoning* (pp. 302–311). San Mateo, CA: Morgan Kaufmann.
Rumelhart, D., & McClelland, J. (1986). On learning the past tense of english verbs. In D. Rumelhart & J. McClelland (Eds.), *Parallel distributed processing: Explorations in the microstructure of cognition* (Vol. 2, pp. 216–271). Cambridge, MA: Bradford, MIT Press.
Schank, R. (1982). *Dynamic memory.* Cambridge, UK: Cambridge University Press.
Schank, R. (1986). *Explanation patterns: Understanding mechanically and creatively.* Hillsdale, NJ: Erlbaum.

Schank, R. (1991). *Tell me a story*. New York: Scribner's Sons.
Schank, R., & Abelson, R. (1977). *Scripts, plans, goals, and understanding*. Hillsdale, NJ: Erlbaum.
Schank, R., Brand, M., Burke, R., Domeshek, E., Edelson, D., Ferguson, W., Freed, M., Jona, M., Krulwich, B., Ohmaye, E., Osgood, R., & Pryor, L. (1990). Towards a general content theory of indices. *Working Notes of the American Association for Artificial Intelligence Spring Symposium on Case-Based Reasoning*. Palo Alto, CA.
Schank, R., Osgood, R., Brand, M., Burke, R., Domeshek, E., Edelson, D., Ferguson, W., Freed, M., Jona, M., Krulwich, B., Ohmaye, E., & Pryor, L. (1990). *A content theory of memory indexing* (Tech. Rep. No. 2). Chicago, IL: Northwestern University, The Institute for the Learning Sciences.
Seifert, C. (1987). *Mental representations of social knowledge: A computational approach to reasoning about relationship*. Unpublished doctoral dissertation, Yale University.
Seifert, C. (1988). A retrieval model for case-based memory. *Unpublished Proceedings of the Case-Based Reasoning Workshop at the Seventh National Conference on Artificial Intelligence* (pp. 120–125). Minneapolis, MN.
Sejnowski, T. & Rosenberg, C. (1986). *Nettalk: A parallel network that learns to read aloud* (Tech. Rep. No. JHU/EECS–86101). Baltimore, MD: Electrical Engineering and Computer Science, Johns Hopkins University.
Subramanian, D., & Woodfill, J. (1990). Subjective ontologies. *Working Notes, American Association for Artificial Intelligence Spring Symposium Series, Symposium on Planning in Uncertain, Unpredictable, or Changing Environments* (pp. 130–135). Stanford, CA.
Tversky, A. (1988). Features of similarity. In A. Collins & E. Smith (Eds.), *Readings in cognitive science: A perspective from psychology and artificial intelligence* (pp. 290–302). San Mateo, CA: Morgan Kaufmann.
Wilensky, R. (1983). *Planning and understanding: A computational approach to human reasoning*. Reading, MA: Addison-Wesley.

4
The Case for Nonconnectionist Associative Retrieval in Case-Based Reasoning Systems*

Piero P. Bonissone, Lisa F. Rau,
George Berg

1. INTRODUCTION

Case-based reasoning (CBR) is the process of using previously acquired solutions to problems as the basis for computing new solutions to new problems. The stored problem descriptions and solutions are *cases*. CBR has been applied to problem solving in many different application areas, for example, legal (Ashley, 1988; Oskamp, Walker, Schrickx, & Vanderberg, 1989; Rissland & Skalak, 1989), medical (Koton, 1988), financial (Bonissone & Dutta, 1990), and engineering (Hennessy & Hinkle, 1991).

Case-based reasoning can provide an alternative to rule-based expert systems, and is especially appropriate when the number of rules needed to capture an expert's knowledge is unmanageable. CBR can respond better than expert systems when the problems are not static. It can work in problem domains where the underlying models used for solutions are not well understood. It has historically had its greatest success in areas where individual cases or precedents govern the decision-making processes, as in case law.

Any CBR system consists of four phases: (a) problem input, (b) case retrieval, (c) case modification, and (d) solution output. We believe that the second phase, case retrieval, is of primary importance to the overall effectiveness of any CBR system, for the following reasons:

1. Retrieving the case that will yield the best solution to a new problem ensures the best solution within the system's capability. This may or may not be the

---
* The authors would like to thank all the anonymous reviewers whose comments greatly improved this chapter in many ways. Saad Ayub was also helpful in preparing the examples, and commented on a draft of the chapter.

case that matches the new problem the most with respect to superficial (i.e., surface or "raw") features.
2. Retrieving the case or cases that yield the best solution to a new problem must include some computation of the similarities and differences between the input problem and the retrieved cases. All subsequent case modification uses this computation as a basis.

The next few sections further detail the importance of retrieval to CBR. We describe our Combining Approximate Reasoning Systems, CARS, and show why its marker passing and intersection search method of case retrieval is more appropriate for CBR than connectionist approaches, despite their intuitive appeal. In detailing the reasoning processes that CARS uses, we indicate places where it is difficult to duplicate the processing using connectionist schemes. We close with a comparison between CARS and other kinds of CBR systems.

1.1. The Importance of Retrieval to CBR

Case-based reasoning systems are only as good as the cases within their case bases. Moreover, even the best of cases are useless if they cannot be appropriately retrieved.

One primary factor that influences the effectiveness of a case-based reasoning system is the effectiveness of the underlying retrieval mechanism that retrieves cases. Ideally, a retrieval mechanism for CBR would exhibit these properties:

> *Associative retrieval:* Any feature of the input case can be a key or index used for retrieval . This is also called *content addressability*. This gives the retrieval system the flexibility to retrieve cases from memory along any of the represented indices of an input case, rather than a prespecified one.
>
> *Pattern completion:* The retrieval mechanism should attempt to find matching cases even if not all of the features of the input case are given.
>
> *Approximate matching:* Cases should be retrieved even when features of the input problem match case features inexactly. For example, a *stock offering* is not the same as a *stock swap*; however, for the purposes of case-based reasoning, it may turn out that the similarities between these two features are more important than the differences. This property is sometimes referred to as *data fault tolerance*.

In addition to being desirable properties for the retrieval mechanism in a case-based reasoner, they are also the properties of distributed representation

NONCONNECTIONIST ASSOCIATIVE RETRIEVAL 171

connectionist networks (also known as Parallel Distributed Processing (PDP) networks). Hinton, McClelland, and Rumelhart (1986) cited these as principal properties—ones which make PDP models worthwhile. Moreover, they claim that these properties cannot be duplicated with more conventional representation schemes. To quote from Rumelhart and McClelland's (1986) *Parallel Distributed Processing*:

> It is, of course, possible to implement some kind of content addressability of memory on a standard computer in a variety of different ways. One way is to search sequentially, examining each memory in the system to find the memory or the set of memories which has the particular content specified in the cue. An alternative, somewhat more efficient, scheme involves some form of indexing—keeping a list, for every content a memory might have, of which memories have that content.
>
> Such an indexing scheme can be made to work with error-free probes, but it will break down if there is an error in the specification of the retrieval cue. There are possible ways of recovering from such errors, but they lead to the kind of combinatorial explosions which plague this kind of computer implementation. (p.26)

In this chapter we show that this claim does not hold true, at least not for the retrieval mechanism for CBR systems. We describe the associative retrieval mechanism of the CARS case-based reasoning system. The mechanism, which is implemented, performs associative retrieval, does pattern completion, and is data fault tolerant. Yet it does not suffer from the combinatorial explosion predicted by Rumelhart and McClelland. There are two primary reasons for this:

1. The index or "list, for every content a memory night have, of which memories have that content" (see above) is implicit in the conceptual, structured hierarchy. For example, a "memory" that has a "content" of MANUFACTURING-FIRM (i.e., MANUFACTURING-FIRM1) can access another memory that has a content of MANUFACTURING-FIRM (i.e., MANUFACTURING-FIRM2) through the links necessarily present relating MANUFACTURING-FIRM1 and MANUFACTURING-FIRM2 to a general category of MANUFACTURING-FIRM.
2. This same structured hierarchy allows for the relaxed and partial matching (allowing errors in the matched objects) also claimed to be impossible without combinatorial explosion. The time to find all memories with contents of MANUFACTURING-FIRMs is not proportional to the number of other concepts present in other memories.

The implicit index allows indexing to proceed as a hashing function (Corman, Leiserson, & Rivest, 1990), so that the time to retrieve related concepts is not more than $O(1)$. That is, a constant amount of time is needed which is independent of the number of concepts. This indexing function occurs once for every slot in a case, and therefore bounds the computational complexity, while still allowing for relaxed matching.

The rest of this chapter describes the prototype CBR system that uses this method of retrieval, presents a simple example, and concludes with a discussion of the advantages of symbolic representation and retrieval over connectionist distributed representations.

2. OVERVIEW

2.1. The CARS System

CARS stands for Combining Approximate Reasoning System. CARS is a prototype system for performing precedent-based reasoning in the domain of corporate mergers and acquisitions. CARS' CBR component is designed to retrieve cases using an existing GE (General Electric) text processing, conceptual information storage and retrieval system called SCISOR (Jacobs & Rau, 1990; Rau, 1987). The SCISOR system reads the text of short stories about mergers and acquisitions, saves a conceptual representation in its database, and recalls to working memory those in its database that are "similar" to an input "probe" case representation. Figure 4.1 illustrates a sample story and conceptual representation of a story read by SCISOR. The SCISOR prototype is used in two ways in the CARS system:

1. SCISOR serves as a front end to the CARS system by automatically populating a case base with surface features extracted from text stories about mergers and acquisitions. These surface features are augmented with abstract features by CARS.
2. The retrieval mechanism used in the SCISOR system to answer natural language queries about the contents of the stories is used to perform the first two stages of retrieval in the CARS CBR system.

The natural language text interpretation technology embodies in SCISOR is not relevant to the operation of the CARS system; it is discussed in detail in (Jacobs & Ray, 1990; Rau, 1987) and elsewhere. The retrieval mechanism is described in more detail here as it is the portion of the CARS system that we believe provides the same functionality as PDP systems without the disadvantages.

2.2. Overview of CARS

What is most distinctive about the CARS system is its integration of several different technologies into one system, such as CBR and RBR (rule-based reasoning), SCISOR, and uncertain reasoning.

Figure 4.1.
Sample Story and Template from SCISOR

```
PHILLIP MORRIS - KRAFT
Mr. John M. Richman, the CHairman and Chief Executive Officer of Kraft, Inc.,
announced a radical restructuring of Kraft in response to a hostile tender
offer by Philip Morris. The offer of $90 a share in cash for all of the out-
standing common stock of Kraft had been announced just five days earlier on
October 18, 1988. Kraft, a maker of foods, is known for its brand names such
as Miracle Whip, Velveeta, Parkay, Chiffon and Breyer's.

         C-CORP-TAKEOVER
             R-SUBEVENT:       OFFER
             R-AMOUNT/SHARE:   $90
             R-DATE:           October 18, 1988
             R-QUALITY:        HOSTILE
             R-TARGET:         C-BUSINESS-ORG
                                   R-NAME:       Kraft, Inc.
                                   R-CEO:        Mr. John M. Richman
                                   R-CHAIRMAN:   Mr. John M. Richman
                                   R-BUSINESS:   FOOD
                                   R-BRANDS:
                                                 Velveeta
                                                 Miracle-Whip
                                                 Parkey
                                                 Chiffon
                                                 Breyer's
                                   R-PRODUCT:    POLYMER RESINS
             R-SUITOR:         C-BUSINESS-ORG
                                   R-NAME:       Phillip Morris
             R-RESPONSE:       RESTRUCTURE
```

In particular, two reasoning modalities are integrated in CARS: RBR and CBR. The reasoning systems implementing these modalities have a common characteristic: their ability to manage the uncertainty intrinsic in complex problems, such as the mergers and acquisition application.

In RBR, uncertainty is present both in the domain knowledge (*plausible rules* and *fuzzy/imprecise* premises) and in the inference techniques used to search the rule graph. The Plausible Reasoning Module (PRIMO) (Aragones, Bonissone, & Stillman, 1990; Bonissone, 1989) is the rule-based reasoner, and integrates the theories of possibilistic and default reasoning.

In CBR, uncertainty is present in the semantics of *abstract features* used to index the cases, in the evaluation and (hierarchical) aggregation of the *similarity measures* computed across these features, in the determination of *relevancy and saliency* of the similar cases, and in the solution adaptation phase. In CARS, most of this uncertainty is modeled by using fuzzy predicates and plausible rules to derive abstract features from the surface features. The prescreening using abstract features and aggregate similarity measures of the database uses a customizable mechanism to evaluate similarity based on surface features contained in the textual description of the case.

The next sections give brief overviews of the application area and the CBR component of CARS.

2.3. The M&A Application

We have built our first CARS application to reason in the domain of mergers and acquisitions (M&A). The M&A area has many attributes which make it an ideal candidate domain for research with CARS. M&A is a field where multiple agents, with different goals and viewpoints, attempt to plan strategies using incomplete, or uncertain information. In addition, M&A cases develop over time, allowing us to work on the problems of representing and reasoning about events in sequences.

Furthermore, the process of analyzing an M&A situation requires the use of case-based reasoning methods (e.g., in the area of antitrust considerations), rule-based reasoning methods (e.g., in the area of strategy identification) or both (e.g., determining the price to offer for shares based on company worth derived from rules or derived from the price paid for the most similar previous offering). While many metrics can be used to judge the ultimate outcome of a takeover attempt, it is possible to have at least one crisp evaluation measure, that is, whether the takeover was ultimately successful or not.

Some of the reasons why M&A is a good application area to perform case-based reasoning research in are also reasons why we feel a purely connectionist approach would be inappropriate. For example, working with temporally related events can be cumbersome with connectionist systems. Secondly, with CBR systems, there is not necessarily one best case from which to perform reasoning with. CARS retrieves a *list* of the best cases, something connectionist systems do not do "naturally." These and other areas where we feel our symbolic approach yields a better architecture than a connectionist architecture are developed more fully in the next section.

The next sections give brief overviews of the case representation, retrieval, and reasoning processes that are used by the CARS system.

2.3.1. Case Representation. The cases in our case database are viewed as situation/solution pairs. The situation is represented by the top-level goal(s) and the starting state. The solution is represented by a network of events and a linear sequence of states. Events and states are related by explanatory information encoded as causal, temporal, and membership links. Subsets of events are grouped into interpretations to facilitate their indexing and reuse.

Given the dynamic nature of M&A cases, we have chosen to divide each case into five phases: initial condition, pre-tender, tender-negotiation, outcome, and long-term results. Each of the phases have fairly well-defined starting points, which allow us to map the incoming information into case representations. It should be noted that the phase partition of a case is orthogonal with the case representation of states and events. Within each phase, the case is represented by state changes, goals, events, and interpretations.

States. The initial state of each object is represented by a set of state variables (surface and abstract features) with their associated values. These state variables represent the known values of the features (slots) of the object instances which define the case. Each state change contains only the slots whose values have changed. State changes are temporally linked with other state changes, forming a complete ordering. The state changes can be indexed from the event network, by one or more events. We can observe the linear state change evolution in Figure 4.2, which illustrates the initial state of the Kraft–Phillip Morris takeover case (*STATE-KPM-PHASE1*) and a transition of state changes (*STATE-KPM-2* and *STATE-KPM-3*).

Goals. Goals specify a state (or partial state) to be reached, by specifying the values the state variables should hold. In addition, the goal contains a measure of goal attainment.

Events. Events are objects that associate action, goal, and state information. Each event has at least two slots: the (instantiated) *action* used to achieve the goal and the *context* (i.e., the state at the time this event occurred). Additional optional slots can be used to describe goal, cost, and time duration of the event.

Events are temporally linked with other events, forming a partial ordering. Known causal relations between events (or between events and state changes) can be represented by *causal* links. In addition, events can be linked to a state which *enabled* the event, thus capturing the action preconditions.

The same Figure 4.2 illustrates the event *KPM-E-TENDER-OFFER-PM-01*, its context (*STATE-KPM-PHASE1*), and two events causally linked to the first one: *KPM-E-REJECT-TENDER-OFFER-K-01* and *KPM-E-ANNOUNCE-RE-STRUCTURE-PLAN-K-01*.

4. Interpretations. Interpretations are explanations for the occurrence of sets of events. They may contain some local knowledge such as a goal, objects affected by the interpretation, etc. The interpretations are currently used to represent the case analysis of a domain expert. At some levels these interpretations can be seen as steps in the hierarchical expansion of a plan and can be used to augment the goal/plan hierarchy. In our example, the two events *KPM-E-REJECT-TENDER-OFFER-K-01* and *KPM-E-ANNOUNCE-RESTRUCTURE-PLAN-K-01* are grouped under the same interpretation. This interpretation describes a defensive strategy adopted by Kraft to oppose the takeover attempt by Phillip Morris.

2.3.2. Case Retrieval. Retrieval in CARS is a three-stage process.

The first stage marks and intersects nodes to retrieve the most likely candidates for case retrieval. It uses a variation on a spreading-activation, or marker-passing, intersection search (Hendler, 1987; Norvig, 1986). As in a traditional marker-passing system, binary (present or not present) marks are placed at nodes in the conceptual hierarchy corresponding to features of the input case.

The conceptual hierarchy itself is implemented in a knowledge representation language formalism similar in spirit to KL-ONE (Brachman & Schmolze, 1985) and Kodiak (Wilensky, 1984). It contains two primary relationships of category

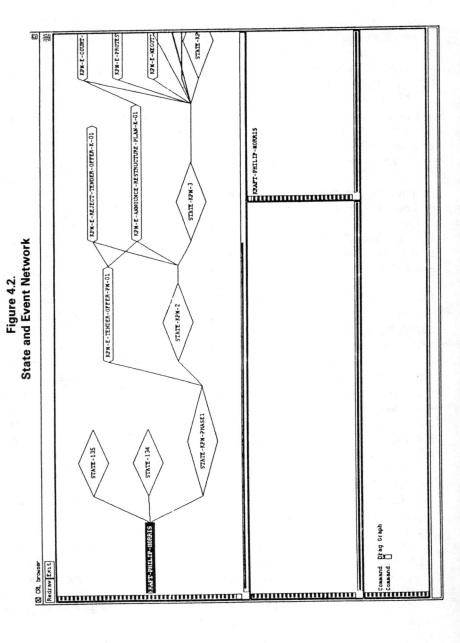

**Figure 4.2.
State and Event Network**

membership ("is-a") and features ("has-a"). The average depth in the hierarchy is six, and it contains lexical mappings between lexical items (i.e., words) and concepts used to represent the meaning of the words (Jacobs & Rau, 1984). Currently, there are over 1,000 abstract concepts in the hierarchy and over 10,000 specific (word-level) concepts.

The marks placed at nodes in the hierarchy are then propagated across the links between concepts, as in a normal intersection search. However, unlike typical marker-passing systems, an *intersection* takes place at the case or cases indexed by the nodes in the hierarchy, not at the conceptual nodes themselves. This allows marker passing to be used to perform case retrieval, as opposed to its traditional use in determining binary (between two nodes) connections between concepts for inferencing (Charniak, 1983; Hendler, 1987; Norvig, 1986). These cases are then examined in subsequent states for their degree of match with the input case. This marking and intersecting process is described below in the *marking* and *intersecting* paragraphs.

The second stage is an evaluation of the candidate cases returned by the first stage with respect to the relationships between the individual elements of the cases. This process is a modified form of graph matching, similar to that described in (Levinson, 1990).

The third stage incorporates reasoning with abstract features of the cases to filter the results of the second stage, and perform some of the case-based reasoning functions. It also uses the *relationships* that exist between surface features for ranking similarity. In the following discussion of the retrieval process, we assume (for maximum generality) that the input case is a *graph* structure consisting of nodes and arcs.

Stage 1: Marking. Each node in the graph causes a set of nodes in the case memory to be *activated*. This set of nodes can be modified depending on such end-use-specific features as the depth and breadth of the conceptual hierarchy and the types of inexact matches that are desirable in the domain. The determination of the set of nodes can be fully automated by making it a function of the total number of instances to be marked. For example, the maximum number of instances of any node in the system can be divided into three parts to provide two thresholds that determine when to use the three conditions described below. Suppose the node with the greatest number of instances is the **company** node, and it has 600 instances. Then a node in the probe that has less than 200 instances would use Condition 3, nodes with between 200 and 400 instances would use Condition 2, and the remainder would use Condition 1.

Hard coding particular rules for how to match particular features may make the system less autonomous than a connectionist implementation, but in return, they can compute more precise and "intelligent" (i.e., domain-specific) similarities.

The most restrictive set of nodes to be activated is the set of all instances of exactly the same **type** as the input node. In Figure 4.3, the input node is a

Figure 4.3.
Activated Node Set: Input Node: Food

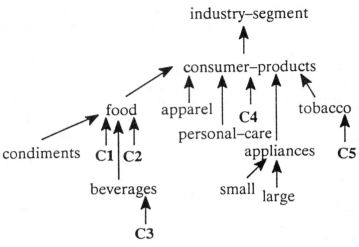

Input Node: **C1**
condition 1: all instances of the exact same type: **C2**
condition 2: all descendants: **C2** and **C3**
condition 3: direct descendants of all ancestors: **C2, C3** and **C4**

category of companies that are in the industry segment with type food. The three conditions are:

> **Condition 1:** All instances of the exact same type (i.e., all instances that have the same *parent*).
> **Condition 2:** All descendants (i.e., all instances in the transitive closure of the *children-of* relationship).
> **Condition 3:** All direct descendants of all ancestors (i.e., all instances that are *children* of any *ancestor*) and all descendants (i.e., all instances in the transitive closure of the *children-of* relationship).

For Condition 1, this set of activated nodes would cause the cases that contained the highest proportion of nodes of the same types to be retrieved. A more relaxed condition on the set of nodes to be activated is the set of all *descendants* of the type of the input node (Condition 2). A still more relaxed condition incorporates all instances that are direct children of all ancestors of an input node (Condition 3), as is graphically depicted in Figure 4.3. Note that this first pass retrieval, computing similarity at the "type" categorization level is augmented in the reasoning stage with abstract features.

NONCONNECTIONIST ASSOCIATIVE RETRIEVAL   179

Intersecting. Every activated node adds one to a score accumulated in its containing case. This is different from the traditional notion of intersection search in that intersections occur at the case level as opposed to the traditional intersection *between two nodes*. An intersection is detected if the case threshold is exceeded. The case threshold is a (again, user-modifiable) proportion of the surface features in the case.

Stage 2: Checking. Most spreading activation systems (e.g., Cohen & Kjeldsen, 1987; Hendler, 1987; Norvig, 1986) contain a path-checking phase during which candidates returned by the first two phases (marking and intersecting) are checked for their goodness of fit to the types of paths desired.

An analogous process to this path-checking phase for intersecting graph structures is a graph matching phase. Graph matching proceeds by taking a node-node match, examining the similar or identical relationships they participate in, and checking if the values in those relationships also match. Consider the example shown in Figure 4.4.

The **selling-2** instance marks the **corporate-takeover-1** instance through Condition 2. The *merchandise* role of **selling-2** unifies with the *target* role of the **corporate-takeover**. The filler of these roles (**Bruck Plastics**) is identical. This process continues until all the nodes are accounted for, backtracking if necessary.

This process results in a rank-ordered list of the best matching cases, based on a combination of how closely the surface features of the cases in the case base match the probe, and the relationships of the features of the match.

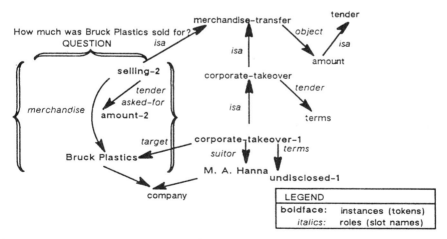

**Figure 4.4.
Question and Answer Representation**

The retrieval mechanism described here is also used to perform natural language question answering in the GE NLToolset (Jacobs & Rau, 1990), and is described more fully in (Rau, 1987).

Stage 3: Reasoning. The results of the first two stages of retrieval (marking/intersecting and checking) are used as input to the abstract feature generation mechanism described in the next sections.

Abstract Features. The raw cases retrieved by the first two stages of retrieval are analyzed and augmented with abstract (derived) features, as indicated in Figure 4.5. Eighteen abstract features have been extracted from fifty-nine surface features. This process is a typical example of integration between CBR and RBR in the CARS system. In this case the case-based reasoner activates the rule-based reasoner to augment the case indexing information.

Figure 4.5 shows a screen dump of CARS. In the top-right window of the screen we can observe a subset of surface features (e.g., *political-attitude*, *public-attitude*, *current-assets*, current-liabilities, etc.) and abstract features (e.g., *short-term-FC*, *long-term-FC*, *coverage*, *profitability*,...) describing Kraft, the target company in the probe.

For each abstract feature we have defined a term set of linguistic values. For instance, from the same Figure 4.5 we can see the linguistic value assigned to each abstract feature: (*short-term-FC* ← *STRONG*), (*long-term-FC* ← *AVERAGE*), (*coverage* ←*VERY-STRONG*), etc. A term set of seven linguistic values, ranging from *VERY-WEAK* to *VERY-STRONG*, was used to define the partial degrees of strength of each abstract feature. The term set is displayed in the second column of Figure 4.9.

Each linguistic value is defined by a label and its semantics. The semantics are represented by the membership distribution of a fuzzy set, defined on the unit interval, establishing a partial ordering among the labels. The meaning of the terms *STRONG*, *VERY-STRONG*, and *AVERAGE* are illustrated in the third column of Figure 4.9 and discussed in the section entitled Feature Value Comparisons. Similarity measures, defined as the complement of metrics between fuzzy sets, are evaluated for each abstract feature. Subsets of these similarity measures are then aggregated to determine higher level similarity.

We can observe that the case description has been augmented by interpretations and judgments about the raider and target's financial conditions, the quality of the tender offer, and other subjective assessments usually provided by a financial analyst. The text itself only provides the explicit information available about a case (surface features), as illustrated in Figure 4.1. In real-world situations, financial analysts supplement that information using domain knowledge. In our case that knowledge has been encoded into a PRIMO rule base, allowing us to generate abstract features such as *short-term financial condition* from industry sector surface features such as *receivable-turnover*, *inventory turnover*, *acid ratio*, and company surface features such as *cost of goods sold*, *inventory*, *annual credit sale*, *accounts receivable*, etc., as illustrated by the graph in Figure 4.6.

Figure 4.5.
Target Surface and Abstract Features

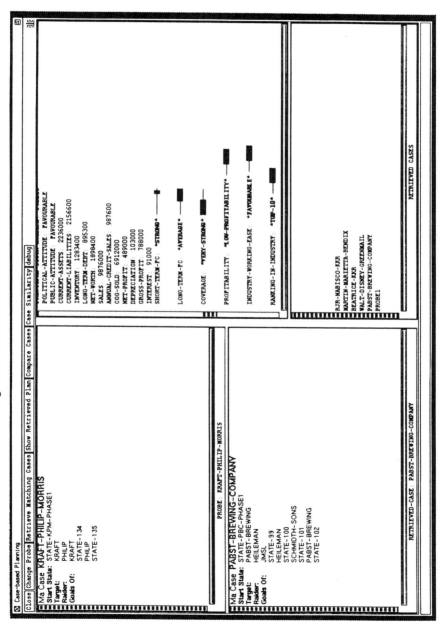

Figure 4.6.
Derivation of Abstract Features From Surface Features

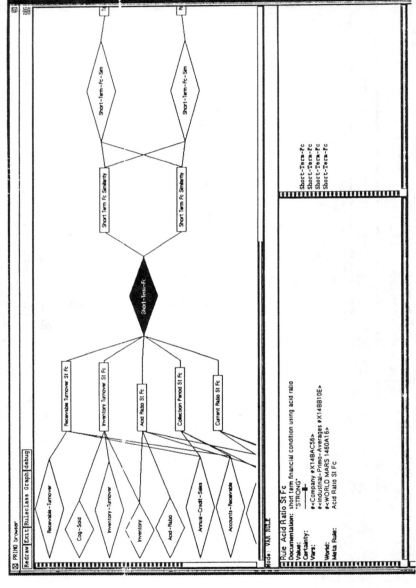

This graph, which is part of the PRIMO browser, illustrates the functional dependency between variables (represented by diamonds) and rules (represented by rectangles). For instance, we can see that the rule *inventory turnover ST FC* uses two company surface features (*cost of goods sold, inventory*), and one industry sector surface feature (*inventory turnover*). We can see that the value of the abstract feature *short-term-financial-condition* is *STRONG*. This value is the result of the aggregation of the output of the five rules. As we will see in the following sections, *STRONG* is a linguistic value from a given term set, defining the relative strength of the target company financial conditions in the short term.

Similarities. Similarities are defined at many levels: between individual abstract features (e.g., *target-short term FC-SIM* (which is the similarity between the target financial conditions in the probe and the retrieved case); and between groups of abstract features (e.g., *target-target similarity* (which is the overall similarity between the target company in the probe and in the case).

For example, Figure 4.7 illustrates a subset of the target abstract feature similarities (from *target short term FC-SIM* to *target-company-mgmt-involvement-sim* and their corresponding linguistic values. The bar following the linguistic value represents the degree of certainty for the value assignment. Certainty is defined on the [0,1] interval. The bar's lower bound is a measure of positive evidence supporting the assignment (i.e., a degree of belief). The distance between the bar's upper bound and one is a measure of evidence refuting the assignment (i.e., a degree of doubt). The bar's width indicates the amount of ignorance in qualifying the assignment (i.e., the lack of commitment in supporting or refuting the value assignment). PRIMO uncertainty calculi maintain and propagate the certainty interval throughout the deductive inference process. The interested reader is referred to references (Aragones, Bonissone, & Stillman, 1990; Bonissone, 1989).

Similarity can be further aggregated by combining *target-target-similarity*, and *raider-raider-similarity* into a similarity measure for each phase. This is discussed in the section entitled *Combinations of Similarities* and illustrated in Figure 4.12.

After cases are retrieved with this initial associative retrieval method, a similarity module incorporates abstract features not currently inferred by the natural language analysis program into the retrieved cases. These cases are analyzed, and the similarities between the input case and the candidate cases evaluated. We briefly describe each of these processes next; more details on the techniques can be found in (Bonissone, Blau, & Ayub, 1990).

2.3.3. Similarity module. The similarity module takes as input the cases returned by the retrieval system, the probe, and information relating to the needs of the reasoner. The retrieved cases and probe are augmented with a set of abstract features. Appropriate similarity measures are chosen and applied based on the needs of the reasoner (e.g., goal satisfaction or establishment of precedent), and the most similar cases are returned.

Figure 4.7.
Similarity Measures of Abstract Features

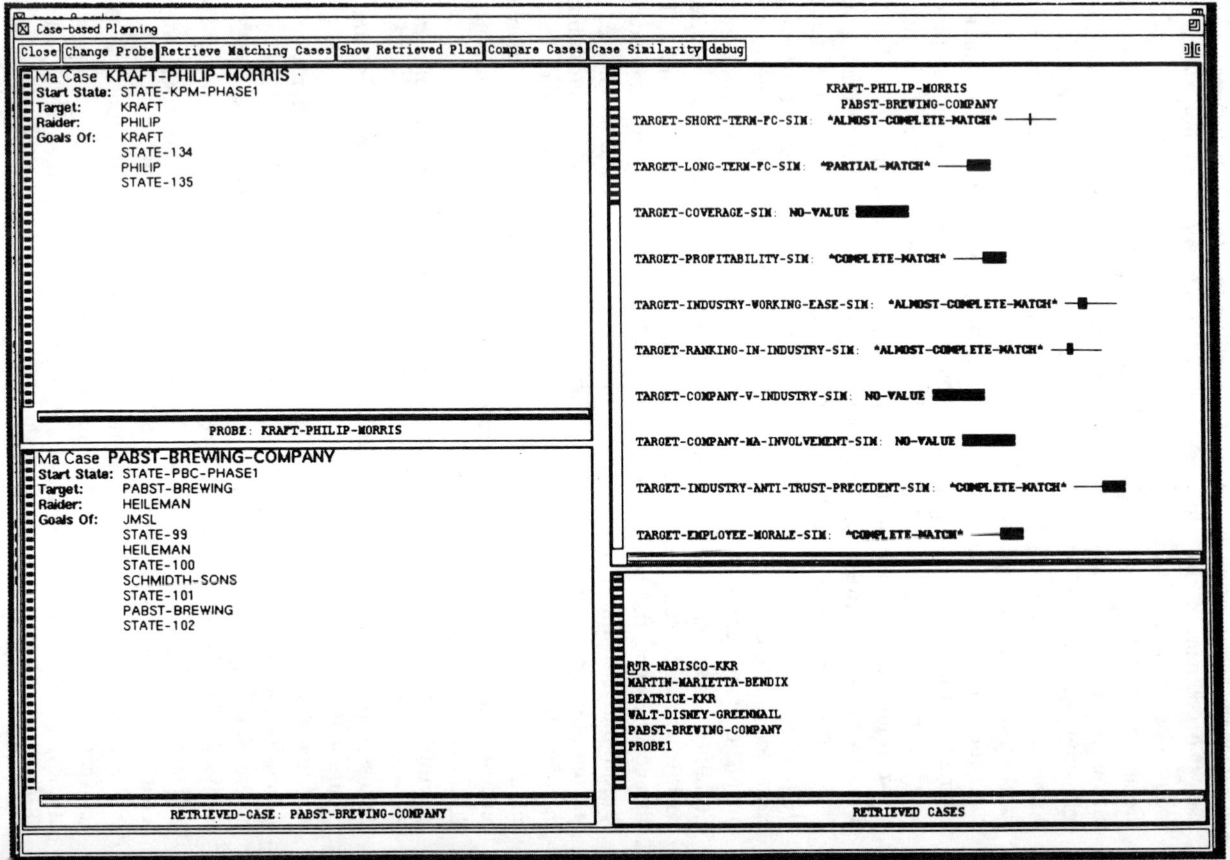

| Close | Change Probe | Retrieve Matching Cases | Show Retrieved Plan | Compare Cases | Case Similarity | debug |

Ma Case KRAFT-PHILIP-MORRIS
Start State: STATE-KPM-PHASE1
Target: KRAFT
Raider: PHILIP
Goals Of: KRAFT
STATE-134
PHILIP
STATE-135

KRAFT-PHILIP-MORRIS
PABST-BREWING-COMPANY
TARGET-SHORT-TERM-PC-SIM: *ALMOST-COMPLETE-MATCH*
TARGET-LONG-TERM-PC-SIM: *PARTIAL-MATCH*
TARGET-COVERAGE-SIM: NO-VALUE
TARGET-PROFITABILITY-SIM: *COMPLETE-MATCH*
TARGET-INDUSTRY-WORKING-EASE-SIM: *ALMOST-COMPLETE-MATCH*
TARGET-RANKING-IN-INDUSTRY-SIM: *ALMOST-COMPLETE-MATCH*
TARGET-COMPANY-V-INDUSTRY-SIM: NO-VALUE
TARGET-COMPANY-MA-INVOLVEMENT-SIM: NO-VALUE
TARGET-INDUSTRY-ANTI-TRUST-PRECEDENT-SIM: *COMPLETE-MATCH*
TARGET-EMPLOYEE-MORALE-SIM: *COMPLETE-MATCH*

PROBE: KRAFT-PHILIP-MORRIS

Ma Case PABST-BREWING-COMPANY
Start State: STATE-PBC-PHASE1
Target: PABST-BREWING
Raider: HEILEMAN
Goals Of: JMSL
STATE-99
HEILEMAN
STATE-100
SCHMIDTH-SONS
STATE-101
PABST-BREWING
STATE-102

RETRIEVED-CASE: PABST-BREWING-COMPANY

RETRIEVED CASES
RJR-NABISCO-KKR
MARTIN-MARIETTA-BENDIX
BEATRICE-KKR
WALT-DISNEY-GREENMAIL
PABST-BREWING-COMPANY
PROBE1

Analysis of cases. The similarity component uses domain-specific rules. These rules are specified for analyzing cases to derive abstract features. These features are assigned a value and a degree of certainty. Values for features (abstract or surface), can be raw data or lexical terms (linguistic values representing fuzzy intervals (Zadeh, 1984) chosen from feature value term sets provided in CARS. The degree of certainty represents the extent to which the abstract features can be inferred from the surface features.

For example, let us refer to Figure 4.6. We can observe that there are five PRIMO plausible rules (denoted by rectangles) that are used to determine the value of the variable *target short term FC Sim*. One of such rules is *acid ratio St Fc*, illustrated in Figure 4.8.

```
(def-rule (acid-ratio-st-fc case-based              ; RULE NAME
                            (resources)             ; RULE CLASS
                            (company*industry-ratios))  ; INSTANTIATION CLASS
    (?company ?industry-ratios)                     ; OBJECT-VARIABLES
    "short term financial condition using acid ratio"  ; ON-LINE DOCUMENTATION
    (lb-pass-threshold                              ; CONTEXT
      (t3 (number-predicate (current-assets ?company))
          (number-predicate (current-liabilities ?company))
          (number-predicate (inventory ?company))
          (number-predicate (acid-ratio ?industry-ratios)))
     250)
    (acid-ratio-pred    (current-assets ?company)   ; ANTECEDENT
                        (current-liabilities ?company)
                        (inventory ?company)
                        (acid-ratio ?industry-ratios))
    (((short-term-fc ?company)                      ; CONCLUSION
      ((acid-ratio-cons   (current-assets ?company)
                          (current-liabilities ?company)
                          (inventory ?company)
                          (acid-ratio ?industry-ratios))
       (i::d3 *certain* *likely* :premise) :INTERSECT))))  ; RULE STRENGTH
```

Figure 4.8.
PRIMO Rule Inferring the Company Short-Term Financial Condition

The rule in Figure 4.8 consists of a *rule name*, *rule class*, *instantiation class*, *object variables*, *online documentation*, *context*, *antecedent*, *consequent*, and *rule strength*. These rule components are used for: (a) rule-base design, (b) rule instantiation, (c) control of inference, and (d) rule evaluation.

1. **Rule-base design:** *Rule name* and *rule class* are used to identify the rule and structure the rule base for the purposes of efficiency in inference and ease of debugging and knowledge engineering.
2. **Rule instantiation:** Rules are written with object variables scoped by an implicit universal quantifier. While rule classes are design partitions of the rule base, *instantiation classes* are instantiation partitions of the same rule base (i.e., they define the subsets of rules to be jointly instantiated when a new instance of an object occurs). Also, *object variables* are instantiated with the corresponding slot values of the new instance. In our example, they are ?company and ?industry-ratios.
3. **Inference control:** The *context* is a precondition that must be satisfied before the antecedent of the rule is evaluated. Typically a context is a conjunctions of predicates on object-level variables (i.e., domain variables) or meta-level variables (i.e., processing resources and requirements). In our example they perform a type checking on the value of the predicates used in the antecedent (to guarantee that all numeric values are available).
4. **Rule evaluations:** The *antecedent* is a conjunction of (possible) fuzzy predicates on object-level variables. The conjunction is implemented using T-norms (Bonissone, 1987), which are described below. The result of the antecedent is the degree to which the conjunct of predicates have been satisfied. The output of the antecedent, in conjunction with the *rule strength* is used to determine the truth value of the *rule conclusion*. In our example we have one predicate acid-ratio-pred, which computes the acid ratio of the company as:

$$\text{Acid Ratio} = \frac{\text{Current Assets - Inventory}}{\text{Current Liabilities}}$$

And normalize with respect to the industry average acid ratio. The mapping, illustrated in Figure 4.9, is then used to select the term that best describes the short-term financial condition of the company, given the acid ratio average of its industry sector.

In our implementation the intervals used in the mapping are actually fuzzy intervals. Therefore, the membership value of the acid ration percentage is computed for each term in the term set. The term with the highest membership value is selected. The corresponding membership value describes the degree of confidence of this linguistic value assignment.

The M&A application built in our system contain 70 PRIMO rules to extract abstract features and evaluate similarities for about 20 M&A cases.

Figure 4.9.
Mapping of Percentage Acid Ratio to Terms Labels and Semantics

Acid Ratio Percentage Interval	Term Label	Term Semantics
[0,60]	*VERY-WEAK*	(0 130 0 20)
[60,80]	*WEAK*	(170 270 20 30)
[80,90]	*BELOW-AVERAGE*	(310 410 30 30)
[90,115]	*AVERAGE*	(450 550 30 30)
[115,140]	*ABOVE-AVERAGE*	(590 690 30 30)
[140,170]	*STRONG*	(730 830 30 20)
[170, ∞]	*VERY-STRONG*	(870 1000 20 0)

Feature value comparisons. By applying this process to the probe and the retrieved case, we obtain a linguistic value for each of their abstract features. It should be noted that each linguistic term has a label and a meaning. This is illustrated in the third column of Figure 4.9.

In the third column of Figure 4.9, a parametric representation is used to describe the membership distribution of each term, N_i. Using this representation we can describe a fuzzy set of a universe of discourse U as the four-tuple: (a,b,α,β). The universe U is the unit interval (represented by an integer representation on the scale from 0 to 1000). The first two parameters (a, b) indicate the interval of the universe of discourse in which the membership value is 1.0; the third and fourth parameters (α, β) indicate the left and right *width* of the distribution. Linear functions are used to define the slopes. Let $\mu_{N_i}(\chi) : X \rightarrow [0,1]$ be the membership function of the fuzzy set N_i, as illustrated in Figure 4.10.

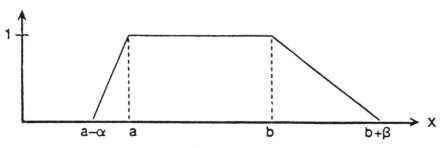

Figure 4.10.
Membership Distributions of $N_i = (a, b, \alpha, \beta)$

We can represent N_i, as the four-tuple $(a_i, b_i, \alpha_i, \mu_i)$ where:

$$\mu_{N_i}(x) = \begin{cases} 0 & \text{if } x < (a_i - \alpha_i) \\ \dfrac{1}{\alpha_i}(x - a_i + \alpha_i) & \text{if } x \in [(a_i - \alpha_i), a_i] \\ 1 & \text{if } x \in [a_i, b_i] \\ \dfrac{1}{\beta_i}(b_i + \beta_i - x) & \text{if } x \in [b_i, (b_i + \beta_i)] \\ 0 & \text{if } x > (b_i + \beta_i) \end{cases}$$

The membership distribution described by the above equation is illustrated in Figure 4.10.

Having established the meaning of the labels used to define each abstract feature value, we now need to compute the similarity measure for each feature. This is done by executing a two step procedure.

First we compute the distance between the fuzzy set representations of the corresponding values. For example, let us assume that the abstract feature *target short-term FC-Sim* has value *STRONG* in the probe and *VERY STRONG* in the retrieved case. The distance between the two corresponding fuzzy sets is computed as the absolute value of their difference. This is done using fuzzy arithmetic operations that are closed under the four-tuple parametric representation (Bonissone & Decker, 1986). Specifically, given two fuzzy numbers $X = (a, b, \alpha, \mu)$ and $Y = (c, d, \gamma, \delta)$ we can define the difference

$$X\text{-}Y = (a-d, b-c, \alpha + \delta, \beta + \gamma)$$

In this example, the difference between *VERY-STRONG* and *STRONG* is (40, 270, 40, 30). This distance is then transformed into a degree of matching by taking the complement with respect to the unit interval. Using the same formula for the difference, by representing the unit as (1000, 1000, 0, 0) we have the degree of matching $1\text{-}X\text{-}Y = (730, 960, 30, 40)$.

The second step, referred to as linguistic approximation, consists in selecting a label (chosen from one of the similarity term sets provided) whose meaning is the closest to that of the computed degree of matching. This semantic closeness is evaluated by a measure of set containment:

$$\frac{\|P \cap D\|}{\|D\|}$$

where P is the similarity term and D is the result of complementing the set distance. This measure, representing the degree of matching between the reference (P) and the date (D), is used as an associated certainty value for the label.

A simple example of a seven term similarity term set is given by Figure 4.11.

Figure 4.11.
Term Set For Partial Matching of Abstract Features

Term Label	Term Meaning
NO-MATCH	(0 130 0 20)
ALMOST-NO-MATCH	(170 270 20 30)
LESS-THAN-PARTIAL-MATCH	(310 410 30 30)
PARTIAL-MATCH	(450 550 30 30)
MORE-THAN-PARTIAL-MATCH	(590 690 30 30)
ALMOST-COMPLETE-MATCH	(730 830 30 20)
COMPLETE-MATCH	(870 1000 20 0)

In the case of our example, the degree of matching was the fuzzy number (730, 960, 30, 40). By using the term set described in Figure 4.11, we can see that the term with the closest meaning (730, 830, 30, 20) is *ALMOST-COMPLETE-MATCH*. The degree of confidence in this label selection is

$$\frac{\|(730,830,30,20) \cap (730,960,30,40)\|}{\|(730,960,30,40)\|} = \frac{125}{265} = 0.47.$$

From the same Figure 14.11 we could see that the term *COMPLETE-MATCH*, with its meaning described by (870, 1000, 20, 0), would have a degree of confidence of

$$\frac{\|(870,1000,20,0)\| \cap (730,960,30,40)\|}{\|(730,960,30,40)\|} = \frac{120}{265} = 0.45.$$

Therefore the term *ALMOST-COMPLETE-MATCH* was used as the value for the similarity measure for the abstract feature *target-short-term FC-SIM*, as shown in Figure 4.7.

Multiple similarity term sets are provided to allow for different "views" of similarity (e.g., the lenient similarity term set has wide fuzzy intervals for the labels representing high similarity and narrower intervals for those representing low similarity. The opposite is true for the strict term set).

Combinations of similarities. The similarity measure can be aggregated or chained (using the transitivity of similarity) according to well-defined operators called triangular norms. Triangular norms (T-norms) are the most general families of binary functions that satisfy the requirements of the conjunction operators. T-norms are two-place functions from [0,1] x [0,1] to [0,1] that are monotonic, commutative, and associative. Their corresponding boundary conditions (i.e., the evaluation of the T-norms at the extremes of the [0,1] interval) satisfy the truth tables of the logical AND operator (Bonissone, 1987). Five uncertainty calculi based on the following five T-norms are used in PRIMO:

$T_1(a,b) = \max(0, a+b-1)$

$T_{1.5}(a,b) = (a^{0.5} + b^{0.5} - 1)^2 \quad$ if $(a^{0.5} + b^{0.5}) \geq 1$
$\qquad\quad\; = 0 \qquad\qquad\qquad\quad$ otherwise

$T_2(a,ba) = ab$

$T_{2.5}(a,b) = (a^{-1} + b^{-1} - 1)^{-1}$
$T_3(a,b) = \min(a,b)$

Their corresponding DeMorgan dual T-conorms, denoted by $S_i(a,b)$, are defined as:

$$S_i(a,b) = 1 - T_i(1 - a^{-1}, - b)$$

These five calculi provide the user with an ability to choose the desired uncertainty calculus starting from the most conservative (T_1) to the most liberal (T_3).

The use of T-norms in aggregating and chaining certainty intervals during the extraction of abstract features is extended in CARS to the aggregation of similarity measures.

This mechanism aggregates similarities by taking as input a list of similarities to be combined, their associated uncertainties, and optional weights indicating the importance of the feature in the aggregation. This mechanism is based on three aggregation operators.

T-norms (used to discount low similarities),
T-conorms (used to enhance high similarities), and
Linear combinations (used to average remaining similarities).

The reader is referred to reference (Dubois & Prade, 1984) for a detailed study of aggregating operators.

In Figure 4.2 we can observe two levels of aggregation of similarity measures: all the raiders' abstract feature similarities (from *raider-industry-anti-trust-precedent-sim* to *raider-performance-as-raider-sim*) are aggregated to determine the *raider-raider-similarity* between probe and case. Similarly, the target abstract feature similarities are aggregated to derive the *target-target similarity*. Finally, *target-target similarity* and *raider-raider similarity* are combined to derive the case *Phase-1 similarity*. It should be noted that during the aggregation process of similarity, we do not account for slots with no values (denoted by the extended certainty bar).

Figure 4.12.
Aggregation of Similarities

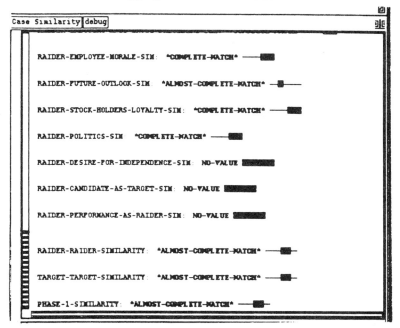

In our example, from Figure 4.7 we can see that most of the target abstract feature similarities range from *COMPLETE-MATCH* to *PARTIAL MATCH*. The raider abstract feature similarities have an identical range of values (a subset of which is shown in Figure 4.2). Their aggregation is performed using T-conorms and linear combination operators and in both cases results into a *ALMOST-COMPLETE-MATCH*. The last aggregation to obtain *Phase-1 similarity* returns the same degree of matching, as shown in Figure 4.12.

The similarity between two cases can be computed by aggregating the five phase similarities in an analogous fashion. It is straightforward to customize this final aggregation to reflect different goals of the retriever, as we will show in the sequel. Let us recall the definition of the five phases: (1) initial condition, (2) pretender, (3) tender-negotiation, (4) outcome, and (5) long-term results.

For instance, by only aggregating Phases 1, 2, and 4 we can stress the need to find successful cases with similar initial and pretender conditions. The result can give us the range of tender-negotiations (plans/counterplans) which are applicable to the current situation.

Alternatively, by only aggregating Phases 2, 3, and 4 we can observe the range of macroeconomic conditions to ascertain raider/target financial assessments, for which a particular (pretender and posttender) plan was successful.

3. DISCUSSION

The CARS system is a working prototype, implemented to demonstrate and validate the concept of a trader's workstation, and the utility of CBR technology. We evaluate its performance with respect to the perceived usefulness of the software to the users.

Ideally, CARS should be evaluated by comparison to connectionist systems designed and implemented to perform the same or similar tasks. However, as detailed below in the section on related work, there are no comparable connectionist systems. In this circumstance, we compare CARS with the general state of the art in terms of the features and abilities of connectionist models.

3.2. Advantages of Retrieval Method

Like distributed connectionist systems, associative symbolic retrieval has distinct advantages over other symbolic indexing schemes, for example, discrimination nets (Kolodner, 1984), or deductive information retrieval (Charniak, Riesbeck, & McDermott, 1980). Among these are associative retrieval, approximate matching, and pattern completion. We now turn to a brief discussion of each of these properties and their manifestation in the symbolic retrieval algorithm used in CARS.

3.2.1. Associative Retrieval. Associative retrieval in CBR allows any and all indices in the problem case to be used as indices in retrieval. This prevents the need to make a priori decisions about which features will be used as indices, and in what order they should be tried. A good discussion of the problems with indexing for CBR can be found in Thagard and Holyoak (1989).

3.2.2. Approximate Matching. The system achieves approximate matching through the relaxation of the set of nodes that are activated (see Figure 14.3). Approximate matching is of particular importance to CBR systems because typically the input case is not *exactly* like an existing case in the case memory. Symbolic retrieval also allows us to specify whether any given feature should be relaxed or not. For example, for certain applications, the type of the company may be an important surface feature and should not be relaxed, whereas for other applications, the industry segment of the company may not be an important feature, and approximate matches are desirable. As discussed below, a general treatment of relaxation is problematic for current distributed representation systems.

3.2.3. Pattern Completion. The system achieves pattern completion, or fault tolerance in that no feature must necessarily be present for a given case to be retrieved. This quality is different from approximate matching in that approximate matching allows for *similar* nodes to match each other. Pattern completion, on the other hand, means that not every node in the input must match a node in the retrieved case, or *vice versa*. Together with approximate matching, this quality is of particular importance to CBR systems because of the virtual guarantee that the input will be neither completely specified nor be exactly like a case in the case memory.

3.3. Comparing Retrieval in CARS and Connectionist Models

As we have shown, the retrieval mechanism implemented in CARS has those features which a PDP-based retrieval mechanism would provide. Both are capable of doing associative retrieval—providing flexibility in terms of which indices can be used to retrieve cases. Both support approximate matching, where the retrieved patterns need not be complete matches with the input case, but only matching important features (possibly partially). Both CARS and PDP models allow cases to be retrieved from incompletely specified input cases.

However, despite the fact that CARS and PDP-based retrieval methods both give us these desired properties, we contend that the CARS method is superior to existing PDP models for retrieval in CBR system.

First, as described above, the CARS mechanism allows us to change our criteria for allowable matches without altering the system. A conventional PDP model would have to be retrained under the new criteria. Another possibility is to use a PDP network which is trained to provide the correct cases when presented with both the probe case and the match criteria as input. It has not been demonstrated, however, that this is possible in practice.

Second, a retrieval mechanism used in a CBR system must often retrieve multiple cases in response to an input case. This puts the PDP-based retrieval mechanism at a severe disadvantage. Whereas the CARS retrieval mechanism can easily return a list of many cases, this poses a problem for PDP models. By virtue of the nature of their distributed representations, the representation for a case is the pattern of activation of the output units of the network. The learning procedure trains the network to always return as output that case which most closely matches the input (although in some circumstances the output may be the conflation of several cases). To get around this limitation, the number of output units could be multiplied by n, to allow n distinct patterns to be output at once, but this is not a general solution. For small values of n, this unnecessarily limits the number of retrievable cases. For larger values of n, we get a *much* larger network (the number of weights between two layers of units increasing with the square of the number of units), and pay the penalty both in run-time of the learning algorithm and again in the increased difficulty of the task being learned (multiple case retrieval).

Training n separate networks to retrieve cases is not a practical alternative either, as there is no way to ensure that the independent networks will retrieve distinct cases. In this situation relevant cases may be unretrieved by any of the networks. If the networks are in some fashion connected in order to constrain them to produce distinct cases, this is in reality the same problem as training an *n*-case network, with the severe disadvantages just described.

Lastly, since the rest of our CBR system is a conventional symbol-processing program, it is easier to integrate the symbolic structured forms of the cases returned by the CARS retrieval mechanism than it is to convert a pattern vector to such a representation. This is a minor point, and one which would not even hold true if either the CBR system were completely connectionist, or if the advantage of using a PDP retrieval mechanism outweighed the conversion penalty. But, since neither of these is true, it underscores the advantage of the CARS retrieval mechanism over PDP models.

One area where the relative advantage of CARS over a PDP model is unclear is training. It is true that training complex distributed representation connectionist models currently is a time-consuming task. It is also true that the knowledge engineering required to build the conceptual hierarchy and case base is not insignificant, although there is research which indicates that this process may be automated (Mooney & Dejong, 1985). However, CARS gets its input case base from natural language text processing which requires knowledge of the domain to operate. Therefore the knowledge-engineering cost is offset by eliminating the time to hand encode a case base, and the knowledge-engineering cost is not fairly assigned as a cost to CARS, as it services the text processing system as well.

Although it might be argued that it is questionable to claim as an advantage for CARS that it does by hard (hand) coding that which a PDP model does by learning, we believe that setting up the learning trials for a PDP system is, in the case of a PDP model for associative retrieval, as much a hand-coding task as is setting a variable in CARS. In addition, depending on the number of different match criteria and the possible combinations, setting up these learning trials greatly complicates the training task to enable the network to provide correct retrieval in all cases.

An additional complication for PDP models is that extending the case base requires retraining the network. For some learning methods (e.g., back propagation) this requires retraining over the entire case base to ensure that all previous cases are retained, rather than being forgotten in the course of learning the new cases.

None of the above objections to the use of PDP models for the retrieval mechanism for a CBR system are absolute or represent limitations in principle on PDP models. It is true, however, that these *are* problems for current and immediately foreseeable connectionist systems. Current research on learning methods which are faster and give better results (Fahlman & Lebiere, 1990), and into ways of representing and processing structured information (such as lists, trees, etc.) and variable binding (Pollack, 1990) may overcome the disadvantages cited above. But, until they have done so, the ability of the CARS retrieval mechanism to provide a computationally tractable model which provides the advantages of PDP networks, but without their current disadvantages, makes it the preferred method.

In this chapter we make the general claim that CARS' retrieval mechanism is superior to existing connectionist methods. Specifically we examine the PDP variety of connectionism. There are of course other types of connectionist models, but, of these only the structured connectionist models (Feldman, Fanty, Goddard, & Lynne, 1988) have been used substantially for building models involving complex knowledge representation.

We do not, however, feel that "structured" (or "localist") connectionist models are comparable to CARS, and are indeed inferior to PDP-based retrieval mechanisms. This claim is based on several points. First, as a retrieval mechanism, a structured network is acting as an intersection search. However, since this search must be implemented using only undifferentiated association, it is more difficult to design the network to perform the complex (and varying) retrieval tasks done by CARS. Also, any pattern completion or approximate matching abilities must be explicitly designed into the structure of the entire network, as there exist neither the control mechanism used by CARS, nor the automatic generalization of PDP learning to provide them. This also makes the networks more difficult to expand, as any such mechanisms must be replicated to provide for new cases. In short, it is our contention that structured connectionist networks are not practical for a general retrieval mechanism for use in CBR systems.

4. RELATED WORK

Memory-based reasoning (Stanfill & Waltz, 1986) is a massively parallel approach to case retrieval and CBR. The main argument for using a parallel architecture for case retrieval is also an argument for using a localist, spreading activation, and intersection search method of retrieval. That is, that indices used to make case retrieval tractable may prevent the best case or cases from being retrieved.

Whereas MBR proponents (i.e., Waltz, 1989) presume the only solution to this problem is parallelism, in fact the retrieval model described here is guaranteed to exhibit the same quality of performance as parallel retrieval within the same order of magnitude time, in *serial*. With N parallel processors, a database with N bases can find best matches in $o(1)$ (i.e., in time independent of N). Marker-passing retrieval performs one $o(1)$ retrieval for each slot in the probe case. Given that any given probe as a constant number of slots in it, a constant number of $o(1)$ retrievals yields $o(1)$ performance. Retrieval of each slot is an $O(1)$ operation in that an instance in the probe directly indexes the set of retrieved instances, directly retrieving the set independent of the number of elements in the set and the total number of concepts in the system.

4.2. Connectionist Approaches to CBR

As mentioned earlier, there are currently no general connectionist CBR systems. There is, however, a small but significant body of research on connectionist approaches to the problems of CBR and related problems. For example, Thrift (1989) has proposed a neural network model for CBR, but as of this writing, it is no more than a proposal (see also Becker, 1988).

Most work in connectionism that is of potential relevance to CBR is actually work in analogical retrieval, for example, the ARCS system of Thagard and Holyoak (1989). Also related is the work by Holyoak, Novick, and Melz (1994) on the ACME system to do analogical mapping. Seifert (1989) pointed out that analogical reasoning typically focuses on *interdomain* retrieval, whereas CBR typically performs *intradomain* retrieval. Also, exact matches are ideal in CBR, but useless in analogical reasoning.

Among other differences, analogical reasoning requires systematic similarity between input and retrieved cases, whereas this requirement may not be needed for CBR as long as the retrieved cases can be used in the new problem situation. In this view, similarity is derived from those features (either surface or abstract) of the retrieved cases likely to be useful in the new situation. This set of features changes from situation to situation, so in this sense, the similarity is not systematic.

Nonetheless, there are substantive similarities between work in connectionist analogy systems and our system, but as of this writing, we have found no specific work in connectionist CBR that demonstrates the advantages we have already seen in our CARS system.

As this chapter has shown, the current generation of connectionist systems lack general solutions to the problems of multiple case retrieval, variables and structured information, excessive training time, incremental learning, and scaling. Until there exist such solutions, connectionist CBR systems must only exist as either proposals or limited proof-of-concept experiments, and not full-scale CBR systems on a par with the existing symbolic ones.

4.3. Prototypical Symbolic CBR

A prototypical symbolic CBR system uses indexing to retrieve relevant cases. These indices form discrimination nets. The choice of what features serve as indices is made after knowledge engineering.

In some CBR domains, for example, in legal reasoning, certain prespecifiable features of input cases are the only features of relevance in finding similar cases, as in HYPO (Ashley, 1988). This constrains the dimensions along which features can usefully be relaxed, and so index traversal is a computationally feasible retrieval method.

4.4. Combining CBR and RBR

The AI community has recently recognized the need to integrate diverse reasoning techniques for effectively solving complex real-world problems. Within case-based reasoning, this trend is represented by the works of Carbonell and Veloso (1988), Veloso and Carbonell (1991) (integration of CBR and classical search problem solvers), Hammond and Hurwitz (1988) (integrating CBR and explanation-based reasoning), Braverman and Wilensky (1990) (integrating CBR and explanation-based learning), Koton (1988), and Goel (1990), (integrating CBR and model-based reasoning), Rissland and Skalak (1989), Rissland, et al (1991); Bonissone and Dutta (1990), Dutta and Bonissone (1991) (Branting, 1991), and Golding (1991) (integrating RBR and CBR).

In particular, we believe that the integration of case-based and rule-based reasoning is a crucial factor for the development of reasoning systems solving realistic problems. RBR and CBR are largely *complementary* reasoning methodologies. RBR can better represent specialized domain knowledge in a modular, declarative fashion, while CBR can better represent past experiences and domain complexity (Riesbeck & Schank, 1989). Significant benefits are possible by combining these two reasoning modalities. For example, CBR can directly enhance RBR by providing a context for screening the knowledge base and by extending the coverage of rules by representing exceptions (to the rule) in the form of cases. Going the other direction, RBR can enhance CBR by expressing domain knowledge to dynamically determine the contextually dependent relevance of a feature set (or attributes of a case) to a given goal and to dynamically select the best similarity/relevance measure to use for case retrieval. There are numerous domains in which it is important to combine RBR and CBR, such as the legal (Oskamp et al., 1989; Rissland & Skalak, 1989) and the financial domains (Bonissone & Dutta, 1990).

From a control viewpoint, there are three possible ways of combining RBR and CBR: (a) a higher level controller (blackboard) decides whether to use the case-based or the rule-based reasoner; (b) the rule-based reasoner explicitly requests the use of the knowledge available from the cases; (c) the case-based reasoner uses the inference capabilities provided by the rules.

The first paradigm is exemplified by Rissland and Skalak's approach (1989). While working in the legal domain of statutory interpretation, they have developed a hybrid reasoning system, called CABARET. The system's architecture consists of two coequal reasoners, a RBR and a CBR, with a separate agenda-based controller. The central controller contains heuristics to direct and interleave the two modes of reasoning and to post and prioritize tasks for each reasoner. In a more recent version of CABARET (Rissland et al., 1991) this type of control is implemented by a blackboard system, GBB.

The second paradigm is illustrated by Bonissone and Dutta's approach

(1990). While working in the domain of mergers and acquisitions (M&A), they have developed a system, MARS, that is controlled by a rule-based system.

In MARS rules are used to represent the domain expertise that is required for structuring various aspects of the M&A deal or deciding upon the next best course of action. Cases provide the prior experiences of other companies involved in similar hostile takeovers. For example, the raider may have certain rules to determine which company to select as a possible target. The system may have similar cases to determine whether the Justice Department will block the takeover to enforce *antitrust* laws.

Rules are used in forward and backward chaining mode to make selected inferences. Whenever the expert (or system designer) feels that CBR is important for deciding about a particular conclusion, a rule to this effect is added in the knowledge base. When this rule is part of an active deductive path, the rule is executed and the CBR is used to generate a parallel proof path. Each proof path is annotated with a certainty interval representing the degree to which the conclusion is supported or refuted. This uncertainty representation is then used to determine the proportionate contribution of each path to the final conclusion/goal.

The first paradigm provides a nice modularity for control. However, it is predicated on finding the right heuristics for the controller (and on being able to extend or customize these heuristics to different domains). The second approach uses more domain-dependent heuristics to determine the activation of the CBR.

The third paradigm is exemplified by the work of Bonissone, Blau, and Ayub in the development of CARS (Bonissone et al., 1990; Blau, Bonissone, & Ayub, 1991). In CARS architecture, the CBR is the dominant reasoner. During case indexing, retrieval, and adaptation, the CBR activates PRIMO, a rule-based reasoner that contains plausible rules of abstraction, evaluation, and modification.

PRIMO rules are used in case indexing to augment the case and probe representation with a set of abstract features derived from subsets of surface features. Each abstract feature has a value (with fuzzy semantics) and a certainty evaluation qualifying the value assignment. In case retrieval, the rules combine the similarity measures computed across the abstract features of probe and cases and provide a partial ordering on the cases. In case adaptation, rule-based inferences are used to perform aspects of derivational adaptation to achieve retrieved subgoals.

5. SUMMARY

This chapter has presented a discussion of the importance of the retrieval process to case-based reasoning system, as well as some important desirable properties in a retrieval mechanism. Despite the fact that parallel distributed processing models have many of these properties, they also have many shortcomings (at least at the present time and in the near future). These problems severely limit their usefulness as part of a large, general case-based reasoning systems.

On the other hand, the modified and augmented marker-passing mechanism described here and implemented in the CARS system for CBR has the capabilities of a PDP model of associative retrieval but without the limitations on dynamically changeable match criteria or extracting multiple matches for a given input case. In addition to using associative retrieval to find the best matching cases along surface feature dimensions, CARS generates abstract features and combines CBR and RBR in a novel way. Given the limitations of current PDP models, we conclude that for associative retrieval in CBR systems, the retrieval mechanism used in CARS is preferred over the use of the current generation of distributed representation connectionist models.

REFERENCES

Aragones, J.K., Bonissone, P.P., & Stillman, J. (1990, July). Primo: A tool for reasoning with incomplete and uncertain information. *Proceedings of the International Conference on Information Processing and Management of Uncertainty In Knowledge-Based Systems (PMU-90)*. Paris, France.

Ashley, K. (1988). *Modelling legal argument: Reasoning with cases and hypotheticals*. Unpublished doctoral dissertation, Computer and Information Science, University of Massachusetts at Amherst.

Becker, L.A., & Jazayeri, K. (1988). A connectionist approach to case-based reasoning. *Proceedings of the Case-based Reasoning Workshop* (pp. 213–217). San Mateo, CA: Morgan Kaufmann.

Blau, L., Bonissone, P.P., & Ayub, S. (1991). Planning with dynamic cases. *Proceedings of Case-Based Reasoning Workshop* (pp. 295–306). San Mateo, CA: Morgan Kaufmann

Bonissone, P.P., & Dutta, S. (1990). A mergers and acquisitions reasoning system. *Journal of Computer Science In Economics and Management, 3*, 239–268.

Bonissone, P.P. & Decker, K.S. (1986). Selecting uncertainty calculi and granularity: An experiment in trading-off precision and complexity. In L. Kanal & J. Lemmer (Eds.), *Uncertainty in artificial intelligence* (pp. 217–247). Amsterdam: North-Holland.

Bonissone, P.P., Blau, L., & Ayub, S. (1990). Leveraging the integration of approximate reasoning systems. *Proceedings of the 1990 AAAI Spring Symposium In Case-Based Reasoning* (pp. 1–6). Stanford, CA.

Bonissone, P.P. (1987). Summarizing and Propagating Uncertain Information With Triangular Norms. *International Journal of Approximate Reasoning, 1*, 71–101.

Bonissone, P.P. (1989). Now that I have a good theory of uncertainty, what else do I need? *Proceeding Fifth AAAI Workshop on Uncertainty in Artificial Intelligence* (pp. 22–23). Amsterdam: North-Holland.

Brachman, R., & Schmolze, J. (1985). An overview of the KL-ONE knowledge representation system. *Cognitive Science*, *9*, 171–216.

Branting, L.K. (1991). Exploiting the complimentarity of rules and precedents with reciprocity and fairness. *Proceedings of Case-Based Reasoning Workshop* (pp. 39–50). San Mateo, CA: Morgan Kaufmann.

Braverman, M.S., & Wilensky, R. (1990). Towards An Unification of Case-Based Reasoning and Explanation-Based Learning. *Proceedings of the AAAI Spring Symposium—Case Based Reasoning* (pp. 80–84). Menlo Park, CA: AAAI.

Carbonell, J., & Veloso, M. (1988). Integrating derivational analogy into a general problem solving architecture. *Proceedings of the Case-Based Reasoning Workshop* (pp. 104–124). San Mateo, CA: Morgan Kaufmann.

Charniak, E. (1983). Passing markers: A theory of contextual influence in language comprehension. *Cognitive Science*, *7*, 171–190.

Charniak, E., Riesbeck, C., & McDermott, D. (1980). *Artificial intelligence programming*. Hillsdale, NJ: Erlbaum.

Cohen, P.R., & Kjeldsen, R. (1987). Information retrieval by constrained spreading activation in semantic networks. *Information Processing and management, Special Issue on Artificial Intelligence for Information Retrieval*, *23*(4), 255–268.

Corman, T.H., Leiserson, C.E., & Rivest, R.L. (1990). *Introduction to algorithms*. Cambridge, MA: MIT Press.

Dubois, D., & Prade, J. (1984). Criteria aggregation and ranking of alternatives in the framework of fuzzy set theory. In H. Zimmermann, L. Zadeh, & B. Gaines (Eds.), *Fuzzy sets and decision analysis* (pp. 209–240). Amsterdam: North-Holland.

Dutta, S., & Bonissone, P.P. (1991). Integrating case based and rule based reasoning: The possibilistic connection. In *Uncertainty in artificial intelligence* (Vol. 6). Amsterdam: North-Holland.

Fahlman, E.E., & Lebiere, C. (1990). The cascade-correlation learning algorithm. In D.S. Touretzky (Ed.), *Advances in neural processing systems 2*. San Mateo, CA: Morgan Kaufmann.

Feldman, J.A., Fanty, J.A., Goddard, N.H., & Lynne, K.J. (1988). Computing with structured connectionist networks. *Communications of the ACM*, *31*(1), 170–187.

Goel, A.K. (1990). Grounding case modification in deep models. *Proceedings AAAI Spring Symposium—Case Based Reasoning* (pp. 41–44). New York: AAAI.

Golding, A., & Rosenbloom, P. (1991). Integrating rule-based and case-based reasoning for name pronunciation. *Proceedings of the National Conference on Artificial Intelligence*. Menlo Park, CA: AAAI Press.

Hammond, K., & Hurwitz, N. (1988). Extracting diagnostic features from explanations. *Proceedings of the Case-Based Reasoning Workshop* (pp. 169–178). San Mateo, CA: Morgan Kaufmann.

Hendler, J. (1987). *Integrating marker passing and problem solving: An activation spreading approach to improved choice in planning*. Hillsdale, NJ: Erlbaum.

Hennessy, D., & Hinkle, D. (1991). Initial results form clavier: A case-based autoclave loading assistant. *Proceedings of Case-Based Reasoning Workshop* (pp. 225–232). San Mateo, CA: Morgan Kaufmann.

Hinton, G.E., McClelland, J.L., & Rumelhart, D.E. (1986). Distributed representations. In D.E. Rumelhart, J.L. McClelland, & The PDP Research Group (Eds.), *Parallel distributed processing: Explorations in the microstructure of cognition, Vol. 1: Foundations*. Cambridge, MA: MIT Press.

Holyoak, K.J., Novick, L.R., & Melz, E.R. (1994). Component processes in analogical transfer: Mapping, pattern completion, and adaptation. In J.A. Barnden & K.J. Holyoak (Eds.), *Advances in connectionist and neural computation theory, Vol. 2: Analogical connections* (pp. 113–180). Norwood, NJ: Ablex.

Jacobs, P.S., & Rau, L.F. (1984). Ace: associating language with meaning. *Proceedings of the Sixth European Conference on Artificial Intelligence* (pp. 137–146). Pisa, Italy.

Jacobs, P.S., & Rau, L.F. (1990a). The GE NLToolset: A software foundation for intelligent text processing. *Proceedings of the Thirteenth International Conference on Computational Linguistics* (Vol. 3. pp. 373–277). Helsinki, Finland.

Jacobs, P., & Rau, L. (1990b). SCISOR: Extracting information from on-line news. *Communications of the Association for Computing Machinery, 33*(11), 88–97.

Kolodner, J. (1984). *Retrieval and organizational strategies in conceptual memory: A computer model.* Hillsdale, NJ: Erlbaum.

Koton, P. (1988). Reasoning about evidence in causal explanations. *Proceedings of the Case-Based Reasoning Workshop* (pp. 260–270). San Mateo, CA: Morgan Kaufmann.

Levinson, R. (1990). *Pattern associativity and the retrieval of semantic networks* (Tech. Rep. No. Ucsc-Crl-90-30). Santa Cruz, CA: Computer Science Department, University of California at Santa Cruz.

Mooney, R., & Dejong, G. (1985). Learning schemata for natural language processing. *Proceedings of the Ninth International Joint Conference on Artificial Intelligence* (pp. 681–687). Los Angeles, CA.

Norvig, P. (1986). *A unified theory of inference for text understanding.* Unpublished doctoral dissertation, Computer Science Division Report UCB/CSD 87/339, University of California, Berkeley, CA.

Oskamp, A., Walker, R.F., Schrickx, J.A., & Vandenberg, P.H. (1989). Prolex, divide and rule: A legal application. *Proceedings of the Second International Conference on Artificial Intelligence and Law.* Vancouver, BC.

Pollack, J.B. (1990). Recursive distributed representations. *Artificial Intelligence, 46,* 77–106.

Rau, L.F. (1987). Knowledge organization and access in a conceptual information system. *Information Processing and Management* [Special Issue on Artificial Intelligence for Information Retrieval], *23,* 269–283.

Riesbeck, C.K., & Schank, R.C. (1989). *Inside case-based reasoning.* Hillsdale, NJ: Erlbaum.

Rissland, E.L., Basu, C., Daniels, J.J., McCarthy, J., Rubinstein, Z.B., & Skalak, D.B. (1991). A blackboard architecture for CBR: An initial report. *Proceedings of Case-Based Reasoning Workshop* (pp. 77–92). San Mateo, CA: Morgan Kaufmann.

Rissland, E.L., & Skalak, D.B. (1989). Interpreting statutory predicates. *Proceedings of the Second International Conference on Artificial Intelligence and Law* (pp. 46–53). Vancouver, BC.

Rumelhart, D.E., & McClelland, J.L. (1986). *Parallel distributed processing: Exploration in the microstructure of cognition, Volume 1: Foundations.* Cambridge, MA: MIT Press.

Seifert, C. (1989). Analogy and case-based retrieval. *Proceedings of the Darpa Case-Based Reasoning Workshop* (pp. 125–129). San Mateo, CA: Morgan Kaufmann.

Stanfill, C., & Waltz, D. (1986). Toward memory-based reasoning. *Communications of the Association for Computing Machinery, 29*(12), 11213–1228).

Thagard, P., & Holyoak, K.J. (1989). Why indexing is the wrong way to think about analog retrieval. *Proceedings of the Darpa Case-Based Reasoning Workshop* (pp. 36–40). San Mateo, CA: Morgan Kaufmann.

Thrift, P. (1983). A neural network model for case-based reasoning. *Proceedings of the Darpa Case-Based Reasoning Workshop* (pp. 334–337). San Mateo, CA: Morgan Kaufmann.

Veloso, M., & Carbonell, J. (1991). Variable-precision case retrieval in analogical problem solving. *Proceedings of Case-Based Reasoning Workshop* (pp. 93–106). San Mateo, CA: Morgan Kaufmann.

Waltz, D.L. (1989). Is indexing used for retrieval? *Proceedings of the Darpa Case-Based Reasoning Workshop* (pp. 41–44). San Mateo, CA: Morgan Kaufmann.

Wilensky, R. (1984). Kodiak—a knowledge representation language. *Proceedings of the Sixth Annual Conference of The Cognitive Science Society*. Boulder, CO

Zadeh, L. (1984). A computational theory of disposition. *Proceedings of the 1984 International Conference On Computational Linguistics* (pp. 312–318). New York: Association for Computational Linguistics.

5
What Is Metaphor?*

George Lakoff

1. INTRODUCTION

Why is the study of metaphor of special interest to those in connectionist cognitive science?

To begin with, connectionist systems are constraint satisfaction systems. Systems of conceptual metaphor are also constraint satisfaction systems. A metaphor system imposes a massive number of constraints on a conceptual system. These constraints greatly limit the possibilities for how situations can be conceptualized, and for how novel linguistic expressions can be understood.

It is a major challenge for connectionist cognitive science to show how such a robust phenomenon as metaphor can be modeled. We know a great deal about metaphor systems—they contain thousands of conventional mappings; new conventional mappings build on existing ones; novel extensions are constrained by the existing fixed system plus certain constraints on mappings, such as the invariance principle (see below).

One of the major results to be surveyed in this chapter is that basic concepts like time, state, attribute, cause, purpose, means, etc., are metaphorical, and that in general, abstract concepts are metaphorically understood in terms of more concrete, typically spatial, concepts. This means that the study of concepts can be broken down into two parts: the nonmetaphorical concrete (typically spatial) basic concepts and the metaphorically characterized abstract concepts. An account of metaphor, therefore, will go a long way in a characterization of human concepts. And a connectionist theory of metaphor will, correspondingly, go a long way toward providing a connectionist theory of the human conceptual system.

---

* This research was supported in part by grants from the Sloan Foundation and the National Science Foundation (IRI-8703202) to the University of California at Berkeley.

The following colleagues and students helped with this chapter in a variety of ways, from useful comments to allowing me to cite their research: Ken Baldwin, Claudia Brugman, Jane Espenson, Sharon Fischler, Ray Gibbs, Adele Goldberg, Mark Johnson, Karin Myhre, Alan Schwartz, Eve Sweetser, and Mark Turner.

This chapter, in surveying the basics of our knowledge about metaphor, characterizes the kinds of things that connectionist models must eventually be able to do. The disparity between the kinds of phenomena discussed in this chapter and the capacities of all existing models will be obvious to any reader. But if progress is to be made, it is important to bring together the empirical results of linguists with the concerns of model builders.

Thus, the questions a connectionist should be asking in reading the following pages should be: How can one model

- individual fixed cross-domain mappings,
- properties of systems (like duality, hierarchy, and inheritance with overrides),
- the invariance principle,
- novel metaphorical extensions,
- image metaphors,
- metaphor superimpositions,
- metaphor schemas (e.g., GENERIC IS SPECIFIC),
- imageable idioms,
- real time processing of new cases using the fixed system,
- the learning of conventional cases given an experiential basis,
- the realizations of metaphor in such diverse cases as instruments (like thermometers), cartoons, rituals, dreams, social practices, and discourse forms.

Anyone who seriously asks these questions will see that the empirical results are very far ahead of present modeling capabilities, and will be for a long time to come. This should be seen, of course, not as a cause for despair, but as a challenge.

In addition, contemporary metaphor research provides an important negative result: It is not the case in general that metaphorical meanings of sentences are produced algorithmically by taking a literal meaning of that sentence as input and applying a linear procedure to yield a metaphorical meaning.

There are two kinds of problems for such an algorithmic approach, which will be discussed below.

The first problem is that conventional metaphorical mappings are static structures, with such standard properties as duality and hierarchy (see below). These static structures serve at least three purposes: (a) understanding—target domain structures are understood in terms of source domain structures plus mappings; (b) learning—at each stage in development, the current static metaphorical structure is the basis for extensions to new conventional static structures; and (c) extension—the static mappings are used as a basis for novel extensions to nonconventional metaphors.

Now consider the second problem. One might think that novel extensions might work by an algorithmic approach like the following: Create an algorithm whose input is (A) static mappings and (B) literal meanings and whose output is (C) novel metaphorical meanings. Any such algorithm would work step by step. But a large proportion of actual poetic metaphors involve simultaneous multiple mappings (see Lakoff & Turner, 1989, pp. 26-34). Simultaneous activation of a number of mappings, as one might get in a connectionist framework, seems to be what is going on in such cases.

These issues should be borne in mind in reading what follows.

2. THE CLASSICAL AND THE CONTEMPORARY THEORIES

Do not go gentle into that good night.

—Dylan Thomas

Death is the mother of beauty...

—Wallace Stevens, "Sunday Morning"

These famous lines by Thomas and Stevens are examples of what classical theorists, at least since Aristotle, have referred to as metaphor: instances of novel poetic language in which words like "mother," "go," and "night" are not used in their normal everyday senses. In classical theories of language, metaphor was seen as a matter of language not thought. Metaphorical expressions were assumed to be mutually exclusive with the realm of ordinary everyday language: everyday language had no metaphor, and metaphor used mechanisms outside the realm of everyday conventional language.

The classical theory was taken so much for granted over the centuries that many people did not realize that it was just a theory. The theory was not merely taken to be true, but came to be taken as definitional. The word "metaphor" was defined as a novel or poetic linguistic expression where one or more words for a concept are used outside of its normal conventional meaning to express a similar concept.

But such issues are not matters for definitions; they are empirical questions. As a cognitive scientists and a linguist, one asks: What are the generalizations governing the linguistic expressions referred to classically as "poetic metaphors?" When this question is answered rigorously, the classical theory turns out to be false. The generalizations governing poetic metaphorical expressions are not in language, but in thought: They are general mappings across conceptual domains. Moreover, these general principles which take the form of conceptual mappings, apply not just to novel poetic expressions, but to much of ordinary everyday language.

In short, the locus of metaphor is not in language at all, but in the way we conceptualize one mental domain in terms of another. The general theory of metaphor is given by characterizing such cross-domain mappings. And in the process, everyday abstract concepts like time, states, change, causation, and purpose also turn out to be metaphorical.

The result is that metaphor (that is, cross-domain mapping) is absolutely central to ordinary natural language semantics, and that the study of literary metaphor is an extension of the study of everyday metaphor. Everyday metaphor is characterized by a huge system of thousands of cross-domain mappings, and this system is made use of in novel metaphor.

Because of these empirical results, the word "metaphor" has come to be used differently in contemporary metaphor research. The word "metaphor" has come to mean "a cross-domain mapping in the conceptual system." The term "metaphorical expression" refers to a linguistic expression (a word, phrase, or sentence) that is the surface realization of such a cross-domain mapping (this is what the word "metaphor" referred to in the old theory). I will adopt the contemporary usage throughout this chapter.

Experimental results demonstrating the cognitive reality of the extensive system of metaphorical mappings are discussed by Gibbs (in Ortony, 1993). Turner's (1987) book, *Death is the Mother of Beauty*, whose title comes from Stevens's great line, demonstrates in detail how that line uses the ordinary system of everyday mappings. For further examples of how literary metaphor makes use of the ordinary metaphor system, see *More Than Cool Reason: A Field Guide to Poetic Metaphor*, by Lakoff and Turner (1989) and *Reading Minds: The Study of English in the Age of Cognitive Science*, by Turner (1991).

2.1. Beyond the Old Literal–Figurative Distinction

A major assumption that is challenged by contemporary research is the traditional division between literal and figurative language, with metaphor as a kind of figurative language. This entails, by definition, that: What is literal is not metaphorical. In fact, the word "literal" has traditionally been defined in terms of a set of assumptions that have since proved to be false.

Some traditional False Assumptions are:

- All everyday conventional language is literal, and none is metaphorical,
- All subject matter can be comprehended literally, without metaphor,
- Only literal language can be contingently true or false,
- All definitions given in the lexicon of a language are literal, not metaphorical, and
- The concepts used in the grammar of a language are all literal; none are metaphorical.

The big difference between the contemporary theory and traditional views of metaphor lies in this set of assumptions. The reason for the difference is that, in the intervening years, a huge system of everyday, conventional, conceptual metaphors has been discovered. It is a system of metaphor that structures our everyday conceptual system, including most abstract concepts, and that lies behind much of everyday language. The discovery of this enormous metaphor system has destroyed the traditional literal–figurative distinction, since the term "literal," as used in defining the traditional distinction, carries with it all those false assumptions.

A major difference between the contemporary theory and the classical one is based on the old literal–figurative distinction. Given that distinction, one might think that one "arrives at" a metaphorical interpretation of sentence by "starting" with the literal meaning and applying some algorithmic process to it (see Searle, in Ortony, 1993). Though there do exist cases where something like this happens, this is not in general how metaphor works, as we shall see shortly.

2.2. What is Not Metaphorical

Although the old literal–metaphorical distinction was based on assumptions that have proved to be false, one can make a different sort of literal–metaphorical distinction: Those concepts that are not comprehended via conceptual metaphor might be called "literal." Thus, while I will argue that a great many common concepts like causation and purpose are metaphorical, there is nonetheless an extensive range of nonmetaphorical concepts. Thus, a sentence like "The balloon went up" is not metaphorical, nor is the old philosopher's favorite "The cat is on the mat." But as soon as one gets away from concrete physical experience and starts talking about abstractions or emotions, metaphorical understanding is the norm.

3. THE CONTEMPORARY THEORY: SOME EXAMPLES

Let us now turn to some examples that are illustrative of contemporary metaphor research. They will mostly come from the domain of everyday conventional metaphor, since that has been the main focus of the research. I will turn to the discussion of poetic metaphor only after I have discussed the conventional system, since knowledge of the conventional system is needed to make sense of most of the poetic cases.

The evidence for the existence of a system of conventional conceptual metaphors is of five types:

- generalizations governing polysemy (i.e., the use of words with a number of related meanings),
- generalizations governing inference patterns (i.e., cases where a pattern of inferences from one conceptual domain is used in another domain),
- generalizations governing novel metaphorical language (see Lakoff & Turner, 1989),
- generalizations governing patterns of semantic change (see Sweetser, 1990),
- psycholinguistic experiments (see Gibbs, 1990).

We will primarily be discussing the first three of these sources of evidence, since they are the most robust.

3.1. Conceptual Metaphor

Imagine a love relationship described as follows:

Our relationship has hit *a dead-end street*.

Here love is being conceptualized as a journey, with the implication that the relationship is *stalled*, that the lovers cannot *keep going the way they've been going*, that they must *turn back*, or abandon the relationship altogether. This is not an isolated case. English has many everyday expressions that are based on a conceptualization of love as a journey, and they are used not just for talking about love, but for reasoning about it as well. Some are necessarily about love; others can be understood that way. For example,

Look *how far we've come*. It's been *a long, bumpy road*. We can't *turn back* now. We're at a *crossroads*. We may have to *go our separate ways*. The relationship isn't *going anywhere*. We're *spinning our wheels*. Our relationship is *off the track*. The marriage is *on the rocks*. We may have to *bail out* of this relationship.

These are ordinary, everyday English expressions. They are not poetic, nor are they necessarily used for special rhetorical effect. Those like *look how far we've come*, which are not necessarily about love, can readily be understood as being about love.

As a linguist and a cognitive scientist, I ask two commonplace questions:

1. Is there a general principle governing how these linguistic expressions about journeys are used to characterize love?
2. Is there a general principle governing how our patterns of inference about journeys are used to reason about love when expressions such as these are used?

WHAT IS METAPHOR? 209

The answer to both is yes. Indeed, there is a single general principle that answers both questions. But it is a general principle that is neither part of the grammar of English, nor the English lexicon. Rather, it is part of the conceptual system underlying English: It is a principle for understanding the domain of love in terms of the domain of journeys.

The principle can be stated informally as a metaphorical scenario:

> The lovers are travelers on a journey together, with their common-life goals seen as destinations to be reached. The relationship is their vehicle, and it allows them to pursue those common goals together. The relationship is seen as fulfilling its purpose as long as it allows them to make progress toward their common goals. The journey isn't easy. There are impediments, and there are places (crossroads) where a decision has to be made about which direction to go in and whether to keep traveling together.

The metaphor involves understanding one domain of experience, love, in terms of a very different domain of experience, journeys. More technically, the metaphor can be understood as a mapping (in the mathematical sense) from a source domain (in this case, journeys) to a target domain (in this case, love). The mapping is tightly structured. There are ontological correspondences, according to which entities in the domain of love (e.g., the lovers, their common goals, their difficulties, the love relationship, etc.) correspond systematically to entities in the domain of a journey (the travelers, the vehicle, destinations, etc.).

To make it easier to remember what mappings there are in the conceptual system, Johnson and I (Lakoff & Johnson, 1980) adopted a strategy for naming such mappings, using mnemonics which suggest the mapping. Mnemonic names typically (though not always) have the form: TARGET DOMAIN IS SOURCE DOMAIN, or alternatively, TARGET DOMAIN AS SOURCE DOMAIN. In this case, the name of the mapping is LOVE IS A JOURNEY. When I speak of the LOVE-IS-A-JOURNEY metaphor, I am using a mnemonic for a set of ontological correspondences that characterize a mapping, namely:

- The lovers correspond to travelers.
- The love relationship corresponds to the vehicle.
- The lovers' common goals correspond to their common destinations on the journey.
- Difficulties in the relationship correspond to impediments to travel.

It is a common mistake to confuse the name of the mapping, LOVE IS A JOURNEY, for the mapping itself. The mapping is the set of correspondences. Thus, whenever I refer to a metaphor by a mnemonic like LOVE IS A JOURNEY, I will be referring to such a set of correspondences.

If mappings are confused with names of mappings, another misunderstanding can arise. Names of mappings commonly have a propositional form, for example, LOVE IS A JOURNEY. But the mappings themselves are not propositions. If mappings are confused with names for mappings, one might mistakenly think that, in this theory, metaphors are propositional. They are, of course, anything but that: metaphors are mappings, that is, sets of conceptual correspondences.

The LOVE-AS-A-JOURNEY mapping is a set of ontological correspondences that characterize epistemic correspondences by mapping knowledge about journeys onto knowledge about love. Such correspondences permit us to reason about love using the knowledge we use to reason about journeys. Let us take an example. Consider the expression, "We're stuck," said by one lover to another about their relationship. How is this expression about travel to be understood as being about their relationship?

"We're stuck" can be used of travel, and when it is, it evokes knowledge about travel. The exact knowledge may vary from person to person, but here is a typical example of the kind of knowledge evoked. The capitalized expressions represent entities in the ontology of travel, that is, in the source domain of the LOVE-IS-A-JOURNEY mapping given above.

> TWO TRAVELERS are in a VEHICLE, TRAVELING WITH COMMON DESTINATIONS. The VEHICLE encounters some IMPEDIMENT and gets stuck, that is, makes it nonfunctional. If they do nothing, they will not REACH THEIR DESTINATIONS. There are a limited number of alternatives for action:

- They can try to get it moving again, either by fixing it or getting it past the IMPEDIMENT that stopped it.
- They can remain in the nonfunctional VEHICLE and give up on REACHING THEIR DESTINATIONS.
- They can abandon the VEHICLE.

> The alternative of remaining in the nonfunctional VEHICLE takes the least effort, but does not satisfy the desire to REACH THEIR DESTINATIONS.

The ontological correspondences that constitute the LOVE-IS-A-JOURNEY metaphor map the ontology of travel onto the ontology of love. In so doing they map this scenario about travel onto a corresponding love scenario in which the corresponding alternatives for action are seen. Here is the corresponding love scenario that results from applying the correspondences to this knowledge structure. The target domain entities that are mapped by the correspondences are capitalized:

> Two LOVERS are in a LOVE RELATIONSHIP, PURSUING COMMON-LIFE GOALS. The RELATIONSHIP encounters some DIFFICULTY, which makes it nonfunctional. It they do nothing, they will not be able to ACHIEVE THEIR LIFE GOALS. There are a limited number of alternatives for action:

- They can try to make it functional again, either by fixing it or getting it past the DIFFICULTY.
- They can remain in the nonfunctional RELATIONSHIP, and give up on ACHIEVING THEIR LIFE GOALS.
- They can abandon the RELATIONSHIP.

The alternative of remaining in the nonfunctional RELATIONSHIP takes the least effort, but does not satisfy the desire to ACHIEVE LIFE GOALS.

this is an example of an inference pattern that is mapped from one domain to another. It is via such mappings that we apply knowledge about travel to love relationships.

3.2. Metaphors Are Not Mere Words

What constitutes the LOVE-AS-JOURNEY metaphor is not any particular word or expression. It is the onotological mapping across conceptual domains, from the source domain of journeys to the target domain of love. The metaphor is not just a matter of language, but of thought and reason. The language is secondary. The mapping is primary, in that it sanctions the use of source domain language and inference patterns for target domain concepts. The mapping is conventional, that is, it is a fixed part of our conceptual system, one of our conventional ways of conceptualizing love relationships.

This view of metaphor is thoroughly at odds with the view that metaphors are just linguistic expressions. If metaphors were merely linguistic expressions, we would expect different linguistic expressions to be different metaphors. Thus, "We've hit a dead-end street" would constitute one metaphor. "We can't turn back now" would constitute another, entirely different metaphor. "Their marriage is on the rocks" would involve still a different metaphor. And so on for dozens of examples. Yet we don't seem to have dozens of different metaphors here. We have one metaphor, in which love is conceptualized as a journey. The mapping tells us precisely how love is being conceptualized as a journey. And this unified way of *conceptualizing* love metaphorically is realized in many different *linguistic* expressions.

It should be noted that contemporary metaphor theorists commonly use the term "metaphor" to refer to the conceptual mapping, and the term "metaphorical expression" to refer to an individual linguistic expression (like *dead-end street*) that is sanctioned by a mapping. We have adopted this terminology for the following reason: Metaphor, as a phenomenon, involves both conceptual mappings and individual linguistic expressions. It is important to keep them distinct. Since it is the mappings that are primary and that state the generalizations that are our principal concern, we have reserved the term "metaphor" for the mappings, rather than for the linguistic expressions.

In the literature of the field, small capitals like LOVE IS A JOURNEY are used as mnemonics to name mappings. Thus, when we refer to the LOVE-IS-A-JOURNEY metaphor, we are referring to the set of correspondences discussed above. The English sentence "Love is a journey," on the other hand, is a metaphorical expression that is understood via that set of correspondences.

3.3. Generalizations

The LOVE-IS-A-JOURNEY metaphor is a conceptual mapping that characterizes a generalization of two kinds:

1. Polysemy generalization—a generalization over related senses of linguistic expressions (e.g., *dead-end street, crossroads, stuck, spinning one's wheels, not going anywhere,* and so on).
2. Inferential generalization—a generalization over inferences across different conceptual domains.

That is, the existence of the mapping provides a general answer to two questions:

1. Why are words for travel used to describe love relationships?
2. Why are inference patterns used to reason about travel also used to reason about love relationships?

Correspondingly, from the perspective of the linguistic analyst, the existence of such cross-domain pairings of words and of inference patterns provides evidence for the existence of such mappings.

3.4. Novel Extensions of Conventional Metaphors

The fact that the LOVE-IS-A-JOURNEY mapping is a fixed part of our conceptual system explains why new and imaginative uses of the mapping can be understood instantly, given the ontological correspondences and other knowledge about journeys. Take the song lyric,

We're driving in the fast lane on the freeway of love.

The traveling knowledge called upon is this: When you drive in the fast lane, you go a long way in a short time and it can be exciting and dangerous. The general metaphorical mapping maps this knowledge about driving into knowledge about love relationships. The danger may be to the vehicle (the relationship may not last) or the passengers (the lovers may be hurt, emotionally). The excitement of the love journey is sexual. Our understanding of the song lyric is a consequence of the preexisting metaphorical correspondences of the LOVE-IS-A-JOURNEY metaphor. The song lyric is instantly comprehensible to speakers of English because those metaphorical correspondences are already part of our conceptual system.

The LOVE-IS-A-JOURNEY metaphor and Reddy's Conduit Metaphor (Reddy, 1979) were the two examples that first convinced me that metaphor was not a figure of speech, but a mode of thought, defined by a systematic mapping from a source to a target domain. What convinced me were the three characteristics of metaphor that I have just discussed:

1. the systematicity in the linguistic correspondences.
2. the use of metaphor to govern reasoning and behavior based on that reasoning.
3. the possibility for understanding novel extensions in terms of the conventional correspondences.

3.5. Motivation

Each conventional metaphor, that is, each mapping, is a fixed pattern of conceptual correspondences across conceptual domains. As such, each mapping defines an open-ended class of potential correspondences across inference patterns. When activated, a mapping may apply to a novel source domain knowledge structure and characterize a corresponding target domain knowledge structure.

Mappings should not be thought of as processes, or as algorithms that mechanically take source domain inputs and produce target domain outputs. Each mapping should be seen instead as a fixed pattern of onotological correspondences across domains that may, or may not, be applied to a source domain knowledge structure or a source domain lexical item. Thus, lexical items that are conventional in the source domain are not always conventional in the target domain. Instead, each source domain lexical item may or may not make use of the static mapping pattern. If it does, it has an extended lexicalized sense in the target domain, where that sense is characterized by the mapping. If not, the source domain lexical item will not have a conventional sense in the target domain, but may still be actively mapped in the case of novel metaphor. Thus, the words *freeway* and *fast lane* are not conventionally used of love, but the knowledge structures associated with them are mapped by the LOVE-IS-A-JOURNEY metaphor in the case of "We're driving in the fast lane on the freeway of love."

3.6. Imageable Idioms

Many of the metaphorical expressions discussed in the literature on conventional metaphor are idioms. On classical views, idioms have arbitrary meanings. But within cognitive linguistics, the possibility exists that they are not arbitrary, but rather motivated. That is, they do not arise automatically by productive rules, but they fit one or more patterns present in the conceptual system. Let us look a little more closely at idioms.

An idiom like "spinning one's wheels" comes with a conventional mental image, that of the wheels of a car stuck in some substance—either in mud, sand, snow, or on ice, so that the car cannot move when the motor is engaged and the wheels turn. Part of our knowledge about that image is that a lot of energy is being used up (in spinning the wheels) without any progress being made, that the situation will not readily change of its own accord, that it will take a lot of effort on the part of the occupants to get the vehicle moving again—and that may not even be possible.

The LOVE-IS-A-JOURNEY metaphor applies to this knowledge about the image. It maps this knowledge onto knowledge about love relationships: A lot of energy is being spent without any progress toward fulfilling common goals, the situation will not change of its own accord, it will take a lot of effort on the part of the lovers to make more progress, and so on. In short, when idioms have associated conventional images, it is common for an independently motivated conceptual metaphor to map that knowledge from the source to the target domain. For a survey of experiments verifying the existence of such images and such mappings, see Gibbs (1990).

3.7. Mappings Are at the Superordinate Level

In the LOVE-IS-A-JOURNEY mapping, a love relationship corresponds to a vehicle. A vehicle is a superordinate category that includes such basic-level categories as car, train, boat, and plane. Indeed, the examples of vehicles are typically drawn from this range of basic-level categories: car (*long bumpy road, spinning our wheels*), train (*off the track*), boat (*on the rocks, foundering*), plane (*just taking off, bailing out*). This is not an accident: In general, we have found that mappings are at the superordinate rather than the basic level. Thus, we do not find fully general submappings like A LOVE RELATIONSHIP IS A CAR; when we find a love relationship conceptualized as a car, we also tend to find it conceptualized as a boat, a train, a plane, etc. It is the superordinate category VEHICLE not the basic-level category CAR that is in the general mapping.

It should be no surprise that the generalization is at the superordinate level, while the special cases are at the basic level. After all, the basic level is the level of rich mental images and rich knowledge structure. (For a discussion of the properties of basic-level categories, see Lakoff, 1987, pp. 31-50.) A mapping at the superordinate level maximizes the possibilities for mapping rich conceptual structure in the source domain onto the target domain, since it permits many basic-level instances, each of which is information rich.

Thus, a prediction is made about conventional mappings: the categories mapped will tend to be at the superordinate rather than basic level. Thus, one tends not to find mappings like A LOVE RELATIONSHIP IS A CAR or A LOVE RELATIONSHIP IS A BOAT. Instead, one tends to find both basic-level cases (e.g., both cars and boats), which indicates that the generalization is one level higher, at the superordinate level of the vehicle. In the hundreds of cases of conventional mappings studied so far, this prediction has been borne out: It is superordinate categories that are used in mappings.

4. BASIC SEMANTIC CONCEPTS THAT ARE METAPHORICAL

Most people are not too surprised to discover that emotional concepts like love and anger are understood metaphorically. What is more interesting, and I think more exciting, is the realization that many of the most basic concepts in our conceptual systems are also comprehended normally via metaphor—concepts like time, quantity, state, change, action, cause, purpose, means, modality, and even the concept of a category. These are concepts that enter normally into the grammars of languages, and if they are indeed metaphorical in nature, then metaphor becomes central to grammar.

What I would like to suggest is that the same kinds of considerations that lead to our acceptance of the LOVE-AS-JOURNEY metaphor lead inevitably to the conclusion that such basic concepts are often, and perhaps always, understood via metaphor.

4.1. Categories

Classical categories are understood metaphorically in terms of bounded regions, or "containers." Thus, something can be *in* or *out* of a category, it can be *put into* a category or *removed from* a category, etc. The logic of classical categories is the logic of containers (see Figure 5.1).

If X is in Container A and Container A is in Container B, then X is in Container B.

This is true not by virtue of any logical deduction, but by virtue of the topological properties of containers. Under the CLASSICAL CATEGORIES ARE CONTAINERS metaphor, the logical properties of categories are inherited from the logical properties of containers. One of the principal logical properties of classical categories is that the classical syllogism holds for them. The classical syllogism,

Figure 5.1.

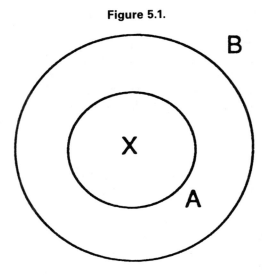

Socrates is a man.
All men are mortal.
Therefore, Socrates is mortal.

is of the form:

If X is in category A and Category A is in Category B, then X is in Category B.

Thus, the logical properties of classical categories can be seen as following from the topological properties of containers plus the metaphorical mapping from containers to categories. As long as the topological properties of containers are preserved by the mapping, this result will be true.

In other words, there is a generalization to be stated here. The language of containers applies to classical categories and the logic of containers is true of classical categories. A single metaphorical mapping ought to characterize both the linguistic and logical generalizations at once. This can be done provided that the topological properties of containers are preserved in the mapping.

The joint linguistic-and-inferential relation between containers and classical categories is not an isolated case. Let us take another example.

4.2. Quantity and Linear Scales

The concept of quantities involves at least two metaphors. The first is the well-known MORE IS UP, LESS IS DOWN metaphor as shown by a myriad of expressions like *prices rose, stocks skyrocketed, the market plummeted*, and so on. A second is that LINEAR SCALES ARE PATHS. We can see this in expressions like:

John is *far* more intelligent than Bill.
John's intelligence *goes way beyond* Bill's.
John is *way ahead* of Bill in intelligence.

The metaphor maps the starting point of the path onto the bottom of the scale and maps distance traveled onto quantity in general.

What is particularly interesting is that the logic of paths maps onto the logic of linear scales (see Figure 5.2).

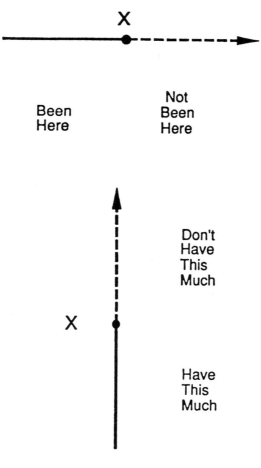

Figure 5.2.

Path inference. If you are going from A to C, and you are now at an intermediate point B, then you have been at all points between A and B and not at any points between B and C.

Example. If you are going from San Francisco to New York along Route 80, and you are now at Chicago, then you have been to Denver but not to Pittsburgh.

Linear scale inference. If you have exactly $50 in your bank account, then you have $40, $30, and so on, but not $60, $70, or any larger amount.

The form of these inferences is the same. The path inference is a consequence of the cognitive topology of paths. It will be true of any path image schema. Again, there is a linguistic-and-inferential generalization to be stated. It would be stated by the metaphor LINEAR SCALES ARE PATHS, provided that metaphors in general preserve the cognitive topology (that is, the image-schematic structure) of the source domain.

Looking at the inferential structure alone, one might suggest a nonmetaphorical alternative in which both linear scales and paths are instances of a more general abstract schema. But when *both* the inferential and lexical data are considered, it becomes clear that a metaphorical solution is required. An expression like "ahead of" is from the spatial domain, not the linear scale domain: "Ahead" in its core sense is defined with respect to one's head—it is the direction in which one is facing. To say that there is no metaphorical mapping from paths to scales is to say that "ahead of" is not fundamentally spatial and characterized with respect to heads; it is to claim rather that "ahead" is very abstract, neutral between space and linear scales, and has nothing to do with heads. This would be a bizarre analysis. Similarly, for sentences like "John's intelligence goes beyond Bill's," the nonmetaphorical analysis would claim that "go" is not fundamentally a verb of motion at all, but is somehow neutral between motion and a linear relation. This would also be bizarre. In short, if one grants that "ahead of" and "go" are fundamentally spatial, then the fact that they can also be used of linear scales suggests a metaphor solution. Indeed, there could be no such neutral sense of "go" for these cases, since "go beyond" in the spatial sense involves motion, while in the linear scale sense, there is no motion or change, but just a point on a scale. Here the neutral case solution is not even available.

4.3. The Invariance Principle

In the examples we have just considered, the image schemas characterizing the source domains (containers, paths) are mapped onto the target domains (categories, linear scales). This observation leads to the following hypothesis, called "The Invariance Principle":

Metaphorical mappings preserve the cognitive topology (that is, the image-schema structure) of the source domain, in a way consistent with the inherent structure of the target domain.

What the invariance principle does is guarantee that, for container schemas, interiors will be mapped onto interiors, exteriors onto exteriors, and boundaries onto boundaries; for path schemas, sources will be mapped onto sources, goals onto goals, trajectories onto trajectories; and so on.

To understand the invariance principle properly, it is important not to think of mappings as algorithmic processes that "start" with source domain structure and wind up with target domain structure. Such a mistaken understanding of mappings would lead to a mistaken understanding of the invariance principle, namely, that one first picks all the image-schematic structure of the source domain, then one copies it onto the target domain unless the target domain interferes.

One should instead think of the invariance principle in terms of constraints on fixed correspondences: If one looks at the existing correspondences, one will see that the invariance principle holds (source domain interiors correspond to target domain interiors; source domain exteriors correspond to target domain exteriors; etc.). As a consequence it will turn out that the image-schematic structure of the target domain cannot be violated: One cannot find cases where a source domain interior is mapped onto a target domain exterior, or where a source domain exterior is mapped onto a target domain path. This simply does not happen.

4.4. Target Domain Overrides

A corollary of the invariance principle is that image-schema structure inherent in the target domain cannot be violated, and that inherent target domain structure limits the possibilities for mappings automatically. This general principle explains a large number of previously mysterious limitations on metaphorical mappings. For example, it explains why you can give someone a kick, even if they don't have it afterwards, and why you can give someone information, even if you don't lose it. This is just a consequence of the fact that inherent target domain structure automatically limits what can be mapped. For example, consider that part of your inherent knowledge of actions that says that actions do not continue to exist after they occur. Now consider the ACTIONS-ARE-TRANSFERS metaphor, in which actions are conceptualized as objects transferred from an agent to a patient, as when one gives someone a kick or a punch. We know (as part of target domain knowledge) that an action does not exist after it occurs. In the source domain, where there is a giving, the recipient possesses the object given after the giving. But this cannot be mapped onto the target domain since the inherent structure of the target domain says that no such object exists after the action is over. The target domain override in the invariance principle explains why you can give someone a kick without his having it afterward.

4.5. Abstract Inferences as Metaphorical Spatial Inferences

Spatial inferences are characterized by the topological structure of image-schemas. We have seen cases such as CATEGORIES ARE CONTAINERS and LINEAR SCALES ARE PATHS where image-schema structure is preserved by metaphor and where abstract inferences about categories and linear scales are metaphorical versions of spatial inferences about containers and paths. The invariance principle hypothesizes that image-schema structure is always preserved by metaphor.

The invariance principle raises the possibility that a great many, if not all, abstract inferences are actually metaphorical versions of spatial inferences that are inherent in the topological structure of image-schemas. What I will do now is turn to other cases of basic, but abstract, concepts to see what evidence there is for the claim that such concepts are fundamentally characterized by metaphor.

4.6. Time

It has often been noted that time in English is conceptualized in terms of space. The details are rather interesting.

Ontology: Time is understood in terms of things (i.e., entities and locations) and motion.

Background condition: The present time is at the same location as a canonical observer.

Mapping:

- Times are things.
- The passing of time is motion.
- Future times are in front of the observer; past times are behind the observer.
- One thing is moving, the other is stationary; the stationary entity is the deictic center.

Entailment:

- Since motion is continuous and one-dimensional, the passage of time is continuous and one-dimensional.

Special Case 1:

- The observer is fixed; times are entities moving with respect to the observer.
- Times are oriented with their fronts in their direction of motion.

Entailments:

- If Time 2 follows Time 1, then Time 2 is in the future relative to Time 1.
- The time passing the observer is the present time.
- Time has a velocity relative to the observer.

Special Case 2

- Times are fixed locations; the observer is moving with respect to time.

Entailment.

- Time has extension, and can be measured.
- An extended time, like a spatial area, may be conceived of as a bounded region.

This metaphor, TIME PASSING IS MOTION, with its two special cases, embodies a generalization that accounts for a wide range of cases where a spatial expression can also be used for time. Special Case 1, TIME PASSING IS MOTION OF AN OBJECT, accounts for both the linguistic form and the semantic entailments of expressions like:

> The time will come when... The time has long since gone when... The time for action has arrived. That time is here. In the weeks following next Tuesday... On the preceding day,... I'm looking ahead to Christmas. Thanksgiving is coming up on us. Let's put all that behind us. I can't face the future. Time is flying by. The time has passed when...

Thus, special Case 1 characterizes the general principle behind the temporal use of words like *come, go, here, follow, precede, ahead, behind, fly, pass*, accounting not only for why they are used for both space and time, but why they mean what they mean.

Special Case 2, TIME PASSING IS MOTION OVER A LANDSCAPE, accounts for a different range of cases, expressions like:

> There's going to be trouble down the road.
> He stayed there for ten years.
> He stayed there a long time.
> His stay in Russia extended over many years.
> He passed the time happily.
> He arrived on time.
> We're coming up on Christmas.
> We're getting close to Christmas.
> He'll have his degree within two years.
> I'll be there in a minute.

Special Case 2 maps location expressions like *down the road, for* + location, *long, over, come, close to, within, in, pass*, onto corresponding temporal expressions with their corresponding meanings. Again, Special Case 2 states a general principle relating spatial terms and inference patterns to temporal terms and inference patterns.

The details of the two special cases are rather different; indeed, they are inconsistent with one another. The existence of such special cases has an especially interesting theoretical consequence: words mapped by both special cases will have inconsistent readings. Take, for example, the *come* of *Christmas is coming* (Special Case 1) and *We're coming up on Christmas* (Special Case 2). Both instances of *come* are temporal, but one takes a moving time as first argument and the other takes a moving observer as first argument. The same is true of *pass* in *The time has passed* (Special Case 1) and in *He passed the time* (Special Case 2).

These differences in the details of the mappings show that one cannot just say blithely that spatial expressions can be used to speak of time, without specifying details, as though there were only one correspondence between time and space. When we are explicit about stating the mappings, we discover that there are two different—and inconsistent—subcases.

The fact that time is understood metaphorically in terms of motion, entities, and locations accords with our biological knowledge. In our visual systems, we have detectors for motion and detectors for objects/locations. We do not have detectors for time (whatever that could mean). Thus, it makes good biological sense that time should be understood in terms of things and motion.

4.7. Duality

The two special cases (location and space) of TIME PASSING IS MOTION metaphor is not merely an accidental feature of our understanding of time. As we shall see below, there are other metaphors that come in such location-object pairs. Such pairs are called "duals," and the general phenomenon in which metaphors come in location-object pairs is referred to as "duality."

4.8. Simultaneous Mappings

It is important to recall that metaphorical mappings are fixed correspondences that can be activated, rather than algorithmic processes that take inputs and give outputs. Thus, it is *not* the case that sentences containing conventional metaphors are the products of a real-time process of conversion from literal to metaphorical readings. A sentence like *The time for action has arrived* is not understood by first trying to give a literal reading to *arrive*, and then, upon failing, trying to give it a temporal reading. Instead, the metaphor TIME PASSING IS MOTION is a fixed structure of existing correspondences between the space and time domains, and *arrive* has a conventional extended meaning that makes use of that fixed structure of correspondences.

Thus, it is possible for two different parts of a sentence to make use of two distinct metaphorical mappings at once. Consider a phrase like, *Within the coming weeks*. Here, *within* makes uses of the metaphor of time as a stationary landscape which has extension and bounded regions, while *coming* makes use of the metaphor of times as moving objects. This is possible because the two metaphors for time pick out different aspects of the target domain. *The coming weeks* conceptualizes those weeks as a whole, in motion relative to the observer. *Within* looks inside that whole, conceptualizing it as a bounded region with an interior. Each mapping is used partially. Thus, while the mappings—as wholes—are inconsistent, there are cases where parts of the mappings may be consistently superimposed. The invariance principle allows such parts of the mappings to be picked out and used to characterize reasoning about different aspects of the target domain.

Simultaneous mappings are very common in poetry. Take, for example, the Dylan Thomas line "Do not go gentle into that good night." Here "go" reflects DEATH IS DEPARTURE, "gentle" reflects LIFE IS A STRUGGLE, with death as defeat. "Night" reflects A LIFETIME IS A DAY, with death as night. This one line has three different metaphors for death, each mapped onto different parts of the sentence. This is possible since mappings are fixed correspondences.

There is an important lesson to be learned from this example. In mathematics, mappings are static correspondences. In computer science, it is common to represent mathematical mappings by algorithmic processes that take place in real time. Researchers in information processing psychology and cognitive science also commonly represent mappings as real-time algorithmic procedures. Some researchers from these fields have mistakenly supposed that the metaphorical mappings we are discussing should also be represented as real-time, sequential algorithmic procedures, where the input to each metaphor is a literal meaning. Any attempt to do this will fail for the simultaneous mapping cases just discussed.

5. EVENT STRUCTURE

I now want to turn to some research by myself and some of my students (especially Sharon Fischler, Karin Myhre, and Jane Espenson) on the metaphorical understanding of event structure in English. What we have found is that various aspects of event structure, including notions like states, changes, processes, actions, causes, purposes, and means, are characterized cognitively via metaphor in terms of space, motion, and force.

The general mapping we have found (for the Event Structure Metaphor) goes as follows:

- States are locations (bounded regions in space).
- Changes are movements (into or out of bounded regions).
- Causes are forces.
- Actions are self-propelled movements.
- Purposes are destinations.
- Means are paths (to destinations).
- Difficulties are impediments to motion.
- Expected progress is a travel schedule; a schedule is a virtual traveler, who reaches prearranged destinations at prearranged times.
- External events are large, moving objects.
- Long-term, purposeful activities are journeys.

This mapping generalizes over an extremely wide range of expressions for one or more aspects of event structure. For example, take states and changes. We speak of being *in* or *out* of a state, or *going into* or *out of* it, of *entering* or *leaving* it, of getting *to* a state or emerging *from* it.

This is a rich and complex metaphor whose parts interact in complex ways. To get an idea of how it works, consider the submapping "difficulties are impediments to motion." In the metaphor, purposive action is self-propelled motion toward a destination. A difficulty is something that impedes motion to such a destination. Metaphorical difficulties of this sort come in five types: blockages, features of the terrain, burdens, counterforces, and lack of an energy source. Examples of each are shown below.

Blockages

> He got over his divorce. He's trying to get around the regulations. He went through the trial. We ran into a brick wall. We've got him boxed into a corner.

Features of the terrain.

> He's between a rock and a hard place. It's been uphill all the way. We've been bogged down. We've been hacking our way through a jungle of regulations.

Burdens.

> He's carrying quite a load. He's weighed down by lot of assignments. He's been trying to shoulder all the responsibility. Get off my back!

Counterforces.

> Quit pushing me around. She's leading him around by the nose. She's holding him back.

Lack of an energy source.

> I'm out of gas. We're running out of steam.

To see just how rich the event structure metaphor is, consider some of its basic entailments.

- Manner of action is manner of motion.
- A different means for achieving a purpose is a different path.
- Forces affecting action are forces affecting motion.
- The inability to act is the inability to move.
- Progress made is distance traveled or distance from goal.

We will consider examples of each of these one by one, including a number of special cases.

Aids to Action are Aids to Motion.

> It is smooth sailing from here on in. It's all downhill from here. There's nothing in our way.

A Different Means of Achieving a Result is a Different Path.

> Do it this way. She did it the other way. Do it any way you can. However you want to go about it is fine with me.

Manner of Action is Manner of Motion.

> We are moving/running/skipping right along. We slogged through it. He is flailing around. He is falling all over himself. We are leaping over hurdles. He is out of step. He is in step.

Careful Action is Careful Motion.

> I'm walking on eggshells. He is treading on thin ice. He is walking a fine line.

Speed of Action is Speed of Movement.

> He flew through his work. He is running around. It is going swimmingly. Keep things moving at a good clip. Things have slowed to a crawl. She is going by leaps and bounds. I am moving at a snail's pace.

Purposeful Action is Self-Propelled Motion To a Destination.

> This has the special cases shown below.

Making Progress Is Forward Movement.

> We are moving ahead. Let's forge ahead. Let's keep moving forward. We made lots of forward movement.

Amount of Progress is Distance Moved.

> We've come a long way. We've covered lots of ground We've made it this far.

Undoing Progress is Backward Movement.

> We are sliding backward. We are backsliding. We need to backtrack. It is time to turn around and retrace our steps.

Expected Progress is a Travel Schedule; A Schedule is a Virtual Traveler who reaches prearranged destinations at prearranged times.

> We're behind schedule on the project. We got a head start on the project. I'm trying to catch up. I finally got a little ahead.

Starting an Action is Starting out on a Path.

> We are just starting out. We have taken the first step.

Success Is Reaching The End of the Path.

> We've reached the end. We are seeing the light at the end of the tunnel. We only have a short way to go. The end is in sight. The end is a long way off.

Lack of Purpose is Lack of Direction.

> He is just floating around. He is drifting aimlessly. He needs some direction.

Lack of Progress is Lack of Movement.

We are at a standstill. We aren't getting any place. We aren't going anywhere. We are going nowhere with this.

External Events Are Large Moving Objects.

Special Case 1: Things.
How're things going? Things are going with me. Things are going against me these days. Things took a turn for the worse. Things are going my way.

Special Case 2: Fluids.
You gotta go with the flow. I'm just trying to keep my head above water. The tide of events... The winds of change... The flow of history... I'm trying to get my bearings. He's up a creek without a paddle. We're all in the same boat.

Special Case 3: Horses.
Try to keep a tight rein on the situation. Keep a grip on the situation. Don't let things get out of hand. Wild horses couldn't make me go. "Whoa!" (said when things start to get out of hand)

Such examples provide overwhelming empirical support for the existence of the event structure metaphor. And the existence of that metaphor shows that the most common abstract concepts—TIME, STATE, CHANGE, CAUSATION, ACTION, PURPOSE, and MEANS—are conceptualized via metaphor. Since such concepts are at the very center of our conceptual systems, the fact that they are conceptualized metaphorically shows that metaphor is central to ordinary abstract thought.

5.1. Inheritance Hierarchies

Metaphorical mappings do not occur isolated from one another. They are sometimes organized in hierarchical structures, in which 'lower' mappings in the hierarchy inherit the structures of the 'higher' mappings. Let us consider an example of a hierarchy with three levels.

> Level 1: The Event Structure Metaphor
> Level 2: A PURPOSEFUL LIFE IS JOURNEY
> Level 3: LOVE IS A JOURNEY; A CAREER IS A JOURNEY

To refresh your memory, recall:
The Event Structure Metaphor
Target Domain: Events   Source Domain: Space

- States are locations (bounded regions in space).
- Changes are movements (into or out of bounded regions).

- Causes are forces.
- Actions are self-propelled movements.
- Purposes are destinations.
- Means are paths (to destinations).
- Difficulties are impediments to motion.
- Expected progress is a travel schedule; a schedule is a virtual traveler, who reaches prearranged destinations at prearranged times.
- External events are large, moving objects.
- Long-term, purposeful activities are journeys.

In our culture, life is assumed to be purposeful, that is, we are expected to have goals in life. In the event structure metaphor, purposes are destinations and purposeful action is self-propelled motion toward a destination. A purposeful life is a long-term, purposeful activity, and hence a journey. Goals in life are destinations on the journey. The actions one takes in life are self-propelled movements, and the totality of one's actions form a path one moves along. Choosing a means to achieve a goal is choosing a path to a destination. Difficulties in life are impediments to motion. External events are large moving objects that can impede motion toward one's life goals. One's expected progress through life is charted in terms of a life schedule, which is conceptualized as a virtual traveler that one is expected to keep up with.

In short, the metaphor A PURPOSEFUL LIFE IS A JOURNEY makes use of all the structure of the event structure metaphor, since events in a life conceptualized as purposeful are subcases of events in general.

A PURPOSEFUL LIFE IS A JOURNEY
Target Domain: Life   Source Domain: Space

•the person leading a life is a traveler.

Inherits Event Structure Metaphor, with:

Events = Significant Life Events
Purposes = Life Goals

Thus, we have expressions like:

He got a head start in life. He's without direction in his life. I'm where I want to be in life. I'm at a crossroads in my life. He'll go places in life. He's never let anyone get in his way. He's gone through a lot in life.

Just as significant life events are special cases of events, so events in a love relationship are special cases of life events. Thus, the LOVE-IS-A-JOURNEY inherits the structure of the LIFE-IS-A-JOURNEY metaphor. What is special about the LOVE-IS-A-JOURNEY metaphor, is that there are two lovers, who are travelers, and that the love relationship is a vehicle. The rest of the mapping is a consequence of inheriting the LIFE-IS-A-JOURNEY metaphor. Because the lovers are in the same vehicle, they have common destinations, that is, common life goals. Relationship difficulties are impediments to travel.

LOVE IS A JOURNEY
Target Domain: Love   Source Domain: Space
•The lovers are travelers.
•The love relationship is a vehicle.
Inherits the LIFE-IS-A-JOURNEY metaphor.

A career is another aspect of life that can be conceptualized as a journey. Here, because STATUS IS UP, a career is actually a journey upward. Career goals are special cases of life goals.

A CAREER IS A JOURNEY
Target Domain: Career   Source Domain: Space
•A careerist is a traveler.
•Status is up.

Inherits LIFE IS A JOURNEY, with:

Life goals = Career Goals
Ideal: To go as high, far, and fast as possible.

Examples include:

He clawed his way to the top. He's over the hill. She's on the fast track. He's climbing the corporate ladder. She's moving up in the ranks quickly.

This inheritance hierarchy accounts for a range of generalizations. First, there are generalizations about lexical items. Take the word *crossroads*. Its central meaning is in the domain of space. But it can be used in a metaphorical sense of any extended activity, of one's life, of a love relationship, or of a career.

I'm at a crossroads on this project. I'm at a crossroads in life. We're at a crossroads in our relationship. I'm at a crossroads in my career.

The hierarchy allows one to state a general principle: that *crossroads* is extended lexically via the submetaphor of the event structure metaphor that says long-term purposeful activities are journeys, and that all its other uses are automatically generated via the inheritance hierarchy. Thus, separate senses for each level of the hierarchy are not needed.

The second generalization is inferential in character. Thus, the understanding of difficulties as impediments to travel occurs not only in events in general, but also in a purposeful life, in a love relationship, and in a career. The inheritance hierarchy guarantees that this understanding of difficulties in life, love, and careers is a consequence of such an interstanding of difficulties in events in general.

The hierarchy also allows us to characterize lexical items whose meanings are more restricted: Thus, *climbing the ladder* refers only to careers, not to love relationships or to life in general.

Such hierarchical organization is a very prominent feature of the metaphor system of English and other languages. So far we have found that the metaphors higher up in the hierarchy tend to be more widespread than those mappings at lower levels. Thus, the event structure metaphor is very widespread (and may even be universal), while the metaphors for life, love, and careers are much more restricted culturally.

5.2. Duality in the Event Structure System

In our discussion of time metaphors, we noted the existence of an object-location duality. There were two related time metaphors. In both, the passage of time was understood in terms of relative motion between an observer and a time. In the object dual, the observer is fixed and times are moving objects. In the location dual, the opposite is true. The observer moves and times are fixed locations in a landscape.

The event structure system that we have seen so far is based wholly on location. But there is another event structure system that is the dual of the one we have just discussed—a system based on objects rather than locations. In both systems, CHANGE IS MOTION and CAUSES ARE FORCES that control motion. The difference is this:

> In the location system, change is the motion of the thing changing to a new location or from an old one.
> In the object system, the thing changing does not necessarily move. Change is instead the motion of an object to, or away from, the thing changing.

In addition, the object in motion is conceptualized as a possession and the thing changing as a possessor. Change is thus seen as the acquisition or loss of an object. Causation is seen as giving or taking. Here are some examples:

- I have a headache. [The headache is a possession]
- I got a headache. [Change is acquisition—motion to]
- My headache went away. [Change is loss—motion from]
- The noise gave me a headache. [Causation is giving—motion to]
- The aspirin took away my headache. [Causation is taking—motion from]

WHAT IS METAPHOR? 231

We can see the duality somewhat more clearly with a word like "trouble":

- I'm in trouble. [Trouble is a location]
- I have trouble. [Trouble is an object that is possessed]

In both cases, trouble is being attributed to me, and in both cases, trouble is metaphorically conceptualized as being in the same place as me (colocation)—in one case, because I possess the trouble object and in the other case, because I am in the trouble location. That is, attribution in both cases is conceptualized metaphorically as colocation. In "I'm in trouble," trouble is a state. A state is an attribute that is conceptualized as a location. Attributes (or properties) are like states, except that they are conceptualized as possessable objects.

Thus, STATES ARE LOCATIONS and ATTRIBUTES ARE POSSESSIONS are duals, since possession and location are special cases of the same thing—colocation—and since states and attributes are also special cases of the same thing—what can be attributed to someone.

Given this, we can see that there is an object version of the event structure metaphor:

- Attributes are possessions.
- Changes are movements (of possessions, namely, acquisitions or losses).
- Causes are forces (controlling the movement of possessions, namely, giving or taking away).

These are the duals of:

- States are locations.
- Changes are movements (to or from locations).
- Causes are forces (controlling movement to or from locations).

Similarly, ACTIONS ARE SELF-PROPELLED MOVEMENTS (to or from locations) has as its object dual ACTIONS ARE SELF-CONTROLLED ACQUISITIONS OR LOSSES. Thus, there is a reason why one can "take" certain actions—you can take a shower, or take a shot at someone, or take a chance.

The submapping PURPOSES ARE DESTINATIONS also has a dual. Destinations are desired locations, and so the submapping can be rephrased as PURPOSES ARE DESIRED LOCATIONS, and ACHIEVING A PURPOSE IS REACHING A DESIRED LOCATION. Replacing "location" by "object," we get the dual PURPOSES ARE DESIRED OBJECTS, and ACHIEVING A PURPOSE IS ACQUIRING A DESIRED OBJECT (or ridding oneself of an undesirable one).

Here are some examples:
ACHIEVING A PURPOSE IS ACQUIRING A DESIRED OBJECT

They just handed him the job. It's within my grasp. It eluded me. Go for it. It escaped me. It slipped through my hands. He is pursuing a goal. Reach for/grab all the gusto you can get. Latch onto a good job. Seize the opportunity. He found success.

There is also a hierarchical structure in the object version of the event structure metaphor. A special case of getting an object is getting an object to eat. Hence,

ACHIEVING A PURPOSE IS GETTING SOMETHING TO EAT

He savored the victory. All the good jobs have been gobbled up. He's hungry for success. The opportunity has me drooling. This is a mouth-watering opportunity.

Traditional methods of getting things to eat are hunting, fishing, and agriculture. Each of these special cases can be used metaphorically to conceptualize achieving (or attempting to achieve) a purpose.

TRYING TO ACHIEVE A PURPOSE IS HUNTING

I'm hunting for a job. I bagged a promotion. The pennant is in the bag.

The typical way to hunt is to use projectiles (bullets, arrows, etc.).

I'm shooting for a promotion. I'm aiming for a career in the movies. I'm afraid I missed my chance.

TRYING TO ACHIEVE A PURPOSE IS FISHING

He's fishing for compliments. I landed a promotion. She netted a good job. I've got a line out on a good used car. It's time to fish or cut bait.

TRYING TO ACHIEVE A PURPOSE IS AGRICULTURE.

It's time I reaped some rewards. That job is a plum. Those are the fruits of his labor. The contract is ripe for the picking.

I will not try to survey all the dualities in the English metaphor system, but it is worth mentioning a few to see how subtle and pervasive dualities are. Take, for example, the LIFE-IS-A-JOURNEY metaphor, in which goals in life are destinations, that is, desired locations to be reached. Since the dual of PURPOSES ARE DESTINATIONS is PURPOSES ARE DESIRED OBJECTS, the dual of LIFE IS A JOURNEY is a metaphor in which life is an activity through which one acquires desired objects. In this culture, the principle activity of this sort is business, and hence, LIFE IS A BUSINESS is the dual of LIFE IS A JOURNEY.

A PURPOSEFUL LIFE IS A BUSINESS

> He has a rich life. It's an enriching experience. I want to get a lot out of life. He's going about the business of everyday life. It's time to take stock of my life.

Recall that LOVE IS A JOURNEY is an extension of A PURPOSEFUL LIFE IS A JOURNEY. It happens that LOVE IS A JOURNEY has a dual that is an extension of the dual of A PURPOSEFUL LIFE IS A JOURNEY, which is A PURPOSEFUL LIFE IS A BUSINESS. The dual of LOVE IS JOURNEY is LOVE IS A PARTNERSHIP, that is, a two-person business. Thus, we speak of lovers as "partners"; there are marriage contracts, and in a long-term love relationship the partners are expected to do their jobs and to share in both responsibilities (what they contribute to the relationship) and benefits (what they get out of it). Long-term love relationships fail under the same conditions as businesses fail—when what the partners get out of the relationship is not worth what they put into it.

Duality is a newly discovered phenomenon. The person who first discovered it in the event structure system was Jane Espenson, a graduate student at Berkeley who stumbled upon it in the course of her research on causation metaphors. Since Espenson's discovery, other extensive dualities have been found in the English metaphor system. However, at present, it is not known just how extensive dualities are in English, or even whether they are all of the location-object type.

At this point, I will leave off discussing the metaphor system of English, even though hundreds of other mappings have been described to date. The major point to take away from this discussion is that metaphor resides for the most part in this huge, highly structured, fixed system. This system is anything but "dead." Because it is conventional, it is used constantly and automatically, with neither effort nor awareness. Novel metaphor uses this system, and builds on it, but only rarely occurs independently of it. But, most interestingly, this system of metaphor seems to give rise to abstract reasoning, which appears to be based on spatial reasoning.

5.3. Invariance Again

The metaphors I have discussed primarily map three kinds of image schemas: containers, paths, and force images. Because of the complexity of the subcases and interactions, the details are intricate, to say the least. However, the invariance principle does make claims in each case as to what image schemas get mapped onto target domains. I will not go through most of the details here, but so far as I can see, the claims made about inferential structure are reasonable ones.

For example, the logic of force dynamics does seem to map, via the submapping CAUSES ARE FORCES, onto the logic of causation. The following are inferences from the logic of forces inherent in force dynamics:

- A stationary object will move only when force is applied to it; without force, it will not move.
- The application of force requires contact; thus, the applier of the force must be in spatial contiguity with the thing it moves.
- The application of force temporarily precedes motion, since inertia must be overcome before motion can take place.

These are among the classic inferential conditions on causation: spatial contiguity, temporal precedence, and that A caused B only if B would not have happened without A.

At this point, I would like to take up the question of what else the invariance principle would buy us. I will consider two cases that arose while Mark Turner and I were writing *More Than Cool Reason* (Lakoff & Turner, 1989). The first concerns image metaphors and the second, generic-level metaphors. But before I move on to those topics, I should point an important consequence of invariance.

Johnson and I argued in *Metaphors We Live By* (Lakoff & Johnson, 1980) that a complex propositional structure could be mapped by metaphor onto another domain. The main example we gave was ARGUMENT AS WAR. Kövecses and I, in our analysis of anger metaphors (Lakoff, 1987, Case Study 1; Kövecses, 1990), also argued that metaphors could map complex propositional structures. The invariance principle does not deny this, but it puts those claims in a very different light. Complex propositional structures involve concepts like time, states, changes, causes, purposes, quantity scales, and categories. If all of these abstract concepts are characterized metaphorically, then the invariance principle claims that what we had called propositional structure is really image-schematic structure. In other words:

> So-called propositional inferences arise from the inherent topological structure of the image schemas mapped by metaphor onto concepts like time, states, actions, causes, purposes, means, quantity, and categories.

The reason that I have taken the trouble to discuss all those abstract concepts is to demonstrate this consequence of the invariance principle; namely, that what have been seen in the past as propositional inferences are really image-based inferences. If the invariance principle is correct, it has a remarkable consequence, namely that:

> Abstract reasoning is a special case of image-based reasoning.

WHAT IS METAPHOR? 235

Image-based reasoning is fundamental and abstract reasoning is image-based reasoning under metaphorical projections to abstract domains.

To look for independent confirmation of the invariance principle, let us turn to image metaphors.

6. NOVEL METAPHORS

6.1. Image Metaphors

There is a class of metaphors that function to map one conventional mental image onto another. These contrast with the metaphors I have discussed so far, each of which maps one conceptual domain onto another, often with many concepts in the source domain mapped onto many corresponding concepts in the target domain. Image metaphors, by contrast, are 'one-shot' metaphors: They map only one image onto one other image.

Consider, for example, this poem from the Indian tradition:

> Now women-rivers
> belted with silver fish
> move unhurried as women in love
> at dawn after a night with their lovers.
> (Merwin & Masson, 1981, p. 71)

Here the image of the slow, sinuous walk of an Indian woman is mapped onto the image of the slow, sinuous, shimmering flow of a river. The shimmering of a school of fish is imagined as the shimmering of the belt.

Metaphoric image mappings work in just the same way as all other metaphoric mappings: by mapping the structure of one domain onto the structure of another. But here, the domains are conventional mental images. Take, for example, this line from André Breton:

> My wife...whose waist is an hourglass.

This is a superimposition of the image of an hourglass onto the image of a woman's waist by virtue of their common shape. As before, the metaphor is conceptual; it is not in the words themselves, but in the mental images. Here, we have a mental image of an hourglass and of a woman, and we map the middle of the hourglass onto the waist of the woman. Note that the words do not tell us which part of the hourglass to map onto the waist, or even that it is only part of the hourglass shape that corresponds to the waist. The words are prompts for us to map from one conventional image to another. Similarly, consider:

> His toes were like the keyboard of a spinet.
> (Rabelais, *The Descriptions of King Lent*, trans. J.M. Cohen)

Here too, the words do not tell us that an individual toe corresponds to an individual key on the keyboard. Again, the words are prompts for us to perform a conceptual mapping between conventional mental images. In particular, we map aspects of the part–whole structure of one image onto aspects of the part–whole structure of another. Just as individual keys are parts of the whole keyboard, so individual toes are parts of the whole foot.

Image mapping can involve more than mapping physical part–whole relationships. For example, the water line of a river may drop slowly and that slowness is part of the dynamic image, which may be mapped onto the slow removal of clothing:

> Slowly slowly
> rivers in autumn show
> sand banks
> bashful in first love woman
> showing thighs.
> (Merwin & Masson, 1981, p. 69)

Other attributes are also mapped: the color of the sand bank onto the color of flesh, the quality of light on a wet sand bank onto the reflectiveness of skin, the light grazing of the water's touch receding down the bank onto the light grazing of the clothing along the skin. Notice that the words do not tell us that any clothing is involved. We get that from a conventional mental image. Part–whole structure is also mapped in this example. The water covers the hidden part of the bank just as the clothing covers the hidden part of the body. The proliferation of detail in the images limits image mappings to highly specific cases. That is what makes them 'one-shot' mappings.

Such mappings of one image onto another can lead us to map knowledge about the first image onto knowledge about the second. Consider the following example from the Navaho:

> My horse with a mane made of short rainbows.
> (*War God's Horse Song I*, Words by Tall Kia ahni. Interpreted by Louis Watchman.)

The structure of a rainbow, its band of curved lines for example, is mapped onto an arc of curved hair, and many rainbows onto many such arcs on the horse's mane. Such image mapping allows us to map our evaluation of the source domain onto the target. We know that rainbows are beautiful, special, inspiring, larger than life, almost mystic, and that seeing them makes us happy and awe inspired. This knowledge is mapped onto what we know of the horse: it too is awe inspiring, beautiful, larger than life, almost mystic. This line comes from a poem containing a series of such image mappings:

> My horse with a hoof like a striped agate,
> with his fetlock like a fine eagle plume:
> my horse whose legs are like quick lightning
> whose body is an eagle-plumed arrow:
> my horse whose tail is like a trailing black cloud.

Image metaphors raise two major issues for the general theory of metaphor:

1. How do they work? What constrains the mappings? What kind of internal structures do mental images have that permit some mappings to work readily, others only with effort, and others not at all?
2. What is the general theory of metaphor that unifies image metaphors with all the conventional metaphors that map the propositional structure of one domain onto the propositional structure of another domain?

Turner and I (Lakoff & Turner, 1989) have suggested that the invariance principle could be an answer to both questions. We suggest that conventional mental images are structured by image schemas and that image metaphors preserve image-schematic structure, mapping parts onto parts and wholes onto wholes, containers onto containers, paths onto paths, and so on. The generalization would be that all metaphors are invariant with respect to their cognitive topology, that is, each metaphorical mapping preserves image-schema structure.

6.2. Generic-Level Metaphors

When Turner and I were writing *More Than Cool Reason*, we hypothesized the existence of what we called "generic-level metaphors" to deal with two problems that we faced—first, the problem of personification, and second, the problem of proverbs, which requires an understanding of analogy. I shall discuss each in turn.

6.3. Personification

In studying a wide variety of poems about death in English, we found that, in poem after poem, death was personified in a relatively small number of ways: drivers, coachmen, footmen; reapers, devourers, and destroyers; or opponents in a struggle or game (say, a knight or a chess opponent). The question we asked was: Why these? Why isn't death personified as a teacher or a carpenter or an ice cream salesman? Somehow, the ones that occur repeatedly seem appropriate. Why?

In studying personifications in general, we found that the overwhelming number seem to fit a single pattern: events (like death) are understood in terms of actions by some agent (like reaping). It is that agent that is personified. We thus hypothesized a very general metaphor, EVENTS ARE ACTIONS, which combines with other, independently existing metaphors for life and death. Consider, for example, the DEATH IS DEPARTURE metaphor. Departure is an event. If we understand this event as an action on the part of some causal agent—someone who brings about, or helps to bring about, departure—then we can account for figures like drivers, coachmen, footman, etc. Or take the PEOPLE ARE PLANTS metaphor. In the natural course of things, plants wither and die. But if we see that event as a causal action on the part of some agent, then that agent is a reaper. So far, so good. But why destroyers and devourers? And what about the impossible cases like teachers and carpenters?

Destruction and devouring are actions in which an entity ceases to exist. The same is true of death. The overall 'shape' of the event of death is similar in this respect to the overall 'shapes' of the events of destruction and devouring. Moreover, there is a causal aspect to death: the passage of time will eventually result in death. Thus, the overall shape of the event of death has an entity that over time ceases to exist as the result of some cause. Devouring and destruction have the same overall 'event shape.' That is, it is the same with respect to causal structure and the persistence of entities over time.

Turner (1987) had noticed a similar case in *Death Is The Mother of Beauty*, his classic work on kinship metaphor. In expressions like "Necessity is the mother of invention," or "Edward Teller was the father of the H-bomb," causation is understood in terms of giving birth or fathering—what Turner (1987) called the CAUSATION IS PROGENERATION metaphor. But, as he observed (pp. 145-148), this metaphor could not be used for just any instance of causation. It could only be used for cases that had the overall event shape of progeneration: something must be created out of nothing, and the thing created must persist for a long time (as if it had a life).

Thus, for example, we can speak of Saussure as the father of modern synchronic linguistics, or of New Orleans as giving birth to jazz. But we cannot use this metaphor for a single causal action with a short-lived effect. Thus, we could not speak of Jose Canseco as the father of the home run he just hit, or of that home run as giving birth to the Oakland A's victory in the game. Though, of course, we could speak of Babe Ruth as the father of modern home-run hitting, and of the home runs giving birth to the era of baseball players as superstars. The overall event shape of the target domain limits the applicability of the metaphor.

Recalling Turner's (1987) observation about CAUSATION IS PROGENERATION, we therefore hypothesized that EVENTS ARE ACTIONS is constrained in the following way: the action must have the same overall event shape as the event. What is preserved across the mapping is the causal structure, the aspectual structure, and the persistence of entities. We referred to this as 'generic-level structure.'

The preservation of generic-level structure explained why death is not metaphorized in terms of teaching, or filling the bathtub, or sitting on the sofa. They simply do not have the same causal and overall event structure, that is, they do not share 'generic-level structure.'

6.4. Proverbs

In Asian figures—proverbs in the form of short poems—the question arises as to what are the limitations on the interpretation of a proverb. Some interpretations are natural; others seem impossible. Why?

Consider the following example from *Asian Figures*, translated by William Merwin (1973).

> Blind
> blames the ditch.

To get some sense of the possible range of interpretations for such a proverb, consider the following application of the proverb:

> Suppose a presidential candidate knowingly commits some personal impropriety (though not illegal and not related to political issues) and his candidacy is destroyed by the press's reporting of the impropriety. He blames the press for reporting it, rather than himself for committing it. We think he should have recognized the realities of political press coverage when he chose to commit the impropriety. We express our judgment by saying, 'Blind/blames the ditch.'

Turner and I (1989) observed that the knowledge structure used in comprehending the case of the candidate's impropriety shared certain things with the knowledge structure used in comprehending the literal interpretations of 'Blind/blames the ditch.' That knowledge structure is the following:

- There is a person with an incapacity, namely, blindness.
- He encounters a situation, namely a ditch, in which his incapacity, namely his inability to see the ditch, results in a negative consequence, namely, his falling into the ditch.
- He blames the situation, rather than his own incapacity.
- He should have held himself responsible, not the situation.

This specific knowledge schema about the blind man and the ditch is an instance of a general knowledge schema, in which specific information about the blindness and ditch are absent. Let us refer to it as the "generic-level schema" that structures our knowledge of the proverb. That generic-level knowledge schema is:

- There is a person with an incapacity.
- He encounters a situation in which his incapacity results in a negative consequence.
- He blames the situation rather than his own incapacity.
- He should have held himself responsible, not the situation.

This is a very general schema characterizing an open-ended category of situations. We can think of it as a variable template that can be filled in in many ways. As it happened, Turner and I were studying this at the time of the Gary Hart scandal, when Hart, a presidential candidate, committed certain sexual improprieties during a campaign, had his candidacy dashed, and then blamed the press for his downfall. "Blind/blames the ditch" fits this situation. Here's how:

- The person is the presidential candidate.
- His incapacity is his inability to understand the consequences of his personal improprieties.
- The context he encounters is his knowingly committing an impropriety and the press's reporting it.
- The consequence is having his candidacy dashed.
- He blames the press.
- We judge him as being foolish for blaming the press instead of himself.

If we view the generic-level schema as mediating between the proverb 'Blind/blames the ditch' and the story of the candidate's impropriety, we get the following correspondence:

- The blind person corresponds to the presidential candidate.
- His blindness corresponds to his inability to understand the consequences of his personal improprieties.
- Falling into the ditch corresponds to his committing the impropriety and having it reported.
- Being in the ditch corresponds to being out of the running as a candidate.
- Blaming the ditch corresponds to blaming the press coverage.
- Judging the blind man as foolish for blaming the ditch corresponds to judging the candidate as foolish for blaming the press coverage.

This correspondence defines the metaphorical interpretation of the proverb as applied to the candidate's impropriety. Moreover, the class of possible ways of filling in the generic-level schema of the proverb corresponds to the class of possible interpretations of the proverb. Thus, we can explain why 'Blind/blames the ditch' does not mean 'I took a bath' or 'My aunt is sitting on the sofa' or any of the myriad of things the proverb cannot mean.

All of the proverbs that Turner and I studied turned out to involve this sort of generic-level schema. And the kinds of things that turned up in such schemas seemed to be pretty much the same in case after case. They include:

- Causal structure.
- Temporal structure.
- Event shape; that is, instantaneous or repeated, completed or open-ended, single or repeating, having fixed stages or not, preserving the existence of entities or not, and so on.
- Purpose structure.
- Modal structure.
- Linear Scales.

This is not an exhaustive list. But what it includes are most of the major elements of generic-level structure that we discovered. What is striking to us about this list is that everything on it is, under the invariance principle, an aspect of image-schematic structure. In short, if the invariance principle is correct, the way to arrive at a generic-level schema for some knowledge structure is to extract its image-schematic structure.

The metaphoric interpretation of such discourse forms as proverbs, fables, allegories, and so on seems to depend on our ability to extract generic-level structure. Turner and I have called the relation between a specific knowledge structure and its generic-level structure the GENERIC IS SPECIFIC metaphor. It is an extremely common mechanism for comprehending the general in terms of the specific.

If the invariance principle is correct, then the GENERIC IS SPECIFIC metaphor is a minimal metaphor that maps what the invariance principle requires it to and nothing more. Should it turn out to be the case that generic-level structure is exactly image-schematic structure, then the invariance principle would have enormous explanatory value. It would obviate the need for a separate characterization of generic-level structure—explaining possible personifications and the possible interpretations for proverbs.

6.5. Analogy

The GENERIC IS SPECIFIC metaphor is used for more than just the interpretation of proverbs. Turner (1991) has suggested that it is also the general mechanism at work in analogic reasoning, and that the invariance principle characterizes the class of possible analogies. We can see how this works with the Gary Hart example cited above. We can convert that example into an analogy with the following sentence: "Gary Hart was like a blind man who fell into a ditch and blamed the ditch." The mechanism for understanding this analogy makes use of:

- a knowledge schema for the blind man and the ditch,
- a knowledge schema concerning Gary Hart, and
- the GENERIC IS SPECIFIC metaphor.

The GENERIC IS SPECIFIC metaphor maps the knowledge schema for the blind man and the ditch into its generic-level schema. The generic-level schema defines an open-ended category of knowledge schemas. The Gary Hart schema is a member of that category, since it fits the generic-level schema given the correspondences stated above.

It appears at present that such analogies use this metaphorical mechanism. But it is common for analogies to use other metaphorical mechanisms as well, for instance, the great chain metaphor and the full range of conventional mappings in the conceptual system. Sentences like "John is a wolf" or "Harry is a pig" use the great chain metaphor (see Lakoff & Turner, 1989, Chapter 4).

A good example of how the rest of the metaphor system interacts with GENERIC IS SPECIFIC is the well-known example of Glucksberg and Keysar (in Ortony, 1993), "My job is a jail." First, the knowledge schema for a jail includes the knowledge that a jail imposes extreme physical constraints on a prisoner's movements. The GENERIC IS SPECIFIC metaphor preserves the image-schematic structure of the knowledge schema, factoring out the specific details of the prisoner and the jail: X imposes extreme physical constraints on Y's movements. But now two additional conventional metaphors apply to this generic-level schema: the event structure metaphor, with the submetaphor ACTIONS ARE SELF-PROPELLED MOVEMENTS, and PSYCHOLOGICAL FORCE IS PHYSICAL FORCE. These metaphors map "X imposes physical constraints on Y's movements" into "X imposes extreme psychological constraints on Y's actions." The statement "My job is a jail" imposes an interpretation in which X = my job and Y = me, and hence yields the knowledge that "My job imposes extreme psychological constraints on my actions." Thus, the mechanism for understanding "My job is a jail" uses very common, independently existing metaphors: GENERIC IS SPECIFIC, PSYCHOLOGICAL FORCE IS PHYSICAL FORCE, and the event structure metaphor.

6.6. The Glucksberg–Keysar Claim

I mention this example because of the claim by Glucksberg and Keysar (in Ortony, 1993) that metaphor is simply a matter of categorization. However, in personal correspondence Glucksberg has written, "We assume that people can judge and can also infer that certain basic level entities, such as 'jails' typify or are emblematic of a metaphoric attributive category such as 'situations that are confining, unpleasant, etc.'" Glucksberg and Keysar give no theory of how it is possible to have such a "metaphoric attributive category"—that is, how it possible for one kind of thing (a general situation) to be metaphorically categorized in terms of a fundamentally spatial notion like 'confining.' Since Glucksberg is not in the business of describing the nature of conceptual systems, he does not see it as his job to give such an account. I have argued in this chapter that the general principle governing such cases is the event structure metaphor. If such a metaphor exists in our conceptual system, then Glucksberg's 'jail' example is accounted for automatically and his categorization theory is not needed. Indeed, the category he needs—"situations that are confining, unpleasant, etc."—is a "metaphoric attributive category." That is, to get the appropriate categories in his categorization theory of metaphor he needs an account of metaphor. But given such an account of metaphor, his metaphor-as-categorization theory becomes unnecessary.

Even worse for the Glucksberg–Keysar theory, it cannot account for either everyday conceptual metaphor of the sort we have been discussing or for really rich poetic metaphor, such as one finds in the works of, say, Dylan Thomas, or for image metaphor of the sort common in the examples cited above from the Sanskrit, Navaho, and surrealist traditions. Since it does not even attempt to deal with most of the data covered by the contemporary theory of metaphor, it cannot account for "how metaphor works."

6.7. More On Novel Metaphor

As common as novel metaphor is, its occurrence is rare by comparison with conventional metaphor, which occurs in most of the sentences we utter. Our everyday metaphor system, which we use to understand concepts as commonplace as TIME, STATE, CHANGE, CAUSATION, PURPOSE, etc., is constantly active, and is used maximally in interpreting novel metaphorical uses of language. The problem with all the older research on novel metaphor is that it completely missed the major contribution played by the conventional system.

As Turner and I discussed in detail (Lakoff & Turner, 1989), there are three basic mechanisms for interpreting linguistic expressions as novel metaphors: extensions of conventional metaphors, generic-level metaphors, and image metaphors. Most interesting poetic metaphor uses all of these superimposed on one another. Let us begin with examples of extensions of conventional metaphors.

Dante begins the *Divine Comedy*:

> In the middle of life's road
> I found myself in a dark wood.

"Life's road" evokes the domain of life and the domain of travel, and hence the conventional LIFE IS A JOURNEY metaphor that links them. "I found myself in a dark wood" evokes the knowledge that if it's dark you cannot see which way to go. This evokes the domain of seeing, and thus the conventional metaphor that KNOWING IS SEEING, as in expressions like "I see what you're getting at," "His claims aren't clear," "The passage is opaque," etc. This entails that the speaker does not know which way to go. Since the LIFE IS A JOURNEY metaphor specifies destinations are life goals, it is entailed that the speaker does not know what life goals to pursue, that is, he is without direction in his life. All of this uses nothing but the system of conventional metaphor, ordinary knowledge structure evoked by the conventional meaning of the sentence, and metaphorical inferences based on that knowledge structure.

Another equally simple case of the use of the conventional system is Robert Frost's

> Two roads diverged in a wood, and I—
> I took the one less traveled by,
> And that has made all the difference.

Since Frost's language often does not overtly signal that the poem is to be taken metaphorically, incompetent English teachers occasionally teach Frost as if he were a nature poet, simply describing scenes. (I have actually had students whose high school teachers taught them that!) Thus, this passage could be read nonmetaphorically as being just about a trip on which one encounters a crossroads. There is nothing in the sentences themselves that forces one to a metaphorical interpretation. But, since it is about travel and encountering crossroads, it evokes a knowledge of journeys. This activates the system of conventional metaphor we have just discussed, in which long-term, purposeful activities are understood as journeys, and further, how life and careers can also be understood as one-person journeys (love relationships, involving two travelers, are ruled out here). The poem is typically taken as being about life and a choice of life goals, though it might also be interpreted as being about careers and career paths, or about some long-term, purposeful activity. All that is needed to get the requisite range of interpretations is the structure of conventional metaphors discussed above, and the knowledge structure evoked by the poem. The conventional mapping will apply to the knowledge structure yielding the appropriate inferences. No special mechanisms are needed.

6.8. Searle's Theory

At this point I will leave off discussion of other more complex poetic examples, since they require lengthy discussion and since such discussion can be found in Lakoff and Turner (1989), Turner (1987), and Turner (1991). Instead, I will confine myself to discussing three examples from John Searle's theory of metaphor (in Ortony, in press). Consider first Disraeli's remark, "I have climbed to the top of the greasy pole."

Certainly, this could be taken nonmetaphorically, but its most likely metaphorical interpretation is via the CAREER IS A JOURNEY metaphor. This metaphor is evoked jointly by source domain structure about pole climbing (which is effortful, self-propelled, destination-oriented motion upward) and knowledge that the metaphor involves effortful, self-propelled, destination-oriented motion upward. Part of the knowledge evoked is that the speaker is as high as he can get on that particular pole, that the pole was difficult to climb, that the climb probably involved backwards motion, that it is difficult for someone to stay at the top of a greasy pole, and that he will most likely slide down again. The CAREER-IS-A-JOURNEY metaphor maps this knowledge onto corresponding knowledge about the speaker's career: the speaker has as much status as he or she can get in that particular career, that it was difficult to get to that point in the career, that is probably involved some temporary loss of status along the way, that it is difficult to maintain this position, and that he or she will probably lose status before long. All this follows with nothing more than the conventional career-as-journey mapping, which we all share as part of our metaphorical systems, plus knowledge about climbing greasy poles.

The second example of Searle's I will consider is "Sally is a block of ice." Here there is a conventional metaphor that AFFECTION IS WARMTH, as in ordinary sentences like "She's a warm person," "He was cool to me," etc. "A block of ice" evokes the domain of temperature, and, since it is predicated of a person, it also evokes knowledge of what a person can be. Jointly, both kinds of knowledge activate AFFECTION IS WARMTH. Since "a block of ice" is something that is very cold and not able to become warm quickly or easily, this knowledge is mapped onto Sally's being very affectionate and not being able to become affectionate quickly or easily. Again, common knowledge and a conventional metaphor that we all have is all that is needed.

Finally, Searle discusses "The hours crept by as we waited for the plane." Here we have a verb of motion predicated of a time expression; the former activates the knowledge about motion through space and the latter activates the time domain. Jointly, they activate the time-as-moving-object mapping. Again the meaning of the sentence follows only from everyday knowledge and the everyday system of metaphorical mappings.

Searle accounts for such cases by his Principle 4, which says that "we just do perceive a connection" which is the basis of the interpretation. This is vague and does not say what the perceived connection is or why we "just do" perceive it. When we spell out the details of all such "perceived connections," they turn out to be the system of conceptual metaphors that I have been describing. But given that system, Searle's theory and his principles become unnecessary.

In addition, Searle's account of literal meaning makes most of the usual false assumptions that accompany that term. Searle assumes that all everyday, conventional language is literal and not metaphorical. He would thus rule out every example of conventional metaphor that is described not only in this chapter, but in the whole literature of the field.

The study of the metaphorical subsystem of our conceptual system is a central part of synchronic linguistics. The reason is that much of our semantic system, that is, our system of concepts, is metaphorical, as we saw above.

7. THE EXPERIENTIAL BASIS OF METAPHOR

The conceptual system underlying a language contains thousands of conceptual metaphors—conventional mappings from one domain to another, such as the event structure metaphor. The novel metaphors of a language are, except for image metaphors, extensions of this large conventional system.

Perhaps the deepest question that any theory of metaphor must answer is this: Why do we have the conventional metaphors that we have? Or alternatively: Is there any reason why conceptual systems contain one set of metaphorical mappings rather than another? There do appear to be answers to these questions for many of the mappings found so far, though they are in the realm of plausible accounts, rather than in the realm of scientific results.

Take a simple case—the MORE IS UP metaphor, as seen in expressions like *Prices rose. His income went down. Unemployment is up. Exports are down. The number of homeless people is very high.*

There are other languages in which MORE IS UP and LESS IS DOWN, but none in which the reverse is true, where MORE IS DOWN and LESS IS UP. Why not? The answer given in the contemporary theory is that the MORE IS UP metaphor is *grounded in experience*—in the common experience of pouring more fluid into a container and seeing the level go up, or adding more things to a pile and seeing the pile get higher. These are thoroughly pervasive experiences; we experience them every day of our lives. They are experiences with a structure—a correspondence between the conceptual domain of quantity and the conceptual domain of verticality: MORE corresponds in such experiences to UP and LESS corresponds to DOWN. These correspondences in real experience form the basis for the correspondence in the metaphorical cases, which go beyond the cases in real experience: in "Prices rose" there is no correspondence in real experience between quantity and verticality, but understanding quantity in terms of verticality makes sense because of the existence of a regular correspondence in so many other cases.

Consider another case—What is the basis of the widespread KNOWING IS SEEING metaphor, as in expressions like: *I see what your saying. His answer was clear. This paragraph is murky. He was so blinded by ambition that he never noticed his limitations.* The experiential basis, in this case, is the fact that most of what we know comes through vision, and that in the overwhelming majority of cases, if we see something, then we know it is true.

Consider still another case: Why, in the event structure metaphor, is achieving a purpose understood as reaching a destination (in the location subsystem) and as acquiring a desired goal (in the object subsystem)? The answer again seems to be correspondences in everyday experience. To achieve most of our everyday purposes, we either have to move to some destination or acquire some object. If you want a drink of water, you've got to go to the water fountain. If you want to be in the sunshine, you have to move to where the sunshine is. And if you want to write down a note, you have to get a pen or pencil. The correspondences between achieving purposes and either reaching destinations or acquiring objects is so utterly common in our everyday existence, that the resulting metaphor is completely natural.

But what about the experiential basis for A PURPOSEFUL LIFE IS A JOURNEY? Recall that that mapping is in an inheritance hierarchy, where life goals are special cases of purposes, which are destinations in the event structure metaphor. Thus, A PURPOSEFUL LIFE IS A JOURNEY inherits the experiential basis for PURPOSES ARE DESTINATIONS. Thus, inheritance hierarchies provide *indirect experiential bases*, in that a metaphorical mapping lower in a hierarchy can inherit its experiential basis indirectly from a mapping higher in the hierarchy.

Experiential bases motivate metaphors, they do not predict them. Thus, not every language has a MORE IS UP metaphor, though all human beings experience a correspondence between MORE and UP in their experience. What this experiential basis does predict is that no language will have the opposite metaphor LESS IS UP. It also predicts that a speaker of language that does not have that metaphor will be able to learn that metaphor much more easily than the opposite metaphor.

7.1. Realizations of Metaphor

Consider objects like thermometers and stock market graphs, where increases in temperature and prices are represented as being up and decreases as being down. There are real man-made objects created to accord with the MORE IS UP metaphor. They are objects in which there is a correlation between MORE and UP. Such objects are a lot easier to read and understand than if they contradicted the metaphor, say, if increases were represented as down and increases as up.

Such objects are ways in which metaphors impose a structure on real life, through the creation of new correspondences in experience. And of course, once such real objects are created in one generation, those objects serve as an experiential basis for that metaphor in the next generation.

There are a great many ways in which conventional metaphors can be made real. Metaphors can be realized in obvious imaginative products such as cartoons, literary works, dreams, visions, and myths. But metaphors can be made real in less obvious ways as well, in physical symptoms, social institutions, social practices, laws, and even foreign policy and forms of discourse and of history.

Let us consider some examples:

Cartoons. Conventional metaphors are made real in cartoons. A common example is the realization of the ANGER IS A HOT FLUID IN A CONTAINER metaphor, in which one can be "boiling mad" or "letting off steam." In cartoons, anger is commonly depicted by having steam coming out of the character's ears. Similarly, social clumsiness is indicated by having a cartoon character "fall on his face."

Literary works. It is common for the plot of novel to be a realization of the PURPOSEFUL LIFE IS A JOURNEY metaphor, where the course of a life takes the form of an actual journey. *Pilgrim's Progress* is a classical example.

Rituals. Consider the cultural ritual in which a newborn baby is carried upstairs to insure his or her success. The metaphor realized in this ritual is STATUS IS UP, exemplified by sentences such as: *He clawed his way to the top. He climbed the ladder of success. You'll rise in the world.*

Dream Interpretation. Conceptual metaphors constitute the vocabulary of dream interpretation. It is the collection of our everyday conceptual metaphors that make dream interpretations possible. Consider one of the most celebrated of all dream interpretations: Joseph's interpretation of Pharaoh's dream from Genesis. In Pharaoh's dream, he is standing on the river bank, when seven fat cows come out of the river, followed by seven lean cows that eat the seven fat ones and still remain lean. Then Pharaoh dreams again. This time he sees seven "full and good" ears of corn growing, and then seven withered ears growing after them. The withered ears devour the good ears. Joseph interprets the two dreams as a single dream. The seven fat cows and full ears are good years and the seven lean cows and withered ears are famine yeas that follow the good years. The famine years "devour" what the good years produce. This interpretation makes sense to us because of a collection of conceptual metaphors in our conceptual system—metaphors that have been with us since Biblical times. The first metaphor used is: TIMES ARE MOVING ENTITIES. A river is a common metaphor for the flow of time; the cows are individual entities (years) emerging from the flow of time and moving past the observer; the ears of corn are also entities that come into the scene. The second metaphor used is ACHIEVING A PURPOSE IF EATING, where being fat indicates success and being lean indicates failure. This metaphor is combined with the most common of metonymies: A PART STANDS FOR THE WHOLE. Since cows and corn were typical of meat and grain eaten, each single cow stands for all the cows raised in a year and each ear of corn for all the corn grown in a year. The final metaphor used is: RESOURCES ARE FOOD, where using up resources is eating food. The devouring of the good years by the famine years is interpreted as indicating that all the surplus resources of the good years will be used up by the famine years. The interpretation of the whole dream is thus a composition of three conventional metaphors and one metonymy. The metaphoric and metonymic sources are combined to form the reality of the dream.

Myths. In the event structure metaphor, there is a submapping EXTERNAL EVENTS ARE LARGE, MOVING OBJECTS that can exert a force upon you and thereby affect whether you achieve your goals. In English the special cases of such objects are "things," fluids, and horses. Pamela Morgan (in unpublished work) has observed that in Greek mythology, Poseidon is the god of the sea, earthquakes, horses, and bulls. The list might seem arbitrary, but Morgan observes that these are all large moving objects that can exert a force on you. Morgan surmises that this is not an arbitrary list. The sea, earthquakes, horses, and bulls are all large moving objects that can exert a significant force. Poseidon, she surmises, should really be seen as the god of external events.

Physical symptoms. The unconscious mind makes use of our unconscious system of conventional metaphor, sometimes to express psychological states in terms of physical symptoms. For example, in the event structure metaphor, there is a submapping DIFFICULTIES ARE IMPEDIMENTS TO MOTION which has, as a special case, DIFFICULTIES ARE BURDENS. It is fairly common for someone encountering difficulties to walk with his shoulders stooped, as if "carrying a heavy weight" that is "burdening" him.

Social institutions. We have a TIME IS MONEY metaphor, shown by expressions like: *He's wasting time. I have to budget my time. This will save you time. I've invested a lot of time in that. He doesn't use his time profitably.* This metaphor came into English about the time of the industrial revolution, when people started to be paid for work by the amount of time they worked. Thus, the factory led to the institutional pairing of periods of time with amounts of money, which formed the experiential basis of this metaphor. Since then, the metaphor has been realized in many other ways. The budgeting of time has spread throughout American culture.

Social practices. There is conceptual metaphor that SEEING IS TOUCHING, where the eyes are limbs and vision is achieved when the object seen is "touched." Examples are: *My eyes picked out every details of the pattern. He ran his eyes over the walls. He couldn't take his eyes off of her. Their eyes met. His eyes are glued to the TV.* The metaphor is made real in the social practice of avoiding eye "contact" on the street, and in the social prohibition against "undressing someone with your eyes."

Laws. Law is major area where metaphor is made real. For example, CORPORATIONS ARE PERSONS is a tenet of American law, which not only enables corporations to be "harmed" and assigned "responsibility" so that they can be sued when liable, but also gives corporations certain First Amendment rights.

Foreign policy. A STATE IS A PERSON is one of the major metaphors underlying foreign policy concepts. Thus, there are "friendly" states, "hostile" states, etc. Health for a state is economic health and strength is military strength. Thus, a threat to economic "health" can be seen as a death threat, as when Iraq was seen to have a "stranglehold" on the "economic lifeline" of the U.S. Strong states are seen as male, and weak states as female, so that an attack by a strong state on a weak state can be seen as a "rape," as in the rape of Kuwait by Iraq. A "just war" is conceptualized as a fairy tale with villain, victim, and hero, where the villain attacks the victim and the hero rescues the victim. Thus, the U.S. in the Gulf War was portrayed as having "rescued" Kuwait. As President Bush said in his address to Congress, "The issues couldn't have been clearer: 'Iraq was the villain and Kuwait, the victim.'"

Forms of discourse. Common metaphors are often made real in discourse forms. Consider three common academic discourse forms: the Guided Tour, the Heroic Battle, and the Heroic Quest. The Guided Tour is based on the metaphor that THOUGHT IS MOTION, where ideas are locations and one reasons "step-by-step," "reaches conclusions," or you fail to reach a conclusion if you are engaged in "circular reasoning." Communication in this metaphor is giving someone a guided tour of some rational argument or of some "intellectual terrain." The present chapter is an example of such a guided tour, where I, the author, am the tour guide who is assumed to be thoroughly familiar with the terrain, and where the terrain surveyed is taken as objectively real. The discourse form of the Heroic Battle is based on the metaphor that ARGUMENT IS WAR. The author's theory is the hero, the opposing theory is the villain, and words are weapons. The battle is in the form of an argument defending the hero's position and demolishing the villain's position. The Heroic Quest discourse form is based on the metaphor that knowledge is a valuable but elusive object that can be "discovered" if one perseveres. The scientist is the hero on a quest for knowledge, and the discourse form is an account of his difficult journey of discovery. What is "discovered" is, of course, a real entity.

What makes all of these cases realizations of metaphors is that in each case there is something real structured by conventional metaphor, and which is made comprehensible, or even natural, by those everyday metaphors. What is real differs in each case: an object like a thermometer or graph, an experience like a dream, an action like a ritual, a form of discourse, etc. What these examples reveal is that a lot of what is real in a society or in the experience of an individual is structured and made sense of via conventional metaphor.

Experiential bases and realizations of metaphors are two sides of the same coin: They are both correlations in real experience that have the same structure as the correlations in metaphors. The difference is that experiential bases precede, ground, and make sense of conventional metaphorical mappings, while realizations follow, and are made sense of, via the conventional metaphors. And as we noted above, one generation's realizations of a metaphor can become part of the next generation's experiential basis for that metaphor.

8. SUMMARY OF RESULTS

As we have seen, the contemporary theory of metaphor is revolutionary in many respects. To give you some idea how revolutionary, here is a list of the basic results that differ from most previous accounts.

8.1. The Nature of Metaphor

- Metaphor is the main mechanism through which we comprehend abstract concepts and perform abstract reasoning.
- Much subject matter, from the most mundane to the most abstruse scientific theories, can only be comprehended via metaphor.
- Metaphor is fundamentally conceptual, not linguistic, in nature.
- Metaphorical language is a surface manifestation of conceptual metaphor.
- Though much of our conceptual system is metaphorical, a significant part of it is nonmetaphorical. Metaphorical understanding is grounded in nonmetaphorical understanding.
- Metaphor allows us to understand a relatively abstract or inherently unstructured subject matter in terms of a more concrete, or at least a more highly structured subject matter.

8.2. The Structure of Metaphor

- Metaphors are mappings across conceptual domains.
- Such mappings are asymmetric and partial.
- Each mapping is a fixed set of ontological correspondences between entities in a source domain and entities in a target domain.
- When those fixed correspondences are activated, mappings can project source domain inference patterns onto target domain inference patterns.
- Metaphorical mappings obey the invariance principle: the image-schema structure of the source domain is projected onto the target domain in a way that is consistent with inherent target domain structure.
- Mappings are not arbitrary, but grounded in the body and in everyday experience and knowledge.
- A conceptual system contains thousands of conventional metaphorical mappings, which form a highly structured subsystem of the conceptual system.
- There are two types of mappings: conceptual mappings and image mappings; both obey the invariance principle.

8.3. Some Aspects of Metaphor

- The system of conventional conceptual metaphor is mostly unconscious, automatic, and is used with no noticeable effort, just like our linguistic system and the rest of our conceptual system.
- Our system of conventional metaphor is "alive" in the same sense that our system of grammatical and phonological rules is alive; namely, it is constantly in use, automatic and below the level of consciousness.
- Our metaphor system is central to our understanding of experience and to the way we act on that understanding.

- Conventional mappings are static correspondences, and are not, in themselves, algorithmic in nature. However, this by no means rules out the possibility that such static correspondences might be used in language processing that involves sequential steps.
- Metaphor is mostly based on correspondences in our experiences, rather than on similarity.
- The metaphor system plays a major role in both the grammar and lexicon of a language.
- Metaphorical mappings vary in universality; some seem to be universal, others are widespread, and some seem to be culture specific.
- Poetic metaphor is, for the most part, an extension of our everyday, conventional system of metaphorical thought.

These are the conclusions that best fit the empirical studies of metaphor conducted over the past decade or so. Though much of it is inconsistent with traditional views, it is by no means all new, and some ideas (e.g., that abstract concepts are comprehended in terms of concrete concepts) have a long history.

9. CONCLUDING REMARKS

The evidence supporting the contemporary theory of metaphor is voluminous and grows larger each year as more research in the field is done. The evidence, as we saw above, comes from five domains:

- generalizations over polysemy,
- generalizations over inference patterns,
- generalizations over extensions to poetic cases,
- generalizations over semantic change, and
- psycholinguistic experiments.

I have discussed only a handful of examples of the first three of these, hopefully enough to make the reader curious about the field.

But evidence is convincing only if it can count as evidence. When does evidence fail to be evidence? Unfortunately, all too often. It is commonly the case that certain fields of inquiry are defined by assumptions that rule out the possibility of counterevidence. When a defining assumption of a field comes up against the evidence, the evidence usually loses! The practitioners of the field must ignore the evidence if they want to keep the assumptions that define the field they are committed to.

Part of what makes the contemporary theory of metaphor so interesting is that the evidence for it contradicts the defining assumptions of so many academic disciplines. In my opinion, this should make one doubt the defining assumptions of all those disciplines. The reason is this: The defining assumptions of the contemporary theory of metaphor are minimal. There are only two:

1. *The generalization commitment*—to seek generalizations in all areas of language, including polysemy, patterns of inference, novel metaphor, and semantic change.
2. *The cognitive commitment*—to take experimental evidence seriously.

But these are nothing more than commitments to the scientific study of language and the mind. No initial commitment is made as to the form of an answer to the question of what is metaphor.

However, the defining assumptions of other fields do often entail a commitment about the form of an answer to that question. It is useful, in an interdisciplinary volume of this sort, to spell out exactly what those defining assumptions are, since they will often explain why different authors reach such different conclusions about the nature of metaphor.

9.1. Literal Meaning Commitments

I started this chapter with a list of the "false assumptions" about literal meanings that are commonly made. These assumptions are, of course, "false" only relative to the kinds of evidence that supports the contemporary theory of metaphor. If one ignores all such evidence, then the assumptions can be maintained without contradiction.

Assumptions about literality are the locus of many of the contradictions between the contemporary theory of metaphor and various academic disciplines. Let us review those assumptions. In the discussion of literal meaning given above, I observed that it is taken as definitional that what is literal is not metaphorical. The "false assumptions and conclusions" that usually accompany the word "literal" are:

- All everyday conventional language is literal, and none is metaphorical.
- All subject matter can be comprehended literally, without metaphor.
- Only literal language can be contingently true or false.
- All definitions given in the lexicon of a language are literal, not metaphorical.
- The concepts used in the grammar of a language are all literal; none are metaphorical.

We will begin with the philosophy of language. The generalization commitment and the cognitive commitment are *not* definitional to the philosophy of language. Indeed, most philosophers of language would feel no need to abide by them, for a very good reason. The philosophy of language is typically not seen as an empirical discipline, constrained by empirical results, such as those that arise by the application of the generalization and cognitive commitments. Instead, the philosophy of language is usually seen as an a priori discipline, one which can be pursued using the tools of philosophical analysis alone, rather than the tools of empirical research. Therefore, all the evidence that has been brought forth for the contemporary theory of metaphor simply will not matter for most philosophers of language.

In addition, the philosophy of language comes with its own set of defining assumptions, which entail many of the false assumptions usually associated with the word "literal." Most practitioners of the philosophy of language usually make one or more of the following assumptions:

- The correspondence theory of truth.
- Meaning is defined in terms of reference and truth.
- Natural language semantics is to be characterized by the mechanisms of mathematical logic, including model theory.

These assumptions entail the traditional false assumptions associated with the word "literal." Thus, the very field of philosophy of language comes with defining assumptions that contradict the main conclusions of the contemporary theory of metaphor.

Consequently, we can see why most philosophers of language have the range of views on metaphor that they have: They accept the traditional literal-figurative distinction. They may, like Davidson (1981), say that there is no metaphorical meaning and that most metaphorical utterances are either trivially true or trivially false. Or, like Grice (1989, p. 34) and Searle (in Ortony, 1993), they will assume that metaphor is in the realm of pragmatics, that is, that a metaphorical meaning is no more than the literal meaning of some other sentence which can be arrived at by some pragmatic principle. This is required, since the only real meaning for them is literal meaning, and pragmatic principles are those principles that allow one to say one things (with a literal meaning) and mean something else (with a different, but nonetheless literal, meaning).

Much of generative linguistics accepts one or more of these assumptions from the philosophy of language. The field of formal semantics accepts them all, and thus formal semantics, by its defining assumptions, is at odds with the contemporary theory of metaphor. Formal semantics simply does not see it as its job to account for the generalizations discussed in this chapter. From the perspective of formal semantics, the phenomena that the contemporary theory of metaphor is concerned with are either nonexistent or uninteresting, since they lie outside the purview of the discipline. Anyone who accepts mathematical logic as the correct approach to natural language semantics, must see metaphor as being outside of semantics proper and, therefore, must also reject the entire enterprise of the contemporary theory of metaphor.

Chomsky's theory of government and binding also accepts crucial assumptions from the philosophy of language that are inconsistent with the contemporary theory of metaphor. Government and binding, following my early theory of generative semantics, assumes that semantics is to be represented in terms of logical form. Government and binding, like generative semantics, thus rules out the very possibility that metaphor might be part of natural language semantics as it enters into grammar. Because of this defining assumption, I would not expect Chomskyan theorists to become concerned with the phenomena covered by the contemporary theory of metaphor, since it is inconsistent with their theoretical assumptions.

Interestingly, much of continental philosophy and deconstructionism is also characterized by defining assumptions that are at odds with the contemporary theory of metaphor. Nietzsche (see Johnson, 1981) held that all language is metaphorical, which is at odds with those results that indicate that a significant amount of everyday language is not metaphorical. Much of continental philosophy, observing that conceptual systems change through time, assumes that conceptual systems are purely historically contingent—that there are no conceptual universals. Though conceptual systems do change through time, there do, however, appear to be universal, or at least very widespread, conceptual metaphors. The event structure metaphor is my present candidate for a metaphorical universal.

Continental philosophy also comes with a distinction between the study of the physical world, which can be scientific, and the study of human beings, which it says cannot be scientific. This is very much at odds with the conceptual theory of metaphor, which is very much a scientific enterprise.

Finally, the contemporary theory of metaphor is at odds with certain traditions in symbolic artificial intelligence and information processing psychology. Those fields assume that thought is a matter of algorithmic symbol manipulation, of the sort done by a traditional computer program. This defining assumption puts it at odds with the contemporary theory of metaphor in two respects.

First, the contemporary theory has an image-schematic basis: The invariance hypothesis both applies to image metaphors and characterizes constraints on novel metaphor. Since symbol-manipulation systems cannot handle image-schemas, they cannot deal with image metaphors (Lakoff & Turner, 1989, pp. 89-96) or with imageable idioms or image-schema transformations (see Lakoff, 1987, Case Study 2, especially pp. 440-461). The essential problem here is that image schemas are topological in character and the symbolic structures of traditional AI are not.

Second, those traditions must characterize metaphorical mapping as an algorithmic process, which typically takes literal meanings as input and gives a metaphorical reading as output. This is at odds with cases where there are multiple, overlapping metaphors in a single sentence, and which require the simultaneous activation of a number of metaphorical mappings. (For a discussion of a detailed example, see Lakoff & Turner, 1989, pp. 26-34.)

I mention all this because it is important to be aware of the often hidden theoretical assumptions that lie behind disciplines like generative linguistics and formal logic, as well as both Anglo-American and continental philosophical approaches to language. Those theoretical assumptions can blind one to the most interesting and extensive contemporary research on conceptual systems in general and metaphor in particular.

REFERENCES

Auster, P. (Ed.). (1984). *The Random House book of twentieth century French poetry.* New York: Random House.
Coolidge, D., & Roberts, M. (1930). *The Navaho Indians.* Boston: Houghton Mifflin.
Davidson, D. (1981). What metaphors mean. In M. Johnson (Ed.), *Philosophical perspectives on metaphor.* Minneapolis: University of Minnesota Press.
Gibbs, R.W., Jr. (1990). Psycholinguistic studies on the conceptual basis of idiomaticity. *Cognitive Linguistics, 1-4*, 417–462.
Grice, P. (1989). *Studies in the way of words.* Cambridge, MA: Harvard University Press.
Johnson, M. (Ed.). (1981). *Philosophical perspectives on metaphor.* Minneapolis: University of Minnesota Press.
Johnson, M. (1987). *The body in the mind: The bodily basis of meaning, reason and imagination.* Chicago: University of Chicago Press.
Kövecses, Z. (1990). *Emotion concepts.* New York: Springer-Verlag.
Lakoff, G. (1987). *Women, fire, and dangerous things: What categories reveal about the mind.* Chicago: University of Chicago Press.
Lakoff, G. (1989). Philosophical speculation and cognitive science. *Philosophical Psychology, 2*, 1.
Lakoff, G., & Brugman, C. (1986). Argument forms in lexical semantics. In V. Nikiforidou, M. Van Clay, M. Niepokuj, & D. Feder (Eds.). *Proceedings of the Twelfth Annual Meeting of the Berkeley Linguistics Society* (pp. 442–454). Berkeley: Berkeley Linguistics Society.
Lakoff, G., & Johnson, M. (1980). *Metaphors we live by.* Chicago: University of Chicago Press.
Lakoff, G., & Turner, M. (1989). *More than cool reason: A field guide to poetic metaphor.* Chicago: University of Chicago Press.
Merwin, W.S. (1973). *Asian Figures..* New York: Atheneum.
Merwin, W.S., & Masson, J. (1981). *The Peacock's Egg* (Trans. Moussaieff). San Francisco, CA: North Point.
Ortony, A. (Ed.). (1993). *Metaphor and thought* (2nd ed.), Cambridge, UK: Cambridge University Press.
Rabelais, F. (1957). *The histories of gargantua and pantagruel* (Trans. J.M. Cohen). Harmondsworth, England: Penguin.
Rothenberg, J. (Ed.). (1985). *Technicians of the sacred.* Berkeley and Los Angeles, CA: University of California Press.

Sweetser, E. (1990). *From etymology to pragmatics: The mind-as-body metaphor in semantic structure and semantic change.* Cambridge, UK: Cambridge University Press.

Talmy, L. (1985). Force dynamics in language and thought. *Papers from the Parasession on Causatives and Agentivity.* Chicago: Chicago Linguistic Society.

Turner, M. (1987). *Death is the mother of beauty: Mind, metaphor, criticism.* Chicago: University of Chicago Press.

Turner, M. (1991). *Reading minds: The study of English in the age of cognitive science.* Princeton: Princeton University Press.

APPENDIX: AN ANNOTATED BIBLIOGRAPHY

Gibbs, R.W., Jr. (1990). Psycholinguistics studies on the conceptual basis of idiomaticity. *Cognitive Linguistics, 1-4,* 417-462.

A survey of psycholinguistic results demonstrating the cognitive reality of conceptual metaphor and imageable idioms.

Johnson, M. (1981). *Philosophical perspectives on metaphor.* Minneapolis: University of Minnesota Press.

The best collection of papers by philosophers on metaphor. The author's introduction is the best short historical survey of the history of metaphor in philosophy.

Johnson, M. (1987). *The body in the mind: The bodily basis of meaning, reason and imagination.* Chicago: University of Chicago Press.

A discussion of philosophical issues arising from the discovery of the system of conceptual metaphor.

Kövecses, Z. (1990). *Emotion concepts.* New York: Springer-Verlag.

A thorough and voluminously documented demonstration that emotion is conceptualized metaphorically.

Lakoff, G. (1987). *Women, fire, and dangerous things: What categories reveal about the mind.* Chicago: University of Chicago Press.

A survey of contemporary literature on categorization and other aspects of conceptual system research, including the role of metaphor in forming categories. Includes a general theory of meaning assimilating conceptual metaphor and other aspects of cognitive semantics.

Lakoff, G. (1989). Philosophical Speculation and Cognitive Science. *Philosophical Psychology, 2,* 1.

A discussion of the differing assumptions behind generative semantics and generative grammar.

Lakoff, G. (1991, January). *Metaphor and War: The Metaphor System Used To Justify War in the Gulf.* Distributed via Electronic Bulletin Boards. [Reprinted in Brien Hallet (Ed.), *Engulfed in war: Just war and the Persian Gulf,* Honolulu: Matsunaga Institute for Peace, 1991; *Journal of Urban and Cultural Studies,* 2(1), 1991; Vietnam Generation Newsletter, vol. 3, no. 2, November, 1991; The East Bay Express, February, 1991.]

An analysis of the metaphorical system used in the public discourse and expert policy deliberations on the Gulf War, together with what the metaphors hid, and a critique of the war based on this analysis.

Lakoff, G., & Brugman, C. (1986). Argument Forms in Lexical Semantics. In Nikiforidou, (Eds.), *Proceedings of the Twelfth Annual Meeting of the Berkeley Linguistics Society* (pp. 442-454).

A survey of the argument forms used in justifying metaphorical analysis and a comparison with corresponding argument forms in syntax and phonology.

Lakoff, G., & Johnson, M. (1980). *Metaphors we live by*. Chicago: University of Chicago Press.

The first book outlining the contemporary theory of metaphor.

Lakoff, G., & Turner, M. (1989). *More than cool reason: A field guide to poetic metaphor*. Chicago: University of Chicago Press.

A survey of the mechanisms of poetic metaphor, replete with examples.

Reddy, M. (1979). The conduit metaphor. In A. Ortony (Ed.), *Metaphor and thought*. Cambridge, UK: Cambridge University Press.

The first thorough linguistic analysis of a conceptual metaphor; it marked the beginning of the contemporary theory.

Sweetser, E. (1990). *From etymology to pragmatics: The mind-as-body metaphor in semantic structure and semantic change*. Cambridge, UK: Cambridge University Press.

The best work to date on the role of metaphor in semantic change, and the metaphorical basis of pragmatics.

Talmy, L. (1985). Force dynamics in language and thought. *Papers from the Parasession on Causatives and Agentivity*. Chicago: Chicago Linguistic Society.

The analysis that led to the study of the metaphorical basis of modality and causation.

Turner, M. (1987). *Death is the mother of beauty: Mind, metaphor, criticism*. Chicago: University of Chicago Press.

A study of the regularities behind all the kinship metaphors from Chaucer to Wallace Stevens, including the role of metaphor in allegory. Turner also noticed the prevalence of the CAUSATION IS PROGENERATION metaphor and the constraint that was the precursor to the invariance principle.

Turner, M. (1991). *Reading minds: The study of English in the age of cognitive science*. Princeton, NJ: Princeton University Press.

A reevaluation of the profession of English and the study of the English language in the light of recent results on the nature of metaphor and other results in the cognitive sciences.

Winter, S.L. (1989). Transcendental Nonsense, Metaphoric Reasoning, and the Cognitive Stakes for Law. *137 University of Pennsylvania Law Review*. The most comprehensive of Winter's many articles discussing the role of metaphor in law.

6
A Structured Connectionist Model of Figurative Adjective–Noun Combinations*

Susan H. Weber

1. INTRODUCTION

Despite the traditional treatment of metaphor as an anomalous semantic form (Black, 1979; Richards, 1937), models that place metaphor on the same footing as "literal" semantics are gaining widespread acceptance (Gildea & Glucksberg, 1983; Lakoff, 1987; Martin, 1988). In the domain of adjective–noun combinations, examples abound of metaphoric word senses with comprehension times comparable to literal senses. A case in point is the word sense of "light" meaning low calorie. Traditional models hold that the phrase "light beer" is initially interpreted as a low-weight (or pale-colored) beer and only upon rejection of this initial "literal" interpretation is the correct word sense arrived. The problem with this account is that the "literal" meaning quite often makes sense (e.g., light-colored beer) so no incentive apparently exists to retrieve the contextually appropriate but more fanciful word sense. A more robust model of metaphor processing uses context-sensitive adjective semantics (Barsalou, 1982) so that the meaning of "light" when used to describe typically calorific food items is immediately assumed to mean low calorie, with no intervening "literal" interpretive steps.

The discussion between "literal" and "metaphoric" word senses, argued here, should not be based on processing but on context sensitivity. The word senses that come to mind on hearing the term in isolation (e.g., when asked to define the term) are the "literal" meanings. The word senses that either come to

---

* This research was supported in part by ONR Grant Number N00014-89-J-1323 while the author was at the International Computer Science Institute, Berkeley, CA.

mind only in specific contexts or carry with them some analogical mapping baggage (e.g., light beer, green recruit) are the "figurative" meanings. There is psycholinguistic evidence (Gildea & Glucksberg, 1983; Inhoff, Lima, & Carroll, 1984; Tabossi, 1986) that since both literal and figurative meanings display the same comprehension timings, they are processed with the same mechanisms. Since selecting the more appropriate of two literal word senses (e.g., light color vs. light weight) is also a context-sensitive process, distinguishing between literal and metaphoric usages requires considering either the default (context-free) semantics, or the historical derivation of the term, or both. The term *light*, for example, is not only used far more commonly to refer to color and weight than to calorie content (if only because foods comprise only a small fraction of all objects with color and weight) but the calorie word sense is also a relatively recent extension to the word's meaning.

So if the context-sensitive semantics of a term is a result of its observed meanings in various contexts, how does one interpret the semantics of an unfamiliar or novel expression? The context-sensitive versus context-free distinction applies only to known meanings of a term. If an adjective is used in an unfamiliar and apparently inappropriate context (e.g., green idea), pragmatics demand that there be some reasonable interpretation of the phrase's meaning. When the usual context-sensitive semantic retrieval process fails to supply any interpretations, there must be a supplemental metaphoric meaning interpretation mechanism available to suggest some possibilities. The proposal is to exploit the term's known meanings in other contexts to suggest meanings in the novel context. For adjective–noun combinations, this involves considering the adjective as proposing feature values for the salient features of the object denoted by the noun.

This chapter presents a connectionist model of the semantics of adjective--noun combinations that features a unified model of literal and metaphoric interpretation. The model is built on mechanisms for dynamic conceptual attribute retrieval, where attributes primed by context will be retrieved in preference to those which are contextually irrelevant. Some of the other features of the model include the ability to draw automatic or direct inferences, the use of property abstraction and scalar-value transference as interpretive mechanisms for novel metaphoric usages, and a frequency-based word-sense acquisition mechanism common to both literal and figurative usages.

The novelty of the work described here lies in the abandonment of the traditional two-stage model of metaphor interpretation described in Weber (1989a) in favor of a unified treatment of both literal semantics and figurative semantics for both conventional or familiar and novel metaphor. Since the components of the model responsible for the context-sensitive lexical semantics and direct inferences are described in detail in Weber (1989a, 1989b, 1989c), only a summary of these results appears here.

2. A CONTEXT SENSITIVE MODEL OF CATEGORY STRUCTURE

2.1. "Literal" Semantics: Direct Inferences and Category Structure

Since the interpretation of novel figurative adjective–noun phrases is based on the semantics of familiar adjective–noun phrases, any discussion of these interpretative mechanisms must be prefaced with an analysis of literal interpretative mechanisms. While a limited form of analogical mapping can be established directly between two scalar property values (e.g., low weight/ saturation mapping to low calorie), the really interesting cases arise when observed correlations between property values are brought into play. When an adjective modifies a noun in a literal context, the category denoted by the noun is cast in a new light. Sometimes the shift in perspective is a minor one: the phrase "green car" carries little additional information over the selection of a specific color. The phrase "green banana," however, entails a significant modification to the default values of bananas: in addition to the color changing from yellow to green, one also infers that a green banana is unripe, difficult to peel, astringent tasting, and so on (see Figure 6.1). It is argued that this (completely different) view of the property values of bananas is maintained within the category itself and does not constitute a proper subcategory.

The habit of inferring changes in property-value settings from the knowledge of one property value is called *direct inferencing*. Direct inferences can be either immediate or mediated. Immediate inferences are the direct inferences available at the level of the category under consideration. They are performed quickly, in a few hundred milliseconds, and without conscious thought (Feldman & Ballard, 1982). These immediate inferences must reflect the structure of stored knowledge, as they are available too quickly and effortlessly to involve any complex

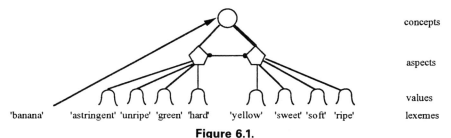

Figure 6.1.
The Coarse Structure of the "banana" Concept, Showing Two Relevant Aspects, One for Ripe Bananas (the default) and One for Unripe. Heavier lines are used to denote preferentially weighted links.

form of information retrieval. The argument is that the patterns of immediate inferences reflect the structure of connections in an underlying spreading activation model, implemented here as a structured connectionist network.

Mediated inferences are the second form of direct inference, where knowledge about a more abstract category is used to supply the information necessary to understand discourse. Mediated inferences take somewhat longer than immediate inferences as they require chaining up the subcategorization hierarchy. For example, questions like "do birds breathe" take longer to answer than questions like "can birds fly," presumably because the answer to the latter question is stored at the same point as the concept *bird*, while information about living organisms in general must be referenced in order to supply an answer to the former (Anderson, 1983). Mediated inferences are not exploited in the figurative interpretation process, however, only the immediate inferences available for a category are used.

With the observation of direct inferences as a starting point, a model of the internal structure of categories can be developed. Given that physical objects possess certain properties with characteristic values, the question is how to represent the correlations between values. The answer suggested by Weber (1989a) is that functional properties of the object supply the necessary organizational structure, as each value of a functional property participates in a distinct *aspect*, or informal coalition of property values, of the category. A functional property is one which is related to a potential use of an instance of the category by an agent. For example, the functional property *ripeness* of fruit, pertinent to the agent's goal *eat fruit*, motivates three distinct aspects of bananas, unripe, ripe, and overripe, each with partially overlapping but distinctive characteristic property values.

Aspects of a category can receive activation from a variety of sources. The direct approach is to name or experience a property value participating in the aspect (e.g., green banana). The same effect is achieved by actually naming the aspect (e.g., unripe banana), since the motivating functional property value also participates in the coalition. Property inheritance can also supply indirect activation to an aspect, by supplying it to a constituent value through scalar transference. If a category happens to stimulate a property value that also participates in an aspect of a superordinate category, then when activation propagates up from the category to the supercategory, that aspect will be preferred (e.g., green banana primes green fruit). Finally, an aspect can be established by default; in the absence of information to the contrary, the most typical aspect of the category will predominate (e.g., ripe for fruit).

It will be shown that aspects, by controlling the priming of correlated property values, support not only straightforward "literal" reference but also metonymy, when one property value is used to refer to another, and unusual or unfamiliar choice of adjectives, when the individual words are known but the meaning of the combination is not. When faced with the need to suggest a semantics for an unfamiliar adjective–noun phrase, a source domain must be established for the analogical mappings of potential meanings. This domain consists of the adjective's connotations in all previously encountered contexts as implemented by conceptual aspects. The connotations considered for the purposes of figurative interpretation are the immediate inferences arising from the aspect primed by the modification of a category commonly associated with the given adjective.

Distinguishing between aspects and categories can be difficult, particularly in light of the argument (Weber, 1989a) that aspects may be considered a form of proto-subcategory, the seed from which a proper subcategory may evolve with sufficient usage (Rosch, Nervis, Gray, Johnson, & Boyes-Braem, 1976). The argument for the existence of intracategory aspects is based on the observation that many property value correlations, despite their crucial role in the priming of direct inferences, do not in themselves constitute a useful (in the information theoretic sense) conceptual category (Gluck & Corter, 1985). One example of such a situation arises when a peach which appears ripe on inspection proves to be either dry, mealy and tasteless, or hard, crunchy and sour on biting into it. It seems untenable to argue that people develop and maintain distinct subcategories for each distinct property value correlation encountered in experience. Category aspects provide a far more economical and plausible model of storing such correlations. Furthermore, multiple aspects of a category can be primed simultaneously, resulting in mutual inhibition between the values in incompatible aspects (e.g., unripe vs. overripe) and mutual reinforcement between compatible aspects. This sort of behavior is difficult to capture with a purely taxonomic approach, even with multiple inheritance (correctly handling the multiple inheritance of incompatible property values is notoriously difficult; see, for example, Shastri, 1985).

2.2. Figurative Interpretation: Property Value Transference

The central component of the model is the use of direct inferences and scalar value transference in interpreting both familiar and fanciful adjective-noun combinations. What is a "green peach"? A "thirsty fern"? A "happy box"? In a literal adjective-noun phrase, the descriptive adjective names a property value of the category denoted by the noun, that is, it indexes a feature value unit associated with the noun. As correlations often exist between feature values (Malt & Smith, 1984), indexing one will tend to excite others, thus supplying the adjective with characteristic connotations, known as direct inferences. For example, while a (ripe) peach is normally pink on the outside and juicy and sweet on the inside, a green peach is unripe, dry and sour in addition to being green in color. These direct inferences suggest themselves so strongly that perceptual property values are often used metonymically to stand for certain (nonobservable) functional or constitutive property values. For example, unripe is an extended word sense of the adjective *green*.

The interesting thing about the phrase "green peach" is that the literal word sense of the adjective (meaning color), while certainly applicable, is not the most appropriate one in the context. Yet it seems difficult to argue that the *unripe* word sense of "green" is a literal one; hence, the suggestion that the metaphoric versus literal distinction should not be made on semantic processing grounds but rather be considered a matter of context sensitivity.

When the modifying adjective indexes a feature value not possessed by the noun, mappings from feature values associated with the adjective in literal noun contexts are used to indirectly index feature values of the noun. A "thirsty fern" is readily understood to be a fern in need of watering, despite the fact that ferns lack the cognitive facilities needed to subjectively experience thirst as humans do. This is an example of what Keil (1979) calls "category error," a situation in which a predicate is applied to a category that does not normally allow it. Keil suggests that natural categories form a "predictability hierarchy," where predictability is defined to be the knowledge of which predicates can be combined with which terms in a natural language. A predicate is said to *span* a term when the predicate can be meaningfully applied to the term and the resulting phrase can be assigned a truth value, be it true or false. A category error occurs when a predicate is used in conjunction with a term it does not span. For example, "green idea" is a category error, since only physical objects can have color as a property. Thus, it is neither true that the idea is green nor that it is not green, since the latter statement implies that the idea has a color, the value of which is something other than green.

When faced with a category error, needless to say, the phrase is far from uninterpretable. Typically, the superficially inapplicable adjective is understood to refer elliptically to a legitimate property of the noun, in this case, hydration. This transference takes place by the spread of activation through the property abstraction hierarchy. Once the relevant property has been activated, the appropriate value (e.g., dehydrated) is made available by separate scalar value transference mechanisms, described in Section 3.

These property and scalar transference mechanisms can be used to supply suggestions for even the most fanciful of expressions such as "happy box." The context surrounding the phrase will usually supply some clues as to the properties of the noun that are being alluded to, but all else being equal the more salient properties of the noun will be favored. The degree of confidence in any such interpretive suggestions falls off with the semantic distance in the property abstraction hierarchy between the mapping's source and target properties.

2.3. Acquiring Lexical Semantics

Another crucial component of the model is context-sensitive lexical semantics. Descriptive adjectives correspond to feature values and nouns to concepts. An adjective–noun phrase is understood by the spread of activation from the corresponding lexemes through the semantic network, where the spread of activation is modulated by the relevance of each intermediate node to the concept under consideration.

The model captures two forms of context sensitivity in descriptive adjectives. In one form, the appropriate word sense of a polysemous lexeme is chosen by spreading activation (Cottrell, 1985). For example, a "green strawberry" is in fact white in color; the adjective is used to refer indirectly to unripeness, a feature of strawberries that is strongly correlated with the color green in the context of other fruits and vegetables (see Figure 6.2).

The other form of context-sensitive semantics involves terms such as *light* and *large*, terms whose meaning is relative to some normative value associated with the noun. A heavy mouse weighs considerably less than even a light elephant, and green leaves are greener than green sea water. One mechanism that could account for this semantic pattern is to have adjectives supply a scaling factor which is applied to the value of the [implicitly] named feature. An adjective indicating a lower than normal value for its property, for example, might carry a scaling factor of 0.8. For example, if mice normally weigh 2 ounces then a light mouse may only weigh 80% of the normal weight, or 1.6 oz. One flaw with this idea is that the variance associated with a given adjective is fixed. The difference in weight between a styrofoam and a lead box is much greater than the difference in weight between a scrawny and an overweight house cat. Nonetheless, for

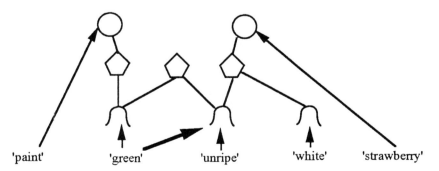

Figure 6.2.
The Component of Network Structure Used to Capture Polysemous Lexical Semantics. Lexemes can have multiple word senses; spreading activation supplies the contextual cues to select the appropriate one.

natural kind terms, the focus of this study, the mechanism seems reasonably appropriate.

There are two situations in which lexical semantics can be learned. In one, an object is presented by the teacher and explicitly named for the student (e.g., "Mommy," "cookie"). In the other, far commoner situation, the exact referent of the lexeme is left up to the student to infer, as when a child is exposed to adult conversation. A crude estimate of the meaning of a term can be made by compiling frequency statistics of use for each lexeme. The meaning hypothesis can be iteratively refined with each new training example, eventually resulting in associations being formed between the lexeme and its referent. The whole process is bootstrapped in experience: the literal meanings of perceptual property terms are learned first, thus supplying a basis for developing abstract features and metaphoric meanings. Each subsequent novel use is interpreted in the light of all previously encountered expressions, so that the semantics of one metaphor can be based on another. For example, the weight and color word sense of *light* would be acquired first, by observing the correlation between the lexeme "light" and certain relative weights and degrees of color saturation. The meaning in the context of beer can be derived by a simple scalar mapping process (e.g., from low weight and low saturation to little taste and/or few calories). The information about which property to target in such a mapping is supplied, if not by the discourse context (e.g., light beer mentioned in a discourse about dieting), then by the salience of the property within the target concept (e.g., since taste is a salient property of beer, a perfectly valid interpretation on first hearing the phrase "light beer" is relatively tasteless beer).

With sufficient repetition this semantic interpretation, initially derived by a simple analogical mapping from previously acquired word senses, is itself catalogued in the dictionary and becomes a figurative word sense in its own right. An even more elaborate example can be devised for the semantics of *green:* the color word sense of *green* is acquired first, by observing the correlation between the lexeme and a certain color hue. Later, the tendency of unripe fruit to be green in color may (with sufficient reinforcement, such as consistent metonymic references to unripeness) become a word sense proper. The interpretation of conventional metaphoric uses, such as the phrase "green recruit," derives not only from the observed correlation between green and unripe but also from the abstraction linking unripeness with inexperience, a salient property of recruits.

3. THE CONNECTIONIST IMPLEMENTATION

This model of adjective–noun semantics is implemented here as an adaptive structured connectionist network. The network operates by allowing activation from the noun to spread through the aspects relevant to the adjective, thus priming all contextually relevant direct inferences, retrieving any relevant stored meanings, and dynamically suggesting novel figurative interpretations based on the available direct inferences, all in parallel. Because the dynamic interpretations are proffered with a relatively low confidence, if a catalogued word sense is available it will be favored over the novel suggestions. Thus, while no explicit attempt is made to catalogue adjective–noun combinations according to their degree of apparent semantic anomaly, the confidence level of interpretation implicitly reflects the distance from a "normal" semantics for the constituent terms.

The network has two distinct learning modes, perceptual feature learning and lexical semantic learning. All unit activation functions are sensitive to either one or the other of the two modes, where the behavior of lexical layer units is affected by the lexical learning signal and all other units, concept, aspect, gaussian and stimulus response, react to the perceptual learning signal. Both signals are implemented with single dedicated control units which can be clamped on or off independently of each other, but in practice the perceptual learning is run before the lexical learning, in order to furnish a coherent lexical semantics as a learning target.

In both learning modes, the net is run by clamping on a single concept node and the subset of the environmental stimulus nodes corresponding to the observed property values of the given exemplar of a concept. For example, a typical training session might start with a concept learning session, in which the system is exposed to the property value correlations that characterize the various aspects of a given concept, by clamping on such values as may correspond to a certain exemplar of the concept. For example, if the concept being learned is *apple*, then two possible exemplars are a ripe, juicy, sweet apple and an unripe, sour, dry apple. The results of training on this input is shown in Figure 6.3 on the

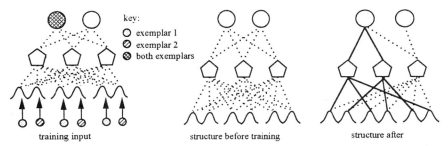

Figure 6.3.
Concept Learning. In this learning mode the conceptual exemplars are stored and generalized, resulting in the model's characteristic multifaceted representation of concepts. Shown on the far right are the results after training on two exemplars of one concept. Dotted lines are used to show links with initial relatively insignificant random weights, with solid lines used for links whose weights have been differentiated by training.

far right: two aspect units get recruited by the apple concept unit to represent the two observed property value cooccurrence patterns.

Once the mental model of apples is in place, a mapping from applicable lexemes to that model can be attempted. Both concept and feature value nodes are considered candidates to supply the semantics for the lexical layer, as depicted in Figure 6.4a. Lexical semantic learning is an iterative process, since the field of possible referents, initially relatively wide, must be narrowed down in a process of elimination. A modified form of Hebbian reinforcement learning is used to successively refine the lexical semantics hypotheses. The first step in this process is shown in Figure 6.4: The lexemes in the phrase "sour apple," when used to describe the observed sour, dry, and unripe apple exemplar, could refer to any one of the four concept and value units currently active (see Figure 6.4b). Eventually, however, after sufficient distinct exemplars of the concept are named in various ways, the field of possibilities is narrowed, often to a single word sense as shown in Figure 6.4c. In order to leave room for potential word-sense extensions, the links between a lexeme and other potential referents are never completely cut.

After both concept acquisition and lexical semantics disambiguation, the net can be used to supply a semantics for not only the adjective–noun phrases on which it was trained, but more interestingly, on novel and even apparently anomalous phrases. The mechanisms described in Weber (1989a, 1989b), once suitably adapted and incorporated into the prestructuring of the net, can be used to supply a basis for dynamic figurative interpretations (see Figure 6.5). The crucial difference in the use of these mechanisms here is that, unlike in the earlier work, the interpretations suggested by these metaphorical mapping mechanisms are made available regardless of whatever other more direct meanings may also be available. The distinction between possibly conflicting

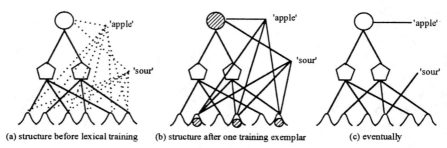

Figure 6.4.
Lexical Learning. In this learning mode lexemes are associated with previously conceptual aspects, as generalized from exemplars. A process of elimination is used to narrow down the field of possible referents for the lexeme. As before, dotted lines represent links with initial, relatively insignificant, weights.

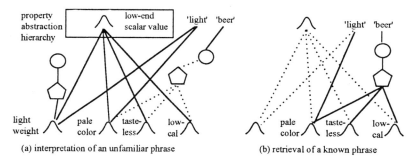

Figure 6.5.
Hypothesizing a Semantics for an Unfamiliar Adjective-Noun Phrase versus Retrieving the Meaning of a Known Phrase. The mechanisms in (b) arise from the structure built after the dynamic interpretation Stage (a). Note the change in relative significance on the weights between the links used for dynamic interpretation and those for retrieval of a familiar phrase, as denoted by the use of dotted lines.

meanings suggested by the various alternative mechanisms is based on confidence measures associated with the interpretations, as opposed to being based on availability (in the traditional two-stage model of metaphor interpretation, metaphoric meanings only become available on failure to determine the literal meaning).

3.1. Representing Feature Values

Properties can be roughly classified into two groups, single valued and multivalued. A single valued property is one for which the various allowable values are mutually exclusive. For example, temperature cannot be both cold and hot at the same time, nor can a given object's weight be simultaneously light and heavy. Single valued properties corresponding to perceptual features tend to be quantitative physical properties of a scalar nature. The allowable values for such a property can be strictly ranked with respect to each other, from least to greatest (Kittay, 1987). One example of this behavior is the *temperature* property, whose values range from freezing through cold, cool, warm, hot, and finally to boiling/burning/blistering, etc. There will generally be two values that typify the positive and negative extremes (e.g., hot and cold) with a third value typifying the neutral setting. There are many possible scales to choose from, the most obvious of which is the intensity scale: temperature ranges from cold to hot, size from small to large, hydration from dry to juicy. Another common scale is the emotional connotations scale: anger is negative, reasonableness positive; sadness opposes happiness, and so on. A property value can participate in any number of scales, but since the various scales are considered to be incomparable, no contradiction is perceived by the system with the assignment of anger, for example, to the positive end of the intensity scale as well as to the negative end of the emotions scale.

Multivalued properties, on the other hand, seem to be nonscalar in nature in that more than one value can legitimately be active at the same time. For example, a cookie can taste at once salt and sweet, and a shirt worn to a party might smell of both smoke and scent. Such multivalued properties are not explicitly represented with a single unit as are single valued properties, but rather are represented implicitly through their property values.

While properties can be classified as multi- or single valued, their constituent property values can be classified as either graded or categorical (Smith & Medin, 1981). Perceptual feature values are all graded, that is, a given value can be present in varying amounts: the shirt worn at a party may only smell faintly of scent. There is considerable similarity between the scalar nature of single-valued properties and the gradedness of perceptual property values. Both can be represented with a unit whose activation level reflects the intensity of the perceptual experience. Orthogonal to this graded or scalar intensity measure is the degree of confidence in the presence or absence of a given property or value. In general, the evidence presented by perception is taken as incontrovertible, while inferences as to properties and values can vary in their reliability. Accordingly, each property and value is represented by a pair of units, one for the scalar intensity measure and the other a separate confidence measure. The resulting connectionist representation of single-valued properties and graded values participating in multivalued properties is shown in Figure 6.6a. (The property and value intensity/confidence pairs are represented in the figure by

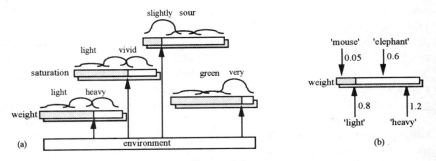

Figure 6.6.
Representing Adjectives. (a) Implementing scalar properties and graded property values. Gaussian units tuned to respond to different scalar value transform the intensity value into a unit-value representation. (b) Adjective semantics are implemented as weights on the links to the corresponding feature unit, so that a heavy elephant weighs more than a (normal) elephant, which is considerably more than a heavy mouse.

FIGURATIVE ADJECTIVE-NOUN COMBINATIONS

overlapping rectangles, with the intensity bars mostly occluding the confidence bars.) Figure 6.6b deals with a related representational issue, that of how to capture the relative nature of descriptive adjectives when used to refer to perceptual property values. When the net is simply being run (as opposed to being trained), the weighted input from the currently active noun supplies the default value for each feature associated with that noun, and the adjectival input supplies modifying signals. The two input values are simply multiplied together, so an adjectival input less than one will lessen the default value while an input greater than one will increase it. This scheme, while suffering from the failing of forcing a semantics of uniform and fixed variance on adjectives, offers the advantage of saving the space required by the combinatoric number of nodes that would be needed to represent the cross product of nouns with adjectives.

3.2. A Brief Example: Drinking Beer

For example, consider the system "tasting" its first beer. The system is already familiar with the scalar properties opacity, effervescence, and alcohol content, and the scalar property values bitter taste and golden-brown color, as shown in Figure 6.7a. The system is also assumed to have already learned the adjective used to refer to each of these values. After exposure to (and training on) exemplars of a pilsner and a stout, a representation for the concept of beer is acquired. As can be determined from Figure 6.7b, the pilsner was pale gold, clear, slightly bitter, or hoppy with a retentive head and moderate alcohol content. The stout, on the other hand, was dark brown, opaque, and very hoppy

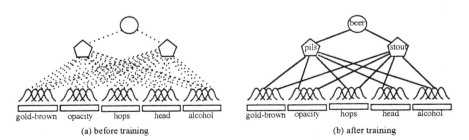

Figure 6.7.
An Example of Learning From Exemplars about Beer. (a) Before training, there are (potentially hundreds of) as yet unrecruited units at both the concept level and the aspect level, such that each level is fully connected to the one below it. (b) After training on two exemplars of the concept, a concept unit and two aspect units have been recruited to represent the new concept.

with no head to speak of and a higher alcohol content. (The scalar quantities shown in the figure are assumed to increase from left to right.) This example will be returned to in the discussion to follow of the system's novel interpretation mechanisms.

3.3. Proposing Novel Interpretations

In addition to the acquisition and retrieval mechanisms for catalogued meanings described above, a few simple analogical mapping mechanisms supply alternative semantic suggestions. Since these alternatives have relatively low-confidence measures, they will only seriously be considered when the stored meaning retrieval mechanisms fail to supply any semantics other than the default or context-free ones. These mechanisms are based on the premise that analogical mappings can be established between two feature values at analogous scalar positions on their respective feature scales. The process of figuratively interpreting an adjective–noun phrase involves setting up mappings from the values primed by the literal connotations of the adjective in various contexts (the source domain) to values of the category denoted by the noun (the target domain). The set of all values activated in this manner form the interpretive basis for understanding a figurative usage. Semantic correspondences must somehow be established between the property value denoted by the adjective and property values belonging to the category denoted by the noun. There are two correspondences to be established, the first being property to property, the second, value to value. For example, when interpreting the phrase "green idea" one must not only establish that the color property in fruit corresponds somehow to development in ideas, but also that the value green maps to underdeveloped. These mappings are discovered by two interlocking interpretive processes, one to establish all property to property mappings, the other to set up the value to value correspondences within related properties.

There are two methods used to establish these semantic correspondences: (direct) value transference and (indirect) scalar correspondence.

Property value transference (Aarts & Calbert, 1978) is applicable when a property value (and hence its associated property) is common to both the source and target fields. Certain relatively straightforward interpretations arise when a property value of the target category is made available through an immediate inference associated with another category. For example, all forms of food and drink share the properties *color* and *taste*. Referring back to the example of beer introduced in Figure 6.7, and assuming that the system has already observed the correlation between green color and sour taste in unripe fruit, the unfamiliar figure of speech "green beer" could be interpreted as denoting sour beer, as shown in Figure 6.8a.

Figure 6.8.
Metaphoric Interpretation. (a) Value transference: The phrase "green beer" is interpreted to mean sour beer, based on the correlation between the color green and a sour taste in fruit. (b) scalar correspondence: The phrase "green beer" is interpreted to mean beer which has not been allowed to ferment for Long enough, by analogical reasoning through the abstraction relating ripening time with processing time.

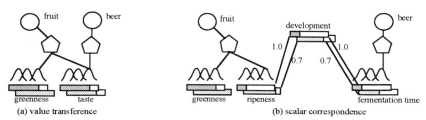

To establish correspondences in the nonoverlapping areas of the source and target fields, however, more indirect mappings must be resorted to. Scalar correspondence mappings exploit the scalar nature of many properties, particularly properties of physical objects. Properties that are quantitative in nature, such as size, weight, density, malleability, and so on, tend to impose a natural scalar ordering on their values (Kittay, 1987). Thus, assuming that two such properties share a common abstraction, the value mappings become obvious. In order to establish a semantic correspondence between the property named by the adjective (e.g., *green* names a color) and properties of the noun (e.g., the experience of recruits), a property abstraction hierarchy relates all the properties in the knowledge base. Each property node is in fact a pair of value-confidence units like the ones used in feature value nodes. As activation propagates through the abstraction hierarchy, the confidence signal is steadily decremented but the intensity signal is maintained at full strength. Since the confidence in the spreading intensity value decays as it propagates, the confidence in a scalar correspondence mapping declines in direct proportion to the semantic distance between the target and its source, a distance defined by the structure of the abstraction hierarchy. Thus, the confidence measures of a value input from the property abstraction hierarchy directly reflects the semantic distance between the source and target. For instance, if ripening time in the source field (fruit) corresponds to fermentation time in the target field (beer), then unripe maps to insufficiently fermented (see Figure 6.8b).

There are two potential plausibility metrics to evaluate the believability of a given figurative interpretation. On the one hand, there is the semantic distance between the properties, as defined by the property abstraction hierarchy. The property-level mapping can occur between the property and itself, in direct-value correspondence, leading to arguably the most plausible suggestions. The degree of plausibility for mappings involving two distinct properties is inversely proportional to the semantic distance between the two in the property abstraction hierarchy. In the worst case, the requirement that a logical relationship pertain between the two properties can be relaxed, leading to the most imaginative suggestions, where apparently arbitrarily related properties are placed in correspondence, albeit with vanishingly small confidence.

On the other hand, there is the choice of source and target domains. Since the target domain consists of the (salient) properties of the noun, a plausible mapping should prefer a more salient property of the category denoted by the noun, but any property is a valid target. This points to the need of a separate salience unit for each property value to augment the current confidence measure. Such a scheme would permit the commonest connotations of the adjective to be used preferentially.

4. IMPLEMENTATION DETAILS

The adaptive structured connectionist network described in the preceding section was developed on the Rochester Connectionist Simulator (Goddard, Lynne, & Mintz, 1988). One of the hallmarks of structured connectionist nets as opposed to PDP style architectures is the heterogeneous use of nontrivial unit functions. The network used to implement the model of adjective-noun interpretation is characteristic in this respect in that while the network is formed of initially fully interconnected layers of units and link weights are adjusted during training to reflect the input data, the connections are recurrent rather than feed forward, and each layer of units employs a distinct activation function. The network blends prestructured elements with adaptive components. The layered architecture (shown in Figure 6.9) reflects certain a priori assumptions about the internal structure of cognitive categories. The links between layers, however, are initially uniform and must develop in response to training input from the environment. To this end, a handful of control units exist to supply reset or enable signals to units in several layers, permitting three distinct operational modes: concept learning, lexical semantic learning, and lexical interpretation. While the three modes of operation are fully interleavable, dependencies do exist in that it is difficult to get sensible interpretations of symbols whose semantics is still fuzzy. Thus, the two explicit learning modes are initially run in sequence, starting with perceptually grounded concept learning, followed by lexical acquisition, after which adjective–noun combinations can meaningfully provide additional implicit data for further extensions to both conceptual and lexical semantics.

Figure 6.9.
The Layered Prestructuring Employed in the Connectionist Implementation. (a) The interconnections, initially complete with small random weights, of the layers. (b) The actual implementation of the "virtual" value units depicted in (a).

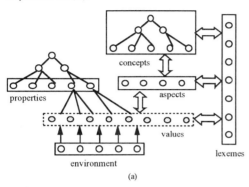
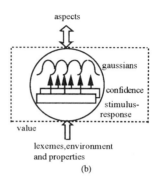

In perceptual learning mode, the network responds to an exemplar, which is defined to be a pattern of cooccurring feature values associated with a single concept. Before running the network in this mode, the user clamps on one concept unit and any (meaningful/appropriate) subset of the environmental stimulus units, where the semantics of each stimulus unit is known to the user but not to the system. That is, even though a given input node may be labeled as representing the feature value green, since it is initially fully connected to the aspect layer (albeit indirectly), an initially uniform semantics for all input units exists. The labels merely provide the teacher with a map to the input unit's supposed relationship with the outside world.

The differences in activation function behavior between the learning modes can be fairly subtle. Stimulus response units, for example, simply transmit their environmental input in both; however, in lexical learning mode if no environmental input is available the unit will respond to suggestions as to its value coming in from alternative internal sources, specifically, from the property inheritance hierarchy used by the figurative interpretation mechanisms.

Gaussian units generally respond to their input from feature units weighted by the input from the corresponding confidence unit. When learning from perceptual sources, they will also recruit themselves to an aspect unit that is emitting the distinguished signal of new recruitment. During gaussian recruitment, the weight on each link is set to the value currently being transmitted. When running in either lexical learning or nonlearning mode, if no inputs are being received from the feature layer, the weighted sum of inputs from any active aspects effects the retrieval of the activation pattern stored on recruitment.

In lexical processing mode, aspects respond with the weighted sum of gaussian and concept layer inputs. During perceptual training, on the other hand, only the gaussian layer inputs are attended to. If an unrecruited unit's response is over a certain threshold and greater than the current maximum of all other aspect units, then it will recruit itself to represent the current pattern of gaussian activity by setting the weights on the incoming links to reflect the values they transmit. This has the effect of severing all links to currently inactive gaussians. If the unit's response equals the maximum of the other aspect units, then there is contention for recruitment, so the weights on the gaussian layer links are rerandomized to (eventually) break the response deadlock. Once a unit has been recruited it will respond as before to gaussian input but will not be eligible to represent a new pattern. The effect of the threshold on the recruitment scheme is to widen the radius of sensitivity of aspect units to include not only the precise pattern it was recruited on, but also reasonably similar patterns, including subpatterns. For an alternative formulation of one-shot recruitment learning, see Dieterich (1989).

Concept units also have distinct behaviors for perceptual learning and both lexical learning and nonlearning modes. The exemplar learning response is tied to the corresponding behavior of aspect units. Immediately after recruitment an aspect unit emits a distinguished value (1.0) as a signal to the concept layer, which is monitoring the responses of aspects to the given stimuli. Only when an aspect has been newly recruited at the gaussian level will a concept node recruit it. Concept layer recruitment involves cutting the links to all but the maximally active aspect, the link to which has its weight boosted to the maximum. This procedure means that while a concept can acquire many aspects, each aspect will be associated with one and only one concept, just as required by the model. In lexical learning and nonlearning mode, however, only the concept unit associated with the currently active noun is activated; all others remain silent.

Lexical units are initially fully connected to both the feature layer and the concept layer, since these two layers contain compact representations of the semantics of adjectives and nouns, respectively. Lexical semantic acquisition is achieved with simple Hebbian weight reinforcement. When a lexical unit is coactivated with either a feature value or a concept node, the strength of the connection between them is augmented, and when the lexeme is active it slightly decrements the weight on all links to inactive values and concepts.

4.1. An Example

Some components of the system's initial structure, as well as the data used during perceptual training, are obtained from the user-supplied input file. A small example of how such an input file looks appears below:

```
sfeature (ripeness: unripe, ripe, overripe, rotten)
sfeature (experience: inexperienced, experienced)
feature (taste: sweet, sour, astringent)
feature (color: green, yellow, red)
concept (apple, banana, recruit)
abstracts (development: ripeness, experience)
exemplar (apple: red, sweet, ripe)
phrase: pomme
exemplar (apple: green, sour, unripe)
phrase: pomme verte
exemplar (banana: yellow, sweet, ripe)
phrase: banane
exemplar (banana: green, astringent, unripe)
phrase: banane verte
exemplar (recruit: inexperienced)
```

There are six statements known to the system: *feature, sfeature, abstracts, concept, exemplar,* and *phrase*. The *feature* statement is used for nonscalar features such as hue (color), saturation, taste, and so on; features for which multiple values are permissible. Separate feature nodes are created for each value associated with the property. The *sfeature* statement is used for scalar features such as temperature, weight, size, and so on; features whose values are mutually exclusive and arranged along an implicit scale. The values named in the statement are assumed to appear in order of increasing scalar magnitude. A single feature node is created for the property, and the given values are allocated scalar positions within the feature node. The *abstracts* statement is used to build the property abstraction hierarchy. The property abstraction hierarchy plays such a crucial role in the novel metaphor interpretation process that it would be better to acquire the structure of the hierarchy during training rather having the user specify it beforehand, but until a solution is found to the problem of automatic abstraction the hand coding is needed. The *concept* statement is somewhat redundant, since concepts appear in exemplars, but was included for implementational simplicity. The statement has no effect on the network's initial structure; its only use is in minimizing the lexical dictionary used to devise training sequences. The *exemplar* statement specifies the form of the perceptual mode training sequences. For example, the first set of cooccurring property values would be red, ripe, and sweet. These values are run with the lexeme *pomme*, which is the French word for apple (*phrases* apply to the previous exemplar). Lexical training with the given set of exemplars results in *pomme* mapping to the apple concept and *banane* to the banana concept, but the best guess as to the semantics of *verte* is that is could equally well refer to either unripe or green, as seems appropriate.

The network produced by these statements consists of three concept nodes

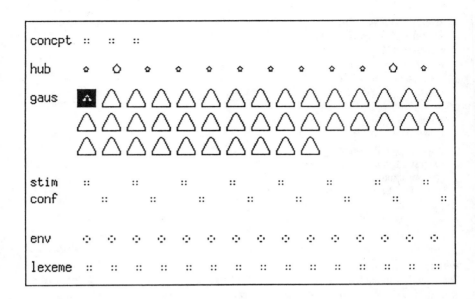

Figure 6.10.
Results of Running the Example on the System Developed on the Rochester Simulator. Before running any exemplars each gaussian unit is fully connected to each aspect unit with small random weights. After training, the connections between the two layers have taken on a structure that reflects the structure present in the exemplars.

(apple, banana, recruit), 12 aspects (the total number of feature values and as good a guess as any), 45 gaussian units (five for each stimulus), 8 stimulus response-confidence pairs (ripeness, experience, sweet, sour, astringent, green, yellow, red), 15 internal environment (i.e., training input) inputs, one for each concept and feature value, and 15 lexical level units, all initially arranged as shown in Figure 6.9. Figure 6.10 shows a pair of before and after connectivity pictures for a selected gaussian unit in the network, where the size of the icons reflect the strength of the link between that unit and the highlighted unit. As shown in the figure, connections between gaussians and aspects (labeled *hub* in the figure) are initialized with small random weights, and each gaussian is fully connected to all others (this interconnectivity is used in the implementation of recruitment learning). After running the exemplars, the connections between the selected gaussian and the aspect layer are no longer uniform: two aspects are strongly associated with the gaussian, two more are moderately related, and the connection between the gaussian and one of the aspect units has been cut entirely (as denoted by the dotted pentagon).

5. SUMMARY AND FUTURE WORK

One challenging task yet to be attempted is to learn property abstractions, rather than building them in according to the user's specifications. The difficulty with learning property abstractions under the current scheme is that properties and their attendant values are not represented at a fine enough grain to support abstraction. Some form of microfeature representation would be the obvious first place to start in remedying this deficiency.

Another intriguing problem raised by the work to this point is the difficulty in integrating dynamic gaussian distribution with the other forms of training supported by the network. Preliminary work on training the gaussian layer to conform to the representational demands of the underlying property values seemed encouraging, but so far all attempts to integrate these techniques with the exemplar training routine have failed. The problem is one of a moving target: The gaussian layer needs a clear indication of the representational capacity of each feature value unit, but at the same time the exemplar training procedure requires a clear signal from the gaussian layer to be effective.

One final suggestion for future work on the system is that it be extended to allow mediated direct inferences to play a role in the metaphor-semantic suggestion mechanisms. Only immediate direct inferences are currently considered when devising dynamic figurative interpretations.

To summarize, the model of lexical semantics for adjective-noun phrases suggested by the observation of direct inferences has three components, functionally organized internal structuring of categories into aspects, context-sensitive lexical semantic retrieval for both literal and figurative usages, and dynamic interpretation mechanisms to suggest figurative meanings of novel usages. The dynamic mechanisms base their interpretive suggestions on catalogued meanings in alternative contexts. These suggestions can, with sufficient repetition or situational reinforcement, be added to the catalogue of known meanings, thus enriching the semantic basis for future figurative interpretations.

REFERENCES

Aarts, J.M.G., & Calbert, J.P. (1979). *Metaphor and non-metaphor: The semantics of adjective-noun combinations*. Tübingen: Verlag.

Anderson, J.R. (1983). A spreading activation theory of memory. *Journal of Verbal Learning and Verbal Behavior, 22*, 161–295.

Barsalou, L.W. (1982). Context-independent and context-dependent information in concepts. *Memory and Cognition, 10*(1), 82–93.

Black, M. (1979). More about metaphor. In A. Ortony (Ed.), *Metaphor and thought*. Cambridge, MA: Cambridge University Press.

Cottrell, G.W. (1985). *A connectionist approach to word-sense disambiguation* (Tech. Rep. No. 154). Rochester, NY: University of Rochester Computer Science Department.

Dieterich, J. (1989). *Spreading Activation and Connectionist Models for Natural Language Processing* (ICSI-Tech. Rep. No. 89–008). Berkeley, CA: International Computer Science Institute.

Feldman, J.A., & Ballard, D.H., (1982). Connectionist models and their properties. *Cognitive Science, 6*, 205–254.

Gildea, P., & Glucksberg, S. (1983). On understanding metaphor: The role of context. *Journal of Verbal Learning and Verbal Behavior, 22*(5), 577–590.

Gluck, M.A., & Corter, J.E. (1985, August). *Information and category utility*. Unpublished manuscript, Computer Science Department, Stanford University, Stanford, CA.

Goddard, N., Lynne, K., & Mintz, T. (1988, May). *The Rochester Connectionist Simulator User Manual* (Tech. Rep. No. 233). Rochester, NY: Computer Science Department, University of Rochester.

Inhoff, A.W., Lima, S.D., & Carroll, P.J. (1984) Contextual effects on metaphor comprehension in reading. *Memory and Cognition, 12*(6), 558–587.

Keil, F.C. (1979). *Semantic and conceptual development: An ontological perspective*. Cambridge, MA: Harvard University Press.

Kittay, E. (1987). *Metaphor, its cognitive force and linguistic structure*. London, UK: Clarendon.

Lakoff, G. (1987). *Women, fire, and dangerous things: What categories reveal about the mind*. Chicago, IL: University of Chicago Press.

Malt, B.C., & Smith, E.E. (1984). Correlated properties in natural categories. *Journal of Verbal Learning and Verbal Behavior, 23*, 250–269.

Martin, J.H. (1988). *A computational theory of metaphor* (Tech. Rep. No. UCB/CSD 88/465). Berkeley: Computer Science Division, University of California, Berkeley.

Richards, I.A. (1937). *The philosophy of rhetoric*. London: Oxford University Press.

Rosch, E., Mervis, C.B., Gray, W.D., Johnson, D.M., & Boyes-Braem, P. (1976). Basic objects in natural categories. *Cognitive Psychology, 8*, 382–439.

Shastri, L. (1985). *Evidential reasoning in semantic networks: A formal theory and its parallel implementation* (Tech. Rep. No. 166). Rochester, NY: Computer Science Department, University of Rochester.

Smith, E.E., & Medin, D. (1981). *Categories and concepts.* Cambridge, MA: Harvard University Press.

Tabossi, P. (1988). Effects of context on the immediate interpretation of unambiguous nouns. *Journal of Experimental Psychology; Language, Memory and Cognition,* 153–162.

Weber, S.H. (1989a). *A structured connectionist approach to direct inferences and figurative adjective-noun combinations* (Tech. Rep. No. 289). Rochester, NY: University of Rochester Computer Science Department.

Weber, S.H. (1989b). Direct inferences and figurative interpretation in a connectionist implementation of language understanding. *Proceedings of IJCNN-91, the International Joint Conference on Neural Networks.* Washington, DC.

Weber, S.H. (1989c). Figurative adjective-noun interpretation in a structured connectionist network. *Proceedings of the 11th Annual Conference of the Cognitive Science Society* (pp. 204–211). Ann Arbor, MI.

7
Back-Propagation Representations for the Rule-Analogy Continuum*

Catherine L. Harris

1. INTRODUCTION

In a review of recent papers on analogical reasoning, Dejong (1989) laments the diversity of topics billed as investigations of analogy. Is this the "curse of an alluring name" or is analogy truly central to thought? It is likely that analogy has become an alluring topic precisely *because* theorists are trying to define the central elements of thought. Like many other cognitive scientists, I hypothesize that the phenomenon I focus on, language, displays organizational principles which are fundamental to human cognition. Analogy theorists have noted that many cognitive abilities may be mediated by a similarity-based processing system (Clement & Gentner, 1991; Collins & Burstein, 1989, Holyoak & Thagard, 1989). In the current chapter, I integrate the ideas of modern analogy theorists with language data, in particular, data relevant to the systems of rules and partial regularities holding between linguistic expressions and their conventional interpretations. I suggest it is not a coincidence that ancient Greek and Roman grammarians and the linguists of the pregenerative era (Bloomfield, 1933; Steinthal, 1881, cited in Esper, 1973) used the term *analogy* to signify regularities of language (e.g., inflectional paradigms and the assimilation of foreign loan words), while today researchers use this term for abstract or creative problem solving (Gentner, 1983, 1989; Holyoak & Thagard, 1989; Johnson-Laird, 1983, 1989). I will argue for a revival of some aspects of the pregenerative approach to language, but with a modern slant: The continuum from abstract rules, to analogical relations to similarity of properties observed for both conceptual and linguistic processing arises from a common substrate, the

---
* I thank John Barnden for crucial suggestions on an early version of this chapter, and am grateful for the extensive comments of four anonymous reviewers.

cognitive microstructure, described by researchers working in the Parallel Distributed Processing (PDP) or connectionist framework (McClelland, Rumelhart, & Hinton, 1986; Smolensky, 1988).

This claim is explored in three steps. I first review some ideas about the relevance of connectionist networks (multilayer pattern associators coupled with a learning algorithm such as back propagation, henceforth "networks") to age-old and yet still current dilemmas in linguistic theory (Esper, 1973; Harris, 1991a; Hockett, 1968). I also briefly note some of the similarities between the representational dilemmas faced by linguists and the dilemmas currently preoccupying analogy theorists (Vosniadou & Ortony, 1989). These ideas are then illustrated with two implementations of PDP models of polysemy (Harris, 1990, 1991b). The specific problem to be solved is identifying the relationship among entities in expressions containing the polysemous prepositions *over, across, through, around, above,* and *below.* The hidden units of the trained network can be analyzed to see how linguistic information is represented, but analysis may also shed light on the questions of interest to the modern analogy theorists, such as whether novel patterns are processed "on analogy" to patterns which share similar features, similar relations, or similar systems of corresponding features. I show how the encodings formed by the hidden units are an emergent property of the similarity structure of the training corpus combined with resource limitations. In the final section, I return to the questions of the nature of mental representation, and compare the similarity-based framework described by Gentner and Clement (1988) and Collins and Burstein (1989) with the schematicity continuum proposed by cognitive linguistics. I suggest that we may not need to posit an architecture of cognition which is equipped with either an explicit "systematicity constraint" or fundamental distinctions between object properties and object relations.

2. LINGUISTIC REGULARITIES, ANALOGY AND PDP

Although there are marked differences between current ideas about language and those of the pregenerative era, the central questions in modern linguistics have been around for millennia: How can observed regularities in language be described in a succinct fashion, and what is the source of the human ability to produce and comprehend novel utterances? I will describe three approaches to answering these questions.

1. The linguists who predate the Chomskian revolution attributed linguistic productivity to the psychological process they called "analogy."
2. Many linguists, following Chomsky (1957, 1965), posit that observed regularities derive from mentally represented rules.

3. Cognitive linguists (Lakoff, 1987; Langacker, 1987, 1991; Talmy, 1985) are less explicit than Chomskians about the nature of mental data structures (although see Deane 1988, 1991, in press), but emphasize the importance of explaining observed grammatical regularities in terms of language-independent principles, such as the nature of human communication and information processing.

2.1. The Pregenerative Era: Appeals to Analogy

The ancient grammarians of Greece and Rome termed the basic orderliness of language "analogy" and introduced the proportional analogy pattern (*dream:dreamt::sleep:slept*) which became the standard method for classifying the similarities among assembled noun and verb stems (Esper, 1973). Observed exceptions to inflectional paradigms, the perturbations caused by foreign loan words, and change over time in words' forms and meanings were noted and were thought to reflect a basic property of human creativity, which was accordingly termed "analogy."

The observation of significant regularity, combined with the frequency of exceptions, led to the often-cited debate between the "analogists" and the "anomalists." The analogists (chiefly the Alexandrian grammarian Aristarchus) argued that the key property of language is conformity to pattern, while the anomalists (the Stoics of the first century B.C.) emphasized the imperfections and irregularities of language. However, Esper (1973) suggests that the anomaly-analogy debate may be a historical fiction. He comments, "Fehling (1956) has made an exhaustive study of the evidence and has concluded that the 'controversy' between the two 'schools' was an invention of the Roman polymath Marcus Terentius Varro (116-127 B.C.) and that none of the alleged adversaries were so stupid as to be unaware that there are systematic regularities in linguistic forms and that there are many exceptions to the regularities" (p. 2).

Up through Bloomfield's day (roughly, the first half of this century) morphological paradigms were identified as a type of proportional analogy insofar as the relationship between stem and suffix is systematic across many examples. But even richer opportunities for systematicities exist because language is inherently relational: A form is paired with a meaning. An analogy can be said to obtain if systematicities exist in this pairing. Wheeler (1887) subsumed under "analogy" eight main linguistic phenomena that involve systematic similarities. For example, he illustrated the idea that a similarity in form can suggest a similarity in meaning by citing the historical change from Old English *brydguma* to Modern English *bridegroom*. Rules of sound change would predict that *brydguma* (cf. Gothic *guma* 'man' = Latin *homo*) should become *bridegoom*. But presumably, with *guma* no longer part of speakers' vocabularies, *groom* made more sense, yielding the current *bridegroom*.

Saussure (1916) noted that if analogy is to be the label for the psychological processes responsible for systematicities of language, then analogy is both innovative and conservative. The innovative role of analogy is to allow new forms to be created on a model, while the conservative role confers stability on a form which is integrated into a system. Important factors in predicting innovation and conservation were thought to be the number of items in a class, and how frequently speakers used each item (Bloomfield, 1933). These factors are reminiscent of networks' extraction of regularities from a corpus using a training algorithm such as back propagation (Plunkett & Marchman, 1991).

Analogy was thus used as a cover label for creative uses of language (including semantic extensions, the effect of cross-linguistic borrowings and analogical reanalysis) and for overlearned or automatic processes like declension and morphology. Although it was assumed that analogy was at root a psychological phenomenon, there were only vague ideas about what mental processing mechanisms were responsible for the observed "analogies" (Saussure, 1916). The following quote from Chomsky (1966, cited in Dineen, 1968) illustrates generative grammarians' insistence that unformalized notions be rejected.

> To attribute the creative aspects of language to 'analogy' or 'grammatical patterns' is to use the terms in a completely metaphorical way, with no clear sense and no relation to the technical usage of linguistic theory. (p. 12)

2.2. Chomskian Linguistics: The Triumph of Succinctness and Abstraction

Currently, morphological as well as syntactic productivity is assumed to be the result of the application of rules (or "constraints," Chomsky, 1981), which are thought to be maximally succinct, abstract descriptions of observed regularities, and are also assumed to be the mental data structures responsible for the existence of observed regularities. One advantage of describing language in terms of rules is the existence of notational systems for their description. These include finite state automata, rewrite rules, push-down stacks, and the formal grammars of the Chomsky hierarchy which have played so large a role in the unfolding of the computational revolution. But perhaps the main advantage of this view was its explicit conception of the relationship between mental structures (data structures, algorithms) and behavior (language production, comprehension, grammatically judgments).

A disadvantage of these notational systems, and the cognitive theories built around them, is their awkward accommodation of partial regularities. A common method for representing both exceptions and rules is to posit separate data structures, one for storing the rules that generate regular expressions, and one for storing vocabulary items and idiosyncratic word combinations (idioms, fixed expressions).[1]

2.3. Cognitive Linguistics: The Schematicity Continuum

The core idea behind the young cognitive linguistics movement[2] is that language is not an autonomous mental faculty but is a joint result of the nature of human cognition (Langacker, 1987) and the forces of communication (Givon, 1989); the emphasis on communication is most representative of the school called functionalist linguistics (Bates & MacWhinney, 1982, 1987; Kuno, 1987; Siewierska, 1991). The most relevant aspect of cognitive linguistics for this chapter are the representational structures and processes that are posited by those working in this framework. A key idea is that structures are needed which can be arbitrarily specific. I will refer to this as the "rule-analogy continuum" (also, the "schematicity continuum"). In this usage "rule" means a maximally abstract generalization and "analogy" refers to a set of systematic correspondences that may hold between just a small set of items (Harris, 1990).

Fillmore and his colleagues (Fillmore, 1986, 1988; Fillmore, Kay, & O'Connor, 1988) have described how a great deal of a language user's competence consists in the manipulation of idioms and stock phrases such as *learn X by heart, know X by heart; cook his/her/NP's goose;I wouldn't VP if you gave me NP, the more S the more T*, etc. The representational structures for these sentences have to be able to store both overtly occurring words (e.g., *goose*) as well as more abstract items (such as an arbitrary noun phrase).

A second key idea is that there need be no conflict between mentally storing a sentence as a well-learned routine, and permitting that mental representation to be part of the matrix of patterns from which generalizations are extracted. That is, an item can be "memorized" and yet still conform to a rule. For example, we are familiar with the phrase *let the cat out* both as a standard request with a specific meaning (conjuring up a door to the outside world, a home, and a pet that likes scenery changes) as well as a rule-governed combination of the component lexical items (Langacker, 1987).

What descriptive constructs are proposed for translating these ideas into a conception of the nature of grammar? Abstracting over differences in terminol-

---

[1] One might wonder if generativists are headed for the cul-de-sac that purportedly trapped the dueling analogists and anomalists. Esper (1973) reported, "The canons or rules which the analogists found necessary to account for apparent exceptions became so numerous that they demonstrated anomaly as much as analogy; the 'fight' thus ended in a draw" (p. 3).

[2] Although it is often presumptuous to declare an idea to be a "movement" or to rate its youthfulness, we can note that the journal *Cognitive Linguistics* (Mouton de Gruyter) began quarterly publication in 1990, while the first conference with "cognitive linguistics" in its name was held in 1986. The linguistic departments of the Berkeley and San Diego campuses of the University of California have held annual cognitive linguistics workshops since 1987.

ogy and emphasis among different theorists (e.g., Bates & MacWhinney, 1982; Fillmore, 1988; Givon, 1989; Langacker, 1987) a grammar is thought to be a conventionalized set of form-meaning pairs and schematization over form-meaning pairs. A **form** is an actual or possible utterance. **Meaning** is broadly conceived to encompass all evoked conceptualization, including communicative function and extralinguistic aspects of the speech act. A **schematization** is a structure that is a less specific variant of the utterance or meaning.

Langacker (1987) refers to an association between a form and a meaning as a **symbolic structure**. Presumably it is "symbolic" because the form is an arbitrary symbol for the meaning, and it is a structure because it has two parts to it. A schema is any symbolic structure that can be instantiated by more than one utterance-meaning pair. For example, the **subject** schema summarizes what is invariant across many utterances where one part of a clause has certain formal properties (e.g., nominal markings and number agreement with a finite verb) and occupies a position of pragmatic prominence within the clause. The symbolic structure is simply the relationship holding between syntactic properties and their meaning and function, which for sentence subject is the signaling of information prominence.

Langacker (1987, p. 446) uses the [verb] + er pattern of subject nominalization as an example of a case where schemas, analogy, and rules are very similar, and perhaps effectively equivalent. Bloomfield (1933; see also Householder, 1971) would describe the production of *striver* given the verb root *strive* with the analogy chains such as *learn:learner::sleep:sleeper::help:helper::strive:striver*. On this view, producing *striver* requires that the speaker represent the parallels across each verb and nominalization. The first member of each pair is a typical type of verb, one that signals an action, and the second is a particular type of noun, an agent of an action. The first contains no suffix, while the second member of each pair ends with '-er.' But if this information about meaning and phonology is mentally represented, it is descriptively equivalent to the schematic symbolic structure posited by Langacker, which itself is tantamount to a nominalization rule.

Nevertheless, there are some differences in the three approaches. One of the shortcomings of Bloomfieldian analogy (i.e., the view of analogy promulgated by Bloomfield, 1933, and other pregenerative linguists) was that it was never clear how to predict when extending one pattern on analogy to another would lead to an unacceptable utterance ("false analogy") and when it would produce a sentence of the language. This question is similar to the one addressed by modern analogy theorists (e.g., Gentner, 1983; Vosniadou & Ortony, 1989) when they ask how a source domain is selected, and why some attributes, but not others, are mapped to the target domain. Dejong (1989) notes that some cases of what appear to be analogical transfer may really be cases of **reinstantiation**; that is, problem solvers are drawing inferences about a new situation by using knowledge about a general mental model or some type of "known abstraction."

The "known abstraction" is essentially the solution to the problem of "false analogies" proposed by Langacker (1987). The schemas described by Langacker are abstractions of the invariances occurring in a huge number of items which form a class due to their statistical distribution in the text (i.e., in the corpus of utterances the language learner is exposed to). The question of what computational mechanisms are responsible for the extraction of schemas from a corpus is not directly answered by Langacker, except for his suggestion that the learning of linguistic regularities be assimilated to the more general problem of regularity detection, and thus connectionist learning procedures may be useful (Langacker, 1991).

There are ways in which the schema approach differs (at least implementationally), from the Chomskian emphasis on symbolic rules. Because schemas emerge from many utterances, they are tied to a corpus in a way that the rules of generative grammar are not. (Indeed, some theorists deny that it is possible for many of the rules or constraints of grammar to be extracted from a corpus; cf. Chomsky, 1980; Crain, 1991.) Langacker (1987) points to one of the repercussions of representations being emergent properties.

> The one remaining issue is whether or not the speaker possesses the constructional schema as a preestablished unit. If he does, *striver* can be actualized without the concomitant activation of *search/searcher, lecture/lecturer*, etc. If he does not, he must activate these forms and extract the requisite schema... The distinction comes down to whether the schema has previously been extracted and whether this has occurred sufficiently often enough to make it a unit. One would presume so in the present instance [the example of *striver*], but we certainly have the ability to extract new schemas and analogize in unpreconfigured directions. (p. 447)

2.4. Regularity and Schematicity Emerge From the Connectionist Microstructure

The ideas that abstract schemas underlie linguistic productivity shares with Bloomfieldian analogy a troubling vagueness. When should we suspect that a speaker has produced a new form on analogy to an existing form sufficiently often enough that the new form becomes a unit? When are there enough similar form-meaning pairs in a corpus for us to suspect that an abstraction over these pairs will be created?

Cognitive linguists characterize a grammar as an inventory of grammatical constructions. As data structures, lists have little appeal. But once a list is conceived as being stored in a distributed format, the computational advantages discovered by PDP theorists accrue to it: Prototypes emerge when similar patterns reinforce each other, irregular patterns are maintained if favored by frequency, and novel patterns can be generated or interpreted on analogy to familiar ones.

I advocate using connectionist networks as an implementation of a particular idealization of language and grammar. We accept that idealizations are useful even though they are demonstrably inexact. One of Chomsky's (1957) contributions was his idealization of language and grammar. He proposed that a language be idealized as a set of strings, and a grammar be idealized as a mechanical device capable of distinguishing set members from nonmembers. An alternative idealization, which I recommend for heuristic purposes, is that language is a corpus of form-meaning pairs (with form and meaning defined as in the previous section), and a grammar is the matrix of weighted connections that implements the form-meaning correspondences. With this idealization, we have a method for predicting what invariances will be extracted, and how the specificity of a schema is related to the pool of utterances it summarizes. The extracted invariances will be those that were instrumental in learning the training corpus, and will thus depend on the type and token frequencies of pattern-set exemplars, and representational resources of the network (i.e., number of weights).

I will make this proposed idealization more concrete by describing the types of hidden-unit representations constructed by two back-propagation networks which were trained to learn form-meaning correspondences. I will also describe how the ideas about generalization from a corpus of examples is related to the similarity-based processing ideas of Gentner (1989) and Collins and Burstein (1989).

3. MODEL 1: THE POLYSEMIES OF *OVER*

Polysemy is the term for lexical items that have a number of related senses. I picked English prepositional polysemy as the domain of exploration because several analyses exist of both the meaning of many spatial expressions, and of the types of mediating structures that are likely to be necessary for a system to embody the constraints on sense selection. In addition, prepositional polysemy is a phenomenon where we have clear cases of generalization according to a pre-established pattern, and cases that have considerable novelty or uncertainty to them.

This first model was trained to activate the correct polyseme of the preposition *over* given an input vector representing a four-word sentence (Harris, 1989, 1990). With this model, I illustrate the abstraction of invariances into internal representations that function akin to rules, yet are tailor made for the statistics of the data set.

One of the most polysemous of the prepositions, *over* is also one whose interconnected senses are the most complicated (Brugman, 1988; Hawkins, 1984; Herskovitz, 1986). Figure 7.1 diagrams some of the most common spatial senses. In describing a relational configuration, it is convenient to differentiate between the entity functioning as **figure**, and the entity functioning as **ground**. In English, the subject of a sentence usually identifies the figure, while the

Figure 7.1.
Diagrams of Four Spatial Sense of *Over*. LM: landmark. TR: trajector

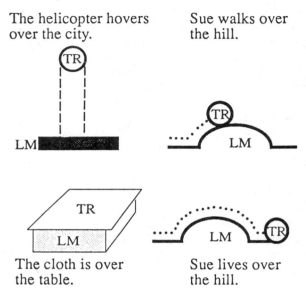

prepositional object signals the ground, as is clear from a comparisons of example sentences (1) and (2). In the terminology of cognitive grammar, the entity which moves or is positioned relative to some reference point is called the **trajector**, while the reference point is called the **landmark**. Many of the details of the *over* schemas, particularly the spatial schemas, were first identified by Brugman (1981).

1. The boy rolled around the bicycle.
2. The bicycle rolled around the boy.

3.1. Main Spatial Schemas

3.1.1. The Above Schema. The trajector is vertically above, but not touching the landmark. *Over* may differ from the preposition *above* by having a connotation of a force pressing down, or in attributing dominance, purview, or surveillance to the spatially superior object, as suggested by comparisons such as (3-5) (Talmy, 1988). (In these and subsequent examples, a ? before a sentence signals some degree of unnaturalness, while a * flags a sentence as semantically or grammatically unacceptable.)

3. The helicopter hovered over the field.
   The helicopter hovered above the field.
4. He stood over me.
   He stood above me.
5. The state flag flew over their house.
   ?The state flag flew above their house.

3.1.2. The Above-Across Schema. The trajector is an object extending (or moving on a path) above a landmark. If there is no contact between the trajector and landmark, usage of *over* to describe the path of movement is fairly unrestricted, as in (6) and (7).

6. The plane flies over the [bridge, hill, field, park, yard, city].
7. The wire stretches over the [bridge, hill, field, park, yard, city].

If contact is present, use of *over* is most felicitous if the path moves *up and over* a vertical barrier, as in *walk over the [bridge, hill, mountain]* or a demarcated boundary, as in *step over the line*. The relative felicity of (7), above, compared to the **contact** versions in (8) below, may be because *plane flies* and *wire stretches* imply paths that are long enough to fully crossover and beyond large two-dimensional regions such as *park, field, yard,* and *city*. On the other hand, *walk* implies a shorter path, one that is typically within the boundaries of these large regions.

8. *The man walked over the [yard, city, park, field].

3.1.3. The Cover Schema. The trajector's two-dimensional length extends to the edges of or beyond the landmark. In most but not all cases, the trajector is construed as vertically above, and in contact with the landmark (9). Note that the trajector is often perceived as exerting a force pressing down upon the landmark.

9. The tapestry stretched over the wall.
10. The spider crawled over the bedclothes.
11. We wrote over the doctor's note.

3.1.4. The End-of-path Schema.

Path schemas require either a verb that indicates extent or motion, or a trajector with significant horizontal extent. If the verb profiles a static relation (e.g., *was, live, stand, sit*) then the frequent interpretation is that the trajector is statically located at the end of a path implied by the preposition and prepositional object (last diagram in Figure 7.1).

12. The grove stands over that mountain.
    I live just over the bridge.
    The ocean lies over the hill.

Summary. These examples show that *over* can signal a number of distinct spatial relationships, and that the meaning evoked by a given sentence can be influenced by all of the words in the clause. In the next section, I describe how the regularities in the mapping from sentences to their meanings can be extracted by a simple back-propagation network.

3.2. Model 1 Implementation

The goal was to use back propagation to learn the regularities inhering in a substantial number of form-meaning pairs. The network was given the task of learning to map "sentences" of the form "trajector (over) landmark" to a representation of the spatial relationship between the trajector and the landmark. This relationship was encoded by turning on specific bits on the output layer that were designated to stand for relations such as **above**, **across**, and **cover**. An additional three bits were turned on to signal **end-of-path**, **up** (upward component to the trajectory), and **contact**. Lexical items were represented in the input layer in a localist fashion: A unique unit designated each word. This meant that the network received no semantic information about the input words. Instead, the input nodes should be viewed as language "form"—as arbitrary strings. Figure 17.2 depicts the number of layers, the connections between layers, and what meaning was assigned to the nodes in the input and output layers.

Semantic features are ultimately not likely to be the right way to think about representing meaning (Brugman, 1988; Lakoff, 1987). Elsewhere (Harris, 1991b, Chapter 6), I have argued that human mental representation of word meaning needs to incorporate both spatial representations and some type of verbal or summary label. However, the present PDP model used bit vectors to code the presence or absence of attributes of a spatial relationship. These bits should be viewed not as semantic primitives, but as summary labels for more complicated information. One can imagine that it is these more complicated data structures that are being referenced when the activation of a unit of the output layer is subtracted from the target activation value in calculating the back-propagation error.

3.2.1. Training Corpus. Eighteen trajectors (plus singular/plural node), 15 verbs, and 15 landmarks were selected in a way that maximized diversity in properties such as dimensionality, size, animacy, motion, and relational configuration of the trajector (TR) and landmark (LM). For each trajector, three to nine verbs agreeing with the selectional restrictions of English were selected. The goal of this selection was to obtain combinations representative of English

Figure 7.2.
Architecture for Network that Learns to Map "sentences" of the Form Trajector Verb (*over*) Landmark to Output Units Standing for Salient Features of Spatial *over* Polysemes. (Because all input patterns corresponded to *over* sentences, including a node for the word *over* was not necessary.) Connectivity between the input layer (which was a localist representation of the vocabulary items) and the first hidden layer was restricted to facilitate inferences about the abstractions constructed by the trained network.

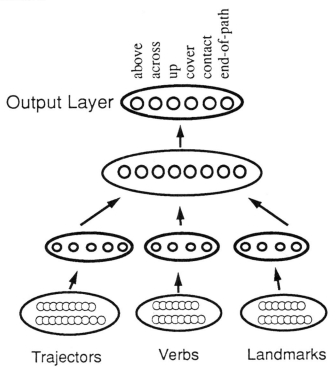

sentences, not to exhaustively list such patterns. These TR-verb combinations plus the plural/singular marker were combined with all possible landmarks to generate 2,700 "trajector verb (over) landmark" patterns. Not all resulting sentences made sense: while balls can roll over floors and tables, they can't roll over oceans. Deleting the anomalous sentences yielded a final set of 1,600 patterns.

Assigning a polyseme of *over* to a given four-word input pattern was essentially done "by hand," although rules were constructed as a guideline for the hand coding (Harris, 1990). The 21 hidden units depicted in Figure 17.2 were the minimal number required for the network to correctly learn all 1,600 patterns. Connectivity between the first and second layer was limited in order to facilitate examination of the types of abstractions the network would produce for a given aspect of the input layer, following Hinton (1986). Weights were modified after every presentation of an input-output pair, and the network was trained until the number of correct patterns no longer increased with continued training. The activation of each output unit had to be within 10 percent of the target activation for a pattern to be considered correct.

3.3. Model 1 Results

3.3.1. Generalization. When the networks was trained on subsets of the pattern set and tested on untrained patterns, the percent of the test set that was correct was an increasing logarithmic function of the size of training set. One hundred percent correct was achieved only when the training set reached the complete size of 1,600 patterns. For example, when trained on 1,400 patterns randomly sampled from the 1,600 patterns (88% of the whole corpus), the network performed correctly on 97% of the remaining 200 patterns. When trained on 50% of the pattern set, the network performed correctly on 87 percent of the 800 untrained patterns. The reason for this is that the input-output pairs in the 1,600-pair corpus varied in how many other input-output pairs out of the 1,600 total could be classified as the same "mapping type." For example, *ocean lies over hill* and *ocean lies over spot* are different mapping types, in that they are paired with different output vectors. (The former was coded having an **end-of-path** meaning, while the latter was coded as having a **cover** meaning.) The fewer input-output pairs that exemplify a mapping type, the less likely it is that enough of them occur the randomly sampled training set for the network to extract the invariances defining that particular mapping type, with the result that the network will assimilate examples in the test to another, slightly different mapping type.

3.3.2. Self-organizations of the Hidden Units. Of the two hidden layers in Figure 7.2, I will focus on the bank receiving connections from the input layer. The activation of each hidden unit in response to each of its inputs was recorded. Each hidden unit is separately graphed in Figures 7.3, 7.4, and 7.5.

Visual inspection of the graphs suggest that the hidden units are selectively responding to inputs of a certain type. The graphs have been annotated with my hypotheses about what types of recoding the network found useful in solving the input-output mapping. (The shaded areas of each figure correspond to the activation values which are thought to from a category. A possible name for the category is the label by the shaded area.)

3.4. Model 1 Discussion

The network clearly succeeds in its task, and appears to use its hidden units to capture intermediary pieces of information that are helpful in learning the input-

Figure 7.3.

Trajector Hidden Units (HUs) 1 and 4 Appear to be Sensitive to the Dimensionalities of the Trajectors, Although the Two Units Make Different Categorizations of the Input. HUs 3 and 2 grouped their inputs according to whether a trajector was typically a *sky* object (not normally in contact with a surface) or a *ground* object. Note that in HU 3, *plane* and *helicopter* are considered *sky* objects while in HU 2 they are considered *ground* objects. This may be because the training set included input patterns in which *plane* and *helicopter* were in contact with the ground, such as when the verb was *roll*. HU 5 was not graphed as it divided the trajectors cleanly into two categories: the items *carpet* and *cloth* in one category, all remaining trajectors in another category. (Shading: see text.)

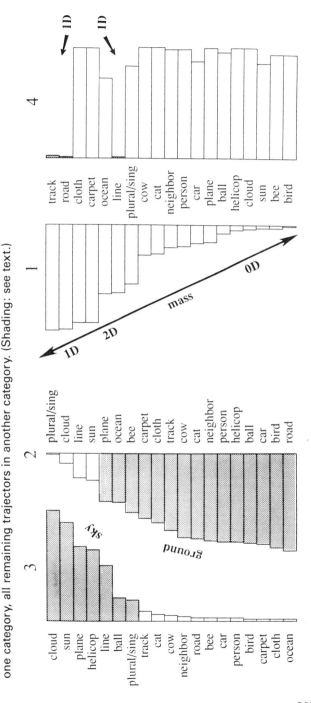

Figure 7.4.
Verb Hidden Units 2 and 3 Differentiate those Verbs which Participate in Path Schemas (shaded) from Those that Do Not. The two hidden units they make different divisions. The verbs that often activate the **end-of-path** bit (*live, belong, is*) are grouped with the other path verbs by HU 3, but grouped with nonpath verbs by HU 2. The groupings in Hidden Units 4 and 1 could be interpreted as affording information about whether the **up** feature should be turned on (inputs that strongly activate HU 3 are shaded and labeled **up** to draw attention to the common feature of these inputs, their common activation of **up**).

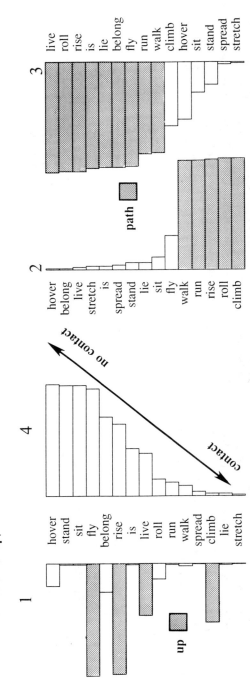

Figure 7.5.

Landmark Hidden Units 1 and 4 both Scale Inputs for Degree of Verticality, although the Scales are Different. Because both hidden units do *not* turn on in response to the tallest landmarks, we can guess that the network has chosen to encode tall landmarks as the default case. The network was probably forced to make as many vertical height distinctions as it did because variations in vertical height determined when the *up* feature would be present for **above-across** sentences.

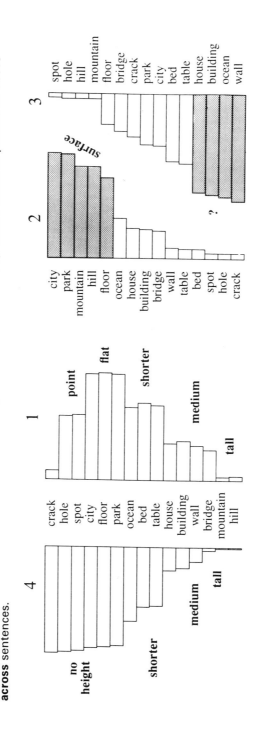

output correspondences. Below I expand on these points, with some emphasis on how PDP concepts mesh with the ideas of the pregenerative linguists, and how they might be appropriate to the needs of modern analogy theorists.

3.4.1. Encodings of Similarity and Differences. The hidden units appear to be classifying the input items along different dimensions. For example, Figure 7.4 shows that Verb Hidden Units 2 and 3 appear to categorize similarly verbs involving paths, such as *roll over hill* and *rise over mountain*. But paths differ in whether they are typically in contact with the ground (and thus activate the **contact** output bit). Verb Hidden Unit 2 is activated by verbs that involve contact, while Hidden Unit 3 is activated by all path verbs. (Note that while *climb* is usually a **contact** verb, it can occur in sentences without ground contact: *plane climbs over mountain*. The verbs *sit* and *stand* are usually not **contact** verbs, since if one *sits over the yard*, one is usually sitting above the yard.)

Landmark Hidden Unit 1 illustrates how the network needed to make two different classifications of vertical height. *Mountain* and *hill* were classified as similar to each other, but distinct from *bridge*. Hidden Unit 4, however, was activated similarly by all three inputs. A reader who was familiar with the training-set mappings could see that the different landmarks were mapped to different types of outputs. For example, the output bit **up** (indicating an upward path) occurred for *bird fly over hill* but not for *bird fly over bridge*.

3.4.2. Varying Schematicity. The hidden units have the ability to encode arbitrarily schematic information. Individual hidden units selectively turned on to varying numbers of input items. At one extreme end, a hidden unit can be activated by just one or two inputs. For example, trajector Hidden Unit 5 was not graphed because it is simple to describe: This hidden unit has an activation of 1.0 when either *cloth* or *carpet* was in the input vector, and 0.0 otherwise. The reason for this is that the *cloth* and *carpet* trajectors mandate activation of the **cover** bit in the training corpus. This relationship was so constant that it was evidently cost effective to dedicate a unique hidden unit for this function. The function is not to recode *cloth* and *carpet* into a more abstract category that contains a number of otherwise dissimilar items. Instead, it is a representation of the information that one of these two words is present in the input vector.

Earlier I mentioned Fillmore's example of a collocation that has only a few variations: *learn X by heart, know X by heart*. Examples such as this cry out for a storage format in which items in different slots can be differentially specific. We could speculate that Fillmore's example is stored in a template of three slots. The first slot is a category that includes *learn, know*, and possibly other semantically similar verbs. The second slot can contain any possible noun phrase, while the third slot is maximally specific in that it contains the phrase *by heart*.

3.4.3. Combinatorial Rules. The limited number of hidden units in the network forced the network to translate information about the identity of a vocabulary item into the salient properties of that item. These salient properties could be interpreted as the abstract variables that are the components of combinatorial rules. For example, from Figure 7.3 we see that the network has recoded the item *person* into the properties "not one-dimensional trajector" and "contact with ground trajector." A rule for activating the **above across up contact** sense of *over* in response to sentences such as *person walks (over) hill* could look like the following:

IF ground TR, *AND* (not one-dimensional TR) *AND* ground-path, *AND* surface LM, *THEN* **above across up contact**

It is sometimes thought that connectionist networks respond to a novel input vector X by activating the output vector of the input pattern Y most similar to X. But this is clearly not the case in the current network. For example, assume that the input pattern in (13) was not in the training set, but (14) and (15) were in the training set.

	input pattern	in training set?	target pattern
13.	person lives (over) bridge	no	above across up end-of-path
14.	person lives (over) spot	yes	above
15.	cow belongs (over) hill	yes	above across up end-of-path

Will the untrained pattern (13) activate an output "on analogy" to (14), the pattern with which it shares two items, or will it activate the same output that is activated by (15), the pattern with which it shares no items? Cleary the latter case is what the network does. The way it does this is via the abstract recodings of the input that are observed in the hidden layer. One can see by checking the activation values in Figures 7.3–7.5 that indeed (13) and (15) activate hidden units similarly, which means they are likely to result in similar output unit values.

3.4.4. Source of Novel Behavior. Above I discussed how the hidden unit recodings function as rules allowing the network to treat untrained patterns in conformity to the form-meaning regularities present in the training set. But these hidden units are also available to be an unlimited source of novel behavior, whereas rules are sometimes thought to be restricted to applying when the appropriate conditions for rule application are met. One method for investigating how the network responds to novel input-word combinations is to invent word combinations which violate the methods used for constructing the training set, and see whether the network can produce reasonable output vectors for these. For example, the patterns in (16) could be hard for the network because they involve trajector-verb combinations which never appeared in the training set.

16. The car flies over the hill.
    The carpet flies over the city.
    The ball sits over the building.

The person flies over the house.
The bees roll over the floor.
The sun hovers over the spot.

Table 7.1 lists ten novel trajector-verb combinations. These ten TR-verb combinations were combined with all 15 landmarks and the trajector-plural/singular marker to create 300 new input vectors. The observed output vectors for each pattern (summarizing over the 30 versions of each) appear in the last column. The question marks indicate an output unit that had an activation value of less than 0.90.

There were two failures to activate features in the manner that probably is closest to what a native speaker would do. The *carpet fly* combination did not activate a unique polyseme. This was apparently caused by the clash between two mutually exclusive targets, the **cover** pattern type, and the **above-across** type. English speakers know that in *carpet flies over* Landmark the two-dimensional nature of the carpet is to be interpreted as a support relationship rather than as a covering relationship. In *car flies over* Landmark, English speakers retain their construal of the car as a trajector in contact with the ground. The network mapped *car* to typically similar items such as *plane* and *helicopter* and thus activated a **no contact** output vector for this pattern.

3.4.5. Relevance to Analogy. One concern of modern analogy theorists is whether there are several types of similarity, and if so, what distinguishes them (Vosniadou & Ortony, 1989). Similarities between two entities can be classified as superficial (such as perceptual similarities, as described by Rips, 1989) or deep, such as when two entities are similar in terms of underlying properties. Gentner (1983, 1989) distinguishes between entities that are similar by virtue of shared attributes (e.g., *car* and *truck* have similar attributes) and entities that are similar by virtue of shared relations. Collins and Burstein (1989) suggest

Table 7.1.
Ten Novel Trajector-Verb Combinations

Trajector-Verb Combination	Output Layer Activations
sun sit	above
cloud sit	above
sun hover	above
cat hover	above
bee roll	above across contact
cloud fly	above across up
ball climb	above across up contact
person fly	above across, up when appropriate
car fly	above across, up when appropriate
carpet fly	above ?across ?cover

that that are three main ways of comparing two entities: (a) a particular property of two entities can be compared, (b) the prototypes of two concepts can be compared, and (c) two entities can be decomposed into components which are then set into correspondence with each other. In this last case, two entities would be judged to be similar by virtue of a "system correspondence" if there was a high number of correspondences between the components of the two entities.

The currency of connectionist networks is similarity. In the case of superficially dissimilar input patterns like *person lives over spot* and *cow belongs over hill* the hidden units are translating nonidentity at the input layer into similarity at the hidden layer. This similarity comparison can be interpreted in the frameworks laid out by Gentner (1989) and Collins and Burstein (1989). In Gentner's framework, we would say that *person lives over bridge* and *person lives over spot* have considerable literal similarity in that two out of three items are identical. But these two sentences do not have much relational similarity because the relation holding among the items are different. On the other hand, *person lives over bridge* and *cow belongs over hill* are relationally similar. In Collins and Burstein's (1989) framework, we would say that these last two examples have a systematic correspondence: the properties of *bridge* that are important in *person lives over bridge* are the same properties of *hill* that are important in *cow belongs over hill*.

3.5. Summary and Preview

This simple connectionist model displays many shortcoming if interpreted as an attempt to completely model polysemy. But like other recent connectionist models, it illustrates a mechanism for generalization from a finite corpus. It also shows how the weighted connections between input and output layers can be interpreted as abstract recodings or *mediating* representations (i.e., structures that mediate an association or correspondence between two different representations). Before discussing how this type of model of linguistic regularities may meet the needs of our two types of analogy theorists (the pregenerative linguists and the current investigators of analogical reasoning) I will review an additional, more complicated model. The new model does not restrict connectivity between the input and hidden layer, uses more vocabulary items, a larger feature vector, and includes six prepositions rather than one.

4. MODEL 2: MULTIPLE PREPOSITIONS

In Harris (1991b) I extended the model of the polysemies of *over* to a model containing six prepositions (*over, above, across, through, around,* and *under*). The model also contained a more diverse set of vocabulary items, so that nonspatial form-meaning mappings (such as *the man talked over the contract* and *we spent around one hundred*) could be included in the training corpus. Four types of regularities were implicit in the training corpus: **lexical categorizations** (categories formed by words occurring in the same sentential slot), **valence matches** (co-occurrence relations, such as argument structure constraints), **schema transformations** (relationships between polysemes that hold for more than one preposition), and **interdomain analogies** (similarities between patterns in different semantic domains, such as *she walked through the woods,* and *she talked through the night*).

We saw that the hidden units of the simple *over* network self-organized to capture aspects of lexical categorization and valence matches. An example of the former was the way the hidden units formed a category for agentive trajectors, and an example of the latter was how one verb hidden unit was activated by verbs that typically co-occur with a mobile trajector, and another was activated by verbs typically co-occurring with a static trajector. In the next section, I will focus on describing how English prepositions exhibit schema transformations and interdomain analogies.

4.1. Interdomain Analogies

The main spatial configurations of *over* were the static **above** sense, the **above-across** sense, (such as *bridge stretches over canyon*), the **cover** sense, and the **end-of-path** sense, which required a surmounting of a barrier, as in *person lives over hill*. The preposition *over* can be used to assert analogous relations among entities in the domains of **time** and **power** and to locate an **amount** on some scale, as shown by (17)–(22). (The analogous semantic feature from the spatial *over* sense is printed in bold next to each example.)

17. **above**: The captain is over the soldier (superior on a scale)
18. **above-across**: We stayed overnight. (temporal path)
19. **above-across**: We ran over budget. (amount moves above and beyond budget fixed point)
20. **cover**: We talked over the contract. (complete coverage of the contract)
21. **end-of-path**: Get over it. (barrier to be surmounted)
22. **end-of-path**: The relationship is over. (focus on end point of path)

Linguists have long been aware that the same word can be used to signal roughly analogous configurations in different domains (Fillmore, 1982; Talmy, 1975; Whorf, 1956). In Langacker's cognitive grammar framework (1987, 1991), the configurational relationship between clausal entities is notated using diagrams such as those in Figure 7.6, with the domain indicated by labeling the space.

Figure 7.6.
The Same Configurational Relationship Can Exist in Different Domains. A notational scheme for this is to draw the relationship, and indicate the domain with a label.

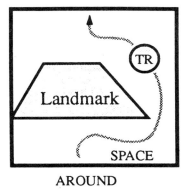
AROUND
(*We ran around the building*)

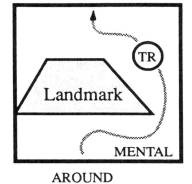
AROUND
(*We got around the problem*)

Some theorists feel that the ability of a word to appear in a huge variety of contexts indicates that the "true" meaning of the word is highly abstract (Ruhl, 1989). An alternative interpretation is that language users have the ability to abstract the relationship among entities from a particular domain and transport it to another domain. In addition, there may be natural mappings set up between common domains such as time and space, mappings which may be the product of early sensorimotor development (Johnson, 1987; Lakoff, 1987).

One reason to view polysemy as a subtype of analogy rather than as a single maximally abstract concept is that usually *all* of the different polysemes of a given preposition are carried into the domains of common use. In these different domains, the prepositional polysemes then structure the entities into a configuration that is analogous to the structure of the entities in the spatial domain. Because often the polysemes conflict with each other (as in the case of *over*) we cannot assume that there is one maximally abstract meaning that can be used in any domain that is desired.

4.2. Schema Transformations

Brugman and Lakoff (1988) observed that prepositions that relate a mobile trajector (e.g., *car*) and a path verb (*run*) can also relate a motionless one-dimensional trajector *road* and a static verb (*is*) They called these *schema transformations* to indicate that a valid schema can be obtained by transforming a given component of one schema into another. (The term "transformation" does not mean that mental representations are literally mutated. Instead, it is a conventional term to signal equivalence of felicity or grammaticality.)

Just as *over* has both an **above-across** and an **end-of-path** sense, so do the prepositions *through, around,* and *across,* as illustrated by (23)–(25).

23. **Path**: The person [walked, ran] through the [woods, tunnel, snow, fog]
    End-of-Path: The person [stood, is, lives] through the [woods, tunnel, snow]
24. **Path**: The person walked across the city.
    End-of-Path: The store is across town.
25. **Path**: The jogger ran around the corner.
    End-of-Path: The store is around the corner.

4.3. Representational Challenges

How should interdomain analogies, such as those in (26) and (27), be represented in bit vectors? The approach taken here could be seen as a rather literal-minded attempt to implement Langacker's heuristic notational system: some features are dedicated for salient aspects of the relational configuration, and additional feature note the domain in which the configuration obtains. There is thus a bit vector with "configurational features" and "domain features." An unattractive aspect of this approach is that it is unclear whether it captures our intuition that the configuration of entities evoked by (26) is analogous, rather than identical to, the configuration of sentence (27). This is because the feature vectors for the meaning of (26) and (27) will be identical except for the features encoding the domain and the features encoding differences in *woods* and *night*.

26. The conspirators walked through the woods.
27. The conspirators talked through the night.

The target feature vectors for these two sentences will thus have identical bits in some slots and opposite bits in others. Current analogy theorists (e.g., Gentner, 1989) urge that the term "analogy" be used to describe an abstraction relation holding between entities, not just a partial similarity.

To defend this method, I can point out that the purpose of the output vector is to capture distinctions in meaning, not to represent the analogical mapping that exists between two separate meanings. In Model 1, I characterized the hidden units as abstract recodings of the inputs values. If dissimilar input items such as *woods* and *night* are categorized as similar at the hidden layer, then we can at least say that a deeper similarity has been captured by the hidden layer. Therefore, it does not seem unreasonable to use the output layer to encode literal similarity and dissimilarity.

4.4. Model 2 Implementation

Vocabulary items for the roles of trajector, verb, and landmark were selected to maximize the diversity of senses that could be obtained by grammatical combinations of the items. Fifty-five semantic features were chosen to distinguish salient aspects of the sentences' meanings (where "meaning" primarily means schematic and relational configuration). These features are not guaranteed to be the *minimal* number of semantic features that would distinguish senses, but they are *sufficient* to distinguish the major differences in meaning. Adding irrelevant bits to the teaching signal does *not* detract from the network's ability to learn mappings to the relevant (i.e., predictable) bits. If the extra bits are redundant with an existing feature, then it will be as if we decided to encode a given feature with two output bits instead of one. If the extra bit is *not* identical to the function of an existing bit, yet is not necessary for capturing our intuitions about how polysemes differ, then it will be equivalent to throwing random variation into the input-output mappings. The presence of unpredictable output bits *does* raise global error, but this does not matter since the worth of the simulation will not be determined by achievement of a low error, but by the types of internal representations that are formed. These will reflect regularities in the corpus regardless of whether irregularities also exist.

Figure 7.7 shows the layers and number of units used to implement the multiprepositional model. The number of hidden units was chosen to be the minimal number which allowed the most important distinctions to be learned by the network. (With fewer hidden units the network overgeneralized less frequent polysemes to the output pattern of frequent polysemes.)

The domain in which an expression takes place was indicated by turning on one of the domain bits **space, mental, time, money,** and **power.** Table 7.2 shows the features that were turned on in the presence of specific vocabulary items, regardless of the other words in the sentence. Table 7.3 shows the features that were turned on to indicate aspects of the general relational configuration, such as the type of path and presence of motion.

A corpus of felicitous "Trajector Verb Preposition Landmark" sentences was obtained by constructing sentence templates such as those in Table 7.4. A total of 171 templates were written. The idea behind the templates was to include as many different uses of the six prepositions as possible, and to include a diversity of types of combinations of vocabulary items. The system for matching semantic features to sentence templates aspired to the following conditions: (a) sentences that appear to have the same configurational meaning (same schema) share more features than sentences which do not share the same schema; (b) polysemes that are related by schema transformations differ by the same features across all prepositions, (c) commonalities of meaning across and within prepositions correspond to presence of common features, (d) prepositions with more perceived "pathness" occur in sentences which are assigned a greater number of

Figure 7.7.
Network Architecture for the Multi prepositional Model. Strictly feed forward, fully interconnected. The vocabulary items and output features are described in the text. Input words are encoded in a localist fashion as in Model 1.

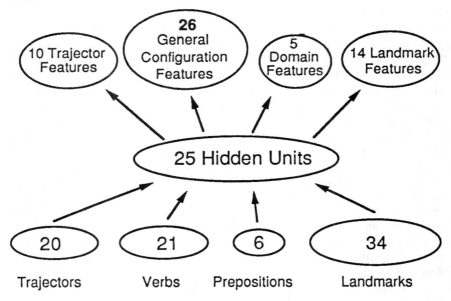

path features, and (e) words which are perceived as semantically similar share features. The 171 templates, when instantiated with vocabulary items, created a total training corpus of 2,617 input-output pairs.

4.5. Training and Learning

All simulation runs used a learning rate of 0.5 and a momentum of 0.9. The entire 2,617 corpus was trained for 10,000 cycles, at which point training error had descended to 0.64 (Training error is the sum of the squared difference between target and observed output activations, averaged over 100 consecutive randomly sampled patterns.) A plot of error decrease as a function of training cycles (Figure 7.8) shows that the point of steepest decrease occurs before 10,000 cycles, although error continues to drop if training is prolonged, with maximum

Table 7.2.
Features for Vocabulary Items

Trajector Features	Vocabulary Items	Trajector Features	Vocabulary Items
1D	fence, road, bridge, river, wire	2D	blanket, snow
person	hiker, soldier, conspirators, children	animate	birds
artifact	blanket, wires, package, game, movie	vehicle	cars, airplane
natural	park, river, snow	structure	building, road, bridge, fence
travelway	bridge, road	place	building, city, park, bridge

Landmark Features	Vocabulary Items	Landmark Features	Vocabulary Items
amount	hundred, thousand	event	lunch, dinner
1D	road, tunnel, bridge, river	natural	park, river
information	mail, game, book, contract, problem	abstract	contract, problem
person	children, captives, captain, clerk	structure	corner, building, bridge, door
travelway	river road bridge	interior	tunnel, woods
height	fence, bridge, hill, corner, tunnel, woods, door, city	place	woods, building, bridge, city, field, hill
2D	woods, building, bridge, city paper, field, hill, blanket, snow	artifact	door, paper, radio, chair, blanket, table, book, contract

Verb Features	Verb Vocabulary Item
action	came, got, flew, moved, walked, ran, played, thought, argued, talked, read, spent, cost
static	had—authority, was—built, was, lived, stood, lay, stretched

error reduction of about 0.23.[3] Figure 7.8 also shows the decrease in training error for networks which were trained on randomly sampled subsets of the 2,617 corpus. We can see that the number of cycles to learn the whole corpus of 2,617 patterns was nearly indistinguishable from the cycles required to learn a training set of 400 patterns.

---

[3] An error of this magnitude could mean that on average every pattern has one of 55 output bits activated at .52 when it was supposed to be 1; $.23 = (1-.52)^2$. Or it could mean that .25 of the output vectors have one bit that is the opposite of its target. Or, it could mean that every pattern has a number of bits which are slightly incorrect. Or, most probably, error comes from all of these sources.

Table 7.3.
Domain and Configuration Features

Domain Features	Example Sentence	Domain	Example Sequence
Space	*soldier walked around city*	Money	*bridge cost over 1000*
Mental	*conspirators talked over problem*	Time	*movie ran over hour*
Power	*soldier is over captain*		

Path Features	Basis for Assignment to a Sentence
extension	Trajectory movies or extends (1D) relative to landmark in any domain. *conspirators moved over hill*
end-to-end	Extension proceeds from one end of landmark to other. *soldier walked across city*
beyond	Extension extends beyond the boundaries of the landmark. *game ran over lunch*
end-point	Focus on the end-point of the path: *game is over*
goal	Goal-oriented aspect to the focus on the path end-point. *children got under table.*

Curved Path Features	Basis for Assignment to a Sentence
curve	Common to all uses of around, minimally means non-straight
turn	Significant turn: *hiker moved around hill*
encircle	Ring around the landmark: *fence was built around building*
winding	Winding path: *children walked around city*

General Configuration Feature	Basis for Assignment to a Sentence
above	Vertical, hierarchical or metaphorical superiority
below	Inferiority in spatial, power, or temporal domains
proximity	Horizontal nearness: *soldier was around captain*
cover	Trajector covers landmark: *snow lay over field*
transverse	Extending across the middle of a plane: *soldier walked across park*
motion	Physical motion occurring with verbs *moved, walked, ran*
ground	Support relation between trajectory and ground
off-ground	Trajectory characteristically not in ground contact (*fly*)
surmount	Trajectory surmounts a physical or metaphorical obstacle
avoid	Trajectory avoids an obstacle
obstacle	Landmark construed as obstacle: *run over hill*
exclude	Trajectory exclusionary: *read through lunch*
addition	Trajector an addition to another trajectory: *talk over lunch*
multi	Trajector is multiplex entity (not used much in current training set)
flat	Trajectory treats landmark as a flat surface: *run across field*

Table 7.4.
Sample Sentence Templates

Templates	Features Assigned
{road fence wires river} {stretched ran} around {river tunnel road corner building hill}	**curved path 1D**
{snow} {lay} across {blanket bridge river tunnel road}	**2D extension**
{birds} lived through {tunnel woods}	**end-point focus**
{airplane city building} stood over {hill bridge}	**end-point focus**
{birds children} {walked ran} under} {table chair}	**below**
{hiker children soldier conspirators} spent over {100 1000}	**money below amount**
{hiker children soldier conspirators} got over {problem suspicion book game}	**got-over-problem**
{hiker children soldier conspirators} was under captain	**under-power**

A test set was obtained by randomly sampling 100 patterns from the full corpus. On each simulation run, different randomly sampled training subsets that constituted 3% to 53% of the 2,617 corpus were trained. The ability of a subset of the corpus to generalize to the whole corpus can be estimated by recording its error to the randomly sampled test set. Figure 7.9 plots mean pattern error on training and testing as a function of training set size.

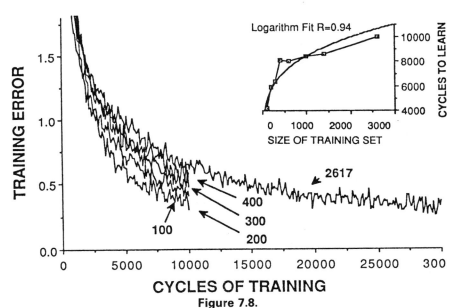

Figure 7.8.
Error Descent During Training for the Whole Corpus (2,617 patterns) and Randomly Sampled Subsets of 100, 200, 300, and 400 patterns. Inset shows that the function relating number of cycles to learn (to criterion of 0.64) and training-set size is logarithmic.

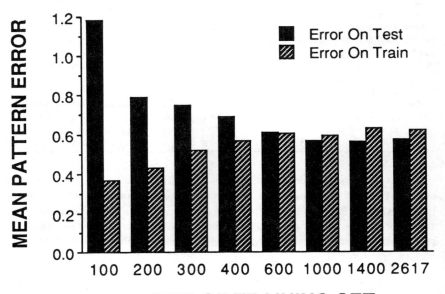

Figure 7.9.
Training Sets of Size 600 and Greater Generalize Equally Well to the Remaining Items in the Corpus.

Randomly sampled subsets of 600 patterns and greater are large enough to encode as many regularities as are extracted during training by the whole corpus. The function relating test error to size of training set is logarithmic ($r = .94$), meaning that small training sets provide a lot of information about the structure of the pattern space, and that each constant addition of new patterns to the training pool is decreasingly informative about input-output invariances. This result demonstrates that the network is indeed encoding invariances rather than storing patterns in a distributed version of a look-up table.

Another way to see the extraction of invariances is to compare the efficiency of training on a single preposition to training on a number of prepositions. There are 604 *over* sentence-meaning pairs in the 2,617 corpus. When trained just on these patterns, the network required 6,000 cycles to reach the same performance on these patterns as was obtained by the whole-corpus network in 10,000 cycles. Whole-corpus training is thus more efficient. Each pattern needs to be presented less than 4 times ($10,000/2617 = 3.8$), while in training just the *over* patterns, each pattern needs to be presented 10 times. This must be because the six prepositions share information about the categories of landmarks and trajectors and the different kinds of paths and configurational relations.

4.6. Model 2 Results

4.6.1. Motivation for Analyses. Part of the appeal of connectionist learning algorithms is thought to be parsimony. The theorist must motivate the task being solved and the input/output specification, but does not need to posit the specific data structures or processes that are necessary to accomplish the computational problem being modeled. But the other side of this coin is that if we are not assured that the network has learned the training corpus and can generalize, we can wonder if we have gained anything beyond knowing that one instantiation of the problem (usually an idealization of the problem) is learnable. Because it is difficult to interpret the weights and hidden unit activations, we may have no new insight into the nature of our problem.

I proposed in the first part of this chapter that a language be idealized as a set of associations between form-meaning pairs, and that the associations be thought of as stored superpositionally (i.e., in a distributed format). The idea that natural language uses a distributed representation is appealing to a number of language researchers (Hinton & Shallice, 1991; MacWhinney, 1989). However, descriptions of the nature of these distributed representations, or illustration of implemented models are still rare. I will use two techniques to examine the properties of the multiprepositional model. The first is principal components analysis, and the second is the technique used to analyze the hidden units of the *over* model, single-unit analysis.

4.6.2. Principal Components Analysis. Principal components analysis is a statistical method for summarizing the dominant regularities in a matrix of numbers, such as the I * H (inputs times hidden units) weights connecting the input layer to the hidden layer. For the current network, this means a 82 * 25 matrix resulted (81 inputs + 1 bias unit, and 25 hidden units). From this matrix, a covariance matrix was calculated and the eigenvectors extracted. The eigenvectors can be ordered by the magnitude of their eigenvalues (how much variance in the covariance matrix they accounted for) and used for redescribing the original input vector. Each of these redescriptions is a principal component, with the first principal component being the one that captures the most information from the original weight matrix.

Elman (1991) and others (Cottrell & Tsung, 1989; Harris & Elman, 1989) have shown that the sequence of state changes in simple recurrent networks can be illustrated by plotting the input patterns in the two-dimensional space formed by two principal components. Usually the implementor picks which two principal components to plot against each other, a decision which is motivated by how informative the resulting plots are. For the current (feed-forward) network, all or some of the 81 input items can be plotted in the two-space formed by two principal components, and the proximity of various items to each other can facilities inferences about the organization of the trained network.

Figure 7.10 shows the relative proximity of input items to each other when

Figure 7.10.
Vocabulary Items are Plotted in Principal-Components Space. Guesses about the function of each part of the space are circled labels. **Prepositions** are in bold, *verbs* are italicized, LANDMARKS are in upper case, trajectors are in lower case.

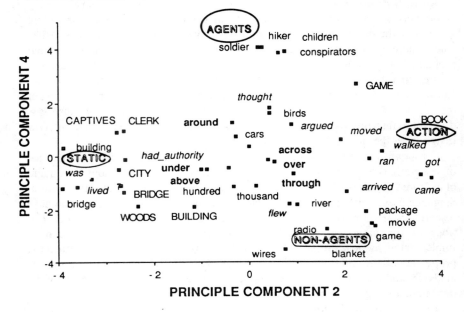

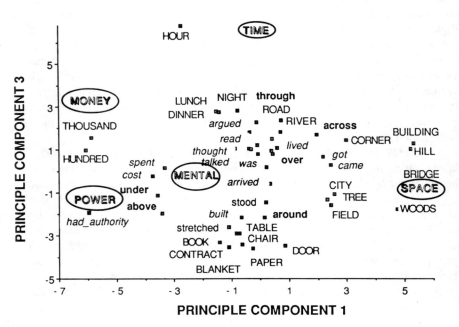

312

they were plotted against the first four principal components of the inputs-to-hiddens weight matrix (two two-dimensional graphs were employed, rather than one four-dimensional graph). To make these plots, I numerically stored the 82 items (81 inputs + bias unit) according to their values on each principal component. My guesses about the function of the principal components derive from characterizing the inputs at either extreme of each dimensions. (These guesses are printed as circled labels in the plots.) Components 1 and 3 were paired to form the two-space in Figure 7.10 as they were concerned with making the main domain distinctions.

> Principle Component 1: space <---> nonspace (power, money, time)
> Principle Component 3: time <---> nontime (mental, space, power)
> Principle Component 2: motion trajectories <---> static configurations
> Principle Component 4: agentive trajectors <---> nonagentive trajectors)

Not all 81 input items could be plotted without items overlapping and decreasing legibility, Items were selected for plotting in each two-space as follows: The ten highest and lowest items of each principal component were plotted. Other words were then selected arbitrarily to fill in the middle regions of each plot.

Landmarks were most important in defining the domain, as indicated by their monopoly of the high and low ends of Principal Components 1 and 3. The trajectors are crucial for defining the function of Principal Component 4. The extreme ends of Principal Component 2, which appears to distinguish motion/action versus stasis, are bounded by both trajectors and verbs. Trajectors convey information about motion and action because trajectors (in this corpus, clausal subjects) like *building, bridge* do not occur in sentences containing motion and action verbs.

These two spaces provide some hints about the encoding of valence matches: items which frequently co-occur together may appear near each other in space. This is clearest with the proximity of *thousand, hundred, spent, cost, under,* and *above* in Principal Component 3.

The reason valence matches are not *more* obvious in these graphs is probably that valence matches capture finger grained distinctions than do the verbs and landmarks which are so important in determining the overall configuration (and thus the majority of features that get turned on in an output vector).

Graphing the principal components of the vocabulary items showed that the hidden units recode in a similar manner items that participate in similar types of lexical categorization and valence matches. In the next section, the weights to and from individual hidden units are analyzed to determine if hidden units are functioning as recognizers for categories larger than a single input term.

4.6.3. Single Hidden-Unit Analyses. Analyzing the weights going into and leaving individual hidden units gives us a close-up picture of how the network implements the function relating input and output patterns. The disadvantage of single hidden-unit analysis is that assigning conceptual labels to what work is being accomplished by a hidden unit requires substantial knowledge of the network's task, which requires familiarity with the method of assigning features to sentences.

For each hidden unit, the incoming and outgoing weights were sorted and listed in decreasing magnitude to facilitate interpreting the function of the hidden unit. Table 7.5 shows a reduced version of eight of these listings. Each hidden-unit entry in the table shows the *n* highest in-coming weights, and *m* lowest out-going weights, separated by "...". Ideally, the cut-off numbers *n* and *m* would include all the inputs which activated that hidden unit. (A hidden unit is activated by any incoming weight higher than its bias weight. In addition, combinations of inputs whose weights sum to a value greater than the bias weight will also activate the hidden unit.) Instead of including all of these weights, I chose *n* and *m* so that at least one big change in weights was included.

To understand Table 7.5, consider the first entry, Hidden Unit 2. The first column gives the vocabulary items that are coming into the hidden unit, followed by the value of the weight on that connection. The vocabulary item that had the strongest weight to Hidden Unit 2 was the landmark (LM) item *field* The item with the second strongest weight was the preposition *through*. The third and fourth columns have the outgoing weights, labeled by the feature of the output vector to which each weight connects. These also are sorted in order of magnitude. We can see that Hidden Unit 2 activated most strongly the output bit that encoded the dimenisonality of the landmark—in this case, two-dimensional. The other output bits are features that usually accompanied sentences containing *through*.

The three vertical dots signal that only the vocabulary items and output bits that were most extreme in value are included in the entry. The vocabulary items that have negative weights to a hidden unit (and thus turn *off* the unit) are usually the ones that are maximally different in meaning, and maximally different in patterns of valency, from the vocabulary items that turn on the hidden unit. As an example of how one can interpret weight differences as a sign of categorization, consider Hidden Unit 2, the first entry in Table 7.5. The weight from input item *lay* is substantially less than the weights from the items *woods, city, paper*. This gap suggests that the hidden unit treats *woods, city*, and *paper* as a category, and perhaps the category of objects with 2-D extent.

The hidden units depicted in Table 7.5 were selected to illustrate a range of types of encodings. We can see from this table that single hidden units encode (i.e., selectively respond to) lexical categories and valence relationships. In addition, a single hidden unit can resemble a "lexical entry." For example, Hidden Unit 9 appears to be sensitive to the single preposition *around*, as it activates the features associated with various *around* polysemes. A single hidden unit can also encode *similarity* among the prepositions. Hidden Unit 11 groups the three prepositions *over, across*, and *above* together, and separates them from *through* and *under*.

Table 7.5.
Highest and Lowest Weights to and from Hidden Units

HU	Input Words		Output Features		Comments
2	LM:field	2.7	LM:2D	4.2	
	through	2.0	LM:interior	2.8	Valence relationships: LMs *Field,*
	LM:blanket	1.9	LM:place	2.5	*woods, city* are most frequent ob-
	LM:woods	1.5	extension	2.3	jects of *through*. *Blanket, paper*
	LM:city	1.5	end-to-end	2.1	share the 2D feature with these
	LM:paper	1.5	end-point	1.9	place LMs.
	lay	.95	mental	1.8	
	.	.	.	.	
	.	.	.	.	
	.	.	.	.	
	above	-2.2	LM:structure	-2.7	
	had_authority	-2.1	LM:1D	-3.2	
5	played	3.7	mental	5.7	*(Played* was assigned mental.) *Ar-*
	LM:hour	2.7	action	5.4	*gued, talked thought, read* were
	argued	2.5	extension	3.7	mapped to both mental and tem-
	talked	1.9	time	2.9	poral schemas. Common to these
	thought	1.8	end-to-end	2.8	schemas is extension and end-to-
	read	1.8	LM:amount	1.9	end traversal of the landmark.
	.	.	.	.	
	.	.	.	.	
	.	.	.	.	
	arrived	-1.7	power	-2.18	
	had_authority	-2.6	space	-2.8	
8	TR:road	3.1	TR:1D	3.7	Trs. *Road, fence,* and *bridge* are
	TR:fence	2.6	TR:structure	3.5	assigned 1D in all output vectors.
	arrived	2.3	space	2.6	*Arrived, came* share outputs of ex-
	came	2.1	extension	2.5	tension and space with the 1D
	TR:bridge	1.9	beyond	2.5	trajectors.
	.	.	.	.	
	.	.	.	.	
	.	.	.	.	
	TR:snow	-2.1	encircle	-2.6	
	TR:park	-2.7	TR:2D	-3.9	*Snow* and *peak* are 2D trajectors.
9	around	4.2	curve	5.0	These are the features used in
	ran	1.9	turn	3.9	*around* schemas, including the
	walked	1.2	proximity	3.7	curved path schema, the vicinity
	came	1.2	avoid	3.7	schema, the ring schema, and the
	got	0.8	encircle	2.9	*talked around problem* sentences.
	corner	0.7	end-to-end	1.5	. .
	.	.	.	.	
	.	.	.	.	*Under* is about as opposite to
	under	-2.0	below	-3.0	*around* as possible

Table 7.5. (*Continued*)

10	LM:bridge	2.4	LM:place	3.5	Landmarks that canonically go with straight-path prepositions to signal end-point focus.
	LM:building	2.3	LM:height	2.9	
	LM:city	2.1	end-point	2.7	
	LM:woods	1.6	LM:structure	2.1	
	lived	1.4	static	2.2	
11	over	2.1	above	5.8	The prepositions *over, across, above* are mapped to outputs that occur with all three of them. Frequent landmarks are also present.
	across	2.0	LM:person	1.9	
	LM:river	1.4	surmount	1.9	
	LM:road	1.2	cover	1.8	
	above	1.0	power	1.6	
	LM:field	1.0	LM:travelway	1.5	
	LM:hill	1.0	addition	1.5	
	.	.	.	.	
	.	.	.	.	
	.	.	.	.	
	through	-2.1	LM:interior	-3.6	
	under	-2.9	below	-3.7	
14	LM:road	2.5	extension	4.4	Straight-path prepositions share the features of extending beyond landmark and having the end-point focus schema.
	LM:tunnel	2.3	beyond	4.2	
	through	2.2	end-to-end	3.4	
	across	2.1	LM:travelway	2.7	
	over	1.7	end-point	2.4	
	.	.	.	.	(*City* and *park* are assigned the feature place but *road* and *tunnel* are not.) Encircle never occurs with end-point focus.
	.	.	.	.	
	.	.	.	.	
	above	-2.6	LM:place		
	under	-3.2	encircle		
	had_authority	-3.2	below	-2.8	
20	ran	3.7	ground	4.0	Extension is common to physical space (movement and 1D) and to mental and time schemas. Input items are 1D trajectors (*wires, (river, fence)* as well as landmarks of the mental domain (*contract, problem, book*).
	walked	2.8	action	4.0	
	LM:contract	1.9	motion	3.5	
	LM:problem	1.8	TR:1D	2.2	
	flew	1.6	avoid	2.1	
	moved	1.1	LM:amount	2.1	
	TR:wires	1.0	money	2.0	
	LM:book	.85	LM:abstract	1.8	
	LM:thousand	0.8	LM:information	.18	
	TR:river	0.8	curve	1.7	The inputs and features of the end-point focus schema are turned off.
	TR:fence	0.5	off-ground	1.7	
	.	.	.	.	
	.	.	.	.	
	.	.	.	.	
	stood	-1.9	beyond	-2.0	
	lived	-2.2	end-point	-2.7	
	was	-2.9	static	-3.6	

An example of a hidden unit that encodes the features common to the **end-point focus** schema is Hidden Unit 14. The inputs with high weights to this HU are two prepositions and their high-match landmarks *through tunnel* and *across road*. The four output bits of the **end-path** schema are present (**extension, beyond, end-to-end and end-point**). In Harris (1991b) I used the **end-of-path** polyseme to show that a network can generalize across prepositions. For each of the three prepositions (*through, above,* and *across*) training sets were constructed which did not have any patterns of the form trajector *lived* preposition landmark. When each network was then tested on the patterns that had been withheld from the training set, the network's correct activation of the **end-of-path** feature was not significantly diminished relative to training on the whole corpus.

4.6.4. Interdomain Analogies. One interesting thing about the training corpus was the presence of "interdomain analogies"—form-meaning pairs that appear to profile the same relational configuration in different domains, such as those in (28) and (29).

28. The conspirators walked over the hill.
29. The conspirators thought over the problem.

It is here that the prepositional model is most transparently relevant to the concerns of theorists studying analogical reasoning in problem solving. The similarity between sentences (28) and (29) is one of systematic correspondences between elements, rather than literal similarity. I suggested earlier that we view the abstract similarity between such sentences as something to be *extracted* by the language processing/representing system, not encoded as part of the form or meaning of these sentences. Recall that in the current network, the configurational similarity between two different senses was captured by turning on similar features (bits in the feature vector).

For example, a possible abstraction for the sentences in (30) is "Agent + *get around the* landmark."

30. The soldiers got around the river.
    The soldiers got around the problem.

How would we determine whether the network has encoded an abstract relationship between the domains of **space** and **mental**, each of which is represented by a different output bit? Our method is to determine whether things which have different representations on the input and output layer are encoded as literally similar at the hidden layer. So, we might look for a hidden unit which is activated by *hill* and *problem* and in turn activates both the output units that stand for the domains of **space** and **mental**.

Hidden Unit 8 (the third entry in Table 7.5) is activated by vocabulary items that commonly appear with *around*, yet does not selectively turn on one of the five domain bits. However, it is difficult to feel confident that this is an encoding of "analogy." It would be better to define a task (or a mapping problem) which required an interdomain analogy for solution.

As human language users, would we be able to understand *got around problem* if we had been exposed to *got around hill* but had never heard *around* used in the **mental** domain before? One thing that would help us with this inference is if we had been exposed to phrases such as *think through the problem* and *get over the problem*

It is easy construct a training corpus which is missing *around* expressions in the **mental** domain. If this is done (but keeping in the examples such as *get around river, get through book, talk over problem, think over contract*), the network does activate the correct target bits for the untrained Agent *got around* [problem, contract]. But it is likely that the network does this by activating a blend of polysemes it has been trained on. It correctly activates the curved-path bits for *around* because in all its experience with *around*, these are always turned on. It then activates **mental** instead of **space** because it has learned that *problem* always activates **mental**, whereas *around* doesn't uniquely turn on a domain bit. So we have the different parts of the input pattern correctly turning on the right output bits, even though the parts have never occurred together.

The blending does not involve explicit correspondences between different domains, just selective activation, and thus does not feel like a satisfying model of analogy. And yet it is not out of the question that many novel human analogies begin this way, with different parts of a stated problem or sentence activating their most frequent interpretations. Our intuition that elements in one domain are set into correspondence with elements of another domain may be after-the-fact computation that allows us to reflect on the blend of elements activated by a novel statement or problem.

4.7. Model 2 Discussion

The primary goal of constructing the multiprepositional model was to better understand the extraction of regularities in patterns of limited compositionality. I will thus briefly discuss the linguistic insights before turning to a more comprehensive discussion of analogy.

Under pressure to learn to activate a sentence's meaning when presented with its form, the hidden units evolved to encode both horizontal co-occurrence statistics (form-form and meaning-meaning) and vertical co-occurrence statistics (form-meaning invariances). Thus, the internal nodes that become strongly activated by the the input node for *walk* are also activated by lexical items which commonly occur with *walk*, such as *over, across, hill*, and *yard*.

The competition of positively and negatively weighted links is reminiscent of Jackendoff's (1983) preference rules, while the sharing of representational structure could be viewed as an implementation of noun and verb valencies (Grimshaw, 1990; Pinker, 1989) or cospecification (Putstejovsky, in press). Connectionism would thus not be seen as an alternative to rules, but as a way to finally get rules implemented in the flexible, yet robust manner that so many linguists have been arguing for.

More radical positions on the relevance of this model to linguistic theory can be entertained. The network solves the problem of polysemy by creating internal categories which conflate semantic attributes of various senses of the polysemous words with their typical contexts of occurrence. If taken seriously as a computational method for handling polysemy, the method violates the traditional separation between lexical information and the rules of contextual integration. In addition, if a "microstructure" of simple processing elements (Hinton, McClelland, & Rumelhart, 1986) is seen as the way to implement flexible rules, then we have a language-independent explanation for why human linguistic rules have the characteristics they have: The strength of rules, and the probability of their generalization in novel contexts, is a joint function of statistical principles (frequency and reliability of form-meaning pairings) and the diachronic and communicative principles that influenced the composition of our training corpora.

5. GENERAL DISCUSSION: UNDERSTANDING ANALOGY

5.1. Partial Regularities and Constraint Satisfaction

In the first section of this chapter, I reviewed how pregenerative linguists used the term "analogy" to refer to systematicities existing across a large set of utterances, such as the analogical proportion *dream:dreamt::sleep:slept*. "Analogy" was also used to mean any partial match between forms, or any systematicity which had known exceptions. There was thus a tension between whether the mechanism underlying linguistic productivity was the creative process vaguely called "analogy," or whether "rules" should supplant analogy as the mechanism of generativity. A shortcoming of the partial-match view of analogy was that it did not explain how speakers avoid "false" analogies. On the other hand, viewing linguistic regularities to be a product of mentally represented rules hindered understanding exceptions to rules, novel extensions of rules, and how lexical rules interact with rules of contextual integration.

I have suggested that a language be idealized as a set of associations between form and meaning. If these associations are understood to be stored in a distributed format, then we resolve the dilemmas described above as follows. We saw in Model 1 (the model of *over* polysemes) that the hidden layers of the network self-organize to be an abstract recoding of the vocabulary items. These abstractions are similar to compositional rules, yet can vary in specificity (i.e., can subsume a small, homogeneous category, or a large, heterogeneous category). The same regularity-extraction mechanism can extract rule-like generalizations if a generalization subsumes a large number of examples, or can extract exceptions to the rules if a generalization is supported by few examples.

Model 2 (the multiprepositional model) illustrates one solution to how aspects of words' meaning interact with context. Individual vocabulary items activate a variety of hidden units. Each hidden unit is involved in a different sense (or usage) of the vocabulary item. For example, one use of *mail* is as a conduit (*book arrived through the mail*), the other is as a physical artifact (*read over the mail*). One of *mail*'s hidden units (the unit that happen to be turned on by *mail*) will be turned on by vocabulary items such as *arrive* and *through*, while another of *mail*'s hidden units will be turned on by items such as *read* and *over*. For this reason, I described the hidden layer of Model 2 as one which conflates word senses with the rules for their contextual integration (Harris, 1992).

Avoiding "false analogies" is achieved in two ways. First, for routinized forms, we have what Dejong (1989) calls "reinstantiation" of a known abstraction rather than induction of a novel schema. But the extraction of any schema depends on constraint satisfaction. Gentner's "systematicity constraint" was at work in the hidden layer of the networks described here.

To understand how the systematicity constraint emerges from constraint satisfaction, we need to be more explicit about the similarity between polysemy and analogical reasoning. Polysemy and analogical reasoning are similar in that some aspects of the "source domain" are deemed important for determining interpretation, and some are not. For example, in Duncker's (1945) fortress/radiation problem, the circular shape of the fortress is important, but not that it is made of stones. In interpreting *blanket is over wall*, the two-dimensional extension of *blanket* and of *wall* are both important in coming up with a **cover** interpretation, whereas in *cat is over wall*, what is important about *wall* is that it separates the conceptualizer from *cat*, not that it is a two-dimensional surface.

In Model 1, we saw that the network recodes the vocabulary items so that each has a number of different salient properties. How does the network "know" when the "obstacle" property of *wall* is important rather than its "two-dimensional surface" property? The node that is most active will be the one that is also activated by other words in the sentence. We can thus say that the interpretation which is selected is the one that participates in a system of relationships with other words in the sentences.

5.2. The Role of Size of Class, Routinization, and Schematicity

While the pregenerative linguists looked at analogies as relations that are systematic across a collection of similar items, cognitive psychologists have focused more on *novel* analogies, especially analogies used for insight (Holyoak,

1985). I suggest that these foci be viewed as the two end-points of a continuum rather than as fundamentally different uses of that alluring name, "analogy." Part of this difference in focus involves the notion of routinization. This notion, readily illustrated by frequency-sensitive algorithms, is under-used in the analogical reasoning literature, which has emphasized the importance of relational systematicity, independent of entrenchment or routinization.

For example, Gentner (1989) has described classes of similarities defined by the number of shared attributes and shared relations. Analogies and abstractions are types of similarity which share many relations but few attributes, while "mere-appearance" matches share only attributes. Gentner's observation that analogies do not turn on the match of surface features has had a decisive impact on the field of analogical reasoning. However, a number of theorists have noticed that the distinction between relational and attributive predicates seems arbitrary (Dejong, 1989; Palmer, 1989). A Relation R holding between X and Z can be recast as an attribute of X by embedding entity Z inside of R. For example, one common attribute of floors in American houses is that they are carpeted. Because this is a routine occurrence, we may prefer to think of carpeting as an attribute of floors, rather than thinking of carpets and floors as two entities joined together by a covering relation. But if carpeting is not tightly associated with covering and floors (or if there are a variety of substances which can cover floors), then we may want to view recast the floor(carpeted) attributive as covering(floor, carpet).

I present in Table 7.6 some dimensions that can be used to compare different cognitive and linguistic phenomena. The dimensions can be described as follows:

Table 7.6.
Dimensions for Comparing Types of Regularities

Cognitive or Linguistic Phenomenon	Number of Items in the Class	Degree of Routinization	Relational Similarity	Known Abstraction Present?
Mere appearance match	varies	varies	low	no
Novel comparison (or novel analogy)	low	low	high	Unclear
Reinstantiation (justified analogy)	possibly high	possibly high	high	yes
Categorization	varies	varies	low	yes
Systematic Correspondences (grammatical rule, valence relation)	high	high	high	yes
Conventional expression, collocation	low	high	low	no

1. *Relational similarity.* I am collapsing Gentner's two dimensions of "Relations Shared" and "Attributes Shared" into one. Two entities can be said to have a high degree of relational similarity if they participate in similar systems of relations. If they are only similar by virtue of sharing an identical property (or if they are literally dissimilar) they will be rated as low in relational similarity. (Collapsing these dimensions means that we are excluding Gentner's categories of "anomaly" and "literal similarity," but these are not categories of similarity, but are instead the definition and antithesis of identity.)

2. Number of items exemplifying a given pattern type or relational similarity. In morphology, this is the number of words which participate in a morphological paradigm. In scientific analogies, there are often only two examples, the source and target examples, as illustrated by the solar system/atom analogy discussed by Johnson-Laird (1989) and others.

3. *Degree of routinization.* Has the information processor been repeatedly exposed to examples of a pattern type, or are they novel? This dimension is likely to be dependent on the previous one. If many items exhibit the same relational similarity, there is likely to be routinization. However, one can have high routinization even if items are relatively idiosyncratic, such as happens with fixed expressions or exceptions to a morphological generalization.

4. *The schematicity (or abstractness) of the representational structure used in interpreting the items* Dejong (1989) points out that the fortress/radiation analogy is almost certainly mediated by the "convergence schema." Yet for other analogies, it is likely that the invariants have not yet been extracted. This dimension may be influenced by the previous two dimensions. Dimensions 1 and 2 quantify characteristics of environmental stimuli (linguistic expressions, problems encountered), while Dimensions 3 and 4 tend to describe the mental structure encoding the items.

A PDP perspective suggests that the extraction of invariants is an automatic consequence of repeated exposure to a class of relationally similar items. In addition, the PDP perspective suggest some qualifications on the type of abstraction that is formed, and how readily novel instances will be assimilated. The degree of abstractness of the representation that is formed after repeated exposure depends on the number of items and their heterogeneity. As seen in the PDP model in this chapter, if many dissimilar entities can fill a given spot in a configuration, then a very abstract category will be constructed for that spot.

Understanding how number of items in the class and routinization interact with relational similarity should be of interest to problem-solving theorists, as studies show that people pay more attention to surface similarity than would be predicted by Gentner's systematicity constraint (Gentner & Landers, 1985, cited in Gentner, 1989). As Dejong (1989) suggests, it is likely that the important variable is whether an abstraction has been induced, and not whether the match is the most systematic of all possible matches.

The PDP perspective is a provocative one in that it provides tools for exploring the continuums of rule governedness, relational similarity, routinization, and abstraction. A deeper understanding of these notions, whether in the domains of language or problem solving, will surely bring us closer to understanding the varieties of human thought.

REFERENCES

Bates, E.A. (1989). Functionalism and the competition model. In B. MacWhinney & E. Bates (Eds.), *The crosslinguistic study of sentence processing*. Cambridge, University Press.
Bates, E.A., & MacWhinney, B. (1982). Functionalist approaches to grammar. In E. Wanner & L.R. Gleitman (Eds.), *Language acquisition: The state of the art*. New York: Cambridge University Press.
Bates, E.A., & MacWhinney, B. (1987). Competition, variation, and language learning. In B. MacWhinney (Ed.), *Mechanisms of language acquisition*. Hillsdale, NJ: Erlbaum.
Bloomfield, L. (1933). *Language*. New York: Holt, Rinehart, & Winston.
Brugman, C. (1981). *The story of over*. Master's Thesis, University of California at Berkeley. Reprinted by the Indiana University Linguistics Club.
Brugman, C. (1988). *The story of 'over': Polysemy, semantics and the structure of the lexicon*. New York: Garland Publishing.
Brugman, C., & Lakoff, G. (19881). Cognitive topology and lexical networks. In G.W. Cottrell, S. Small, & M.K. Tannenhause (Eds.), *Lexical ambiguity resolution: Perspectives from psycholinguistics, neuropsychology and artificial intelligence*. San Mateo, CA: Morgan Kaufman.
Chomsky, N. (1957). *Syntactic structures*. The Hague, Netherlands: Mouton.
Chomsky, N. (1965). *Aspects of the theory of syntax*. Cambridge, MA: MIT Press.
Chomsky, N. (1966). *Cartesian linguistics: A chapter in the history of rational thought*. New York: Harper & Row.
Chomsky, N. (1980). *Rules and representations*. London: Basil Blackwell.
Chomsky, N. (1981). *Lectures on government and binding*. Dordrecht, Netherlands: Coris Publications.
Clement, C., & Gentner, D. (1991). Systematicity as a selection constraint in analogical mapping. *Cognitive Science, 15*, 89–132.
Collins, A., & Burstein, M. (1989). A framework for a theory of comparison and mapping. In S. Vosniadou & A. Ortony (Eds.), *Similarity and analogical reasoning*. Cambridge, MA: Cambridge University Press.
Cottrell, G., & Tsung, F. (1989). Learning simple arithmetic procedures. In *Proceedings of the 11th annual cognitive science society conference*. Hillsdale, NJ: Erlbaum.
Crain, S. (1991). Language acquisition in the absence of experience. *Behavioral and Brain Sciences, 14*.
Deane, P.D. (1988). Polysemy and cognition. *Lingua, 75*, 325–361.
Deane, P.D. (1991). Limits to attention: A cognitive theory of island phenomena. *Cognitive Linguistics, 2*, 1–64.

Deane, P.D. (in press). *Grammar in mind and brain: Explorations in cognitive syntax.* New York: Mouton de Gruyter.

Dejong, G. (1989). The role of explanation in analogy; or, The curse of an alluring name. In S. Vosniadou & A. Ortony (Eds.), *Similarity and analogical reasoning.* Cambridge, MA: Cambridge University Press.

Dineen, F. (1968). Analogy, langue and parole. *Lingua, 21,* 98–103.

Duncker, K. (1945). On problem solving. *Psychological Monographs, 58* (270).

Elman, J.L. (1991). Distributed representations, simple recurrent networks, and grammatical structure. *Machine Learning, 7,* 195–225.

Esper, E.A. (1973). *Analogy and association in linguistics and psychology.* Athens: University of Georgia Press.

Fehling, D. (1956). Varro und die grammatische Lehre von der Analogie und der Flexion [Varro and the grammatical teaching of analogy and inflection]. *Glotta, 35,* 214–270.

Fillmore, C.J. (1982). Towards a descriptive framework for spatial deixis. In R.J. Jarvella & W. Klein (Eds.), *Speech, place and action.* London: John Wiley.

Fillmore, C.J. (1986). *On grammatical constructions.* Unpublished manuscript, Linguistics Department, University of California. Berkeley, CA.

Fillmore, C.J. (1988). The mechanisms of "construction grammar." *Berkeley Linguistics Society, 14,* 35–55.

Fillmore, C.J., Kay, P., & O'Connor, M.C. (1988). Regularity and idiomaticity in grammar: The case of Let alone. *Language, 64,* 501–538.

Gentner, D. (1983). Structure-mapping: A theoretical framework for analogy. *Cognitive Science, 7,* 155–170.

Gentner, D. (1989). The mechanisms of analogical learning. In S. Vosniadou & A. Ortony (Eds.), *Similarity and analogical reasoning.* Cambridge, MA: Cambridge University Press.

Gentner, D., & Clement, C. (1988). Relational selectivity in metaphor. In G.H. Bower (Ed.), *The psychology of learning and motivation.* New York: Academic Press.

Gentner, D., & Landers, R. (1985). Analogical reminding: A good match is hard to find. *Proceedings of the International Conference on Systems, Man, and Cybernetics.* Tucson, AZ.

Givon, T. (1989). *Mind, code and context: Essays in pragmatics.* Hillsdale, NJ; Erlbaum.

Grimshaw, J. (1990). *Argument structure.* Cambridge, MA: MIT Press.

Harris, C.L. (1989). A connectionist approach to the story of 'over'. *Proceedings of the Fifteenth Annual Meetings of the Berkeley Linguistics Society, 1989.* Berkeley, CA: Berkeley Linguistics Society.

Harris, C.L. (1990). Connection and cognitive linguistics. *Connection Science, 2,* 7–34.

Harris, C.L. (1991a). Can connectionist advance linguistic theory? Three areas where the answers are yes, no and maybe. *Working Notes of the 1991 AAAI Spring Symposium on Connectionist Natural Language Processing.*

Harris, C.L. (1991b). *Parallel Distributed Processing Models and Metaphors for Language and Development.* Unpublished doctoral dissertation. University of California. San Diego, CA.

Harris, C.L. (1992). *The conflation of word senses with the rules for their contextual integration.* Paper presented at the 1992 University of Madison-Wisconsin Linguistics Symposium.

Harris, C.L., & Elman, J. (1989). Representing variable information with simple recurrent networks. *Proceedings of the Eleventh Annual Meeting of the Cognitive Science Society* (pp. 404–411). Hillsdale, NJ: Erlbaum.
Hawkins, B. (1984). *The semantics of English spatial prepositions.* Unpublished doctoral dissertation, University of California, San Diego.
Herskovitz, A. (1986). *Language and spatial cognition: An interdisciplinary study of the prepositions in English.* Cambridge, MA: Cambridge University Press.
Hinton, G.E. (1986). Learning distributed representations of concepts. *Proceedings of the 8th Annual Conference of the Cognitive Science Society.* Hillsdale, NJ: Erlbaum.
Hinton, G.E., & McClelland, J.L., & Rumelhart, D.E. (1986). Distributed representations. In D.E. Rumelhart & J.L. McClelland (Eds.), *Parallel distributed processing: Explorations in the microstructure of cognition* (Vol. 1). Cambridge, MA: MIT Press.
Hinton, G.E., & Shallice, T. (1991) Lesioning an attractor network—Investigations of acquired dyslexia. *Psychological Review, 98,* 74–95.
Hockett, C.F. (1968). *The state of the art.* The Hague, Netherlands: Mouton.
Holyoak, K.J. (1985). The psychology of analogical transfer. In G.H. Bower (Ed.), *The psychology of learning and motivation.* New York: Academic Press.
Holyoak, K.J., & Thagard, P. (1989). Analogical mapping by constraint satisfaction. *Cognitive Science, 13,* 295–355.
Householder, F. (1971). *Linguistic speculations.* Cambridge, England: Cambridge University Press.
Jackendoff, R.S. (1983). *Semantics and cognition.* Cambridge, MA: MIT Press.
Johnson, M. (1987). *The body in the mind: The bodily basis of mental experience.* Chicago: University of Chicago Press.
Johnson-Laird, P.N. (1983). *Mental models.* Cambridge, MA: Harvard University Press.
Johnson-Laird, P.N. (1989). Analogy and the exercise of creativity. In S. Vosniadou & A. Ortony (Eds.), *Similarity and analogical reasoning.* Cambridge, MA: Cambridge University Press.
Kuno, S. (1987). *Functional syntax: Anaphora, discourse and empathy.* Chicago: University of Chicago Press.
Lakoff, G. (1987). *Women, fire, and dangerous things: What categories reveal about the mind.* Chicago: Chicago University Press.
Langacker, R.W. (1987). *Foundations of cognitive grammar, Vol. 1: Theoretical prerequisites.* Stanford, CA: Stanford University Press.
Langacker, R.W. (1991). *Foundations of cognitive grammar, Vol. II: Descriptive applications.* Stanford, CA: Stanford University Press.
MacWhinney, B. (1989). Competition and lexical categorization. In R. Corrigan, F. Eckman, & M. Noonan (Eds.), *Linguistic categorization.* Amsterdam: Benjamins.
McClelland, J.L., Rumelhart, D.E., & Hinton, G. (1986). The appeal of parallel distributed processing. In D.E. Rumelhart & J.L. McClelland (Eds.), *Parallel distributed processing: Explorations in the microstructure of cognition* (Vol. 1). Cambridge, MA: MIT Press.
Palmer, S.E. (1989). Levels of description in information-processing theories of analogy. In S. Vosniadou & A. Ortony (Eds.), *Similarity and analogical reasoning.* Cambridge, MA: Cambridge University Press.
Pinker, S. (1989). *Learnability and cognition.* Cambridge, MA: MIT Press.

Plunkett, K., & Marchman, V. (1991). U-shaped learning and frequency effects in a multi-layer perceptron: Implications for child language acquisition. *Cognition, 38,* 1–60.
Pustejovsky, J. (in press). *The generative lexicon.* Cambridge, MA: MIT Press.
Rips, L. (1989). Similarity, typicality and categorization. In S. Vosniadou & A. Ortony (Eds.), *Similarity and analogical reasoning.* Cambridge, MA: Cambridge University Press.
Ruhl, C. (1989). *On monosemy.* Albany, NY: State University of New York Press.
Saussure, F. (1916). *Cours de linguistique Generale.* Paris: Payot. [1959 Translation: *Course in general linguistics.* New York: McGraw-Hill.]
Siewierska, A. (1991). *Functional grammar.* New York: Routledge.
Smolensky, P. (1988). On the proper treatment of connectionism. *Behavior and Brain Sciences, 11,* 1–74.
Steinthal, H. (1881). *Einleitung in die Psychologie und Sprachwissenschaft* [Introduction to psychology and linguistics]. Berlin: Erster Teil.
Talmy, L. (1975). Semantics and syntax of motion. In J. Kimbal (Ed.), *Syntax and semantics* (Vol. 4). New York: Academic Press.
Talmy, L. (1985). Lexicalization patterns: Semantic structure in lexical forms. In T. Shopen (Ed.), *Language typology and syntactic description* (Vol. 3). Cambridge, MA: Cambridge University Press.
Talmy, L. (1988). Force dynamics in language and cognition. *Cognitive Science, 12,* 49–100.
Vosniadou, S., & Ortony, A. (1989). Similarity and analogical reasoning: a synthesis. In S. Vosniadou & A. Ortony (Eds.), *Similarity and analogical reasoning.* Cambridge, MA: Cambridge University Press.
Wheeler, B.I. (1887). *Analogy and the scope of its application in language.* Ithaca, NY: Cornell University Studies in Classical Philolohy, No. 2.
Whorf, B.L. (1956). *Language, thought and reality.* Cambridge, MA: MIT Press.

8
On the Connectionist Implementation of Analogy and Working Memory Matching*

John A. Barnden

1. INTRODUCTION

This chapter pursues two related themes, both concerned with largely unexplored connections between analogy and connectionism. The first theme is that analogy-based reasoning provides a bridge over the gap between traditional AI and connectionism. The second is to do with the types of structural matching that human-like cognition requires. I claim that it requires WM/WM matching—the construction of a structural mapping between two data structures that are both sitting in working memory. The required mapping often has an analogical quality—the mapping obtained may only address a part of each of the two structures, and it may relate nonidentical items to each other. WM/WM matching is of course a normal activity in symbolic systems, whether for analogy or not, but it presents a problem for connectionism. This is because, in traditional connectionist models, the matching that goes on is almost always WM/LTM, that is, between a working memory item (in the form of an input activation pattern) and *long*-term memory items (implicit in the weights).

In this extended introductory section, Subsection 1.1 explains the first theme, Subsection 1.2 the second, and Subsection 1.3 sets out the plan for the rest of the chapter.

---

* The work was supported in part by Grant CDA-8914670 from the National Science Foundation, Grant AFOSR-88-0215 from the Air Force Office of Scientific Research, and Grant NAGW-1592 under the Innovative Research Program of the NASA Office of Space Science and Applications.

I am grateful to Keith Holyoak and Tom Eskridge for valuable comments, and to Tom Eskridge and Heather Pfeiffer for help with system implementation.

1.1. A New Motivation for Connectionist Analogy

The other chapters in this book that apply connectionism to analogy share a motivation for doing so, namely the premise that analogy is an important part of human cognition (and/or, it should be an important part of artificial cognition). I subscribe to this assumption, but I have a further motivation for applying connectionism to analogy, namely my claim that

> one promising way of bridging the gap between connectionism and traditional symbolic AI, while keeping to *fully* connectionist systems, is to make the systems do ABR (analogy-based reasoning).

This appears to be a novel strategy for bridging the gap, although Domeshek (1989) briefly suggests something close to it, and Sun (1991) pursues a related course in which he overcomes the brittleness of rule systems by allowing rule conditions to match working memory data fuzzily.

To appreciate why ABR could help bridge the gap, one needs not only to understand in some detail what the gap is perceived as being, but also to realize that that perception is oversimplified in crucial ways. The perception consists largely of the ideas that

> (AIg) traditional AI is GOOD at encoding/manipulating complex, dynamically arising data structures, such as interpretations of natural language sentences,
> (AIb) but BAD at being flexible and robust (tolerant of input noise and internal failures; adaptive; etc.)
> *whereas,*
> (CNg) connectionism is GOOD at being flexible and robust,
> (CNb) but BAD at encoding/manipulating complex, dynamically arising data structures (see this volume's introduction).

My claim is that connectionist ABR allows the good in (AIg) and CNg) to be preserved, therefore avoiding the bad in (AIb) and (CNb).

The four statements (AIg–CNb) are potentially misleading, and I will be noting some necessary refinements as we go along. My main argument is to the effect that ABR, considered as part of AI, achieves much of the flexibility and robustness that connectionism claims, even when the ABR is implemented in a conventional symbolic way. Nelson, Thagard, and Hardy (1994, Sections 2 & 4) also point out the flexibility of analogical processing. There is a similarity to the claim of Bonissone, Rau, and Berg (this volume) that, in the context of retrieval in case-based systems, the advantages of parallel distributed processing can be obtained by suitable use of symbolic techniques. That the flexibility and robustness of ABR are not attended to in most discussions of the symbolic/connectionist gap is surprising, but I conjecture that it is attributable to the fact that analogy-based reasoning is (still) not regarded as a typical, traditional AI technique. This is despite the major amount of work that has been done on analogy within symbolic AI (Hall, 1989). Thus, we must carefully distinguish between *symbolic* AI in general and its narrower subfield, *traditional* symbolic AI. The latter includes, for instance, standard rule-based reasoning, theorem-proving, inferences using nonmonotonic logic, and most symbolic approaches to natural language parsing and meaning extraction. Symbolic ABR is within nontraditional symbolic AI.

As a further complication, though, symbolic ABR nevertheless uses traditional symbolic data structures (lists, trees, semantic network fragments, etc.) and traditional basic procedures for manipulating such structures (e.g., traversals of semantic network fragments, matching of fragments). Thus, what is nontraditional about analogy-based reasoning is not the basic computational substrate but rather the particular style of high-level processing supported by the substrate. The term "traditional" means different things at different levels of description.

So, the claim is that symbolic ABR frees us to a large extent from (AIb) while keeping us within the confines of traditional symbolic data structures and manipulations. Let us turn to (CNb). This statement is only partially true. There have been several well-known endeavors in so-called "implementational connectionism," which is the use of connectionist networks to implement, more-or-less directly, traditional symbolic data structures and their manipulations. By contrast, "nonimplementational" connectionism tries to avoid any direct implementation of symbolic data structures and algorithms. In an implementational connectionist system, part of the state of the network at any moment is an implementation of some collection of symbolic data structures. Processing events in the system are implementations of traditional symbol-processing steps. Thus, the only major architectural differences from standard symbol processing as implemented on computer hardware is that it is implemented on connectionist "hardware" instead. It is accurate and natural to describe an implementational connectionist system, at a high level, as executing a symbolic algorithm that operates on symbolic data structures. Therefore, (CNb) does not apply to implementational connectionism.[1] Since the usual view of implementational connectionism is that it implements *traditional* symbolic AI, statement (CNg)

---

[1] The "implementational" epithet is from Pinker and Prince (1988, pp. 76–77). We may apply it to the techniques in such works as Barnden (1988a, 1988b, 1989, 1991a), Lange and Dyer (1989), Shastri and Ajjanagadde (1989), Smolensky (1990), and Touretzky (1990). Touretzky there casts his work as "revisionist" rather than implementational, but there is considerable slipperiness in the latter notion (Barnden, 1992). Nonimplementational connectionism includes "subsymbolic" connectionism as a special case, in which the system can only rather *approximately* be described at a high level as manipulating symbolic structures (cf. Smolensky, 1988a, 1988b).

also largely fails for implementational connectionism as commonly understood. Such connectionism runs the danger of inheriting the inflexibility of traditional AI.

Now consider the strategy of *using implementational connectionist techniques to implement the symbolic structures and manipulations involved in symbolic ABR*. If this strategy can be successfully pursued, we will have fully connectionist systems that manipulate complex dynamic data structures while still having flexibility and robustness *by virtue of engaging in ABR*. The impasse apparently set up by (AIg, AIb, CNg, CNb) will therefore be penetrated.

So far it may look as though the suggestion to implement ABR in *connectionism* may appear unmotivated. In fact, however, there is an ABR-specific reason for using an implementation that is at least partially connectionist. A full analogy system needs an efficient and effective way of using information in a target analog in working memory to access appropriate source analogs in a long-term memory that contains a large number of such sources. Efficient source access still remains a major problem area for the symbolic analogy field. (The problem is often skirted, though, since most work on the mechanistic details of analogy focuses on analogical mapping/transfer rather than retrieval.) The problem in particularly acute when it is desired to use structures taken from the target, rather than atomic target features, as indices into long-term memory. Such a structure might for instance be a logical proproposition containing a predicate and several arguments. Structured indices are a problem because they seem to require that some sort of fairly complex structural matching take place not only in the mapping phase of analogy but also as part of retrieval (as happens in the symbolic system of Cook (1991), where however efficiency is sought by means of massively parallel symbol processing). But there is reason to think that certain connectionist techniques (based on "reduced descriptions"—Hinton, 1988, 1990; Pollack, 1990; Plate, 1991; Sumida & Dyer, 1989; see also Murdock, 1983) could help to provide an efficient and effective source-retrieval mechanism, one that allows indices containing structural information but does not require complex matching. Furthermore, these same connectionist techniques could be helpful in streamlining the process of matching a target analog to a source analog that has already been retrieved from long-term memory. I will be discussing these points later.

Two qualifications are needed. Bonissone et al. (this volume) argue that connectionism is not required for the source-retrieval operation of case-based reasoning systems, and that in the current state of the connectionist art, at least, symbolic processing centered on marker passing and some graph matching can do just as well. Indeed, I do not claim that connectionism is *necessary* for efficient source retrieval, but only that it is convenient for that purpose. Also, as pointed out in this volume's introduction, Lange and Wharton's chapter contains the interesting claim that structure-sensitive retrieval may not be needed in any explicit sense; instead, different ways of structuring the components of a target lead to different elaborative inferences, and the different concepts activated by these inferences lead to different retrievals from long-term memory.

We will need to be more careful than we have been so far to clarify what particular sorts of flexibility and robustness are achieved by ABR on the one hand and by connectionism on the other. The sorts are related but not identical, and a further benefit of implementing ABR in connectionism is that we gain some types of flexibility/robustness not achieved by ABR alone. Conversely, implementing *analogy-based reasoning* in connectionism may add types of flexibility and robustness not achieved by connectionism alone.

As I have said, the present article aims at fully connectionist systems that have the advantages of symbolic AI, although hybrid systems are certainly interesting from some points of view. (As in the introductory chapter, a hybrid system has both some connectionist aspects and some aspects with no specified connectionist realization.) Why not go for hybrid systems? My answer to this is threefold. First, to the extent that one sees connectionist systems as an idealization of biological networks and one is interested in seeing how biological networks perform cognition, it behooves one to produce a fully connectionist model of cognition. Secondly, it is quite simply interesting from the point of view of computational science to see whether and how a fully connectionist system could perform cognition. Thirdly, it seems likely that a fully connectionist system would allow a smoother and more complete integration of different aspects of the system than a hybrid system would.

Finally, we need to consider the possibility of analogy-based reasoning being realized in connectionist systems that do not use *implementational* connectionist tools. After all, Harris (this volume) presents a nonimplementational connectionist system that is plausibly claimed to effect a type of analogical processing; and, more generally, the standard connectionist phenomenon of generalization from training examples could possibly be viewed as analogical processing. (See Holyoak, Novick, and Melz, 1994, for more on this, in the context of a system built by Hinton.) However, we come up against disadvantage (CNb) of nonimplementational connectionist systems—such systems do not do a good job of manipulating dynamically arising information with complex structure. Therefore, the complexity of the analogs they can deal with is relatively limited. In using implementational connectionist tools to realize ABR, I am aiming for a degree of structural and processing complexity comparable to that involved in symbolic ABR.

1.2. WM/WM Matching

If a connectionist ABR system works by bringing a source analog down from long-term memory into working memory (WM), for the purpose of comparing it with a target analog already in WM, then we are faced with the task of matching two complex structures in WM with each other. The fact that connectionism is good at some types of matching may blind one to the fact that non-implementational, fully connectionist systems have not been shown to be adept at matching working memory structures (of the high-level type of interest in this chapter) *with each other*. The type of matching for which connectionism is normally congratulated is a form of WM/LTM matching—associative matching of some working memory item, encoded typically as a short-lived activation pattern, to a *long*-term memory item, which is typically implicit in the connection weights. One might suggest achieving connectionist WM/WM matching by computing some general measure of similarity of activation vectors, but we will see that this approach faces difficult problems. There is some reason to think that a network that learns to compare reduced descriptions to each other may be adequate for WM/WM matching, but again there are problems.

WM/WM matching is needed for purposes other than as a component process in ABR, and I have therefore elevated it to the status of second theme of the chapter. I will be showing that one must take natural language understanding to require various kinds of WM/WM matching, often amounting to analogical mapping, unless one is prepared to adopt some very ad hoc and unnatural assumptions.

1.3. Plan of the Chapter

Sections 2–5 are on the first theme, namely implementing ABR in connectionism. Section 2 reviews some advantages that are usually associated with connectionism and that account for the claims of flexibility and robustness in statement (CNg) above. Section 3 argues the flexibility and robustness of ABR, even when it is entirely symbolic, by showing ABR's parallels to most of the advantages in Section 2. Section 4 gives a thumbnail sketch of a connectionist ABR system I am currently implementing. More importantly, perhaps, it suggests that suitable versions of the reduced description idea in connectionism could help us achieve efficient source-analog retrieval using structured indices, efficient matching of source propositions to target propositions, and flexible internal structuring of complex propositions.

Section 5 switches to the second theme, and shows how certain types of WM/WM matching arise in natural language understanding. The section also argues that it is not easy to see how such mapping could be achieved using standard connectionist techniques without simply implementing standard symbolic matching procedures. The section does not claim that the matching definitely cannot be achieved without such implementation, and indeed I express the hope that connectionist reduced descriptions could be helpful in this regard. Section 6 concludes the chapter.[2]

---

[2] Sections 2 and 3 are a condensation of an argument in Barnden (1993). A preliminary version of the connectionist ABR system sketched in Section 4 is described in detail in Barnden and Srinivas (1992). Section 5 is based on a fuller discussion in Barnden (1992) but additionally discusses some recent work on structure matching via reduced representations (Stolcke & Wu, 1992).

2. STANDARD CONNECTIONIST ADVANTAGES

Here I review some advantages that standard connectionist systems are often claimed to have. They are listed in the left-hand column of Table 8.1. For the sake of argument I will uncritically assume that these claims are justified.

A system is said to exhibit *graceful degradation* when it can tolerate significant corruption of its inputs and/or its internal workings and still give reasonable performance. We can therefore distinguish between graceful degradation with respect to *input corruption* and graceful degradation with respect to *system corruption*. Connectionist systems, especially distributed ones, often exhibit one or both types. Input corruption takes the form of noise in an input activation vector. System corruption usually takes the form of node or link deletions or corruptions of the connection weights. (System corruption also includes phenomena such as the corruption of bindings in Smolensky's, 1990, tensor scheme when too many of them are stored.)

It is fair to say that traditional AI systems tend not to degrade gracefully. For definiteness, I will consider a straightforward rule-based system. A small corruption of an input data structure is likely to make it fail to match the precise form expected by the rules which would have applied to the uncorrupted data structure. (See also Holyoak, 1991, p. 313, on this point.) For instance, if a rule R expects to see a list whose first element is a symbol A (which is not a variable), and A in the actual input has been replaced by a different (nonvariable) symbol B, then the rule will typically no longer be triggered. This is the case even if there is no other rule that matches the input more closely than R does. Also, corruptions that take the form of deletions of items, rather than a replacement of items by incorrect ones, will also typically cause large changes in the performance of the system. For instance, either drastically too few rules might be triggered, or new rules that lead to run-time errors might now be triggered. As for lack of graceful degradation with respect to system corruption, damage to some component of a rule in a rule-based system can have large effects on how

Table 8.1.
Advantages of Various Types of System

STANDARD CONNECTIONIST	TRADITIONAL AI	ANALOGY-BASED
graceful degradation	no	yes
representation completion	no	yes
similarity-based generalization	no	yes
learning	yes	yes
emergent rules	no	yes
emergent exceptions	no	yes
content-based access	(no)	(no)
holistic structure processing	no	no
soft constraint-satisfaction	no	no
no	complex temp info structures	yes

the system operates. The corruption might even have the effect of making the system break down, rather than merely giving a wrong answer.

In a connectionist system, we often find a *representation completion* property (more usually called the *pattern completion* property). This can take two basic forms. An incomplete pattern of activation on an input bank of units can lead to a known completion of the pattern appearing on an output bank. Or, an incomplete pattern on some bank units can lead to a known completion appearing on that same bank. (What it means to say that a pattern is incomplete varies somewhat with the specific nature of the system.) Clearly, the pattern completion property of connectionist systems can be seen as just a special case of graceful degradation with respect to input corruption.

Connectionist systems are also widely noted for their capability for *automatic similarity-based generalization*. This property is closely related to, if not a special case of, the property of graceful degradation with respect to input corruption. Previously unseen inputs that are sufficiently similar to inputs on which the system has been trained lead to behavior that is usefully similar to that elicited by the training inputs.

A strongly related property of standard connectionist systems is their ability to *learn* generalizations or category prototypes by virtue of exposure to instances of the generalizations or categories. These generalizations or prototypes are implicit in the weights, that is, implicit in the way the system operates. Notice that learning, in a wide variety of forms, is intensively studied in traditional AI. Perhaps, however, it is fair to say that certain types of learning are more intrinsically and wholeheartedly supported by connectionism.

It has been claimed that connectionism provides a framework in which a system can have *merely emergent rule-like behavior*. Such a system can be described (approximately, at least) as following rules, without actually operating by means of the interpretation of explicit rules (Rumelhart & McClelland, 1986; Smolensky, 1988a, 1988b). One potential benefit of emergence is that the system's actual operation can be more subtle and more sensitive to nuances of the situation than would be possible, in any practical way, in explicit rule interpretation.

As a dual of emergent rule-like behavior, one can point also to *merely emergent exceptions*. A connectionist system need not explicitly note or work out that something is an exception. For instance, in the past-tense model of Rumelhart and McClelland (1986), rules and exceptions to them develop without the system ever having to become aware of the *fact that* irregularities are indeed exceptions to the regularities. On the other hand, a traditional AI learning system that developed its own rules during training might have to construct rules dedicated to particular irregularities or sets of irregularities. To that extent it would have to observe the fact that regularities are being violated, and reason about that fact.[3]

---

[3] To be fair, however, it is by no means clear that the merely emergent quality of exceptions in connectionist systems is actually an advantage. I expand on this point in Barnden (in press). I also

Connectionism has an intrinsic capability for efficient *content-based access* (or *associative access*) to long-term memory, in two different senses. First, given that a standard connectionist system's long-term memory is its weight matrix, and that specific situations that the system has encountered have left their mark on that matrix, the manipulation of an input vector by the network can be thought of as the bringing to bear of relevant long-term memories on that vector. Secondly, a heteroassociating connectionist network can be thought of as outputting activity patterns encoding long-term memories that are in some specific sense relevant to the input vector. Content-based access is not so easily provided in symbolic systems, as implemented on conventional computers, although to some degree it can be obtained by sophisticated indexing schemes (in, e.g., Kolodner, 1983a, 1983b, and Bonissone et al, this volume), associative computer memories (see, e.g., Hwang & Briggs, 1984), or hashing (see, e.g., Standish, 1990).[4]

A large number of connectionist systems are cast as performing efficient, parallel *soft-constraint satisfaction*. Broadly put, some hypotheses compete and cooperate with each other, gradually influencing each other's levels of confidence until a stable (though not necessarily totally consistent) set of hypotheses is found. An example of this is the ACME system (see Holyoak & Thagard, 1989, and Holyoak et al., 1994).

3. FLEXIBILITY AND ROBUSTNESS OF ABR

Here I argue that ABR can achieve variants of most of the advantages associated with connectionist systems. These advantages were reviewed in Section 2 and listed in Table 8.1. I believe that an awareness of the advantages underlies much of the work on analogy, although they are rarely argued for in explicit detail.

I am not claiming that ABR intrinsically provides parallels for all the connectionist advantages mentioned. In particular, there is nothing in traditional ABR that directly corresponds to efficient, parallel soft-constraint satisfaction. Also, ABR has a *need* for efficient content-based access to long-term memory items (source structures) that stand a good chance of being relevant to a given target structure through being somewhat similar to it. But it does not of itself provide any particular mechanism for achieving the access, although, of course, particular ABR systems have included specific mechanisms.

I first need to mention some general assumptions I make about ABR.

---

point out there that traditional symbolic AI systems are by no means forced to have any awareness of exceptions, or special mechanisms for them. For instance, the normal inheritance process in semantic networks, which chases up links from a given node, handles exceptional information in the same way that it handles additional information at nodes, and need not be aware of the exceptionality.

[4] However, Touretzky (1990) points out some deficiencies of hashing as compared to connectionist associative retrieval.

3.1. Some Assumptions about ABR

It seems to be generally accepted that in ABR the sources are *explicit* individuals, separately encoded in memory. That is, ABR appears not to be taken to encompass styles of reasoning that do depend indirectly on similarities to past cases but where memory has no record of those cases as individuals. For instance, a symbolic or connectionist reasoning system that relies on generalizations or prototypes *distilled from* examples that it has encountered, and does not make direct explicit appeal to those examples themselves, is not normally cast as an ABR system. The matter is really one of degree: the more that a system makes direct appeal to individual examples and the more that the long-term memory consists of separate explicit memories of individual examples, the more we are inclined to say that the system does ABR. Although an extreme form of ABR system would not contain any generalized sources—structures obtained by generalizing over groups of sources—ABR systems in general may contain them (Kolodner & Simpson, 1989).

ABR can, when necessary, make inferences about a target on the basis of a *single* source (where, moreover, that source may well encode a situation encountered only once). Indeed, that is the usual case studied in the ABR literature.[5] However, in a standard connectionist learning system, trained with a large number of examples, it is usual for no single example to have a huge effect on the generalizations encoded in the weights.

The ABR paradigm allows the degree or goodness of match between the target and a source to influence the degree of confidence with which information is transferred from the source.[6] That is, transferred information is only ever tentative, ABR being a form of merely plausible reasoning. The worse the match between source and target, the less the confidence that should be attached to transfers. Also, I will allow the tentativeness of a transfer from a source to be influenced by the degree of confirmation from other sources. Thus, if another source matches the target well but fails to generate the same transfer, or generates a transfer that is inconsistent with it, then the transfer should be more tentative than it would otherwise be.

ABR work has concentrated to a considerable extent on one-to-one mappings. This is especially so within the psychology literature (K.J. Holyoak, personal communication, October 1991; and see the review in Gentner, 1989). Systems are typically limited to making a mapped item in the source correspond to at most one item in the target, and making an item in the target correspond to at most

---

[5] This is not to say that the system has actually encountered the situations encoded in its sources. Often the sources are constructed by hand, although we might be asked to imagine that the system has encountered them.

[6] I use "transfer" to mean just the process of moving information from a source to a target to which it has already been mapped, perhaps modifying the information on the way.

one item in the source. For instance, the Structure Mapping Engine (Falkenhainer, Forbus, & Gentner, 1989) throws out non-one-to-one mappings during the construction of global maps, although it seems that the underlying theory (Gentner, 1983) need not in principle be committed to one-to-one-ness, and in later work Falkenhainer (1990) allows non-one-to-one maps. However, in this chapter it is important to allow non-one-to-one mappings, although I do not deny that one-to-one-ness can be adopted as a default or first preference. Barnden (in press) argues in detail that non-one-to-one maps are desirable. I omit the argument here in view of the fact that some prominent analogy systems, such as ACME (Holyoak et al., 1994), allow it.

3.2. Graceful Degradation

ABR systems are much less susceptible than traditional AI systems are to bad consequences from system and input corruptions, under suitable natural assumptions. To take a simple example of input corruption first, suppose that the system observes John kissing Mary, and therefore constructs a target analog T, consisting of the single proposition *John kissed Mary*. Suppose that T analogically matches a certain source analog S, and causes S to be retrieved from memory. Let S be an analog saying that *David kissed Susan, Susan slapped David*, and that *the kissing caused the slapping* (Table 8.2). Structure T and S therefore match to some moderate degree, so let us assume that the tentative conclusions that Mary slapped John and that the kissing caused the slapping are added to T. Now suppose that T had been corrupted during construction, so that its single proposition had been *John kissed ?????* where *?????* was some corrupted symbol, even perhaps one previously unknown to the system. Obviously, the analogical retrieval, matching and transfer could have proceeded just as before, except that the constructed tentative conclusions would have said that *?????* slapped John and that the kissing caused the slapping. Such a modification is a simple example of graceful degradation that drops directly out of the very nature of analogy.

This example does not go much beyond what a rule-based system could do using a variabilized rule saying that if X kisses Y then Y slaps X. For a different type of example, suppose now that the uncorrupted T says that *John kissed Mary* and *Mary disliked John,* and S says that *David kissed Susan, Susan disliked*

Table 8.2. Input-Corruption in ABR

TARGET	SOURCE
John kissed Mary.	David kissed Susan.
	Susan slapped David.
	The kissing caused the slapping.

David, Susan slapped David, and that the kissing and dislike, in combination, causing the slapping (see Table 8.3). Much as before, the tentative conclusion that the John/Mary kissing and dislike caused Mary to slap John is added to *T.* Now suppose *T* had been corrupted, only this time the corruption took the form of the omission of the whole proposition that Mary disliked John. Then we would still have obtained a partial match with *S,* and the same tentative conclusion (augmented now with the proposition that Mary disliked John) would still have been produced. However, the match would have been less good than with the uncorrupted *T,* since fewer propositions are being matched. Therefore, the conclusion would have been more tentative, but this effect is, precisely, a desirably graceful sort of degradation.

These examples show that it is possible for significant corruptions to a target analog *T* to stand a good chance of only altering the analogical inferencing to a graceful extent. The essential point here is that ABR is specifically designed to tolerate large deviations of target analog from source analog, so that further deviations caused by input corruption may well not cause any great harm.

Consider now the following more complex example. Suppose *S* and the uncorrupted *T* are as in Table 8.3, but that the corruption merely causes the *John kissed Mary* proposition to be changed to *John kissed ?????.* The proposition that *Mary disliked John* is preserved unharmed (see Table 8.4). We have a problem now with how the corrupted *T* matches *S.* Without the corruption, *Susan* in *S* can be coherently mapped to *Mary* in *T*, as can be seen from Table 8.3. But with the corruption the most complete mapping would be to map the occurrence of *Susan* in *Susan disliked David* to *Mary* but to map the occurrence of *Susan* in *David kissed Susan* to *?????.* This is a difficulty if one insists on one-to-one mappings. However, I posited earlier that a hard one-to-one constraint is unwarranted. In our example, we may therefore map *Susan* both to *?????* and to *Mary.*

This then raises the issue of how to treat the element *Susan* in transferring the source proposition that *Susan slapped David.* Should the analogical inference be that *Mary slapped John,* or that *????? slapped John,* or what? My current suggestion is that both these propositions should be tentatively proposed as conclusions. As a variant of this, they could be joined together as a disjunction.

Table 8.3. Input-Corruption in ABR

TARGET	SOURCE
John kissed Mary.	David kissed Susan.
Mary disliked John.	Susan disliked David.
	Susan slapped David.
	The kissing and dislike caused the slapping.

Table 8.4. Input-Corruption in ABR

CORRUPTED TARGET	SOURCE
John kissed ?????.	*David kissed Susan.*
Mary disliked John.	*Susan disliked David.*
	Susan slapped David.
	The kissing and dislike caused the slapping.

But whatever choice is made on this issue, the behavior is a graceful degradation of the behavior in the uncorrupted case.[7]

I turn now to the other variety of graceful degradation, concerned with system corruption. Once again, there is a sense in which ABR inherently provides such gracefulness. This is especially so if an analogical inference becomes the less tentative the greater the number of sources that support the inference. For instance, in our kissing/slapping examples, there might be several or many sources in which a kissing cause the appropriate slapping. Then the loss or corruption of some significant proportion of this set of sources would not, by itself, demolish the conclusion that Mary slapped John, but merely make it more tentative. Of course, if there were other source structures in which the kissee did *not* slap the kisser then the mentioned source corruption might reduce the number of slap sources to a level lower than the number of slapless sources. In this case the slapping conclusion might, at best, be posted merely as an improbable possibility rather than as something that is probable. But this is not wrong behavior on the part of the system, and is analogous to what would happen in a connectionist system where one corrupted weights to such an extent that other weights, mediating distinctly different behavior, began to take over.

Even if the system is using only one source to derive analogical inferences for a target, considerable corruption can be gracefully tolerated. The observations that can be made are very similar to those we made for target corruption, but now involving the corruption of individual items within the source rather than in the target. The observations are spelled out in Barnden (1993).

Altogether, therefore, it is reasonable to suggest that ABR (especially when liberalized to allow non-one-to-one mappings) exhibits useful forms of graceful degradation. Notice that I have not argued that ABR can achieve the *same* forms of graceful degradation as connectionism can. But that does not put ABR at a

---

[7] The *?????* is therefore treated much as if it were an "internal query variable" in ACME (Holyoak & Thagard, 1989, pp. 308, 314, 333–337). Such a variable in a target is intended to be mapped to the same source item as some other item *t* in the target. This observation then raises the possibility that one result of the matching process in our example could be the conjecture that *?????* is, in fact, to be identified with *Mary*.

disadvantage with respect to connectionism, because, conversely, it has not been established that connectionism (except when implementing symbolic ABR!) can achieve the forms of graceful degradation that ABR can. Nor has it been shown what sorts of graceful degradation are actually most useful in practice.

In this discussion, we have considered ABR only at the level of symbols and propositions. Instead, should we look at it at the level of bit strings and so forth in a *computer implementation* of ABR? In that case, corruptions could take forms that are not readily translatable into the types of high-level corruption we have been considering in this section. The whole low-level integrity of a high-level data structure such as a proposition might be compromised by a small corruption at the implementational level, leading perhaps to seriously corrupted analogical inferences or even run-time crashes of the system. Also, a small corruption of the addressing machinery or logic circuitry could well have disastrous high-level effects. Therefore, ABR implemented on a (conventional) computer has the same lack of graceful degradation that any system implemented on such a computer has.[8] However, this carries with it the implication that is not *analogy-based reasoning* as such that lacks graceful degradation. Rather, conventional computer implementations lack it. I believe this distinction of the level at which one might analyze graceful degredation has seriously confused discussions of the relative merits of symbolicist computing and connectionism.

One can either view connectionist systems as low-level computational architectures, on the same level as computer hardware, or as high-level virtual machines on the same level as rule-based systems, ABR systems, and so on. In the former case, one can say that connectionist systems degrade more gracefully than conventional computer architectures do, and more gracefully than systems *implemented on these architectures* do. However, if one views connectionist systems as high-level virtual architectures, one should be comparing their graceful degradation properties with those of rule-based systems, ABR systems, or what have you, without bringing in a specific style of implementation. We should not forget that a connectionist system in the high-level virtual machine view can itself be implemented on a conventional computer, without in any way impugning its status as a connection system. But, of course, under such an implementation the connectionist system itself inherits the lack of graceful degradation of the conventional computer.

Notice that an ABR system implemented in some connectionist framework qua low-level computational architecture could avoid the lack of graceful degradation of conventional computers and could gain forms of graceful degradation for which connectionism is noted. A scheme of this sort will be outlined in Section 4.

---

[8] In the case of computers, graceful degradation with respect to system corruption is usually referred to as fault tolerance. Under the heading of conventional computers I am excluding fault-tolerant ones, for simplicity of discussion.

3.3. Representation Completion

It is clear that ABR systems do have a representation-completion property (see Section 2). Suppose a source analog S in memory contains propositions P_i to P_n, and the system is presented with a target structure T consisting of just some nonempty proper subset of this set of propositions. Then, T will match S to a degree dependent on the size of that subset. The ordinary process of transferring information from source to target will then complete T to form a copy of S. The tentativeness of the completion can be made to depend on the goodness of the match. These observations can easily be generalized to the case where T is not identical to a subset of S but can be mapped to such a subset. This type of representation completion is discussed by Holyoak et al. (1994).

3.4. Automatic Similarity-Based Generalization

In Section 2 we characterized the property of automatic similarity-based generalization, in connectionist systems, as holding when previously unseen inputs that are sufficiently similar to inputs on which the system has been trained lead to behavior that is usefully similar to that elicited by those training inputs. Of course, this is exactly the quality on which ABR is founded, if for "training inputs" one reads source structures in the system's memory.

It is difficult to compare the similarity-based generalization obtained in ABR systems with that obtained in connectionism, since the two paradigms have largely been applied to different sorts of problem. In particular, few connectionist systems can cope with the complex structures of information used in typical ABR systems.

3.5. Learning

Connectionism provides interesting, simple approaches to learning. But ABR also provides a simple approach—the continual addition of source structures to memory. (There are other possible types of learning, such as the creation of explicit generalizations and the refinement of the source-retrieval scheme, to name just two.) The gradual accumulation will gradually alter the pattern of analogical inferencing done by the system. The alterations may sometimes merely be adjustments in the tentativeness levels assigned to analogical inferences, but may be more far reaching. In a population of sources that contribute analogical inferences to a target T, different sources can conflict—some could suggest that Mary slapped John, some could suggest that she did not. As the numerical balance of such sources changes, the system could flip from preferring one of the conclusions to preferring the other.

3.6. Merely Emergent Rules and Exceptions

ABR systems can exhibit merely emergent rule-like behavior. Suppose a target structure T contains the single proposition that *John kissed Mary,* and that a source structure S says that *David kissed Susan,* and that *this caused Susan to slap David.* The system can use S to add tentative analogical inferences to T, to the effect that John's kissing Mary caused her to slap him. This effect has nothing specifically to do with the fact that T involves John and Mary in particular—the process would have worked just as well for Peter and Sally instead. With such targets, therefore, the system can be construed by an outside observer as executing a rule of the form: *If X kisses Y then the kissing causes Y to slap X.* Nevertheless, there has been so interpretation of an explicit rule to this effect. This point becomes yet clearer if we consider that the same S could be used with a target T that says that Mary slapped John. The tentative analogical inference would be that John kissed Mary, and this caused the slap. In this case the system appears to be following the converse rule: *If Y slaps X then the slapping is caused by X kissing Y.*

ABR systems can also exhibit merely emergent exceptions. Suppose that, as well as sources in which there is kissing and slapping as above, there are sources in which someone kisses someone but where the kissee is meek and does *not* slap the kisser. Now consider a target T which says that John kissed Mary and Mary was meek. This target matches both our former, nonmeek, sources to some degree, but also our new, meek sources; and it has a stronger match to the latter. Hence, the hypothesis that Mary slapped John that could otherwise come from nonmeek sources can be weakened, and perhaps blocked, by the presence of the meek sources. This is on the assumption that a stronger target/source match leads to higher confidence in the appropriateness of the source for illuminating the target, other things being equal. Whatever the precise mechanism, the important point is that in our example the system is not required to notice that the meek sources are exceptional with respect to other sources. Rather, the effect just drops out of a general scheme for paying more attention to more strongly matching sources. (Nevertheless, an ABR system could be equipped with a mechanism for explicitly noticing exceptions, and such a facility might be valuable.)

4. ABR IMPLEMENTED IN CONNECTIONISM

We have seen that symbolic ABR intrinsically provides (versions of) many of the advantages attributed to connectionism. Therefore, it is worthwhile to implement ABR in connectionism using implementational-connectionist tools, as a way of bridging the symbolicist/connectionist gap. Here we briefly look at the task of implementing the mapping and transfer stages of analogy using implementational-connectionist tools, and implementing source-analog retrieval using a connectionist spreading activation mechanism.

The overall, general scheme I propose is as follows: The system, which is fully connectionist, has a large subnetwork that acts as a long-term data base of source analogs. There is also a subnetwork acting as a working memory (WM) capable of holding a set of proposition-like data structures. The working memory is realized by means of implementational-connectionist tools. The data structures it can contain could be akin to logic formulae, semantic network fragments, frame-based representations, or whatever. At any time, the propositions in WM are deemed to constitute either: (a) a target analog, or (b) a target analog plus a source analog retrieved from the source database. Case (a) obtains at the start of an episode of attempted ABR. Indexing cues generated from the target propositions then cause the stimulation of source analogs in the database, to varying degrees. The most highly stimulated source is then retrieved (i.e., converted to a set of new propositions in WM). Mapping between the source propositions and the target propositions is now attempted. If mapping is successful, source propositions are transformed (according to the mapping established) and become additions to the target. The added propositions can be given a strength that reflects their degree of nontentativeness. This degree depends on how well the source was mapped to the target.

Notice that it is not assumed that sources residing in the long-term database are themselves implemented using implementational-connectionist techniques (although this possibility is available in principle). Since sources are not subject to intricate manipulations until they reach the working memory, it may be possible to use a form of representation in the database that is adequate to encode the complex structure in sources but is not adequate for complex manipulations. Such a representation technique would therefore fail to be an implementational-connectionist technique. My own system, described below, uses a representation of this type. Sources in the database are encoded in weight settings, whereas a source retrieved into the working memory is realized as an activation pattern.

The implementational-connectionist tools for implementing the working memory and the mapping and transfer processes within it could be drawn from the work of any one of a number of investigators, notably Lange and Dyer (1989), Shastri and Ajjanagadde (1989), Smolensky (1990), and Touretzky (1990), as well as from my own work (Barnden, 1989, 1991a). Which particular tools are used does not make much difference from the point of view of the present chapter, as long as they can encode complex propositional structure and can efficiently support the mapping and transfer processes. This requires, for one thing, that working memory should be easily able to hold a variable number of propositions, that new propositions can be easily added to the working memory, and that propositions can easily be matched with each other. I would suggest that the tools in Barnden (1989, 1991a) more readily satisfy the whole set of requirements than do the techniques of the other authors just mentioned (although those techniques may have certain advantages over my own in other respects). I will therefore give a very rough sketch of the working memory used in my connectionist analogy-based reasoning system, ABR-Conposit. (See Barnden & Srinivas, 1992, for a description of an initial version of the system.) Although this system is still in the course of being implemented, the working memory representational techniques are based on those used in an older fully implemented rule-based system, Conposit, which manipulates complex data structures in complex ways.[9]

In ABR-Conposit, the working memory consists mainly of a two-dimensional array (arbitrarily chosen to be of size 32 × 32) in which the elements are small connectionist subnetworks called *active registers* (see Figure 8.1). The registers are said to be active because they perform fundamental processing functions of significant complexity—they are not just static information repositories like registers in a computer. At any moment, a given active register holds an activation pattern deemed to consist of two vectors: a *symbol* and a *highlighting vector*. The highlighting vector's elements are binary valued, but the symbol's elements are real numbers. Most active registers at any given moment will have a *null* symbol (an all-zero vector). A nonnull symbol is deemed to represent some specific domain entity, such as a particular person or the class of all person-loves-person situations.[10] Active registers containing nonnull symbols are deemed to represent, currently, whatever those symbols represent. The highlighting vector is used for a variety of purposes, such as specifying the roles of active registers involved in propositions, or for temporary marking purposes during manipulations of propositions.

An atomic proposition such as *John loves Mary* is realized as the presence of suitable symbols and highlighting states in a "clump" of active registers, as sketched in the top-right sector of Figure 8.1. A clump consists of a "head" register, standing for the proposition as whole, together with one or more neighboring "role" registers. For our example proposition, one role register currently represents the loving predicate, by virtue of currently containing the symbol that denotes all conceivable loving situations, and the other two role registers represent John and Mary by virtue of containing the JOHN and MARY symbols. The role registers are distinguished from each other and from the head register by having different highlighting. Notice that the basic structuring primitive used within a clump is *adjacency of registers*. Mary, John, and loving come to be related to each other within a proposition by virtue of being (temporarily) represented by active registers that are adjacent to the head register. The within-clump structuring is thus a type of *relative-position*

---

[9]The main existing version of the rule-based Conposit system (see Barnden, 1989, 1990) manipulates Johnson-Laird style mental models for the purpose of syllogistic reasoning (Johnson-Laird, 1983).

[10] Informally, in the latter case the symbol can be thought of as denoting the *loves* predicate.

Figure 8.1.
A Temporary State of an 8 × 8 Region of the Working Memory in ABR-Conposit. Each square illustrates an active register, which is a connectionist subnetwork. Only neighboring registers are directly connected to each other. Words, and *X* and *Y*, stand for the "symbol" activation patterns sitting in the registers currently. Squares shown with no symbol shown have the "null" symbol currently. A small letter, bullet mark, or triangle mark indicates a current ON value for a specific element of the highlighting vector in the register. The head registers (see text) are the ones containing a triangle mark. The other nonnull registers are all role registers.

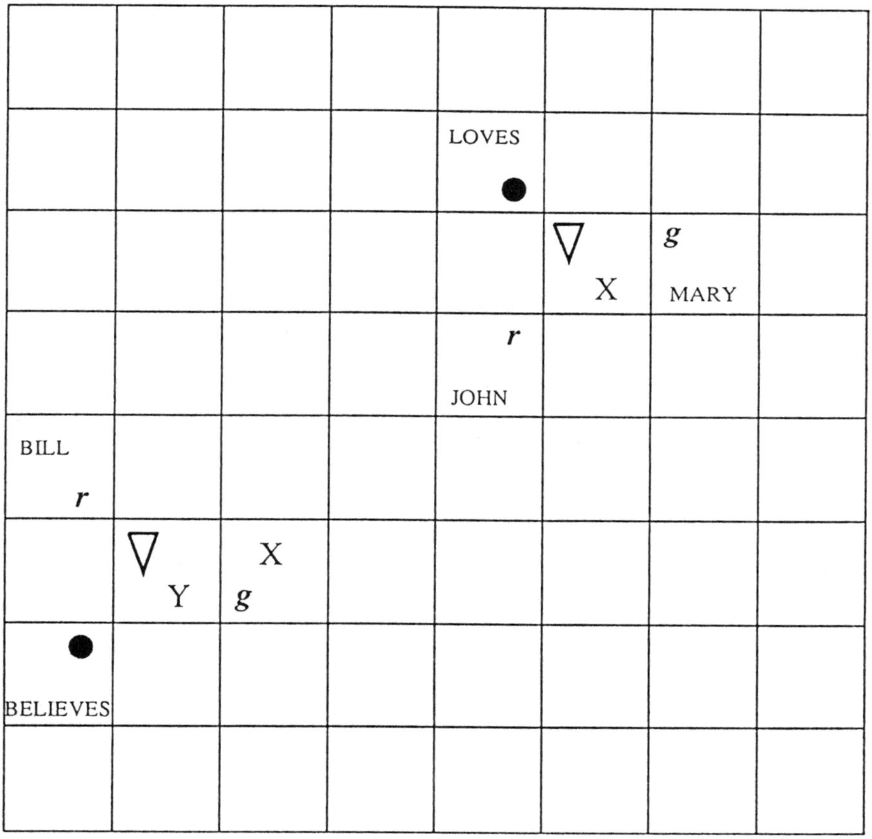

				LOVES ●			
					▽ X	g MARY	
				r JOHN			
BILL r							
	▽ Y	X g					
● BELIEVES							

encoding, a general structure-encoding strategy of considerable power (Barnden & Srinivas, 1991).

Nonatomic propositions such as *Bill believes that John loves Mary*, and so on to more levels of embedding, can also be encoded. The basic technique is again illustrated in Figure 8.1. In our example, there is one clump for *the John loves*

Mary subproposition and another clump for the *Bill believes*... part. The two clumps are linked together by means of the appearance of the symbol X in both clumps. For the moment, take X to be "unassigned" symbol that does not permanently represent anything and is akin to a variable in predicate logic. Nevertheless, because X appears in the head register of the love clump, it is deemed to represent, currently, the John-loving-Mary situation. Similarly, because it appears in the patient role register of the believing clump, it is deemed to represent what is believed by Bill. Altogether, then, we get the effect we want. The technique of linking representational structures (the clumps in our case) together by means of symbol-sharing is an instance of *pattern-similarity association*, which is another general structure-encoding strategy of great power (Barnden & Srinivas, 1991).[11] Notice that relative-position encoding and pattern-similarity association achieve temporary structuring of information without having to change connection weights or use binder nodes. The significance of this is discussed by Barnden and Srinivas (1991).

Symbols such as X and Y in Figure 8.1 are actually *reduced representations* generated automatically from the data structures within working memory. More specifically, the head register of every proposition is given such a reduced representation as its "symbol." (Recall that a symbol is just an activation pattern.) The symbol is the result of applying a certain "reduction" function to the symbols and highlighting vectors in the surrounding role registers. For instance, for the *John loves Mary* proposition in Figure 8.1, the reduction function applies to the JOHN symbol and the highlighting in the register containing that symbol, the MARY symbol and the highlighting accompanying it, and the LOVES symbol and the highlighting accompanying it. The derived reduced representation, X in Figure 8.1, reflects the nature of the whole proposition, yet is just a single symbol. The reduced representations play a fundamental role in both target/source matching and in source retrieval, as we will see in a moment, quite apart from supplying pattern-similarity association between clumps.

Once a source has been retrieved from the database and placed in working memory together with the target, a mapping process ensues. This is effected by a flowchart-like connectionist subnetwork attached to the working memory. Each node in the flowchart sends a *command signal* identically to all active registers. The registers respond differently according to their different current states. The

---

[11] I include the time-phase binding technique of Shastri and Ajjanagadde (1989) under the general heading of pattern-similarity association, for reasons given in Barnden and Srinivas (1991), although it is markedly different from the pattern-similarity association technique used in my own systems. The signature-based binding technique of Lange and Dyer (1989)—see also Lange and Wharton (this volume)—can also be viewed as a type of pattern-similarity association. Anyone familiar with associative memories in computers (Hwang & Briggs, 1984) will find the general idea of pattern-similarity association an unsurprising technique, but, surprisingly, it has not been widely exploited in connectionism.

effects of a command signal on a register can include a change of symbol or highlighting vector, or the broadcasting of the register's symbol to all other registers. The effect is, largely, dependent on the state of the register itself and of its neighbors, and each register is in charge of managing its own state change. The state changes for different registers proceed in parallel with each other, subject to some qualifications spelled out by Barnden (1991a). Details of command signals and the flowchart nets can be found in that paper, where their use in rule-based reasoning is described. The basic way they are used in ABR-Composit for target/source mapping and other purposes is substantially the same as in the rule-based reasoning system. Sequences of command signals can easily effect operations such proposition creation, proposition deletion, proposition modification, and traversal of complex propositions.

Now, it would be perfectly possible to use command signals to effect an exact implementation of a symbolic proposition-matching process, as used in symbolic analogy systems. However, ABR-Composit substantially avoids this by exploiting the reduced representations. Mapping proceeds as follows. The process sequences through the source propositions in an arbitrary order.[12] For each proposition, the reduced representations in its head is broadcast to all the other active registers. Every head register of a target proposition compares the broadcast symbol to its own symbol (reduced representation). If a sufficient degree of match is found, then the register causes a central degree-of-match value to be incremented.

The source/target matching process as just described clearly deals with the case where we want an exact match between propositions in source and target, because identical propositions have almost-identical reduced representations.[13] However, it is more common in ABR to want nonidentical matching. For instance, we may want a target that says that Mary's kissing John caused John to slap Mary to match a source that says that Peter's kissing Susan caused Susan to slap Peter. Also, if target or source can be a result of generalization and therefore contain variable-like elements, we will need to be able to establish maps involving such variables. Barnden and Srinivas (1992) suggest one, rather cumbersome, method for dealing with nonidentical mapping. However, work is now proceeding on a new method based on relaxation. The relaxation scheme gradually alters symbols (including reduced representations) so as to make putatively corresponding ones approach each other.

---

[12] This arbitrary sequencing is effected by the temporal-winner-take-all technique of Barnden, Srinivas, and Dharmavaratha (1990) and Barnden and Srinivas (1993).

[13] The reduction function includes an addition of a small random vector. This is done to avoid certain structuring confusions that might otherwise arise by virtue of the fact that reduced representations are used also to supply pattern-similarity association. Therefore, identical propositions have reduced representations that differ by a small random amount.

If a sufficiently strong match is found between source and target, transfer occurs. Symbols in source propositions are replaced by the target symbols they have been found to correspond to, and source propositions that mapped to target propositions are deleted. The effect of this is to convert nonmapped source propositions into extensions of the target.

The reduced representations are also the backbone of the source indexing/retrieval process. The encoding method for sources in the database that has been used so far is as follows. There is a *retrieval buffer*, which is a two-dimensional array of registers isomorphic to the working memory. For each source S, there is a single connectionist unit u_s that is connected to all the symbol-vector and highlighting-vector units in all the active registers in the retrieval buffer. These connections from u_s are *retrieval connections*. The weights on these connections are such that if u_s sends activation down them, the activation levels caused to appear on the units in the retrieval buffer are exactly those required for the working memory encoding of the source. (The propositions in the retrieval buffer are then copied into the working memory in such a way as to avoid interfering with the target propositions already there.) Thus, a source S is long-term encoded in the weights on links from u_s to the retrieval buffer.

There are *indexing connections* from the symbol and highlighting units in working memory to every unit u_s. These connections are converses to the connections from u_s to the retrieval buffer. It is easy to use the symbols in the target as indices into the database, in the following way. Each target symbol is considered in sequence.[14] It is first broadcast to all registers in working memory. These simply pass the symbol up on the indexing connections to all the source units u_s. The result is that any u_s that encodes a source that *contains the symbol in any position* gains some extra degree activation. Since the symbol can be a reduced representation in a proposition head register, we see that the indexing is on the basis of propositions (of any complexity), not just to basic symbols such as JOHN. The result of the indexing is that u_s units acquire activation in varying degrees. A winner-take-all process selects the one that is allowed to load its source into the retrieval buffer. Preliminary simulations suggest that this retrieval scheme is effective in retrieving sources relevant to the target, at least for fairly simple targets.

Just as target/source mapping must not be confined to the case of identity between target propositions and source propositions, so the retrieval of sources must not be confined to the case of identity. In our current work, we are experimenting to see whether the reduced representations for propositions such as *Mary loves a dog* and *Peter loves a dog* can be made similar enough to have a useful indexing effect (over and above the effect obtained merely by virtue of the use of the KISSES symbol and DOG symbols as indices). To this end we are

---

[14] In arbitrary order, again by means of temporal-winner-take-all.

experimenting with the natural connectionist idea of having the symbols for people be somewhat similar to each other (whereas in the old, rule-based system they were just arbitrary activation patterns). However, no matter what is achieved in this direction, we do *not* aim to make the indexing be sensitive to overall structural consistency of match between target and sources. At most, indexing picks out sources that stand a good chance of turning out to have a structurally consistent mapping to the target during the mapping process within working memory.

Finally, ABR-Conposit is designed to have multiple working memories, not just one, and to be simultaneously pursuing different mapping attempts in different working memories. The mechanism for this is sketched in Barnden and Srinivas (1992), and plays a role in making ABR achieve the flexibility claimed in Section 3, but, for the sake of brevity, I will not describe the mechanics here. One intended effect of the multiplicity is to allow inconsistencies between pieces of advice given by different sources concerning a single target to be noticed. The target would be copied to different working memories, and different sources would be mapped to the target in the different working memories. Conflict between propositions transferred from different sources would be noticed, after copying of all transferred propositions to another, single working memory. Such conflict would serve to reduce the degree of confidence (increase the degree of tentativeness) of the conflicting propositions.

Although the description in this section has been sketchy, and ABR-Conposit is only partially implemented as yet, my hope is that the section will have conveyed that the connectionist implementation of symbolic ABR is possible using implementational connectionist tools, and that the connectionist technique of reduced representations can play a fundamental role in streamlining the mapping process and the process of retrieving relevant source analogs.

5. WM/WM MATCHING

The style of connectionist ABR outlined in the previous section involves WM/WM matching (i.e., the discovery of mappings between complex structures within working memory). I proposed a connectionist implementation of this task. However, the idea that WM/WM matching is an important task in cognition is not dependent on the arguments of the previous sections. Considerations of, for instance, natural language discourse understanding show that such mapping is needed for independent reasons. (Gasser & Smith, 1991, have made a similar point.) This presents something of a problem to nonimplementational connectionism. This is because the structural matching of working memory items (encoding propositions, sentence interpretations, etc.) with each other, rather than with long-term memories implicit in weight matrices, is not well served by standard connectionist techniques. Specifically, general methods for comparing activation patterns are unlikely to do the job.

WM/WM matching has to some extent been considered in connectionism. Apart from the work of Gasser and Smith just mentioned, there has been some work on performing logical unification in connectionist networks (Ballard, 1986; Hölldobler, 1990; Pinkas, 1992; Stolcke & Wu, 1992). However, Gasser and Smith's model only deals with working memory items of very limited complexity, Ballard's model is hybrid in the sense of this volume's introduction, since it involves the dynamic creation of networks, Stolcke and Wu's approach is a huge abstraction away from what we need (as I will explain later), and anyway the type of matching we need is looser than logical unification.

5.1. Working-Memory Representations and Matching: Preliminaries

By *working-memory representations, items,* or *structures* I mean representations that are rapidly created in the course of natural language processing, reasoning, and so on, and perhaps thrown away soon after. A working-memory representation might encode some interpretation of an incoming natural language sentence, or an intermediate product of some reasoning process. I make no a priori assumptions about the form or semantics of working-memory representations. For instance, representations akin to logic formulae are encompassed by the notion, but so are, say, the mental models of Johnson-Laird (1983).

There is a danger that the term "working-memory representation" will suggest that a system necessarily has a separate module called its working memory, or that a system must necessarily have just a small set of well-distinguished memory types (e.g., iconic, working, intermediate, long term, or whatever). I make no commitment on these matters either way. (The particular commitments made in ABR-Conposit are irrelevant in the rest of this chapter.) Connectionist systems generally do have just two types of memory—long term, in the weights, and short term or working memory, in the activation state—but all I commit to in general is the premise that working-memory representations encode temporary information, and can be rapidly created and modified. Also, I make no assumption that people are consciously aware of what is in their working memories.

In connectionist systems, a working-memory representation is almost always an *activity pattern* (on an input, hidden, or output layer, say), whereas the long-term encoding of knowledge is in the *weights*. However, some connectionist systems allow fast weight modulation (see, e.g., McClelland, 1985, 1986; Pollack, 1987; von der Malsburg & Bienenstock, 1987). Rapidly set weights could be used as an alternative to activity patterns as a basis for working-memory representations, as suggested by Goddard (1980) among others. Also, some hybrid symbolic/connectionist systems allow dynamic creation of new connectionist circuitry that holds temporary working information in its topology (e.g., Eskridge, this volume; Goldstone & Medin, 1994; Holyoak et al., 1994; Nelson, Thagard, & Hardy, 1994; Lehnert, 1991).

A response of a traditional symbolicist so far might well be: why this emphasis on the case of *working-memory* structures and WM/WM matching? In traditional symbolic AI, implemented on computers, working-memory representations are typically the same general sort of "stuff" as long-term ones—they are all data structures constructed out of records and pointers sitting in the main computer memory.[15] Even when the long-term knowledge of an AI system is in its rules, the rules are themselves just data structures. As a result, computational mechanisms developed for matching an input against a piece of long-term information—whether the latter is a memory of a past situation, or the condition part of a long-term rule—can equally well be used for matching two working-memory representations to each other, or, for that matter, two long term structures to each other. So, there is no motivation for splitting the discussion of matching into different cases according to whether the objects being matched are long term or in working memory.

However, the working-memory/long-term memory distinction does make a difference in connectionism. A matching operation performed by a connectionist system has almost always been between a working-memory *activity pattern* and some long-term memories as encoded in the *connection weights*.[16] As was explained in Section 2, this WM/LTM matching happens in the following highly implicit manner. The system's long-term memory is its weight matrix, on which specific inputs that the system has encountered have their mark. The system responds to a new input in a way that is (typically) governed by the similarity of that input to the previous inputs, but of course it is not the case that the input is directly and explicitly compared to those previous inputs.

As a result, standard connectionist matching does not throw much light on the problem of designing a connectionist system that is to match two working-memory representations (which are usually activation patterns) to each other. The matching of *two* activation patterns with each other is simply not something that one can perform using existing techniques for matching an activation pattern into a set of weight-encoded memories. Certainly, certain simple WM/WM matching tasks can be performed by just testing whether two activation vectors are equal (to within some small tolerance). This is easy to do with standard connectionist circuitry. However, the matching task in general is much more demanding than this. Matching might need to be highly partial, or to require some form of variable binding, or to require mappings to be forced between entities which may have not particular intrinsic similarity (as in some cases of analogy). I will give examples later, and will argue that it is by no means

---

[15] Of course, data structures can be stored on disks and other secondary storage media, but to be computed upon they must be brought into main memory.

[16] The systems of Gasser and Smith (1991) and Stolcke and Wu (1992) are important recent exceptions. These authors are in the minority who stress the cognitive importance of subjecting working memory items to matching operations. See also the symmetry detection network in Rumelhart, Hinton, and Williams (1986).

clear how existing connectionist approaches could effect the matching without resorting to implementational connectionist techniques, at least in part.

The alternative of having working-memory representations take the form of rapidly set connection weights rather than activation levels does not help much either. The required matching is now between *two subnetworks whose weights have been rapidly altered*—again, the matching is not the standard, implicit connectionist matching of an input activation pattern to weight-encoded memories. Little attention has been given to the matching of connectionist *subnetworks* with each other. The fundamental problem is that, in almost all connectionist systems, weights are not data that can be analyzed by the system itself, except, of course, in the very limited senses that weights are involved in the summation of inputs and can be modified during learning.

In sum, the problem is that existing approaches to matching in connectionism are between disparate types of encoding, namely activation patterns and weight settings, whereas what we want is a form of matching that works between two encodings of the same type.

5.2. Working-Memory Matching in Natural-Language Discourse

Section 4 discussed the connectionist matching target and source analogs within working memory, in the service of analogy-based reasoning. Considerable flexibility and complexity of matching was involved, because of the need to allow partial matches, constant/constant mappings (e.g., Peter mapped to John), and so on. However, there are other cognitive tasks that involve complex, flexible WM/WM matching. In this subsection, we will look at various different cases arise in natural language understating (going considerably beyond the brief comments on the matter in Gasser & Smith, 1991, although our discussion will be far from exhaustive). Some of the cases can naturally be classed as analogy. In Section 5.4 we will turn to some resulting task requirements imposed upon connectionism.

It is important to bear in mind in the present section that *both* partners in a WM/WM matching event are, typically, representations built on the fly rather than being retrieved from long-term memory. Therefore, the otherwise-available option of using standard connectionist WM/LTM matching, after converting one representation into WM form if both are in LTM form, will not be directly relevant.

Our first case of WM/WM matching in natural language understanding is the reasoning involved in coherently understanding two sentences that are saying the same thing at different levels of detail. Consider:

Go along this street for a while. Go for three blocks and turn right.

This example, adapted from one in Hobbs (1985), requires an understanding that just one going-along is probably being advocated—the speaker is probably not telling the listener to go along the street for a while and *then* to go for three blocks. The listener must, among other things, detect the match between going along the street for a while and going along the street for three blocks. This match is approximate, in virtue of pairing the vague notion of "a while" with the more precise notion of "three blocks." Another case is exemplified by the following discourse fragment:

DAVID: *If John loves Susan, he'd better marry her.*
PETER: *John loves Susan*

Here, presumably, we are to assume that both David and Peter can now infer that John had better marry Susan.[17] This example illustrates the frequent need in discourse for the participants to match working-memory representations with each other. (I will consider in Section 5.3 possible objections to this claim that are based on the idea that some of the information might be in long-term form.)

The example involves an *exact* match between Peter's claim and the antecedent of the condition stated by David. However, more complex examples involve partial matches. Consider:

DAVID: *If John loves Susan and has his head screwed on right, he'd better marry her.*
PETER: *John loves Susan.*

Here, it is reasonable to presume that Peter and David infer that: *If John has his head screwed on right, he'd better marry Susan.* Certainly, there is an exact match between Peter's claim and one of the conjuncts in David's condition antecedent. Nevertheless, it is important for our purposes that there is now merely a partial match between Peter's claim and the *whole* of the antecedent. One may not appreciate the significance of this point if one never looks outside the traditional symbolic framework. There, the typical thing to do in any case is to match Peter's claim sequentially against the various subpropositions of the antecedent.[18] However, it would generally be thought undesirable for a nonimplementational connectionist system to be forced to undertake such sequencing through parts.

Another type of partial mapping arises in:

DAVID: *If John loves Susan, he'd better marry her.*
PETER: *John doesn't love Susan.*

---

[17] More precisely, under suitable assumptions of sincerity and well-informedness, David and Peter can infer this. Under other assumptions, we would presume that Peter can infer only, say, that David now believes that John had better marry Susan. I will ignore such complications in what follows.

[18] In view of the optimization techniques commonly used in production systems (e.g., see Forgy, 1982), this sequential process is an oversimplification. However, the optimized systems still contain the type of sequential processing that many connectionists wish to avoid.

In this case, we might not expect an inference, on the basis of these two statements alone, about whether or not John should marry Susan. Rather, we might expect the metalevel inference (by David and Peter) that David's statement turns out to be irrelevant and should not now be paid attention to. The partialness of the match lies in the need to match the David antecedent to just part of Peter's claim.[19]

Match inexactness can be more fundamental than mere partialness. Consider the task of understanding a sentence that explicitly states an analogy.

Just as John hates his brother for being taller, Sally hates her sister for being thinner.

The system should presumably represent the fact that a correspondence is being set up between John and Sally, between brother-of and sister-of, and between taller-than and thinner-than. This should happen even when the system does not have the long-term knowledge either that John hates his brother for being taller or that Sally hates her sister for being thinner. Hence, one could not have recourse to WM/LTM matching as opposed to WM/WM matching.

The analogy in our example involves the correspondence between taller-than and thinner-than. But the system may not previously have been aware of any significant similarity between these relationships (other than they are both physical size comparison relationships). Rather, the sentence may have the effect of *making* the system aware that taller-than and thinner-than are in some sense analogous (in the sense of having analogous effects on people's opinions or emotions). This may lead, for instance, to the system asking for clarification and being told that being taller and being thinner are regarded by many people as advantages. I mention this point to weaken (though not entirely defuse) the possible claim that connectionism has a head start with doing analogical processing through being founded on notions of similarity. This claim only makes sense to the extent that the similarities involved in an analogy are preexisting, rather than introduced by the analogy itself. Holyoak and Thagard (1989, p. 316) point out that ACME can find similarities between predicates by virtue of constructing a mapping, and comment that "this creative aspect of analogy is not well captured by models of mapping that are more highly dependent on preexisting similarities or identities."

WM/WM matching can also arise in less explicit ways:

Micky asked for a kite and a red-striped ball. But the store only had ones with green stripes.

---

[19] Of course, there is the possibility that David and/or Peter will in fact unsoundly infer that John should not marry Susan. But this humanly realistic possibility only serves to strengthen our argument for the frequency with which working memory matching is done and needs to be done. (*Needs* to, by David—if he is to appreciate what Peter has done if the latter happens to make the unsound inference.)

ANALOGY AND WORKING MEMORY MATCHING   355

In order to see that the word "ones" probably refers to balls, the understander must notice the analogy between the desired object and the available ones (cf. Carbonell & Brown's, 1988, discussion of "parallelism," that is analogy, in the service of anaphora). The analogy in our example involves the mapping of green-stripedness to red-stripedness.

It would be implausible to suggest that the understanding of "ones" as balls rather than kites (or something else) could follow exclusively from aspects of the sentence other than this analogy. First, the mere ordering of "kite" and "ball" in the first sentence is not a reliable basis for the anaphor resolution, since that sentence could equally well have been *Micky asked for a ball with a red stripe, and a kite.* Secondly, a kite is no less able to be striped than a ball, so there would be nothing semantically anomalous about taking "ones" to refer to kites. Nor is it the case that kites are excluded from being the reference of "ones" in virtue of their not being mentioned as striped. After all, "ones" does refer to kites in the following sentence: *Micky asked for a kite. But the store only had green-striped ones.* This presents a puzzle to the listener—does poor Micky not like green stripes on things?—but it is nevertheless clear that the reference is to kites.

Actually, anaphora is not the crucial element in the general point I wish to make with the stripes example. Consider:

Micky asked for a ball with a red stripe. But the store only had balls with red spots.

The point here is that spots and stripes are being contrasted, and that the contrast explains the "but." However, the contrast can only be understood through the analogy between the desired object and the available one.

5.3. The Assumed Lack of a Long-Term Encoding

In all this I have assumed that no long-term encoding of the information conveyed in the example discourse fragments is made or already present. However, it might be objected that, for all we know, information in natural language sentences *is* encoded into long-term memory as it is read or heard, even when there is no apparent reason for this action to be desirable. Then, where I have claimed above that working-memory representation A must be matched to working-memory representation B arising a moment later, our objector might say that, instead, B could be matched against a *long*-term memory holding the information in A. Thus, existing connectionist WM/LTM techniques (Section 5.1) might give us the desired result.[20]

---

[20] I am not saying that I know of a good way of doing all this. I am just giving my imagined objector the benefit of the doubt.

However, this objection faces major problems of its own. Notice that for it to work, it must, essentially, insist that a long-term encoding of A is *always* formed, before the required matching to B takes place. It is not enough just to observe that *sometimes* people remember information conveyed in discourse even when there is no apparent need for them to have do so. But the ubiquitous use of long-term encoding is an extremely strong requirement, and is an entirely ad hoc solution to the problem of how to get a connectionist system to match newly encountered pieces of information to each other. We would at least need some other motivation for the scheme, and some experimental evidence, for it to be all reasonable.

In the last paragraph I said that the objection must "essentially" insist that the long-term encoding of A is always formed. The reason for the caveat is that it might be that the long-term encoding is only formed when B is encountered. Perhaps some very simple feature-overlap process between the working-memory representations of A and B, even when they are structurally complex, could determine that A *might* be relevant to B. This overlap could be construed as a sufficient warrant for going to the trouble of giving A a long-term encoding and trying to match B to it. However, this scheme is ad hoc, cumbersome, and again lacking in any motivation other than that of avoiding WM/WM matching.

5.4. The Problem for Connectionism

The question from here on is: how are we to get nonimplementational connectionist systems to perform the necessary types of WM/WM matching? Specifically, how can we cope with partial matches and constant/constant mappings,[21] without resorting to nonconnectionist system features or to a straightforward connectionist implementation, at least in part, of symbolicist matching techniques?

5.4.1. A Fast-Weight Approach. What is of interest to us in this chapter is whether *fully* connectionist systems can perform WM/WM matching. Therefore, hybrid symbolic/connectionist systems are not our concern, although they are interesting in their own right. It is useful nevertheless to consider one prominent hybrid system that performs complex matchings that are on the track of what we are looking for, because in a moment we will consider the possibility of devising a fully connectionist reworking of the system.

The system in question is the ACME analogy-based reasoning system (Holyoak et al., 1994). The system is a hybrid symbolic/connectionist one. It is given symbolic representations of the two analogs, and dynamically constructs,

---

[21] An example of a constant/constant mapping is the putting of John, in one structure, in correspondence with Bill, in another. Clearly, such possibilities are just special cases of a broader class that includes more complex possibilities, like putting John in correspondence with the-father-of-Peter. I will mostly stick to the constant/constant case for simplicity of presentation.

by means of symbolic information processing, a connectionist network that contains a unit for each reasonable "match hypothesis." For instance, a given match hypothesis might encode the hypothesis that a certain object in one analog corresponds to a certain object in the other. Similarly, a match hypothesis can relate two predicates or two propositions. Match hypothesis units are mutually linked, by excitatory connections if they are consistent with each other, and by inhibitory connections if they conflict with each other. An impression of this scheme is given by Figure 3.2 in Holyoak et al. (1994). The figure shows part of the matching network that would be created for matching two family-tree structures. One includes the people Alfonso, Emilio, and Marco, where Emilio's father is Roberto and Alfonso's father is Marco. The other structure includes Arthur and Christopher, where Arthur's father is Christopher. The analogy, if any, is determined by a parallel connectionist relaxation process over the matching network. The network is meant to settle into a state in which some set of mutually consistent match-hypothesis units are highly activated, and match hypotheses units inconsistent with those have low activation. Some entities in one analog might end up not being matched, because no match hypotheses involving them are highly active. Therefore, matches can be partial, on either side. Clearly, arbitrary constant/constant matches can be found. The system gets advantages from being connectionist—in particular, constraints can be violated. For instance, although inhibitory connections like those between the *Arthur = = Alfonso* unit and the *Arthur = = Emilio* unit exist, both these units might end up being highly activated if they have sufficient support from other match-hypothesis units. Thus, the system can deliver non-one-to-one matches, even though it prefers one-to-one matches. The system prefers predicate/predicate correspondences in which the two predicates are taken to be semantically similar, but, again, this constraint can be violated.

Although the intention in ACME is that one of the analogs be a structure retrieved from long-term memory and made into a working-memory representation, whereas the other be a working-memory representation derived from some current input, the system could in fact be used as it stands to try to match any two working-memory representations to each other. Thus, given the properties mentioned in the previous paragraph, it is a very interesting system in its own right, from the view of getting the task of WM/WM matching done. However, it throws little direct light on how the required sorts of WM/WM matching could be done in a fully connectionist system with a fixed topology.

We might therefore consider the possibility of devising a fully connectionist system that emulates ACME. The most obvious possibility here is to exploit the idea of rapidly modulated connection weights, referred to in Section 5.1, as follows. Assume that the analogy task is initiated when two temporary subnetworks are "created," one implementing the target and one implementing the source. The nodes and links in these subnetworks were already present, but the links had zero weight, so that it was as if they were not there; this in turn means that the nodes were "free" (unrecruited). Then, the ACME matching subnetwork is "created" in the same sense; nodes for this subnetwork are recruited, and links between them as well as links to nodes in the target and source subnetworks are made nonzero.

Thus, we must assume that there is a large pool of units, very densely connected to each other and to "permanent" parts of the network by zero-weight connections, such as that at the appropriate moment certain links can be made nonzero. A weight on a connection is made nonzero by means of a suitable signal on a modulatory connection impinging on that connection. The task requirements are therefore as follows, on the assumption that the two potential analogs are initially presented to the system as activation patterns.

> (TR1) The input activation pattern for the analogs must be processed in such a way that they lead to signals on modulatory connections that change some of the zero weights to non-zero weights, thereby having the effect of recruiting units for the source and target networks, and, within each of these subnetworks separately, connecting the units together in just the right way.
>
> (TR2) During or after the construction of the source and target networks, further modulatory signals must be generated that change some other zero weights to nonzero weights, with the effect of recruiting units for the matching network, connecting them to the source and target networks in just the right way, and connecting them to each other by excitatory or inhibitory links in just the right way.

Bear in mind that *all* the processing involved in (TR1) and (TR2) must be done by normal activation spread within the overall network. But both requirements involve the emulation of aspects of ACME's target processing that have considerable complexity. For instance, the system must be able to notice that it must excitatorily connect the match-hypothesis unit for the *Arthur-has-father-Christopher/Alfonso-has-father-Marco* correspondence to the units for the *has-father/has father* correspondence, the *Arthur/Alfonso* correspondence, and the *Christopher/Marco* correspondence. That is, the actual task of doing the WM/WM matching can only take place after the effect of some *complex symbolic processing* in ACME has already been achieved. To my knowledge there is no way, currently, of achieving this processing in a fully connectionist network without resorting to implementational connectionism. Nonimplementational connectionist systems have not yet been developed to the stage where they can achieve processing whose complexity is anywhere near what is needed.[22]

---

[22] Holyoak et al. (this volume) recognize that significant hurdles must be jumped to cash out the symbolic aspects of ACME into fully connectionist terms. However, that is not an aim of theirs.

Instead of using rapidly modulated connections, one could propose replacing each such connection by a chain of two or more connections interspersed with gating units (cf. the dynamic connections of Feldman, 1982). The modulatory signals now go to the gating units, which only let signals pass along the chain when they are highly active. This variant keeps us closer to prototypical connectionism, but does not get us any further forward with the task requirements just noted.

5.4.2. The Direct and Indirect Mapping Models. The Direct Mapping Model of Hummel, Burns, and Holyoak (1994) can be thought of as a variant of ACME in which the mapping units are replaced by quickly enabled links, which I will call mapping links here. The source and target are represented initially by symbolic expressions as in ACME, and these expressions are used to construct networks realizing them. The task of creating the right links within the source and target networks, and of enabling just the right mapping links between these networks is very similar to the corresponding task in the above imaginary reworking of ACME.

By contrast, the Indirect Mapping Model of Hummel et al. (1994) departs markedly in its architecture from ACME, and a fully connectionist reworking of it would appear to involve less in the way of complex set-up processing of the sort labeled as TR1 and TR2 above. This is because the modifiable links in the Indirect Mapping Model are gradually enabled in a simple, uniform way by the constraint-satisfaction search for a target/source mapping. However, it is still the case that just the right links have to be set up between the Hummel et al.'s "SP" nodes in the target analog and the object nodes and predicate nodes. This requires set-up processing of appreciable complexity, although probably not as complicated as in TR1 and TR2. Also, the Indirect Mapping Model is representationally impoverished, in deliberate ways discussed by Hummel et al., and it could well happen that an enriching of the representations would make the set-up processing much more complex again.

5.4.3. Exact Match and Variability of Implementation. I reiterate that there is no particular difficulty for standard connectionism, under certain assumptions, in dealing with the matching of identical structures. For instance, consider our first David and Peter example above, repeated here:

DAVID: *If John loves Susan, he'd better marry her.*
PETER: *John loves Susan.*

For the sake of argument, let us assume that the antecedent and consequent parts of the rule David utters are encoded as activation patterns, A and C, respectively, that are sitting on disjoint sets of units. Let us also assume that the pattern P constructed for Peter's statement is sitting on a third set of units (see Figure 8.2). Given that David's antecedent and Peter's statement are the same proposition, then there is a good chance that A and P are identical. They can then be matched

Figure 8.2.
Activation Patterns Residing on Separate Sets of Units in a Connectionist Network. The dotted boxes depict the unit sets.

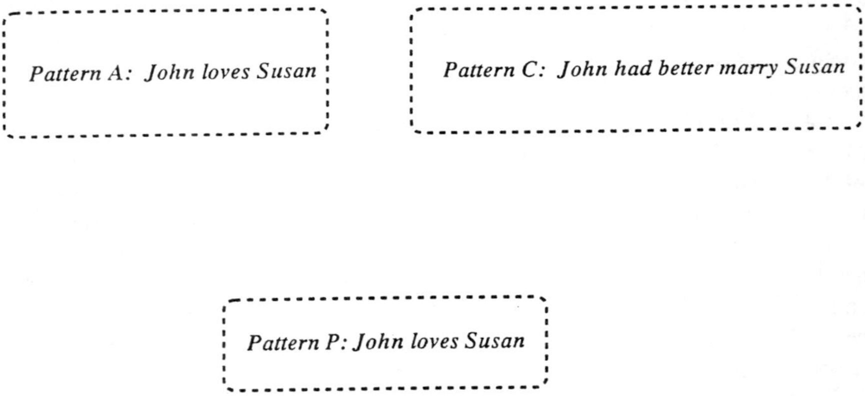

```
┌──────────────────────────────┐   ┌──────────────────────────────────────┐
│  Pattern A: John loves Susan │   │  Pattern C: John had better marry Susan │
└──────────────────────────────┘   └──────────────────────────────────────┘
```

```
        ┌──────────────────────────────┐
        │  Pattern P: John loves Susan │
        └──────────────────────────────┘
```

by simple connectionist circuitry. Note that this argument needed to make no assumption about the intrinsic nature of A and P or about how simple David's antecedent and Peter's statement are. In particular, A and P could be reduced representations of complex propositions.

I said that there is a "good chance" that patterns A and P are identical, and mentioned "certain assumptions." The reason for these caveats is the often-neglected *variability of implementation* issue. To explain this, it is helpful to digress briefly and consider how a proposition like *John loves Mary* might be implemented in a typical AI system. If Lisp is the programming language used, then the implementation is likely to be a linked list structure of the type schematically depicted in Figure 8.3. Each of the double boxes in the figure depicts a small *dynamically allocated* area in main memory. The arrows depict pointers, which are addresses of such areas. Crucially, on different occasions on which the proposition that John loves Mary is created, *different* areas are likely to be allocated, causing different pointers to be used. (The allocated areas may be in memory in a different order from before, or their relative spacing in memory may be different.) Therefore, the exact implementation of the proposition varies in important ways from occasion to occasion. A similar thing happens when associative addressing (see, e.g., Hwang & Briggs, 1984) is used in a computer in place of pointers (see Barnden, 1992, for details).

One must therefore ask whether connectionist encoding schemes can lead to the variability of implementation effect. In fact, they can. The connectionist representation schemes of Touretzky (1990) and of Barnden (1989, 1990, 1991a) are close enough to associative addressing in computers to suffer from a close analog of the variability of implementation in that method. In short, the

Figure 8.3.
Typical Linked-List Representation of Proposition *John loves Mary*. The boxes depict small areas (cells) at arbitrary positions within computer memory. The empty box compartment contains a null pointer. The three "representations" are themselves configurations of cells.

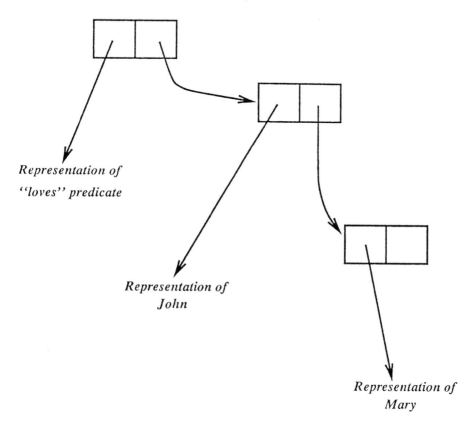

activation pattern implementing *John loves Mary* will differ widely from occasion to occasion. This precludes detecting the identity of propositions, let alone the similarity of nonidentical propositions, by any simple method for comparing the activation vectors to each other. The differences, in the Touretzky case, will be in the use of different "tags" as names of tuples. In the Barnden case, they will partly be the use of different "unassigned symbols" as names of the "clumps" in working memory.

On the other hand, reduced representation schemes, such as in Pollack (1990) and in my own system as described in the previous section, can avoid variability of implementation. For instance, the proposition *Susan hopes that David believes that John loves Mary* will get the same reduced representation on each occasion, because the representation is produced by a fixed way of mixing together the activation patterns for the component items—Susan, believing, etc.[23] (Reduced representations were not included in the Conposit systems described in Barnden, 1989, 1990, 1991a.)

The upshot is that even the matching of quite simple, identical propositions is likely to involve considerable complexity of processing if the representation scheme for the working-memory representations being matched exhibits the variability of implementation effect.

5.4.4. The Embedding Problem. Although we have just cast reduced representations in a favorable light, they face problems when embedding is brought into the picture. Consider the following variant of one of our earlier examples:

DAVID: *If John loves Susan, he'd better marry her.*
PETER: *Well, Cynthia thinks that John loves Susan.*

It is natural to infer the following: *If Cynthia's right, then John had better marry Susan.* We have a partial-match issue: David's antecedent matches only the embedded part of Peter's statement. The difficulty of a reduced-representation approach is therefore to ensure that the reduced representation of *John loves Susan* is sufficiently similar to the one for *Cynthia thinks that John loves Susan* for the system to be able to notice that a match exists. We must be a little more careful with this example, though. One scenario is for Cynthia to be taken by Peter or David to be a reliable witness, so that an inference occurs from Peter's statement to the bare statement that John loves Susan. This then does have an exact match with David's antecedent, as in a previous example. However, in a case where David or Peter is not sure whether Cynthia is reliable, this escape from the embedding issue is unavailable. The embedding cannot now just be thrown away.

Of course, the embedding problem could be solved by expanding the reduced representation of *Cynthia thinks that John loves Susan* to find reduced representations of its components. It could then be noticed that one of these components is the reduced representation of David's antecedent, *John loves Susan*. However, this strategy subverts a major motivation for using reduced representations in the first place, namely to achieve *holistic* processing, processing that avoids the traditional symbolic need to analyze structures continually during processing.

Plate (1991) does provide grounds for hoping that (certain types of) reduced representation allow a structure S to be partially matched, holistically, to a

---

[23] If the system is still in the process of learning its representations, as happens in some reduced representation approaches (Pollack, 1990), the representation may change significantly between occasions widely spaced in time. However, we are considering occurrences of the proposition encountered close together in time.

structure S' of which S is a part. More specifically, if S' is a superposition of reduced representations, including one for S, then a certain simple type of vector match between the S activation pattern and the S' activation pattern may be able to yield a high match value. However, there is no evidence to suggest that the technique can be scaled up to deal with multiple levels of embedding, as in:

DAVID: *If John loves Susan, he'd better marry her.*
PETER: *Tom says Cynthia thinks that John loves Susan.*

Nor is there any evidence to suggest that the technique can be scaled up to deal with cases where there is partialness on *both* sides of the match, as in:

DAVID: *If John loves Susan and has his head screwed on right, he'd better marry her.*
PETER: *Cynthia thinks that John loves Susan.*

A natural inference is that: *If John has his head screwed on right and Cynthia is right, then John had better marry Susan.*

Notice that in these more elaborate examples, we do not even need to consider the question of whether the system is able to arrive at the available conclusions. A more basic issue than that of forming a conclusion is the question of how the system is to notice in the first place that there is a partial match between David's statement and Peter's.

A consideration that we have suppressed throughout is the point that, in all our Peter/David examples, David's antecedent is embedded in a larger structure, namely the whole rule or conditional he states. We assumed earlier that the antecedent and consequent were implemented as separate activation patterns. At the time, that assumption may have looked innocent enough, but in the context of reduced representations we really have no business making it. The separation of David's statement into separate antecedent and consequent representations is already a partial subversion of reduced representations.

Finally, we should note that symbolic matching itself will be the more inefficient the more embedding that there is, because embedding may necessitate elaborate searching. However, what is at issue is whether a connectionist system can do the matching *at all* without resorting to implementational connectionism or subverting its own motivations (such as refraining from analyzing reduced representations).

5.4.5. Segmented Activation Patterns. One simple technique for achieving nonvariability of implementation (at least in simple cases), without using reduced representations, is to represent propositions as separated (segmented) activation patterns in the way suggested by Figure 8.4. There is no problem here with *identical* matching of either simple or complex propositions. However, partialness and embedding do cause problems again. For example, matching the

Figure 8.4.
Propositions Represented as Segmented Activation Patterns. The figure should not be taken literally in a spatial sense. The segments are just disjoint activation patterns over nonoverlapping sets of units in the overall network.

| LOVES | JOHN | MARY |

| THINKS | CYNTHIA | LOVES | JOHN | MARY |

pattern for *John loves Mary* to the pattern for *Cynthia thinks that John loves Mary* requires finding a segment of the latter pattern that matches the former. Bearing in mind the possibility of multiple embedding and of partialness on both sides of the match, we see that it is by no means trivial for a connectionist net to detect partial matches without undertaking a sequential search process of some sort. But the use of such a process would turn the whole WM/WM matching approach into an exercise in implementational connectionism. The representations being matched are themselves implementational connectionist in style, because of the rigid segmentation, so to avoid implementational connectionism we would want, presumably, something more flexible and sophisticated than a simple sequencing through the components of the propositions.

5.4.6. Constant/Constant Matches and Other Matters. In some examples above we saw that a WM/WM matching can involve placing unequal items in correspondence. This raises difficulties for a matching scheme based on measuring the similarity of the activation vectors encoding the items to be matched. Thus is so, irrespective of whether the vectors are segmented activation patterns or reduced representations. This subsection considers the difficulties, and then goes on to consider another approach to matching.

Consider the task of matching the connectionist encodings of the following two statements:

loves(Mary, Peter) $\Rightarrow$ grateful(Peter, Mary)
loves(John, Susan) $\Rightarrow$ grateful(Susan, John)

Assume that each is encoded as a vector (possibly a reduced representation). Observe that, in each statement, there are four occurrences of individual constants (**Mary, Peter, John, Susan**), but only three of other elements, namely the predicate symbols (**loves, grateful**) and the implication symbol. Hence, assuming that the vector encoding **Mary** alone is not very similar to the one encoding **John** alone, and similarly for **Peter** and **Susan**, it is reasonable to suppose that the vectors for the two statements will not be very similar. The dissimilarities between the statemetns are greater than the similarities.

Of course, if the statement vectors are segmented patterns, one could suggest suppressing any comparison of those segments corresponding to the constant occurrences. But, the resulting type of matching could not constitute the whole of the general WM/WM matching process, since the system would typically need to find out whether the correspondence between constituents of the matched structures are identities (as between **John** and **John**) or nonidentities (as between **John** and **Mary**). Therefore, with our current example, the suppression idea requires a further stage in which the segments for the constant occurrences are indeed compared. We are, again, on a slippery slope towards straightforward implementation of a symbolic matching alogrithm.

Another suggestion on the same lines would be to have predicates, connectives, etc., make a considerably greater contribution to a statement vector than constant occurrences do. However, we would again be in trouble with the requirement of finding out whether the component correspondences were identities or not. It would seem difficult to have, let's say, the degree of match (a single number) encode the information about which correspondences were identities and which were not. Also, the suggestion gets into trouble with the need to respect the degree of *consistency* in the match. In our example as it stands, both occurrences of **Mary** correspond to occurrences of **John,** and similarly for **Peter** and **Susan**. But consider now a less consistent variant, in which a match is attempted between the following two statements:

loves(Mary, Peter) ⇒ grateful(Peter, Mary)
loves(John, Susan) ⇒ grateful(Susan, David)

The match is now worse, since one occurrence of **Mary** must correspond to **David**. Yet there is no reason for the strength of match as found by a similarity measure between the two statement vectors to be any less than it was before. It could even be greater, if it just happened that the **Mary** and **David** vectors were more similar than the **Mary** and **John** vectors were. So, a further process is needed to examine consistency. It is often important, presumably, for the system to know about the degree of consistency.

Similar comments would apply to a suggestion that, contrary to our earlier suggestion, the two statement vectors in our (original, consistent) example would in fact be similar, given that the vectors for all people are rather similar to each other. (This could happen, for instance, if the vectors for **Mary, John,** etc., were themselves reduced representations constructed from complex descriptions of those people.) If the people vectors are similar enough for this purpose, they would be similar enough to make the inconsistent version of the example yield a degree of match comparable to that of the consistent version. Anyway, we would again have the problem of needing to discover whether the component correspondences were identities.

It is probable, therefore, that we need to look for a more complex matching process than mere computation of vector similarity. One immediate suggestion is to feed the two vectors to be matched through a standard feed-forward net, letting the hidden units combine information from the two input patterns (Figure 8.5). This would certainly work for cases of doing identical matching by detecting the identity of the two input vectors—it is easy to hand-design a feed-forward net to do the job.

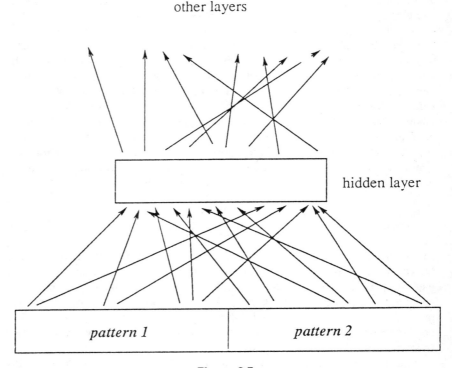

Figure 8.5.
How a Feed-Forward Network Might be Used for the Matching of Two Activation Patterns

However, it is by no means clear how to get the net to compute the degree of consistency of the match. Such computation involves not only comparing each vector to the other, but also, in a sense, comparing aspects of that very comparison with each other. For instance, in our example, consider the aspects of the overall comparison that embody the putting of the two **Mary** occurrences in correspondence with **John** occurrences. These aspects must be compared, in some sense, with each other, to establish that **Mary** is mapped to the same thing in each case.

The problem is actually much worse than is apparent from our example. Consider instead the problem of matching:

loves(Mary, Peter) ⇒ **grateful(Peter, Mary)**
loves(father-of(boss-of(John))), Susan) ⇒ **grateful (Susan, father-of(boss-of(David))).**

Here the consistency check must in some way get the effect of comparing the complex expressions **father-of(boss-of(John))** to **father-of(boss-of(David))** to detect the inconsistency, even though these are part of just one side of the original match. The indirect comparison of these two **father-of(...)** terms is itself a complex match.

It is worth noting that even though such a subsidiary match is between expressions from just one side, it cannot be properly dealt with just by processing that side. The lack of a complete match between the two **father-of(...)** terms would not matter if it were not for the fact that they are meant to correspond to two occurrences of **Mary** on the other side of the overall match. If, instead, the second of these occurrences had been **Cynthia**, the inconsistency we are considering would not have existed.

Finally, notice that although it can be desirable to establish constant/constant correspondence between one side of the match and the other, it will *not* usually be desirable to equate different constants on the same side of the match. In the example just displayed, we would presumably not want to equate John and David in order to get the two structures to match better overall. Thus, the requirements on within-same-side matching are different from those of the overall matching.

Barnden (1992) continues the discussion by considering what happens when one or both structures being matched contain variables. This arises from examples in which one or both analogs in a WM/WM matching task involve quantification.

Very recently, some interesting work on doing WM/WM matching by means of reduced representations has appeared (Stolcke & Wu, 1992). This work shows that tree structures encoded as reduced representations in the RAAM style of Pollack (1990) can be matched by a feed-forward net. Indeed, this can be done even without a hidden layer. The matching net is similar to the net sketched in Figure 8.5, but with the output layer replacing the shown hidden layer. The output is a reduced representation of the merge of the two input trees, themselves encoded as reduced representations (Patterns 1 and 2 in Figure 8.5). The trees of Stolcke and Wu may even contain variables. A variable in one tree can match a subtree of any sort in the other. Stolcke and Wu found good generalization properties in the matching net. However, we should note the current limitations of the work.

The trees are a huge abstraction away from the structures we might want to match. First, a leaf in a tree is restricted to being either 0 or 1. Each 0 leaf acts as a variable, and 1 plays the role of a nonvariable atomic symbol. Different occurrences of 0 act as different variables, so there is no matching-consistency issue at all—matching consistency being, of course, one of the important (though not universally required) aspects of our desired WM/WM matching. Secondly, good generalization has only so far been found when seeking a match of one whole tree to another whole tree, or of one whole tree to a predetermined internal node of another. Stolcke and Wu state that they have so far encountered poor generalization in the more ambitious task of trying to match a whole tree into a nonpredetermined place in the other tree. The work has also not addressed the possible presence of partialness on *both* sides of the match (i.e., when the match found does not encompass the whole of either tree). Thirdly, good generalization was reliably found only when the RAAM network (which transforms the reduced representations to and from fuller representations) was trained along with the matching net. That is, the strategy of training the matching net using a *fixed* reduced representation regime sometimes led to poor generalization. Finally, the net does not output the correspondences between matching items—it just outputs the merge of the two trees.

It is quite possible that the Stolcke and Wu work can be extended to overcome these limitations, especially as the extra benefits of adding a hidden layer to the matching net remain to be elucidated. I have pointed the limitations out only to emphasize the nature of the issues one faces in trying to use reduced representations for structure matching.

5.4.7 ABR-Conposit Again. The above qualifications of the promise of reduced representations with regard to WM/WM matching may appear to subvert the ABR-Conposit project described in Section 4. In reality, they do not, because the discussion has only cast doubt on an approach with a *whole-hearted* reliance on reduced representations. Such an approach rejects the idea of analyzing a reduced representation into its "parts" in order to get processing done, and rejects any resort to implementational connectionism. However, in my own approach I use reduced representations only insofar as they are clearly useful and I am quite happy to resort to implementational connectionism when necessary.

In particular, it should be observed that ABR-Conposit has relatively little trouble with the embedding problem of Section 5.4.4. When ABR-Conposit's working memory contains a complex proposition such as *Bill believes that John loves Mary,* it contains not only the reduced representation for it (Y in Figure 8.1) but also the full representation (everything else in Figure 8.1). One consequence is that the full representation for *John loves Mary* is present as a part of the whole; and this means that the *reduced* representation X for *John loves Mary* is also present. Therefore, it is easy to detect the partial match between *Bill believes that John loves Mary* and, say, *if John loves Mary then he'd better marry her*, by noting the presence of activation vector X (to within the small random variations mentioned above) inside the representation of each of these two propositions.

6. CONCLUSION

I have pursued two distinct but related themes. To take the second one first, I have claimed that demanding types of WM/WM matching (i.e., matching between items in working memory that need not have come from long-term memory) are required in human-like cognition, but that it presents something of a challenge to nonimplementational connectionism. The need for it was argued through examples from natural-language discourse understanding, but arises in other types of cognition also. For instance, if a truck swoops dangerously in front of your car at one moment and a bicycle fails to stop at an intersection you are crossing a couple of moments later, you are likely to notice the analogy between these alarming situations.

WM/WM matching is currently not well catered for by connectionism unless it resorts, at least in part, to an implementation of: (a) conventional symbolic structure-matching, or (b) other elaborate symbolic processes. (I mention (b) to allow for the possibility of implementing an ACME-style system in a fully connectionist system. We saw that an elaborate process was needed to set up the match-hypothesis net.) At present, it seems that the most promising avenue by which (a) and (b) might be avoided is to encode the working-memory structures as reduced representation schemes (Stolcke & Wu, 1992), and such schemes are in a position to avoid the problem of variability of instantiation (the problem of the very same abstract structure having different concrete implementations on different occasions). Nevertheless, important problems remain, including the following.

1. dealing with embedding on both sides of the match (i.e., the structures matched might only match on a substructure of each);
2. dealing with mappings between nonidentical items that are not variables;
3. noticing match inconsistencies (i.e., non-one-to-one correspondences for some items);
4. and outputing the discovered correspondences, as opposed to merely reporting match success or producing a merged structure.

Notice, incidentally, that 1–3 take us considerably beyond what ordinary logical unification achieves. The unification of two logical expressions finds a match between the *whole* of both structures, only allows nonidentical atomic items to match when at least one of them is a variable, and disallows match inconsistencies. (In analogy, we may need to *notice* inconsistencies, but as I noted in Section 3 they are useful in some situations.)

The first main theme pursued in this chapter was the use of *implementational connectionism as applied to analogy-based reasoning* as a novel way of combining the benefits of connectionism and traditional symbolic AI. Analogy-based reasoning, when implemented in a traditional symbolic way, gives us many advantages often claimed by connectionists. These advantages include types of flexibility and robustness, simple approaches to learning, and the ability to give rise to emergent rules and exceptions. Nevertheless, the precise versions of the advantages differ, and for each individual advantage it is not yet clear which side has the better version, or whether we need both versions. Also, there are potential benefits that connectionism can offer that are not obtained through analogy-based reasoning under a traditional symbolic implementation. These include the use of parallel spreading activation for long-term memory retrieval, the use of reduced representations as structure-sensitive indices in such retrieval, and the usefulness of reduced representations in helping quick structure matching within working memory.

REFERENCES

Ballard, D.H. (1986). Parallel logical inference and energy minimization. *Proceedings of the 5th National Conference on Artificial Intelligence (AAAI-86)*, 411–415. Philadelphia.

Barnden, J.A. (1984). On short-term information processing in connectionist theories. *Cognition and Brain Theory*, 7(1), 25–59.

Barnden, J.A. (1988a). The right of free association: Relative-position encoding for connectionist data structures. *Proceedings of the 10th Annual Conference of the Cognitive Science Society* (pp. 503–509). Hillsdale, NJ: Erlbaum.

Barnden, J.A. (1988b). Conposit, a neural net system for high-level symbolic processing: Overview of research and description of register-machine level. *Memoranda in Computer and Cognitive Science* (No. MCCS-88-145). Las Cruces, NM: Computing Research Laboratory, New Mexico State University.

Barnden, J.A. (1989). Neural-net implementation of complex symbol-processing in a mental model approach to syllogistic reasoning. *Proceedings of the 11th International Joint Conference on Artificial Intelligence* (pp. 568–573). San Mateo, CA: Morgan Kaufmann.

Barnden, J.A. (1990). Syllogistic mental models: Exercising some connectionist representation and control methods. *Memoranda in Computer and Cognitive Science* (No. MCCS-90-204). Las Cruces, NM: Computing Research Laboratory, New Mexico State University.

Barnden, J.A. (1991a). Encoding complex symbolic data structures with some unusual connectionist techniques. In J.A. Barnden & J.B. Pollack (Eds), *Advances in connectionist and neural computation theory,* Vol. 1: *High-level connectionist models* (pp. 180–240). Norwood, NJ: Ablex.

Barnden, J.A. (1992). Connectionism, structure-sensitivity, and systematicity: Refining the task requirements. *Memoranda in Computer and Cognitive Science* (No. MCCS-92-227). Las Cruces, NM: Computing Research Laboratory, New Mexico State University.

Barnden, J.A. (1993). On using analogy to reconcile connections and symbols. In D.S. Levine & M. Aparicio (Eds.), *Neural networks for knowledge representation and inference.* (pp. 27–64) Hillsdale, NJ: Erlbaum.

Barnden, J.A., & Srinivas, K. (1991). Encoding techniques for complex information structures in connectionist systems. *Connection Science, 3*(3), 263–309.

Barnden, J.A., & Srinivas, K. (1992). Overcoming rule-based rigidity and connectionist limitations through massively-parallel case-based reasoning. *International Journal of Man-Machine Studies, 36,* 221–246.

Barnden, J.A., & Srinivas, K. (1993). Temporal winner-take-all networks: A time-based mechanism for fast selection in neural networks. *IEEE Transactions on Neural Networks, 4*(5), 844–853.

Barnden, J.A., Srinivas, K., & Dharmavaratha, D. (1990). Winner-take-all networks: Time-based versus activation-based mechanisms for various selection goals. *Proceedings of the IEEE International Symposium on Circuits and Systems* (pp. 215–218), New Orleans.

Carbonell, J.G., & Brown, R.D. (1988). Anaphora resolution: A multi-strategy approach. *Proceedings of the 12th International Conference on Computational Linguistics (COLING-88)* (pp. 96–101), Budapest.

Cook, D.J. (1991). The base selection task in analogical planning. *Proceedings of the Twelfth International Joint Conference on Artificial Intelligence* (pp. 790–794). San Mateo, CA: Morgan Kaufmann.

Domeshek, E. (1989). Parallelism for index generation and reminding. *Proceedings of the Case-Based Reasoning Workshop* (pp. 244–247). San Mateo, CA: Morgan Kaufmann.

Falkenhainer, B. (1990). Analogical interpretation in context. *Proceedings of the Twelfth Annual Conference of the Cognitive Science Society* (pp. 69–76). Hillsdale, NJ: Erlbaum.

Falkenhainer, B., Forbus, K.D., & Gentner, D. (1989). The structure-mapping engine: Algorithm and examples. *Artificial Intelligence, 41*(1), 1–63.

Feldman, J.A. (1982). Dynamic connections in neural networks. *Biological Cybernetics, 46,* 27–39.

Forgy, C.L. (1982). Rete: A fast algorithm for the many pattern/many object pattern match problem. *Artificial Intelligence, 19*(1), 17–37.

Gasser, M., & Smith, L.B. (1991). The development of the notion of sameness: A connectionist model. *Proceedings of the 13th Annual Conference of the Cognitive Science Society* (pp. 719–723). Hillsdale, NJ: Erlbaum.

Gentner, D. (1983). Structure-mapping: A theoretical framework for analogy. *Cognitive Science, 7*(2), 95–119.

Gentner, D. (1989). The mechanisms of analogical reasoning. In S. Vosniadou & A. Ortony (Eds.), *Similarity and analogical reasoning* (pp. 199–241). Cambridge, UK: Cambridge University Press.

Goddard, G.V. (1980). Component properties of the memory machine: Hebb revisited. In P.W. Jusczyk & R.M. Klein (Eds.), *The nature of thought: Essays in honor of D. O. Hebb*. Hillsdale, NJ: Erlbaum.

Goldstone, R., & Medin, D. (1994). Similarity, interactive activation, and mapping: An overview. In K.J. Holyoak & J.A. Barnden (Eds.), *Advances in connectionist and neural computation theory* (Vol. 2). Norwood, NJ: Ablex.

Hall, R.P. (1989). Computational approaches to analogical reasoning. *Artificial Intelligence, 39*, 39–120.

Hinton, G.E. (1988). Representing part-whole hierarchies in connectionist networks. *Proceedings of the 10th Annual Conference of the Cognitive Science Society* (pp. 48–54). Hillsdale, NJ: Erlbaum.

Hinton, G.E. (1990). Mapping part-whole hierarchies into connectionist networks. *Artificial Intelligence, 46*(1–2), 47–75.

Hobbs, J.R. (1985). *On the coherence and structure of discourse* (Report No. CSLI-85-37). Stanford, CA: Center for the Study of Language and Information, Stanford University.

Hölldobler, S. (1990). *CHCL, a connectionist inference system for Horn logic based on connection method and using limited resources* (Tech. Rep. No. 90-042). Berkeley, CA: International Computer Science Institute.

Holyoak, K.J. (1991). Symbolic connectionism: Towards third-generation theories of expertise. In K.A. Ericsson & J. Smith (Eds.), *Toward a general theory of expertise* (pp. 301–335). Cambridge, UK: Cambridge University Press.

Holyoak, K.J., Novick, L.R., & Melz, E.R. (1994). Component processes in analogical transfer: Mapping, pattern completion, and adaptation. In K.J. Holyoak & J.A. Barnden (Eds.), *Advances in connectionist and neural computation theory* (Vol. 2, pp. 113–180). Norwood, NJ: Ablex.

Holyoak, K.J., & Thagard, P. (1989). Analogical mapping by constraint satisfaction. *Cognitive Science, 13*(3), 295–355.

Hummel, J.E., Burns, B., & Holyoak, K.J. (1994). Analogical mapping by dynamic binding: Preliminary investigations. In K.J. Holyoak & J.A. Barnden (Eds.), *Advances in connectionist and neural computation theory* (Vol. 2) (pp. 416–445). Norwood, NJ: Ablex.

Hwang, K., & Briggs, F.A. (1984). *Computer architecture and parallel processing*. New York: McGraw-Hill.

Johnson-Laird, P.N. (1983). *Mental models: Towards a cognitive science of language, inference and consciousness*. Cambridge, MA: Harvard University Press.

Kolodner, J.L. (1983a). Maintaining organization in a dynamic long-term memory. *Cognitive Science, 7*, 243–280.

Kolodner, J.L. (1983b). Reconstructive memory: A computer model. *Cognitive Science, 7*, 281–328.

Kolodner, J.L., & Simpson, R.L. (1989). The MEDIATOR: Analysis of an early case-based problem solver. *Cognitive Science, 13*(4), 507–549.

Lange, T.E., & Dyer, M.G. (1989). High-level inferencing in a connectionist network. *Connection Science, 1*(2), 181–217.

Lehnert, W.G. (1991). Symbolic/subsymbolic sentence analysis: Exploiting the best of two worlds. In J.A. Barnden & J.B. Pollack (Eds.), *Advances in connectionist and neural computation theory* (Vol. 1, pp. 135–164). Norwood, NJ: Ablex.

McClelland, J.L. (1985). Putting knowledge in its place: A scheme for programming parallel processing structures on the fly. *Cognitive Science, 9*(1), 113–146.
McClelland, J.L. (1986). The programmable blackboard model of reading. In J.L. McClelland, D.E. Rumelhart, & the PDP Research Group (Eds.), *Parallel distributed processing* (Vol. 2). Cambridge, MA: MIT Press.
Murdock, B.B., Jr. (1983). A distributed memory model for serial order information. *Psychological Review, 90,* 316–338.
Nelson, G., Thagard, P., & Hardy, S. (1994). Integrating analogy with rules and explanations. In K.J. Holyoak & J.A. Barnden (Eds.), *Advances in connectionist and neural computation theory* (Vol. 2, pp. 181–206). Norwood, NJ: Ablex.
Pinkas, G. (1992). Constructing proofs in symmetric networks. In J.E. Moody, S.J. Hanson, & R.P. Lippmann (Eds.), *Advances in neural information processing systems* (pp. 217–224). San Mateo, CA: Morgan Kaufmann.
Pinker, S., & Prince, A. (1988). On language and connectionism: Analysis of a parallel distributed processing model of language acquisition. In S. Pinker & J. Mehler (Eds.), *Connections and symbols*. Cambridge, MA: MIT Press, and Amsterdam: Elsevier. [Reprinted from *Cognition, 28,* 1988.]
Plate, T. (1991). *Holographic reduced representation* (Tech. Rep. No. CRG-TR-91-1). Toronto: Dept. of Computer Science, University of Toronto, Canada.
Pollack, J.B. (1987). Cascaded back-propagation on dynamic connectionist networks. *Proceedings of the 9th Annual Conference of the Cognitive Science Society* Hillsdale, NJ: Erlbaum.
Pollack, J.B. (1990). Recursive distributed representations. *Artificial Intelligence, 46*(1–2), 77–105.
Rumelhart, D.E., Hinton, G., & Williams, R. (1986). Learning internal representations by error propagation. In D.E. Rumelhart, J.L. McClelland, & the PDP Research Group (Eds.), *Parallel distributed processing* (Vol. 1, pp. 318–364). Cambridge, MA: MIT Press.
Rumelhart, D.E., & McClelland, J.L. (1986). On learning the past tenses of English verbs. In J.L. McClelland, D.E. Rumelhart, & the PDP Research Group (Eds.), *Parallel distributed processing, Vol. 2*. Cambridge, MA: MIT Press.
Shastri, L., & Ajjanagadde, V. (1989). *A connectionist system for rule-based reasoning with multiplace predicates and variables* (Tech. Rep. No. MS-CIS-8905). Philadelphia: Computer and Information Science Dept., University of Pennsylvania.
Smolensky, P. (1988a). The constituent structure of connectionist mental states: A reply to Fodor and Pylyshyn. In T. Horgan & J. Tienson (Eds.), *Connectionism and the philosophy of mind*. Memphis, TN: Dept. of Philosophy, Memphis State University. [Supplement to Vol. XXVI of *The Southern J. of Philosophy.*]
Smolensky, P. (1988b). On the proper treatment of connectionism. *Behavioral and Brain Sciences, 11,* 1–74.
Smolensky, P. (1990). Tensor product variable binding and the representation of symbolic structures in connectionist systems. *Artificial Intelligence, 46*(1–2), 159–216.
Standish, T.A. (1980). *Data structure techniques*. Reading, MA: Addison-Wesley.
Stolcke, A., & Wu, D. (1992). Tree matching with recursive distributed representations (Tech. Rep. No. 92-025). Berkeley, CA: Computer Science Division, University of California.
Sumida, R.A., & Dyer, M.G. (1989). Storing and generalizing multiple instances while

maintaining knowledge-level parallelism. *Proceedings of the Eleventh International Joint Conference on Artificial Intelligence.* San Mateo, CA: Morgan Kaufmann.

Sun, R. (1991). Connectionist models of rule-based reasoning. In *Proceedings of the 13th Annual Conference of the Cognitive Science Society* (pp. 437–442). Hillsdale, NJ: Lawrence Erlbaum.

Touretzky, D.S. (1990). BoltzCONS: Dynamic control structures in a connectionist network. *Artificial Intelligence, 46*(1–2), 5–46.

von der Malsburg, C., & Bienenstock, E. (1987). A neural network for the retrieval of superimposed connection patterns. *Europhysics Letters, 3*(11), 1243–1249.

Author Index

A

Aarts, J.M.G., 272, *280*
Abelson, R., 31, 33, 34, 40, 42, 48, 85, *93*, 99, 100, 102, 103, *125*, 140, 149, *168*
Adelson, B., 97, *122*
Agre, P., 139, *166*
Aizawa, K., 15n, *24*
Ajjanagadde, V., 45, 54, 87, *90, 93*, 329n, 343, 346n, *373*
Alba, J.W., 111, *121*
Allen, S.W., 105, *121*
Ambs, P., 136n, *167*
Anderson, J.R., 45, *90*, 105, *124*, 262, *280*
Aragones, J.K., 173, 183, *199*
Ashley, K., 111, *124*, 135, *166*, 169, 196, *199*
Auster, P., *256*
Ayub, S., 183, 198, *199*

B

Bain, W.M., 110, *121*
Ballard, D.H., 5, *25*, 159, *167, 280*, 350, *370*
Bareiss, R., 111, *121*
Barnden, J.A., 2, 3, 11n, 13n, 14, 15, *25*, 45, 80, *90*, 329n, 332n, 334n, 337, 339, 343, 344, 346, 346n, 347, 347n, 349, 360, 362, 367, *370, 371*
Barsalou, L.W., 259, *280*
Basu, C., 197, *201*
Bates, E.A., 286, 287, *323*
Becker, L.A., 196, *199*
Belyaev, L., 75, *92*
Bienenstock, E., 350, *374*
Black, J.B., 100, *125*
Black, M., 259, *280*
Blank, D.S., 11, *25*
Blau, L., 183, 198, *199*
Bloomfield, L., 282, 285, 287, *323*

Bonissone, P.P., 169, 173, 183, 186, 190, 197, 198, *199, 200*
Boyes-Braem, P., 263, *280*
Brachman, R., 175, *200*
Brand, M., 134, *168*
Branting, L.K., 197, *200*
Braverman, M.S., 197, *200*
Briggs, F.A., 335, 346n, 360, *372*
Brooks, L.R., 105, *121*
Brown, R.D., 355, *371*
Brugman, C., 289, 290, 292, 303, *323*
Burke, R., 134, 134n, *166, 168*
Burr, D.J., 114, *122*
Burstein, M., 97, *121, 122*, 282, 283, 289, 300, 301, *323*

C

Calbert, J.P., 272, *280*
Carbonell, J.G., 10, *25*, 105, *122*, 149, *166*, 197, *200, 202*, 355, *371*
Carroll, P.J., 260, *280*
Cesa, I.L., 32, *92*
Chalmers, D.J., 11, *25*
Chandler, S.R., 2, *25*
Chandrasekaran, B., 110, *122*
Chapman, D., 139, *166*
Charniak, E., 41, *90*, 177, 192, *200*
Chomsky, N., 283, 285, 288, 289, *323*
Clement, C., 282, 283, *323, 324*
Cohen, P.R., 179, *200*
Collins, A., 282, 283, 289, 300, 301, *323*
Cook, D.J., 330, *371*
Coolidge, D., *256*
Corman, T.H., 171, *200*
Corter, J.E., 263, *280*
Cottrell, G., 43, 66, *90*, 265, *280*, 311, *323*
Crain, S., 288, *323*

AUTHOR INDEX

D

Daniels, J.J., 197, *201*
Davidson, D., 254, *256*
Deane, P.D., 284, *323, 324*
Dejong, G., 194, *201*, 282, 287, 320, 321, 322, *324*
Dharmavaratha, D., 347n, *371*
Dieterich, J., 276, *280*
Dineen, F., 285, *324*
Dinsmore, J., 2, 15, *25*
Dolan, C.P., 43, *91*
Domeshek, E., 134, 139, 144n, *166, 168*, 328, *371*
Downing, P.E., 32, *93, 94*
Dubois, D., 190, *200*
Duncker, K., 320, *324*
Dutta, S., 169, 197, 198, *199, 200*
Dyer, M.G., 10, *26*, 33, 34, 35, 36, 38, 40, 42, 45, 47, 48, 50, 51, 68, 86, *91, 92*, 100, *122, 125*, 162, *167*, 320, 329n, 343, 346n, *372, 373*

E

Edelson, D., 134, *168*
Eiselt, K.P., 41, *91*
Elman, J., 311, *324, 325*
Esener, S., 136n, *167*
Esper, E.A., 282, 283, 284, 286n, *324*

F

Fahlman, E.E., 194, *200*
Falkenhainer, B., 31, 32, *91*, 105, *122*, 337, *371*
Fanty, J.A., 195, *200*
Faries, J.M., 99, 105, *124*
Fehling, D., 284, *324*
Feldman, J.A., 5, *25*, 159, *167*, 195, *200*, *280*, 359, *371*
Ferguson, W., 134, *168*
Fillmore, C.J., 286, 287, 302, *324*
Fodor, J.A., 11, 13n, 14, *25*
Forbus, K.D., 31, 32, 47, 75, 84, *91*, 105, *122*, 337, *371*
Forgy, C.L., 353n, *371*
Freed, M., 134, *168*
Fuenmayor, M., 75, *92*

G

Gasser, M., 349, 351n, 352, *371*
Gentner, D., 10, *25*, 31, 32, 47, 75, 84, *91, 92*, 99, 104, 105, 106, 107, 108, 116, *122, 124*, 282, 283, 287, 289, 300, 301, 304, 321, 322, *323, 324*, 336, 337, *371*

Gibbs, R.W., 99, *122*, 208, 214, *256*
Gick, M.L., 10, *25*, 31, 32, *91*, 98, 105, *122*
Gildea, P., 259, 260, *280*
Givon, T., 286, 287, *324*
Gluck, M.A., 263, *280*
Glucksberg, S., 41, *91*, 259, 260, *280*
Gochfeld, D., 47, 75, 84, *93*, 113, 114, *125*
Goddard, G.V., 350, *372*
Goddard, N.H., 195, *200*, 274, *280*
Goel, A.K., 197, *200*
Goldstone, R., 350, *372*
Granger, R.H., 39, *91*
Gray, K.C., 105, 106, 107, *122*
Gray, W.D., 263, *280*
Grice, P., 254, *256*
Grimshaw, J., 319, *324*

H

Hall, R.P., 10, *25*, 105, *122*, 329, *372*
Hammond, K., 31, 46, *91*, 96, 105, 106, 107, 110, 111, *122*, 126, 134, 139, 140, *167*, 197, *200*
Hanson, S.J., 114, *122*
Hardy, S., 328, 350, *373*
Harris, C.L., 283, 286, 289, 292, 293, 301, 311, 317, 320, *324*
Hasher, L., 111, *121*
Hawkins, B., 289, *325*
Helmholtz, H.L.F. von, 4, 7, *25*
Hendler, J., 41n, *91*, 175, 177, 179, *200*
Hennessy, D., 169, *200*
Herskovitz, A., 289, *325*
Hinkle, D., 169, *200*
Hinton, G.E., 2, 5, 6, 7, 10, 13, 13n, 15, *25, 26*, 42, 43, 58, *93*, 127, 151, *167*, 171, *200*, 283, 294, 311, *325*, 330, 351n, *372, 373*
Hobbs, J.R., 352, *372*
Hockett, C.F., 283, *325*
Hodges, J., 75, *92*
Hofstadter, D., 46, *91*
Holbrook, J.K., 41, *91*
Holland, J., 121, *122*
Hölldobler, S., 45, *91*, 350, *372*
Holyoak, K.J., 7, 8, 9, 10, *25, 26*, 31, 32, 47, 75, 84, 86, *91, 92, 93, 94*, 96, 98, 105, 113, 114, 121, *122, 123, 125*, 192, 196, *201, 202*, 282, 321, *325*, 331, 333, 335, 337, 339n, 341, 350, 354, 356, 357, *372*
Householder, F., 287, *325*
Hunter, L., 111, *123*

Hurwitz, N., 197, *200*
Hwang, K., 335, 346n, 360, *372*

I

Indurkhya, B., 3, *26*
Inhoff, A.W., 260, *280*

J

Jackendoff, R.S., 319, *325*
Jacobs, P.S., 172, 177, 180, *201*
Jacoby, L.L., 111, *123*
Johnson, D.M., 263, *280*
Johnson, H.M., 108, 121, *123*
Johnson, M., 3, *26*, 209, 234, 255, *256*, 303, *325*
Johnson-Laird, P.N., 282, 322, *325*, 344, 350, *372*
Jona, M., 134, *168*
Jones, E., 148, *167*
Jordan, M., 158, *167*

K

Kass, A., 111, *123*
Kawamoto, A.H., 42, *92*
Kay, P., 286, *324*
Keane, M., *91*
Kedar-Cabelli, S., 121, *123*
Keil, F.C., 264, *280*
Kintsch, W., 30, 33, 39, 41, 41n, 43, 45, *91, 93*
Kittay, E., 269, 273, *280*
Kjeldsen, R., 179, *200*
Koh, K., 32, *91*, 98, 104, *122*
Kohonen, T., 46, *91*, 159, *167*
Kolodner, J., 31, 33, *91, 92*, 97, 110, 111, *123*, 126, 135, 163, 165, *167*, 192, *201*, 334, 336, *372*
Koton, P., 169, 197, *201*
Kövecses, Z., 234, *256*
Kreuz, R.J., 39, *91*
Krishnamoorthy, A., 136n, *167*
Krulwich, B., 134, *168*
Kruschke, J.K., 112, 114, *123*
Kuno, S., 286, *325*

L

Lakoff, G., 3, *26*, 205, 206, 208, 209, 214, 234, 237, 239, 242, 243, 244, 255, 256, *256*, 259, *280*, 284, 292, 303, *323, 325*
Landers, R., 31, 32, *91*, 99, 104, 105, 106, 107, 108, 116, *122*, 322, *324*
Langacker, R.W., 284, 286, 287, 288, 302, *325*

Lange, T., 32, 34, 35, 36, 38, 41, 43, 45, 47, 48, 50, 51, 58, 60, 68, 75, 80, 86, *92, 93, 94*, 329n, 346n, *372*
Leake, D.B., 31, *93*, 111, *123*
Lebiere, C., 194, *200*
Lebowitz, 33, 40, *92*
Lehnert, W.G., 100, *123*, 139, *167*, 350, *372*
Leiserson, C.E., 171, *200*
Levin, L., 41, 41n, *91*
Levinson, R., 177, *201*
Lima, S.D., 260, *280*
Lynne, K.J., 195, *200*, 274, *280*
Lytinen, S., 38, 40, 48, *92*

M

MacWhinney, B., 286, 287, 311, *323, 325*
Maier, N.R.F., 4, *26*
Malt, B.C., 263, *280*
Marchand, P., 136n, *167*
Marchman, V., 285, *326*
Marr, D., 7, *26*
Marshall, J.B., 11, *25*
Martin, C.E., 41, *93*
Martin, J.H., 259, *280*
Masson, J., 235, 236, *256*
McCarthy, J., 197, *201*
McClelland, J.L., 5, 6, *26*, 42, *92, 93*, 96, 112, *123, 124*, 162, *167*, 171, *200, 201*, 283, 319, *325*, 334, 350, *372, 373*
McDermott, D., 163, *167*, 192, *200*
McGarry, S.J., 32, *91*
McKoon, G., 31, 34, 85, *93*, 99, 100, 102, 103, *123, 125*
Medin, D., 270, *281*, 340, *372*
Meeden, L.A., 11, *25*
Melz, E., 86, *92*, 196, *201*, 331, 335, 337, 341, 350, 356, 357, *372*
Mervis, C.B., 263, *280*
Merwin, W.S., 235, 236, 239, *256*
Meyer, D.E., 99, 101, *123*
Miikkulainen, R., 42, 46, *92*, 162, *167*
Mintz, T., 274, *280*
Mitchell, M., 46, *91*
Mooney, R., 194, *201*
Mozer, M.C., 112, 114, 117, 119, 120, *123*
Mross, E.F., 39, *93*
Murdock, B.B., Jr., 320, *373*

N

Nelson, G., 47, 75, 84, *93*, 113, 114, *125*, 328, 350, *373*
Nisbett, R., 121, *122*
Norman, G., 105, *121*

AUTHOR INDEX

Novick, L.R., 196, *201*, 331n, 335n, 337, 341, 350, 356, 357, *372*
Norvig, P., 33, 41, *92*, 175, 179, *201*

O

O'Connor, M.C., 286, *324*
Ohmaye, E., 134, *168*
Ortony, A., 206, 207, 242, 244, 254, *256*, 283, 287, 300, *326*
Osgood, R., 134, *168*
Oskamp, A., 169, 197, *201*
Owens, C., 31, *92*, 111, 112, *123*, 134n, 137, *167*

P

Palmer, S.E., 321, *325*
Pazzani, M.J., 120, 121, *123*, *124*
Pinkas, G., 350, *373*
Pinker, S., 319, *325*, 329n, *373*
Pirolli, P.L., 105, *124*
Plate, T., 10, *26*, 320, 362, *373*
Plunkett, K., 285, *326*
Poggio, T., 7, *26*
Pollack, J.B., 2, 3, 10, 11, 13n, 14, 15, *25*, 33, 43, 44, 60, *93*, 194, *201*, 320, 350, 361, 362n, 367, *373*
Prade, J., 190, *200*
Prince, A., 329n, *373*
Pryor, L., 134, *168*
Pylyshyn, Z.W., 11, 13n, 14, *25*

R

Rabelais, F., *256*
Ram, A., 111, *124*
Ratcliff, R., 31, 34, 85, *93*, 99, 100, 102, 103, *123*, *125*
Ratterman, M.J., 31, *92*, 99, 104, 105, 106, 107, 116, *124*
Rau, L.F., 172, 177, 180, *201*
Read, S.J., 32, *92*
Reeves, J.F., 40, *92*
Reiser, B.J., 99, 105, *124*
Rho, S.H., 39, *91*
Richards, G., 3, *26*
Richards, I.A., 259, *280*
Riesbeck, C.K., 41, 46, *92*, *93*, 96, 97, *124*, 197, *200*, *201*
Rips, L., 300, *326*
Rissland, E., 11, *124*, 135, *166*, 169, 197, *201*
Rivest, R.L., 171, *200*
Roberts, M., *256*
Rosch, E., 263, *280*

Rosenberg, C., 162, *168*
Rosenbloom, P., 197, *200*
Ross, B.H., 32, *93*, 99, 105, 116, *124*
Rubinstein, Z.B., 197, *201*
Ruhl, C., *326*
Rumelhart, D.E., 5, 6, *26*, 42, *93*, 95, 96, 112, 113, 114, 115, 116, *123*, *124*, *125*, 162, *167*, 171, *200*, *201*, 283, 319, *325*, 334, 351n, *373*

S

Saussure, F., 285, *326*
Schank, R.C., 29, 31, 33, 40, 42, 46, 47, 48, 87, *93*, 96, 97, 98, 99, 100, 102, 103, 109, 110, 112, *124*, 129, 134, 140, 149, *169*, *168*, 197, *201*
Schmolze, J., 175, *200*
Schrickx, J.A., 169, 197, *201*
Schvaneveldt, R.W., 99, 101, *123*
Siefert, C.M., 31, 34, 85, *93*, 97, 99, 100, 102, 103, 105, 106, 107, 108, 110, 113, 116, 121, *122*, *123*, *124*, *125*, 137, 148, *168*, 196, *201*
Sejnowski, T., 162, *168*
Shallice, T., 311, *325*
Shastri, L., 15n, *26*, 45, 54, *93*, 263, *281*, 329n, 343, 346n, *373*
Siewierska, A., 286, *326*
Simpson, R., 32, *92*, 111, *123*, 126, *167*, 336, *372*
Skalak, D.B., 169, 197, *201*
Sloman, S.A., 113, *125*
Small, S., 43, 66, *90*
Smith, E.E., 263, 270, *280*, *281*
Smith, L.B., 349, 351n, 352, *371*
Smolensky, P., 5, 6, *26*, 43, *91*, 112, 114, 117, 119, 120, *123*, 283, *326*, 329n, 333, 334, 343, *373*
Spellman, B.A., 8, 9, *26*
Spencer, R.M., *93*
Srinivas, K., 11n, 13n, 14, 15, *25*, 80, *90*, 332n, 344, 345, 346, 346n, 347, 347n, 349, *371*
Standish, T.A., 335, *373*
Stanfill, C., 195, *201*
Steinthal, H., 282, *326*
Stillman, J., 173, 183, *199*
St. John, M., 42, *93*
Stolcke, A., 11, *26*, 332n, 350, 351n, 367, 369, *373*
Subramanian, D., 139, *168*

Sun, R., 45, 54, *93*, 328, *373*
Sumida, R.A., 10, *26*, 320, *373*
Sweetser, E.E., 3, *27*, 208, *257*
Swinney, D.A., 39, 45, *93*
Sycara, K., 31, *92*
Sycara-Cyranski, K., 126, *167*

T

Tabossi, P., 260, *281*
Talmy, L., 284, 290, 302, *326*
Thagard, P., 7, *26*, 47, 75, 84, *93*, 96, 105, 113, 114, 121, *122, 123, 125*, 192, 196, *202*, 282, *325*, 328, 335, 339n, 350, 354, *372, 373*
Thrift, P., 196, *202*
Till, R.E., 39, *93*
Tomabechi, H., 41, 41n, *91*
Touretzky, D., 43, 58, *93*, 329n, 335n, 343, 360, *374*
Tsung, F., 311, *323*
Turner, M., 205, 206, 208, 234, 237, 238, 239, 241, 242, 243, 244, 255, 256, *256, 257*
Tversky, A., 95, 112, *125*, 155, 156, *168*

V

Vandenberg, P.H., 169, 197, *201*
van Gelder, T., 3, *27*
Veloso, M., 197, *200, 202*
von der Malsberg, C., 350, *374*
Vosniadou, S., 283, 287, 300, *326*

W

Walker, R.F., 169, 197, *201*
Waltz, D., 33, 43, 44, 60, *93*, 195, *201, 202*
Weber, S.H., 260, 262, 263, 268, *281*
Weisberg, R.W., *93*
Wharton, C., 32, 86, *92, 93, 94*
Wheeler, B.I., 284, *326*
Whorf, B.L., 302, *326*
Wickens, T.D., 32, *93, 94*
Wilensky, R., 40, *94*, 142, 168, 175, 197, *200, 202*
Williams, R., 351n, *373*
Woodfill, J., 139, *168*
Wu, D., 11, *26*, 332n, 350, 351n, 367, 369, *373*

Z

Zadeh, L., 185, *202*

Subject Index

A

Abby, Ch. 3
ABR, *see* Reasoning
ABR-Conposit, 23, 24, 344–350, 368–369
Abstraction, 16, 20–23, 32, 34, 102, 106, 107, 116, 117, Ch. 4, Ch. 5, 260, 264, 266, 273, Ch. 7, 369
Access, content-based, 333, 335
ACME (Analogical Constraint Mapping Engine), 5, 7, 8, 10, 11, 17, 20, 350, 368, 369
ACT, 45
Activation, 7, 10, 11, 12, 14–16, 20–22, Ch. 1, 96, 99, 102, 103, 112, Ch. 4, 205, 256, 262, 265, 267, 270, 274, Ch. 7, 332, 334, 343, 345–349, 357–364, 370
   evidential, 43–46, 50, 52–75, 88
   interactive, 7
   of cases, 21
   patterns, 332, 343, 345–349, 357–364
   spreading activation, 2, 12, 16, 21, 34, 35, 41, 43–48, 52, 57–60, 83, 89, 90, 175, 179, 195, 262, 265, 370
Adaptation OR adaptiveness, 10, 12, 16, 17, 171, 173, 198, 328
AI, *see* Artificial intelligence
Ambiguity, 5, 7, 37, 39, 40, 43, 45, 46, 52, 58, *see also* Disambiguation, Language, Polysemy
AMBR, 18
Analog Retrieval by Constraint Satisfaction, *see* ARCS
Analogical Constraint Mapping Engine, *see* ACME
Analogy-based reasoning, *see* Reasoning
ANON, 137
Approximate reasoning, *see* Reasoning

ARCS (Analog Retrieval by Constraint Satisfaction), 3, 5, 7, 9, 10, 46, 75, 76, 84, 85, 89, 90
Artificial intelligence (AI), 2, 20, 23, 24, 30, 39, 127, 129, 135, 137, 163, 255, Ch. 8 *see also* Symbolic approach
Associative retrieval, *see* Retrieval
ASTRA, 17, 18
Attention, 115, 119, 120, 148
Attributes, 19, 20, 23, 197, 231, 236, 243, 260, 292, 300, 319, 321, 322
Awareness, 4, 99

B

Back-propagation, 194, Ch. 7
Binding, 11, 14, 17, 19, 20, 21, Ch. 1, 134–135, 150, 153, 160–162, 194, 333, 346, 351, *see also* Variables
Biological [neural] networks, 15, 24, 331
BORIS, 40
BRAINSTORMER, 148

C

CA, 40
CABARET, 197
Capacity, 19
CARE (Connecting Analogies with Rules and Explanations), 17
CARS, 22, 169, Ch. 4
Case-based reasoning, *see* Reasoning
Cases, 21, 31, 42, 60, Ch. 2, Ch. 3, Ch. 4, 204, 228, 229
   case-roles, 42, 60
Categories, 128, 214–216, Ch. 6, 302, 310, 319, *see also* Concepts
Categorization, 42, 242–243, 294–298, 302, 321, *see also* Classification

SUBJECT INDEX 381

Causation, 120, 130, 140, 146, 174, 175, 203, 206, 207, 215, 230, 233, 234, 238, 239, 258, 337–339, 342
CBR, *see* Reasoning
CHEF, 111
Chunking, 19
Clamping, 35, 44, 52, 53, 62, 63, 113–115, 267
Classification, 7, 8, 18, 128, 152, *see also* Categorization
    semantic, 7, 8, 18
Combinatorial explosion, 57, 162, 271
Competition, 32, 57, 335
Complexity, 1, 11–13, 15, 18, 19, 22, 24, 75, 172, 224, 233, 234, 331
Comprehension, 20, Ch. 1, 97, 108, 259, *see also* Language, Understanding
Compressed representations, 10, *see also* Reduced descriptions
Computation, 96, 105, 172, 288
Computers, 15, 19, 21, 335, 340, 360
Concepts, 16, 19–23, Ch. 1, 129, 132, 162, 163, 175, Ch. 5, Ch. 6, Ch. 7, *see also* Categories
    spatial, 22, Ch. 5
Confidence, 15, 264, 267, 269–275, 336, 342, 349
Connecting Analogies with Rules and Explanations, *see* CARE
Connectionist/symbolic gap, 1, 2, 10, 329, 342
Conposit, 344, 362, *see also* ABR-Conposit
Consistency, 7, 47, 83, 85, 90, 223, 365–367
Constraints, 1, 4, 6, 7, 10, 17, 46, 86, 114, 116, 133–135, 153, 203, 219, 238, 242, 255, 258, 283, 288, 302, 319, 320, 333, 335
    constraint satisfaction, 1, 4, 46, 86, 203, 333, 335
Context, 21, 23, 39, 61, 88, 95, 107, 110, 112, 116, 119–121, 175, 197, Ch. 6, 303, 319
Controllers, 3, 15, 197
Copycat, 4, 7, 16, 46
Correspondences, 5, 7, 8, 23, 53, Ch. 5, Ch. 6, 289, 301, 317, 318, 321, 367, 369
Corruption, 333, 334, 337–340
Creativity, 16
Cross-contextual reminding, 34, 78, 97, *see also* Interdomain analogies
Cross-domain mappings, Ch. 5, *see also* Interdomain analogies
Crossmapping, 86
Crosstalk, 58–61, 89
CYRUS, 111, 165

D

Data structures, 10, 24, 35, 40, 47, 97, 99, 103, Ch. 5, 284, 288, 327, 329, 330, 333, 346, 351, *see also* Knowledge, Representation, Symbolic structure
Decay, 53, 88
Deduction, 183, 192, 198, 215
Direct Mapping Model (DMM), 359
Disambiguation, 20, Ch. 1, *see also* Ambiguity
DISCERN, 46
Discourse, 30, 186, 204, 241, 247, 250, 257, 262, 352, 355–356, 369, *see also* Language, Stories
Distributedness, 3, 11, 19, 22, 23, 42, 43, 46, 50, 51, 112–113, 116–117, 172, 193–195, 198–199, Ch. 7, 328, 333
DMM, *see* Direct Mapping Model
Duals, 222–233
Duncker radiation problem, *see* Radiation problem

E

Efficiency, 23
Elaboration, 12, 21, 30, 84, 165, 331
Embedding, 345, 362–364, 369
Emergence, 45, 96, 333, 334, 342
Encodings, 12, 22, 47, 65, 66, 97, 103, 126, 127, 135, 136–139, 151, 153, 154, 159, 298, 304, 311, 313, 314, 326, 344–346, 352, 355–356, *see also* Compressed encodings, Representation
Episodes, 20–22, Ch. 1
Evaluation, 10, 16, 165, Ch. 4
Evidential activation, *see* Activation
Exceptions, 333, 334, 342, 370
Explanations, 10, 17, 19, 46, 109–111, 174, 175, 197
Extensions, 204, 223, 243, 285

F

False analogies, 287, 288, 319, 320
Features, 21, 22, 29, 46, 47, 62, 66, 69, 75, 78, 84, 89, Ch. 2, Ch. 3, Ch. 4, Ch. 6, Ch. 7, 330, 333
    selection, 115–120, 135–155
    structural, 105, 137
    surface, 47, 75, 78, 84, 89, 105–107, 127, 134, 135, Ch. 4
    vectors, 22, 113–121, Ch. 3, 304, 333
    weighting, 112–120, 157, 164

SUBJECT INDEX

Feedforward networks, 159, 274, 306, 311, 366–367
Flexibility, 16, Ch. 8
Frames, 24, Ch. 1, 136, 343, *see also* Schemas, Scripts
Fuzzy logic, 173, 180, 185–190, 198, 327

G

Gating, 54, 60, 117–119, 157, 359
Generalization, 1, 12, 42, 95, 113, 121, 130, 195, 208, 212, 216, 218, 229, 230, 252, 294, 309, 319, 320, 333, 334, 336, 341, 347, 368
Generation, 180, 199, 288
Gestalts, 4, 5, 42
Goals, 7, 21, 29–31, 35, 38–40, 46–49, 56, 62, 66, 84, 87, Ch. 2, Ch. 3, 174, 175, 183
Goodness, 336, 341
Graceful degradation, 333, 334, 337–340
Grammar, 206, 209, 215, 253, Ch. 7, *see also* Language, Syntax
Graphs, 137, Ch. 4, 313, 330

H

Heteroassociation, 335
Hidden units, 23, 42, 43, Ch. 7, 350, 366–368
Hierarchies, 204, 227–233, 264, 273
Holistic processing, 2, 10–12, 19, 20, 43, 80, 85, 331, 333, 350, 356, 362
Hybrid systems, 2, 14, 16–21, 331, 350, *see also* Symbolic-connectionist systems
Hypotheses, 5, 7, 17, 335, 342, 369

I

Inconsistencies, 223, 366–367
Idioms, 204, 213–214, *see also* Language
Images, Ch. 5
IMM, *see* Indirect Mapping Model
Implementational connectionism, 11, 23, 24, 329–332, 342–343, 352, 359, 363–364, 370
Indexing, 21, 23, 31, 33, 35, 46, 47, 62, 66, 88, 89, 98, 111, 112, 121, Ch. 3, 175, 177, 192, 195, 196, 198, 263, 264, 330, 335, 348, 349, *see also* Retrieval
Indirect Mapping Model (IMM), 359
Inferences, 4, 10, 16, 17, 20, 21, Ch. 1, 107, 110, 120, 129, 137, 149, 151, 165, 166, 173, 177, 183, 198, 197, Ch. 5, Ch. 6, 293, Ch. 8, *see also* Problem Solving, Reasoning

direct, 261–263, 267, 279
immediate, 261–263, 272, 279
dynamic, 42–43
mediated, 261, 262, 279
Inheritance, 204, 215, 227–230, 247, 262, 263
Instantiations, 13, 34, 36, 38, 42, 49, 63, 66, 175, 186, 369
Integration, 1, 4, 16, 17, 21, 23, Ch. 2, 172, 331
Interdomain analogies, 302–304, 317, 318, *see also* Cross-contextual reminding, Cross-domain analogies
Interpretations, 9, 19, 23, Ch. 1, 129, 130, 165, 207, 239–245, 248, Ch. 6, 318, 320, 334
Invariance, 204, 218–220, 223, 233–234, 255, 288, 289, 310, 322
Isomorphism, 7, 12, *see also* One-to-one correspondences

J

JUDGE, 110

K

Knowledge, 29, 34, 35–37, 40, 41, 43, 48, 50, 54, 62, 75, 96, 120, 126, 127, 172, 173, 175, 180, 194, 195, 197, Ch. 5, Ch. 6, 350, 351, 354

L

Language, 3, 13, 14, 20, 23, 30, 43, 139, 140, 172, 180, 183, 194, Ch. 5, Ch. 6, Ch. 7, 328, 332, 352, 369, *see also* Ambiguity, Comprehension, Discourse, Embedding, Grammar, Idioms, Lexical semantics, Literal meaning, Meaning, Metaphor, Metonymy, MOPS, Polysemy, Scripts, Stories, Syntax, Understanding
Learning, 1, 12, 51, 88, 99, 113, 119, 120, 127, 136, 138, 161, 193–194, 203, 267–269, 274, 275, Ch. 7, 333, 334, 341
Levels, 3, 13, 14, 15, 17, 340, *see also* Multilevel models
Lexical semantics, Ch. 6, *see also* Ambiguity, Language, Meaning, Polysemy
Linguistics, 23, Ch. 5, Ch. 7
Literal meaning, 204–207, 222, 223, 239, 245, 253–255, Ch. 6, *see also* Language
Load, 19

SUBJECT INDEX 383

Localist connectionism, 3, 7, 20, 22, 23, 43–46, 195, 306, *see also* Structured connectionism

M

MAC/FAC, 47, 75, 76, 84, 85, 89, 90
Mapping, 4, 7, 9–11, 16, 17, 19, 20, 22, 42, 86, 121, 129, 131, 148, 153, 155, 163, 166, 177, 196, Ch. 5, Ch. 6, 293, 294, 303, 305, Ch. 8, *see also* Cross-domain mappings, Isomorphism, Matching
Markers, 2, 11, 18, 22, 41, 43, 54, 60, 175, 177, 195, 330
MARS, 198
Match hypotheses, *see* Hypotheses
Matching, 11, 12, 21, 22, 24, 50, 96, 112–114, 121, 133–136, 155–157, 166, Ch. 4, 223, 302, 319, Ch. 8, *see also* Mapping, Relaxed matches
  associative, 192, 332,
  pattern matching, 50, 192
  partial, 133–136, 155–157, 166, Ch. 4, 223, 319, 338, 351–353, 356–357, 368
Meaning, 29, 39, Ch. 5, Ch. 6, Ch. 7, 329, *see also* Ambiguity, Language, Lexical semantics, Literal meaning, Polysemy
Memory, 12, 18, 20, 21, 24, Ch. 1, Ch. 2, Ch. 3, 195, Ch. 8
  long-term, 12, 24, 62, 66, 335
  organization packets (MOPs), 102–103, 149
  short-term, 350
  working, 24, Ch. 8
Mental pressure, 16
Mental models, 287, 344, 350
Metaphor, 1–3, 10, 15, 20, 22–24, Ch. 5, 259, 266, 279, *see also* Language, Personification
Metonymy, 248, 262, 263, 266, *see also* Language
Microfeatures, 42, 51, 151–155
Modules, 2, 18, 350
MOPs, *see* Memory; *see also* Language, Scripts

N

Natural Language, *see* Language
Nesting, 10, 13, *see also* Embedding
Nonimplementational connectionism, 329–332, 352, 356, 359, 369
Non-one-to-one correspondences, 337, 339, 369

O

One-to-one correspondences, 7, 336, 338, *see also* Isomorphism
Ontologies, 209–213, 251
Overriding, 204, 219

P

Paradyme, 163–165
Parallelism, 1, 2, 4, 5, 11, 16, 19, 21–23, 40, 87, 96, 126–128, 135, 137, 155, 163–165, 195, 198, 328, 330, 335, 347, 355, 357, 370, *see also* Synchrony
Pattern completion, 22, 192, 195, 334, *see also* Representation completion
Pattern matching, *see* Matching
Pattern recognition, 14, *see also* Perception, Vision
Pengi, 138
Perception, 1, 3–5, 7, 9, 16, 24, 245, 267, 270, 274, 275, 300, *see also* Vision
Personification, 237, 238, 241
Plans, 21, 29–31, 35, 38–40, 46–49, 52, 56, 62, 66, 84, 87, 108–110, 117, Ch. 3
Pointers, 15, 21, 134, 351, 360–361
Polysemy, 23, 208, 212, 252, Ch. 7, *see also* Ambiguity, Language
Pragmatic factors, 7, 80, 260
Predicates, 7, 12, 19, 186, 344, 354, 357, 358, 361, *see also* Properties, Relations
Priming, 33, 39, 44, 68, 74, 80, 88, 99, 260, 262
  semantic, 99
PRIMO, 173, 185
Problem solving, 30, 31, 105, 128, 140, 148, 164, 169, 282, 287, 317, 322, *see also* Inferences, Reasoning
Productions, 45, 353, *see also* Rules
Properties, 23, Ch. 6, Ch. 7, *see also* Predicates, Relations
  functional, 262, 264
  perceptual, 264, 270
Property values, Ch. 6
  categorical, 270
  graded, 270
  multivalued, 269–271
  single valued, 269–271
Proportional analogies, 284, 319
Propositions, 84, 209–210, 234, Ch. 8
Prototypes, 112–113, 172, 288, 301, 334, 336

R

RAAMs, *see* Recursive auto-associative memories

SUBJECT INDEX

Radiation problem, 322
Randomness, 115, 120, 305, 310, 347
Reasoning, 4, 10, 13, 14, 16–24, Ch. 2, Ch. 3, Ch. 4, 208, 210–213, 223, 233, 234, 241, 250, 251, 282, 320, 321, Ch. 8, *see also* Deduction, Inferences, Problem solving
   analogy-based (ABR), 16, 17, 20, 23, 24, 241, 282, 320, 321, Ch. 8
   approximate OR uncertain, Ch. 4
   case-based (CBR), 20–22, 31–34, 46, 47, 66, 80, 83, 84, 89, Ch. 3, Ch. 4, *see also* Cases
   nonmonotonic, 329
   rule-based, *see* Rules
   spatial, 233
Recruitment, 80, 88, 275–276, 358
Recurrent networks, 42, 43, 46, 274, 311
Recursive auto associative memories (RAAMs), 367–368
Reduced descriptions, 10, 11, 12, 23, 330, 332, 346–349, 361–363, 367–370, *see also* Compressed encodings
Relations, 23, 49, 85–86, 106, 108, 127, 152, 153, 160, 161, 175, 179, Ch. 5, 274, Ch. 7, 354, *see also* Predicates, Properties
Relational structure, 4, 5, 9
Relaxation, 6, 7, 43, 113, 115–116, 178, 192, 196, 347, *see also* Relaxed Matches, Settling
Relaxed matches, 113–116
Relevance, 23, 335, 348, 349, 354, 356
REMIND, 20, 21, Ch. 1
Reminding, 20, 21, 24, Ch. 1, Ch. 2, 126, 144, 145, 148, 155, 159, 160, 162, 164, 165
   thematic, Ch. 1, 107
Representation, 1, 4, 5, 7, 10, 12, 14, 20, 22, 33–35, 45, 96, Ch. 2, Ch. 3, Ch. 4, 247, 255, 271, 279, Ch. 7, Ch. 8, *see also* Encodings
   completion, 333, 334, 341, *see also* Pattern completion
   graphical, 20
   symbolic, 127, Ch. 4, 328–330, 336–349, 360–361, 367–370, *see also* Data Structures, Implementational connectionism, Symbolic structure
Retrieval, 1, 10–12, 18, 20–23, Ch. 1, Ch. 2, Ch. 3, Ch. 4, 259, 260, 263 273, 330, 337, 343, 346–349, 370, *see also* Indexing
   associative, 22, 42, Ch. 4
Rigidity, 365, *see also* Flexibility, Robustness
ROBIN, 34, 36–39, 48, 52–61, 86, 87
Robustness, 42, 333–342, *see also* Flexibility, Rigidity
Rules, 3, 17, 23, 24, 34, 36, 37, 39, 40, 42, 43, 48, 49, 51–55, 75, 80, 87, 95, 119, 130, 135, Ch. 4, 214, Ch. 7, Ch. 8, *see also* Productions

S

SAARCS, 86
Schemas, 21, 113, Ch. 5, Ch. 7, *see also* Frames, Scripts
Schematicity, Ch. 7
SCISOR, 172
Scripts, 38, 42, 48, *see also* Frames, MOPs, Language, Schemas
Search, 104, 133, 175, 177, 179, 195, 363
Segmentation, 19, 363–364
Self-organization, 294, 320
Semantics, *see* Lexical semantics, Meaning
Semantic networks, 14, 20, 21, Ch. 1, Ch. 6, 329, 343
Settling, *see also* relaxation, 70, 357
SIAM, 19
Signatures, 21, Ch. 1, 346
Similarity, 1, 7–9, 11, 12, 18, 21, 23, 24, Ch. 2, 127, 128, 155–159, 164, Ch. 4, 251, Ch. 7, 332, 334, 341, 346, 347, 354, 361, 366
   featural, 23, 30
   semantic, 7, 8, 18, 21
   surface, 30–32, 75, 79, 127, 322
Slots, 141, 172, 175, 186, 190, 195, 302, 304
SME, *see* Structure Mapping Engine
Spreading activation, *see* Activation
STAR, *see* Structured Tensor Analogical Reasoning
Stories, 29, 30, 40, 42, 46, 48, 50, 99, Ch. 2, Ch. 3, 172, *see also* Discourse, Language
Strategic processing, 21
Structural consistency, *see* Consistency
Structure Mapping Engine (SME), 31, 337
Structure sensitivity, 13, 330–331, 370
Structured connectionism, 3, 23, 43–46, 47, 50, 54, 60, 80, 163, 195, Ch. 6, *see also* Implementational connectionism, Localist connectionism

SUBJECT INDEX 385

Structured Tensor Analogical Reasoning (STAR), 1, 5, 19
Subsymbolic models, 329
Symbolic approach OR processing, 1, 2, 11, 12, 17, 18, 24, 39, 40, 45, 255, 327–332, 335–342, *see also* Artificial intelligence
Symbolic/connectionist gap, *see* Connectionist/symbolic gap
Symbolic-connectionist systems, 17, 43–46, 356, *see also* Hybrid systems
Symbolic representation, *see* Representation
Symbolic structure, 10, 15, 22, 24, 329–330, *see also* Data structures, Representation: symbolic
Synchrony, 11, 20, *see also* Parallelism
Syntax, 34, 35, 42, 47, 85, 87, 90, 136, *see also* Grammar, Language
Systematicity, 7, 13, 14, 213, 196, Ch. 7

T

TAUs, 100–101
Tensors, *see also* Structured Tensor Analogical Reasoning, 19, 333
Themes, 86, 100–102, 116, 140–155
Thematic reminding, *see* Reminding
Thematic structure, 21, 47
Thinking, 3–5, 9, 10, 15, 24, 31, 205, 211, 213, 227, 252, 255, 282

Topology, 218–220
Transfer, 7, 16, 17, 105, 109, 114, 180, Ch. 6, 336–338, 341–343, 349
Transformation, 303–305
Traversal, 196, 329, 347
Trees, 329, 368
Type/token distinction, 153, 154, 178–179, 289

U

Uncertainty, 173, 183, 190, 198, *see also* Confidence, Reasoning
Understanding, 20, 21, Ch. 1, 97, 99, 105, 110, 138, Ch. 5, 332, 352, 356, *see also* Comprehension, Language

V

Variables, 17, 20, 36, 37, 45, 46, 50, 54, 56, 60, 88, 134, 135, 150, 151, 153, 160, 175, 183, 186, 194, 196, 337, 347, 351, 367, 368, *see also* Binding
Vectors, 10, 19, 96, 113, 194, Ch. 7, 332, 335, 344, 346–347, 364–366, *see also* Features
Vision, 4, 7, *see also* Perception

W

Winner-take-all (WTA), 57, 58, 347, 348
Working memory, *see* Memory